THE ROMANTIC COMEDY

To
MY WIFE
THIS VOLUME IS
DEDICATED

THE ROMANTIC COMEDY

by

D. G. JAMES

ἀλλ' ὅ τι τοῦ ζῆν φίλτερον ἄλλο
σκότος ἀμπίσχων κρύπτει νεφέλαις.
τοῦ δ' ὅ τι τοῦτο στίλβει κατὰ γῆν
δυσέρωτες δὴ φαινόμεθ' ὄντες,
δι' ἀπειροσύνην ἄλλου βιότου
κοὐκ ἀπόδειξιν τῶν ὑπὸ γαίας·
  μύθοις δ' ἄλλως φερόμεσθα.

EURIPIDES: *Hippolytus*

GEOFFREY CUMBERLEGE
OXFORD UNIVERSITY PRESS
LONDON NEW YORK TORONTO

Oxford University Press, Amen House, London, E.C.4
GLASGOW NEW YORK TORONTO MELBOURNE WELLINGTON
BOMBAY CALCUTTA MADRAS CAPE TOWN
Geoffrey Cumberlege, Publisher to the University

First published 1948
Second Impression 1949

Printed in Great Britain

NOTE

THIS essay was finished in 1940, and its publication delayed by the war. The delay has brought advantage and disadvantage. The advantage is that it was read by Dr. A. C. Ewing, whose friendship I had the good fortune to make, under circumstances surprising to both of us; and what philosophical shortcomings the essay now has are certainly not his fault. The disadvantage is that I am even more conscious than I was six years ago of the faults of what I have written. I have made a number of small changes. But more, circumstance and other work have forbidden me to do.

I am again indebted to my sister, Mrs. Frank Blackmore, for her excellent typing of very difficult manuscript. I wish also to thank my friend Mr. Henry Gifford, who has read the proofs with great care and has made many valuable suggestions.

D. G. J.

May 1947

'The argument shows, then, that . . . tragedy and comedy alike afford pleasure and pain; a mixture of pleasure and pain is also evoked by the drama of life which is at once tragic and comic.'—PHILEBUS

CONTENTS

PROLOGUE

THOSE who write what is called literary criticism are for the most part, I think, best described as historians. The title of critic should perhaps be reserved for those whose work it is to pass judgement on the creative work of their own day as it comes before the public; the title of literary historian seems to be best suited to those who undertake to speak, whether of a period or an individual in the past, whether remote or near, of literature. In any case, the difference between the historian and the critic is at most one of degree; for every historian, of whatever kind, is necessarily a critic, whether he knows it or not. The mere compiler of facts (if such a person exists or could exist) is no less a historical monstrosity than a monument of literary dullness.

This is more than a matter of mere names and designations. For if the writer about the past of literature is best called a historian, there is implied in this a responsibility and a limitation. Professor Alexander in an admirable phrase once spoke of the 'natural piety of the historian'; he was suggesting, if I remember rightly, that the philosopher might benefit from an infection of this piety. Whether he was right in this, is no concern of ours. But I think it likely that the 'critic' of past figures and periods in literature, so far as he may properly be called a historian, will acknowledge an obligation to avoid the catchword, the fashionable cry of the schools, the neat and finished explanation, the self-assured and doctrinaire judgement. His historical imagination should go along with a sense of the unlimited fecundity of the given and the likelihood of destructive blows being directed, by a world which defies exhaustive analysis, upon any polished and tidy conceptual schemes he may evolve out of his brain. Plato beheld the Forms as only inadequately mirrored in the sensible world; he knew that the world would resist resolution into perfect ideal patterns. The irrational, the incalculable, and the individual always occur to baffle the Form-discerning mind of man. This is true, no doubt, of physical science; it is still more true of historical science; and a historical imagination, alive to this truth, will employ itself in humility before the irresoluble complexity of things and seek to impose no haughty terms upon a world it foolishly imagines it has conquered with an epigram, a tart saying, or a slick formula.

This is not to say, of course, that we ought, even if it were possible, to abandon the hope of discerning prevailing patterns in the data we study; or that we ought to drown what is absolute in a mere stream of history. The wise scientist acknowledges the awkward but undeniable and 'brute' particularity of things; but he may not forsake his quest of law. Also, if he wisely recognizes the tentativeness and uncertainty of his conclusions, he will not and cannot forsake his feeling that he is helping to bring the human mind, by routes however circuitous and temporarily perhaps misleading, to a final goal of truth. And it is with the historian as it is with the scientist.

I have tried, with however little success, to write about English Romanticism in this spirit. This implies two things. The first is, that this book is neither an attack upon nor a defence of the English Romantic writers. To make either would be a piece of impertinence of which, whatever other faults may be discerned here, I am not guilty. The second is, that I have tried not to approach my subject with any preconceived and exhaustive definition of Romanticism. Definitions are the specific concern of the philosopher; only in a subsidiary way are they the concern of the historian, who, though he must have an eye to these things, must walk warily in the face of his multitudinous data. We are at liberty to remark of the philosopher, *How absolute the knave is*, and to let his knavery and his absoluteness be on his own head.

It will be obvious to the reader that in the compass of a book of this size, I have not tried to write a full history of Romanticism in England. What narrative and analysis follows proceeds by drastic omission; and not only have I not mentioned several of the most remarkable figures in the literature of the period, I have also not undertaken to make anything like exhaustive study of those men of whom I have spoken. This was inevitable. But if I have proceeded by omission and selection, I have nevertheless tried to convey a sense of what may properly be called a 'movement'. We ordinarily use the word in speaking of Romanticism—the phrase, the Romantic Movement, has become widely habitual in speaking of that phase in our literature which began with Blake and (let us say vaguely) ended with the *Aids to Reflection.* In using the word in this way, I suppose we have generally in mind the stirring of a spirit of reaction against eighteenth-century habits of thought and feeling. But so far as what follows is concerned, we might interpret the word to signify a spirit, alive over a period of years, which changed and developed, grew and came to a kind of maturity as it caught and inhabited the minds of a number of men. That there was such a development in Romanticism, which brought great changes, yet did not proceed by any sharp discontinuities, is what I have tried to show.

But in this development, remarkable enough in its speed and in the great changes it produced in Romanticism, certain features are fairly enduring. These are, first, the need to employ mythology; second, certain beliefs about human knowledge and imagination; and third, a sense of the strange and unknown. Some-

PROLOGUE

THOSE who write what is called literary criticism are for the most part, I think, best described as historians. The title of critic should perhaps be reserved for those whose work it is to pass judgement on the creative work of their own day as it comes before the public; the title of literary historian seems to be best suited to those who undertake to speak, whether of a period or an individual in the past, whether remote or near, of literature. In any case, the difference between the historian and the critic is at most one of degree; for every historian, of whatever kind, is necessarily a critic, whether he knows it or not. The mere compiler of facts (if such a person exists or could exist) is no less a historical monstrosity than a monument of literary dullness.

This is more than a matter of mere names and designations. For if the writer about the past of literature is best called a historian, there is implied in this a responsibility and a limitation. Professor Alexander in an admirable phrase once spoke of the 'natural piety of the historian'; he was suggesting, if I remember rightly, that the philosopher might benefit from an infection of this piety. Whether he was right in this, is no concern of ours. But I think it likely that the 'critic' of past figures and periods in literature, so far as he may properly be called a historian, will acknowledge an obligation to avoid the catchword, the fashionable cry of the schools, the neat and finished explanation, the self-assured and doctrinaire judgement. His historical imagination should go along with a sense of the unlimited fecundity of the given and the likelihood of destructive blows being directed, by a world which defies exhaustive analysis, upon any polished and tidy conceptual schemes he may evolve out of his brain. Plato beheld the Forms as only inadequately mirrored in the sensible world; he knew that the world would resist resolution into perfect ideal patterns. The irrational, the incalculable, and the individual always occur to baffle the Form-discerning mind of man. This is true, no doubt, of physical science; it is still more true of historical science; and a historical imagination, alive to this truth, will employ itself in humility before the irresoluble complexity of things and seek to impose no haughty terms upon a world it foolishly imagines it has conquered with an epigram, a tart saying, or a slick formula.

This is not to say, of course, that we ought, even if it were possible, to abandon the hope of discerning prevailing patterns in the data we study; or that we ought to drown what is absolute in a mere stream of history. The wise scientist acknowledges the awkward but undeniable and 'brute' particularity of things; but he may not forsake his quest of law. Also, if he wisely recognizes the tentativeness and uncertainty of his conclusions, he will not and cannot forsake his feeling that he is helping to bring the human mind, by routes however circuitous and temporarily perhaps misleading, to a final goal of truth. And it is with the historian as it is with the scientist.

I have tried, with however little success, to write about English Romanticism in this spirit. This implies two things. The first is, that this book is neither an attack upon nor a defence of the English Romantic writers. To make either would be a piece of impertinence of which, whatever other faults may be discerned here, I am not guilty. The second is, that I have tried not to approach my subject with any preconceived and exhaustive definition of Romanticism. Definitions are the specific concern of the philosopher; only in a subsidiary way are they the concern of the historian, who, though he must have an eye to these things, must walk warily in the face of his multitudinous data. We are at liberty to remark of the philosopher, *How absolute the knave is*, and to let his knavery and his absoluteness be on his own head.

It will be obvious to the reader that in the compass of a book of this size, I have not tried to write a full history of Romanticism in England. What narrative and analysis follows proceeds by drastic omission; and not only have I not mentioned several of the most remarkable figures in the literature of the period, I have also not undertaken to make anything like exhaustive study of those men of whom I have spoken. This was inevitable. But if I have proceeded by omission and selection, I have nevertheless tried to convey a sense of what may properly be called a 'movement'. We ordinarily use the word in speaking of Romanticism —the phrase, the Romantic Movement, has become widely habitual in speaking of that phase in our literature which began with Blake and (let us say vaguely) ended with the *Aids to Reflection.* In using the word in this way, I suppose we have generally in mind the stirring of a spirit of reaction against eighteenth-century habits of thought and feeling. But so far as what follows is concerned, we might interpret the word to signify a spirit, alive over a period of years, which changed and developed, grew and came to a kind of maturity as it caught and inhabited the minds of a number of men. That there was such a development in Romanticism, which brought great changes, yet did not proceed by any sharp discontinuities, is what I have tried to show.

But in this development, remarkable enough in its speed and in the great changes it produced in Romanticism, certain features are fairly enduring. These are, first, the need to employ mythology; second, certain beliefs about human knowledge and imagination; and third, a sense of the strange and unknown. Something of what is involved in these three things I shall try to make clear as we go along. But I have said of them that they are only 'fairly' enduring to safeguard myself against undue dogmatism. For, to use the first by way of illustration, Wordsworth, who is generally accounted (and I should say rightly) the most remarkable figure in English Romanticism, showed no desire to employ mythology, in contrast to Blake, Shelley, and Keats; and to use the third, a part of Blake's objection to religion and Christianity was that it was 'dark' and had too much 'mystery' about it. Even so, there are respects in which Wordsworth and Blake satisfy these generalizations; for after all, Wordsworth discovered a *μῦθος* and Blake was certainly not without a sense of 'unknown modes of being'.

Finally, I suggest, or perhaps it would be better to say, repeat (for the point is not, I think, new) that Romanticism may be seen as, from the beginning to the end, a quest for a literary form adequate to itself. We observe it casting around, perhaps desperately, for expressive form; and we also observe it failing to obtain what it wants. For this reason, I have paid some attention to some of the Romantic efforts in allegory, narrative, and drama. This matter is seen to be closely bound up with the interest of these poets in mythology, and this matter in turn is of course bound up with their beliefs, about which also I have had something to say.

But in those aspects of English Romanticism I have mentioned, and which are treated in this essay, it is the use of mythology which more than any other gives unity to what I have written. This, I think, is the crucial thing. And that is why I have placed upon the title-page the remarkable words of the nurse in *Hippolytus*. We cannot come to proof and certainty; and therefore we cannot dispense with myth and story. Still, the narrative I have to tell does not end with story merely; or, if it ends with story, it is story with which there goes along, also, authority.

Part One

THE GOSPEL OF HELL

§ 1

WRITING about Blake is a hazardous enterprise. A body of work of such obscurity and difficulty as his can only too conveniently be fitted into as many frameworks as his various interpreters choose to bring along. I may perhaps therefore in some measure disarm the reader's natural suspicion of yet another essay on Blake by saying that I have at least no one framework into which I have pushed Blake's poetry; or it might be better to say that I believe that there is no framework into which Blake can be fitted. He defies any neat or consistent interpretation and lends himself to no argument. I believe, that is to say, that Blake's mind was extremely confused; and that the huge difficulty and obscurity of his work arises from an intellectual and imaginative disorder. I believe also that we can understand Blake to any considerable degree only if we recognize that this was so. If we can acknowledge the disorder of which I have spoken, we can at least see the disorder at work; and this is a kind of understanding. At least, I suggest that it is a wider understanding than we shall have if we proceed obstinately on the assumption that Blake's mind was really, despite innumerable evidences to the contrary, clear and whole. In saying this I am aware of the disagreement into which I am thrown with a writer as authoritative as Mr. Middleton Murry.[1] It is a natural and even desirable thing to be predisposed to think a writer of such genius as Blake more ordered and consistent than we with our lesser powers are inclined to believe at least at first and even second sight. Even so, I think that efforts to justify this predisposition must, where Blake is concerned, end in failure; and I shall try in the course of this chapter to say in what the confusions and disorders in Blake's mind of which I have spoken consist.

I shall begin with the *Songs*. Between the two groups, the *Songs of Innocence* and the *Songs of Experience*, there is a great difference of feeling and attitude. Blake describes them as 'showing the two contrary states of the human soul'. I need be at no pains to describe the spirit of the *Songs of Innocence*; they express a deep and innocent joy, removed altogether from anger and resentment. Their tenderness and love is the tenderness and love of Chris-

[1] I am, however, very much in the debt of Mr. Murry's book on Blake.

tianity; and their God is the God who takes account of the fall of every sparrow.

For Mercy, Pity, Peace and Love
Is God, our father dear,
And Mercy, Pity, Peace and Love
Is Man, his child and care.[1]

In the world of the *Songs of Innocence* the suffering of the chimney sweeper and the spectacle of the charity children evoke no anger.

Now like a mighty wind they raise to heaven the voice of song,
Or like harmonious thunderings the seats of Heaven among.
Beneath them sit the aged men, wise guardians of the poor;
Then cherish pity, lest you drive an angel from your door.

The chimney sweeper and the charity children recur in the *Songs of Experience*; and *here* it is the sense of their suffering which animates the poetry, the appeal away from

Mercy, Pity, Peace and Love,

to the need for justice and to the assertion of wrong. What we may call the acquiescence of the earlier *Songs* gives way to moral indignation; indeed, the earlier acquiescence, pity, and charity become contemptible.

Pity would be no more
If we did not make somebody Poor;
And Mercy no more could be
If all were as happy as we.

And mutual fear brings peace,
Till the selfish loves increase:
Then Cruelty knits a snare
And spreads his baits with care.

He sits down with holy fears,
And waters the ground with tears;
Then Humility takes its root
Underneath his foot.

Blake no longer sees Jerusalem but London—

But most thro' midnight streets I hear
How the youthful Harlot's curse
Blasts the new born Infant's tear,
And blights with plagues the Marriage hearse.

[1] Quotations from Blake's writings are made from the excellent Nonesuch edition (1927) of his work in one volume, ed. Geoffrey Keynes. I give page references to that edition for all quotations other than those from the *Songs of Innocence*, *Songs of Experience*, and *The Marriage of Heaven and Hell*.

The God who in the *Songs of Innocence*

> gives to us his joy
> That our grief he may destroy,

has become by 1793 'old Nobodaddy' and 'father of Jealousy', to whom he says,

> Why darkness and obscurity
> In all thy words and laws,
> That none dare eat the fruit but from
> The wily serpent's jaws? (p. 93)

The fathers in these later songs are symbols of repression. Fathers, the Bible, and God are one in symbolizing a deathliness for the soul:

> But his loving look,
> Like the holy book,
> All her tender limbs with terror shook.

These then are the two 'contrary states of the human soul'; the one is innocence, joy, worship, and pity; the other is moral indignation and contempt for religion, for pity, and humility. Now there is, so far as I know, no reason to believe that Blake originally planned to write the two series of songs. By 1789 he had completed the *Songs of Innocence*; he etched them and issued them as a separate volume. In 1794 he added the *Songs of Experience*, issuing them together with the *Songs of Innocence*. It is likely therefore that the second series shows a change in Blake's mind and means that he had deserted his former way of feeling. Now in *The Marriage of Heaven and Hell*, etched about 1793, that is, a year before the *Songs of Experience* were etched, we find the following observations:

'Without Contraries is no progression. Attraction and Repulsion, Reason and Energy, Love and Hate, are necessary to Human existence.

'From these Contraries spring what the religious call Good and Evil. Good is the passive that obeys Reason. Evil is the active springing from Energy.

'Good is Heaven. Evil is Hell.'

In 1793 therefore he regarded the spirit of the *Songs of Innocence* as being what the religious call good; that of the *Songs of Experience* what the religious would call evil. But he says that both are necessary to human existence—Attraction, Reason, and Love, on the one hand; and on the other, Repulsion, Energy, and Hate. We cannot assume that this was his belief when he wrote the *Songs of Innocence*, and these certainly do not suggest an author who believed that Repulsion and Hate were necessary to human existence.

Now although he says in *The Marriage* that Love and Hate, 'good' and 'evil', the spirit of the *Songs of Innocence* and of the *Songs of Experience*, are both necessary to human existence, and in spite of the title *The Marriage of Heaven and Hell*, we hear little else in the book than the gospel of Hell. There is little enough of Heaven in it. He may still say that 'Heaven' and 'good' are necessary; but *The Marriage* is given up to 'energy' as are the *Songs of Experience*; and he shows no disposition to turning his hand to expressing Attraction, Reason, and Love. It is not unreasonable to suspect that although he assents to the need of these qualities, he is himself drawn to their contraries; and the *Songs of Innocence* had been completed at least four years before he etched *The Marriage* and five years before he etched the *Songs of Experience*. In any case, it is certain that these two latter works glorify Satan, 'evil', and 'hell'; and if the *Songs of Innocence* do not suggest an author who believed Hate to be necessary, the later *Songs* and *The Marriage* do not suggest an author who has retained even as a 'contrary' the joy and simplicity of the *Songs of Innocence*.

§ 2

It is very important to consider carefully what is involved in this notion of 'contraries' and of the need of both for human life. Now the first contrary is the spirit of the *Songs of Innocence*. Their spirit is wholly religious; in it pity and mercy and love fill the mind; there is no room for a moral attitude, of judgement or condemnation; all is worship and acquiescence. Now this extraordinarily pure religious sensibility, which, as the rain falls on just and unjust, embraces all things in its love and tenderness, is necessarily difficult to maintain, and unstable. It is unstable because it is too great a flight from the every day and healthy attitude of morality.

> Pity would be no more
> If we did not make somebody Poor;
> And Mercy no more could be
> If all were as happy as we.

In the *Songs of Experience* Blake reacts into a moral attitude. The spectacle of injustice, oppression, and cruelty intelligibly throws him into a perception of life as thoroughly moral as the perception of the *Songs of Innocence* was thoroughly religious. And he says, again quite intelligibly, that both these attitudes are necessary; he also says, with truth, that they contradict each other, that there is a sharp antagonism between the religious and moral ways of seeing the world. They are 'contrary' states; both are desirable, but irreconcilable in a single moment of the spirit.

If I am at all right in saying that considerations such as these were at work in Blake's mind, we can agree that Blake is observing one of the perpetual paradoxes of the religious life. Religion must both transcend morality and remain earnestly moral; to be merely moral and to be deaf to moral considerations are the Scylla and Charybdis of religion. But Blake's mind was a rash one, and he lost patience quickly with religion which seeks to unite the religious and the moral with whatever of balance and order it can. This I think is what he means in *The Marriage of Heaven and Hell* where, having spoken of 'two classes of men' corresponding, as I take it, to the two contraries, he says of them that 'they are always upon the earth, and they should be enemies: whoever tries to reconcile them seeks to destroy existence'. And he then adds: 'Religion is an endeavour to reconcile the two.' It is quite true that religion does try to reconcile them as best it may. But Blake has no patience with it for doing so; and hatred of religion becomes a notable feature of Blake's writing. Hatred, that is to say, of Christianity, for although Blake makes great play throughout his prophetic writing with the word Christianity, he does not at all intend by it what is ordinarily intended by the word. That this is so cannot be too much emphasized.

The two sets of lyrics then, the *Songs of Innocence* and the *Songs of Experience*, when taken together reveal a deeply religious mind in reaction against religion. The 'experienced' Blake finds the acquiescence and worship of the 'innocent' Blake intolerable. The humility, mercy, meekness of the earlier days are dismissed —they are religious and Christian virtues. Also, in the *Songs of Experience* he shows his hatred of the Church and of what he says goes along with religion—mystery. It is of especial importance and interest to notice Blake's contempt, which continues throughout his writings, for the *mysteriousness* of religion. He regards it as a device in the hands of Priest and King for securing power and for working on the credulity of the people. In the poem 'A Little Boy Lost' in the *Songs of Experience* he even upholds Reason against the 'mystery' of religion, accepting, as a temporary ally against the hated cause of religion, what through the body of his work he regards as the greatest enemy of life. There is in the *Songs of Experience*, however, little enough that is positive; they are chiefly songs of rejection and contempt, of what he himself calls repulsion, energy, hate. Now I have suggested that though he speaks, in the subtitle of the collected *Songs* and in *The Marriage of Heaven and Hell*, of innocence and experience as 'contraries' which are both necessary, we have the impression that the gospel of repulsion, energy, and hate has become his choice; if we could not be sure of this from the *Songs of Experience*, we may be sure of it from a reading of *The Marriage*, which is full of what he chooses to call the 'gospel of Hell'.

We must now consider this 'gospel of Hell'. I have said that Blake, so religious in the *Songs of Innocence*, falls, in the *Songs of Experience*, into a fanatical reaction. Blake's mind moved in extremes of emotion and belief, violently and with little consideration. Rejecting Christianity, its worship, mystery, and virtues, he is not content to adopt, like so many people, a moral attitude which tries to be independent of any form of religious belief. Had Blake been a more ordinary person, this might well have happened. Instead, swinging into a drastic extreme, he exalts principles of action directly opposed to Christianity, which Christianity would certainly label evil; also, and most important, he erects them into a gospel and a religion. Hence, if the *Songs of Experience* embody a reaction from Christianity in favour of morality, they also react into an anti-Christian morality, into, that is to say, a religious morality of a very different kind from that which Christianity upholds. Blake, to speak crudely, had religion in his blood; and if he could not have Christianity, he would have an anti-Christian religion and morality. He will erect what Christianity calls evil into a religion; he will have a religion of 'devils', a gospel of 'Hell'.

This is a very surprising situation; and I do not at all imagine that I can explain it. But that Blake fell into a reaction of this sort is certain enough. It is of course clear that when Blake parades his doctrine of 'Hell' he is not adopting a religion of evil for its own sake. On the contrary he is saying, in his perverse way, that only by following the teaching of 'Hell' can we come to 'Heaven'. He has now, he says, a religion and a morality better than the Christian, and in a spirit of vainglory he is willing enough to let it be called devilish. If we wish for life and for life more abundantly, the gospel of 'Hell' will secure it. We find 'Heaven' through the way of 'Hell'. Hence the title *The Marriage of Heaven and Hell*. If we are to come to 'innocence' it must be not by the road of Christianity, which enjoins denial and duty, which exalts mercy and pity, and thereby acquiescence in a world in which there is cruelty and persecution. There must be another way, the way of the 'devil', so hated by Christianity. He is not abjuring the hope of innocence, of a reign of peace and love. But he is denying the rightness of the Christian way to its establishment. What he judges to be the right way he sets out in *The Marriage*.

The following is the substance of the 'gospel of Hell' to which, as I have said, he seems deeply committed by the year 1794. 'Energy', he says, 'is Eternal Delight'; and again, 'Those who restrain desire do so because theirs is weak enough to be restrained;

and the restrainer or reason usurps its place and governs the unwilling'. We are told that 'the road of excess leads to the palace of wisdom', and that 'he who desires but acts not, breeds pestilence'. Such is the ethic of Hell. In the second place, Blake says that by 'an improvement of sensual enjoyment', by which he appears to mean the removal of restraint upon desire, the 'doors of perception' will be 'cleansed' and everything will 'appear to man as it is, infinite'; and he adds that 'man has closed himself up, till he sees all things thro' narrow chinks of his cavern'. The release of desire then brings with it a renewal of imagination; to give rein to desire is to pass on to the perception of infinity in all things. 'For the cherub with his flaming sword is hereby commanded to leave his guard at the tree of life; and when he does, the whole creation will be consumed and appear infinite and holy, whereas it now appears finite and corrupt.' Thirdly, there goes with his gospel of desire and imagination a pantheistic belief. 'God only Acts and Is, in existing beings or men.' Again, 'The worship of God is: Honouring his gifts in other men, each according to his genius, and loving the greatest men best: those who envy or calumniate great men hate God; for there is no other God.'

Thus Blake has adopted an ethic which will not allow of conflict between reason and desire; he also adopts a pantheistic religion. This is the reaction from the Christianity of the *Songs of Innocence* whose meekness gives way to 'energy'. The tygers of wrath are wiser than the horses of instruction. So long as there is cruelty and suffering, the Christian virtues of meekness and humility, mercy and pity are vicious; we must rid the world of its suffering and evil by another way, the way of wrath and spontaneity; and this way will bring the world to an innocence in which love and joy will not be asked to exist in the face of the misery of men. We must recognize that if Blake's ethic of Hell is a highly unorthodox and even eccentric one; if it may seem very immoral by seeking the release of desire from restraint, its motive is yet passionately moral. It is set upon destroying evil for a first requirement. Then, with evil destroyed, then and only then can religion exist without shame; only then will the acquiescence and delight of religion be supportable. But in thus giving an absolute priority to moral claims, the nature of religion as Blake conceives it is changed. It is no longer theistic and a 'mystery'; it is pantheistic and naturalistic. A theistic religion tries to unite religion and morality. Blake for his part, in an access of moral indignation, breaks with Christianity. In doing so he none the less adopts a naturalistic form of 'religion'. Now it is a feature of such naturalistic religion that it believes that good and evil may not be absolutely distinguished; it is a distinction which derives from theistic and 'mystery' religion. And it was a part of Blake's life-long teaching that religion, by insisting on the absoluteness of the distinction between good and evil, is one of the chief enemies of the soul of man. We must no longer, he urged, be plagued by the opposition of right to wrong, of duty to desire, of law to impulse; we must be only 'natural', place no restraint upon desire, be 'ourselves'. This is the core and paradox of Blake's mind and doctrine, that, actuated by the strongest moral impulse, he comes to a denial of morality; reacting from Christianity precisely from a wish to give emphasis to the ethical, he comes to acknowledge no law but that of desire. A man of unusual moral passion, he destroys the foundation of morality. He rejected Christianity with scorn because he believed it weakened the ethical; he himself adopted a religion which did not admit of the ethical.

There is another feature of Blake's doctrine which we must take notice of. Although in the *Songs of Experience* and in *The Marriage of Heaven and Hell* he places himself in the sharpest antagonism to Christianity, he never ceases to claim that what he is teaching is 'real' or 'true' Christianity. Christianity is altogether mistaken; but what Blake teaches and what Jesus taught are one and the same thing. He will gladly give up any claim on Christianity; he will not give up his claim to Jesus. Early in his life (in *The Marriage*) and as late as 1818, the year in which he wrote *The Everlasting Gospel*, he asserted that his doctrine is the original Christianity, and the only true Christianity. 'Jesus was all virtue, and acted from impulse, and not from rules.' So he announces in *The Marriage*, and this theme he elaborates in *The Everlasting Gospel*. How, in the body of his allegorical writings, he interprets Christianity in this eccentric way, we shall see at a later stage. We remark now only that when Blake speaks of Christianity and Christ he does not mean what we ordinarily understand by these words. I shall give one example of Blake's practice in this matter. In the prose introduction to *The Everlasting Gospel* Blake wrote the following words:

> 'There is not one Moral Virtue that Jesus Inculcated but Plato and Cicero did Inculcate before him: what then did Christ Inculcate? Forgiveness of sins. This alone is the Gospel, and this is the Life and Immortality brought to light by Jesus. . . .' (p. 131)

On this there are two observations to be made. First, that in the opening words, Blake tacitly acknowledges that Jesus *did* inculcate 'moral virtues', what it is the purpose of the poem to show he did not do. This has some importance, for it shows that

Blake was not easy and comfortable in his attitude towards the founder of Christianity. He desired him for an ally, but acknowledges, obliquely, that he was not what Blake wishes to believe he was. Secondly, when Blake says that the only novelty in the teaching of Jesus is his insistence on the forgiveness of sins, he means by 'forgiveness of sins' something different from what Christ or any Christian intends to convey by the phrase. Blake urges forgiveness of sins because in his doctrine sins are not, really, sins; in his opinion the moral law has no legitimate claims upon us and offences against it are not therefore in effect offences at all. By *his* gospel of forgiveness, Blake means only this. But this is certainly not what Jesus meant, nor what the Christian means. On the contrary, in the teaching of Christ forgiveness is a real thing; it is a forgiveness of real sins, which cannot be condoned, but can none the less be forgiven. Blake may think what he will; but forgiveness of sins, as he teaches it, is in no sense of the word Christian.

§ 3

It is clear that in the writings which succeeded the *Songs of Innocence* up to and including the first version of *Vala*, Blake set himself to express, apparently with conviction, the gospel of Hell which he has expounded in *The Marriage of Heaven and Hell*. The substance of this gospel I have already described by quotations from the book. His exposition of it in allegorical and mythological form in the works referred to I shall discuss at a later stage. For the present I wish to make some observations about this kind of belief which will be relevant also to a later phase of Blake's naturalistic ethic. These observations will also be relevant to aspects of the work of certain other Romantic writers with whom we shall deal in Part II.

Writing in 1802, in the course of some notes on Sir Thomas Browne, Coleridge remarked that 'strong feeling and an active intellect conjoined, leads almost necessarily, in the first stage of philosophising, to Spinozism'. This remark, however wild a generalization, has considerable truth so far as the English Romantic movement is concerned. By 'Spinozism' we may take Coleridge to mean, not discipleship to the writings of Spinoza primarily, but the adoption of a naturalistic ethic which yet is accompanied by a warmth of feeling and metaphysical excitement which (in a vague enough way) may be thought to merit the description of 'religious'. In fact Coleridge himself read Spinoza[1]

[1] So far as I know, Blake never read Spinoza. Had he done so, I have no doubt that, in his endless perversity, he would have damned him as he damned Wordsworth, for a 'Heathen Philosopher at enmity with all True Poetry'.

with great avidity, and handed on his enthusiasm to Wordsworth; but in saying that 'Spinozism' was found congenial by the Romantic poets, we have in mind certain features in belief and feeling of which Spinoza has become the typical and greatest representative.

Now the perennial interest of Spinoza and his work consists chiefly in two things: the first is that he was a man of intense religious feeling who set himself to evolve an ethic and a metaphysic which, with any rigorous regard for language, we must call irreligious. Spinoza had all the moral and religious passion and austerity of his race. These feelings are shown in his works, which however, as systems of belief, are set upon the destruction of all such doctrines as the Jewish people have given to mankind. His feelings are religious, his beliefs atheism; his system of philosophy is of such a kind as to try to satisfy both. Probably Spinoza never recognized how much his pantheistic philosophy owed to past generations of his people in their worship of a righteous and transcendent God.

The second thing is that Spinoza's ethic is an attempt to unite the notion of man as an animal whose essence, like everything else (he said), is to persevere in its own nature, with the belief that man may achieve a rational and impersonal good. To effect a union of these two ideas, even with the appearance of success, is obviously a task of the greatest difficulty; and Spinoza's system is set in paradoxes which quickly prove to be radical contradictions. On the one hand, the end of our lives is said to be, to become wholly ourselves; and there is nothing in our nature which can destroy us and act against that self-realization; on the other hand Spinoza believed that we can fall into a state of self-frustration and of wretched bondage to our passions. If we are naturally directed towards the true goal of life, we may yet miss the mark. Man's ideal good is strictly natural, and there can, in strictness, be no conflict in us between what is animal and what is not; and the understanding, whereby we are raised out of the bondage of passion into the freedom of reason, must belong to the natural and grow out of it. Yet he sought, and could not fail to seek, to place understanding over against desire. He must both oppose them and make them equally a part of nature; and therefore his ethic may be said to consist in a denial of the problem which ethics ordinarily set out to solve.

Now in regard to the first of these things, Blake may fittingly be compared with Spinoza. For Blake had, if anyone ever had, the *anima naturaliter christiana*, which shows itself in his writings. But he also set his face firmly against the Christian tradition in which he was reared and combated it throughout much the greater part of his work. In regard to the second, Blake, like Spinoza, exalts desire to a place of the highest importance. Spinoza had indeed to resort to understanding, at the price of consistency, for salvation; but in the doctrine of *The Marriage of Heaven and Hell* we hear little of understanding and reason. If they are mentioned, it is to call them the 'usurpers of the place of desire'; they are the enemies of 'energy' and therefore of the emancipation of the senses and of the imagination. Now Spinoza's theoretical inconsistency, though deplorable philosophically, rescues his ethic and gives it a peculiar importance in the history of human thought. But Blake's ethic, so far as Blake may be said to develop it, although consistent, hardly merits being taken seriously. Spinoza acknowledges, in effect, however unwillingly, that advance to the life of freedom is through conflict between 'desire' and 'understanding'; Blake appears to believe that any such conflict should cease and that desire should be given free rein. He wishes us, that is to say, to be as 'natural' as possible, and thinks that we can, if we wish, be entirely natural. To be natural, to be ourselves, as he thinks, through placing no restraint upon ourselves, would be to have freedom and an immense enrichment of our lives and of our imaginations.

So much at least Blake certainly appears to believe. But he shows little if any sign of having thought with any care concerning this strange doctrine. In fact, it requires little thought to see that what Blake says is both confused in itself and contrary to the facts of experience. It is not difficult to show, in the first place, how confused it is. He wishes us to be creatures of desire and imagination, *not* of moral restraint and reason; a violent anti-intellectualism goes along with his desire that mankind should release itself from a moral state in which check is placed upon impulse. Now animals have not reason, nor do they choose. But Blake does not, we may presume, wish us to become animals in the sense that we shall become incapable of reason; or if, in his vague dreaming, he did desire this, he could only do so by forgetting that if we had not reason we certainly would not have imagination. For it is certain that imagination, whatever it may or may not be, cannot possibly act in independence of the knowledge afforded us by the processes of thought. Without power of thought awareness of a world of objects as objects is not possible. It is foolish to think that, our intellectual nature destroyed, we could then be possessed of imagination, whether or not apprehending infinity in all things. If the imagination may ever, in any sense, be said to transcend thought, it can do so, we may be sure, only, in part at least, through the previous aid of thought; and with this Spinoza, for his part, would have emphatically agreed, for his 'scientia intuitiva' is no mere collapse below the level of the rational, but a consummation of the rational. Without the aid of thought, the imagination has no world in which to act, no materials to refashion. It may be indeed that, as Kant said, thought without imagination is helpless; but it is certain that imagination without thought is stillborn. It is all very well to be vaguely and grandly anti-intellectualist; and no doubt it may well be that the intelligence has its limits. But whatever the intelligence may not do, it is the height of folly and vague emotionalism to overlook what in fact it does do. Spinoza was wiser in trying to see (however vainly) man's rational and moral life as a part of what he regarded (however falsely) as man's animal nature.

Let us therefore acquit Blake of so extreme and mistaken a view, more perhaps for the sake of the argument than in confidence that he did not think something like this. If he desired that we should remain intelligent creatures, he seems nevertheless to have thought that through the continued practice of not restraining our desires we should reach a state of equilibrium in which, acting wholly on impulse, we should be happy, stable, and social. This of course assumes a great deal as to what human nature is really like, and as to what it 'naturally' is. But putting this aside, it requires a curious lack of thought to believe that beings whose intelligence is at all more noticeable than that of animals (even if their life be lived for ever in a Garden of Eden or happy South Sea island) could live in ignorance of the experience of choosing. Blake of course is aware that the presence in us of reason is part and parcel of our lives as moral beings. But if we are at all to live an intelligent (and therefore imaginative) life, it is inconceivable that we can with any show of sense hope for our release from a moral state in which we are constantly confronted with alternative lines of action. No doubt we can sympathize with his longing for wholeness of mind and freedom; but it is certain that his doctrine, offering this way of finding these things, is very confused.

In the second place, if his idea is confused in itself, it is also clear that he could only have envisaged, however vaguely, this kind of innocence and freedom by overlooking certain important factors; and another Romantic writer, writing indeed without any knowledge of Blake, though aware that this kind of belief was abroad at the time, observed what these factors are. Keats said in one of his letters that he did not 'at all believe in this sort of perfectibility'.

'The nature of the world', he went on, 'will not admit of it—the inhabitants of the world will correspond to itself. Let the fish Philosophise the ice away from the Rivers in winter time and they shall be at continual play in the tepid delight of Summer. Look at the Poles and at the Sands of Africa, Whirlpools and volcanoes—Let men exterminate them and I will say that they may arrive at earthly Happiness—The point at which Man may arrive is as far as the parallel state in inanimate nature and no further—For instance suppose a rose to have sensation, it blooms on a beautiful morning it enjoys itself—but there comes a cold wind, a hot sun—it cannot escape it, it cannot destroy its annoyances—they are as native to the world as itself . . .'

But this is not all.

'The most interesting question that can come before us is, How far . . . mankind can be made happy—I can imagine such happiness carried to an extreme—but what must it end in?—Death—and who could in such a case bear with death—the whole troubles of life which are now frittered away in a series of years, would then be accumulated for the last days of a being who instead of hailing its approach would leave this world as Eve left Paradise.'[1]

So do Keats's almost casual remarks demolish Blake's vague day-dreaming. It required a curious perversity to overlook the considerations which occupy Keats's sentences, and in disregard for them to try to see in an obscurely conceived 'natural innocence' what might be an end for human life.

Finally, Blake's beliefs appear to rest on the assumption that our desires are somehow good and must lead to happiness. But the great mass of opinion agrees that there is little or no ground for this belief; and that on the contrary the experience of the race leads us to conclude that human nature is in part at least naturally evil. This is also the view of Christianity, and Blake himself, irritatingly enough, appears to have thought so from time to time (here, however, again he went to extremes—'Man is only evil' he said). Now if this is so, and the human will mysteriously infected with evil, only a supernatural agency can save it. The Christian belief, whether right or wrong, is that the evil natural to us is finally expunged by the grace and act of God. That act, moreover, does not restore us to the innocence of an Adam in Eden; we are 'made new in Christ' and in that state indeed are redeemed from time in the knowledge of God. The evil in man is overruled by God to serve the purposes of a new creation. But these beliefs are altogether opposed to those of *The Marriage of Heaven and Hell*, and Blake cannot have them both. Sooner or later he must come to acknowledge, if not Christianity, the absurdity of his belief in 'desire'. But it will be a long time before this acknowledgement comes; and in the first group of prophetic works, to which we shall now turn, it is the gospel of desire which he preaches.

1 *Letters of Keats*, ed. Buxton Forman, Oxford, 1935, p. 335.

In them he appears to look, not for the 'innocence' of eternal life which Christianity promises, but a wholly natural innocence. He will try, in these prophetic books, to set out in poetry a notion and ideal, confused in itself, and divorced from the plain facts of the world and of life.

§ 4

I have completed a brief general exposition of Blake's thought, and I shall now pass on to study the first group of allegorical writings. It is convenient to divide Blake's work into three sections. The first consists of the *Songs of Innocence*; the second of his work from *The French Revolution* (1791) up to and including the first six books of *Vala or The Four Zoas*; the third from the concluding books of *Vala* to his last work *Jerusalem*. Why a division must be made in the middle of *Vala* will be explained at a later stage. We shall now consider the second group of works. The *Songs of Experience* of course fall within this group; but I shall no longer be concerned with them but shall confine myself to the allegorical works in this section of Blake's writings. I shall not attempt to give an account of each one in turn. It will be enough for our purpose to point out certain general features in Blake's allegories, or as they may perhaps be called, mythologies. I shall be chiefly concerned with *The French Revolution*, *The Daughters of Albion*, *Europe*, *The First Book of Urizen*, *The Book of Ahania*, and *The Song of Los*.

These works have this in common that they all expound, in their (to some extent) different ways, the teaching which Blake has expounded in *The Marriage of Heaven and Hell*, that is to say, the gospel of 'Hell'. Now in all these works Blake opposes a revolutionary and 'fiery' personage to a cold, cruel, tyrannical, and repressive one. This is the main feature of his mythology. In *The French Revolution*, Orleans and Fayette are opposed to the King, the archbishop, and the nobles. Orleans is the 'generous' orator of the new ideal and Fayette its hero. Fayette, 'like a flame of fire', 'stood before dark ranks, and before expecting captains':

On pestilent vapours around him flow frequent spectres of religious men, weeping
In winds; driven out of the abbeys, their naked souls shiver in the keen open air;
Driven out by the fiery cloud of Voltaire, and thund'rous rocks of Rousseau,
They dash like foam against the ridges of the army, uttering a faint feeble cry.
(p. 188)

The French Revolution is, indeed, fairly clear. No doubt we are helped by the familiarity of the situation which he treats. He does not, however, treat it at all realistically, but enlarges the figures of the nobles and their opponents to a suitable mythological hugeness. These figures also possess, like all the figures to come in Blake's mythology, a certain nightmarish quality. At the end of *The Marriage of Heaven and Hell* there occurs *A Song of Liberty* which is a transition piece from *The French Revolution* to the later poems of pure mythology. Now in *A Song of Liberty* there appear two figures who are to remain throughout the group of poems with which we are now dealing. In *A Song of Liberty* they are called the 'New Born Terror' (who is a version of Fayette and Orleans) and the 'Starry King' respectively. The former is also called the 'Son of Fire' and is the spirit who is moving Europe to revolution; and the 'Starry King' is also called Urthona. He is the 'tyrant', who is also 'Rome' and the promulgator of the 'ten commands'. In the poems which follow, the opposition between the two forces symbolized by these figures remains. Urthona is sometimes called Urizen, and the 'Son of Fire' sometimes Orc, sometimes Los, sometimes Luvah. Why Blake should thus change the names is not clear, and I shall not stop to discuss the matter at this point. Now Orc, to give him his most frequent name, is a rebel; he is the 'energy' of the gospel of Hell, fighting to overcome the 'stony law' and the 'ten commands' for which Urizen (to give him the name he most often goes by) is responsible. We have a revolutionary and a tyrant. Also, Orc is a creature of fire and is young; Urizen is cold and old, always associated with snow, ice, and mountains. The former is fluid and moving, the latter hard and metallic. Urizen stands for political tyranny, the church, religion, the 'law'; and against them Orc flames in rebellion. This is the central situation in Blake's mythology, and it is one which is familiar enough. We think of Shelley's *Prometheus Unbound*; for Urizen recalls Jupiter, Orc Prometheus.

Indeed, there is some reason to think that the story of Prometheus was present in Blake's mind in the making of his mythology. I shall refer to a number of passages in these poems which suggest that this was so. There is an echo of the Prometheus legend in the following lines in *The Marriage of Heaven and Hell*: 'The Giants who formed this world into its sensual existence, and now seem to live in it in chains, are in truth the causes of its life and the sources of all activity. . . .' We naturally think of the Titans, overthrown by Zeus, and of Prometheus chained to his rock. Again, in the *Visions of the Daughters of Albion* we find two characters, Oothoon and Theotormon, who symbolize sexual innocence and sexual shame respectively, man innocent and man fallen; and they are alternative versions, in certain respects, of Orc and Urizen. There occur the following lines:

Oothoon weeps not; she cannot weep! her tears are locked up;
But she can howl incessant writhing her soft snowy limbs
And calling Theotormon's Eagles to prey upon her flesh.

The Eagles at her call descend and rend their bleeding prey:
Theotormon severely smiles; her soul reflects the smile,
As the clear spring, mudded with feet of beasts grows pure and smiles.
(p. 207)

Blake is using the Eagles in an original way. But his use of them to devour a victim is interesting, and may well be not wholly original. But more important, we find Orc himself bound to a rock on the top of a mountain. In *The First Book of Urizen* 'his young limbs' are 'chain'd to the rock'

With the Chain of Jealousy
Beneath Urizen's deathful shadow. (p. 255)

Again, in *The Song of Los*,

Orc on Mount Atlas howl'd, chain'd down with the Chain of Jealousy
(p. 273)

In *Vala* we find Orc crying to Urizen—

King of furious hail storms
Art thou the cold attractive power that holds me in this chain?
I well remember how I stole thy light and it became fire
Consuming. (p. 371)

Here the description of Urizen as 'king of furious hail storms' would suit the Greek Zeus accurately; and this along with Orc's theft of light and fire makes it reasonably certain that Blake had the Prometheus myth in mind.

Now in addition to these passages and to others which might be quoted, the suitability of Prometheus to Blake's purposes is clear enough. Prometheus was originally a God of Fire and Orc is a 'Son of Fire'; Prometheus was a fire-bringer, and a champion of mankind against oppression. Also, Prometheus was a patron of the crafts and the arts, which might help to make him attractive in Blake's eyes. Nowhere indeed is Blake explicit in his use of the myth; but this was natural in one who was at pains to express his contempt for the Greek mind. Similarly, Zeus, in his tyranny over Prometheus, might well occur to Blake and suggest to him possible aspects of the mythology he was trying to create.

But it is not only of the Prometheus myth that we hear echoes. I have already referred to Blake's mention of Titans. In *The First Book of Urizen* we hear of the sons of Urizen; and in this book and in *The Book of Ahania* and in *Vala* we read of their rebellion against their father. In the first of these poems we read—

> Most Urizen sicken'd to see
> His eternal creations appear,
> Sons and daughters of sorrow on mountains
> Weeping, wailing. First Thiriel appear'd
> Astonish'd at his own existence,
> Like a man from a cloud born; and Utha
> From the waters emerging, laments;
> Grodna rent the deep earth, howling
> Amaz'd; his heavens immense cracks
> Like the ground parch'd with heat, then Fuzon
> Flam'd out, first begotten, last born;
> All his eternal sons in like manner;
> His daughters from green herbs and cattle, . . .
>
> He in darkness clos'd view'd all his race,
> And his soul sicken'd! he curs'd
> Both sons and daughters . . . (p. 256)

Of the sons it is Fuzon who, in *The Book of Ahania*, leads the rebellion.

> 'Shall we worship this Demon of smoke,'
> Said Fuzon, 'this abstract non-entity,
> This cloudy God seated on waters,
> Now seen, now obscur'd, King of Sorrow?' (p. 259)

There follows a narrative of the conflict between Fuzon and Urizen. Now this suggests (though, it must be admitted, vaguely enough) the struggle of Kronos against Uranos; as Kronos the last born of the Titans especially hated his father, so does Fuzon, who is last born, hate his. Both Uranos and Urizen are jealous gods and fathers. I do not wish to erect a vague enough similarity into a show of certainty; but the matter is at least worth consideration. Also, it is worth noticing the following passage. In the Third Night of *Vala*, Urizen, addressing Ahania, says:

> O bright Ahania, a Boy is born of the dark Ocean
> Whom Urizen doth serve, with Light replenishing his darkness.
> I am set here a King of trouble, commanded here to serve
> And do my ministry to those who eat of my wide table.
> All this is mine, yet I must serve, and that Prophetic boy
> Must grow up to command his Prince; *but hear my determin'd decree*:
> Vala shall become a Worm in Enitharmon's Womb,
> Laying her seed upon the fibres, soon to issue forth,
> And Luvah in the loins of Los a dark and furious death.
> Alas for me! what will become of me at that dread time? (p. 320)

This passage, like most in Blake's work, is obscure enough. But whatever else Urizen may be saying, it seems clear that he anticipates that a child will be born, presumably of Los and Enitharmon (the significance of whom we need not here pause to consider), who will overthrow Urizen—'that Prophetic boy must grow up to command his Prince'. Now in fact a child (Orc) is born to Los and Enitharmon—a 'fiery child' (*Vala*, Fifth Night); and it is he who overthrows the power of Urizen. In the Seventh Night of *Vala* Urizen is terrified by the appearance of Orc, whom he recognizes as fulfilment of a prophecy. I suggest that here also we have an adaptation of Greek myth. Both Uranos and Zeus feared the power of a child yet to be born and that this child would overthrow them. We can plausibly believe that any mythology representing rebellion against and overthrow of a God would attract Blake's interest. Rebellion against established Deity was a favourite theme with him as it was to be with Shelley. Certainly, if Blake was drawing, consciously or unconsciously, on Greek mythology, he took little care to follow the myths closely; but this indeed could hardly be expected, for reasons which will become clear later on.

We shall return again to this matter. For the present, we must observe two other strands which went to the making of the tangle of Blake's mythology.[1] They are Milton's version of the conflict of God and Satan, and the story of the life and death of Christ. That he should use the former of these two was inevitable, for *The Marriage of Heaven and Hell* is based on Blake's trick of reversing the roles of God and Satan in *Paradise Lost*. Milton never failed, right up to the end, as *Milton* shows, to fascinate Blake, and the great bulk of the group of poems we are considering is quite unintelligible without reference to *Paradise Lost*. In *The Marriage of Heaven and Hell* Blake says that the Jehovah of the Bible is 'no other than he who dwells in flaming fire'. 'It indeed appear'd to Reason as if Desire was cast out; but the Devil's account is, that the Messiah fell and formed a Heaven of what he stole from the Abyss.' Thus, what Milton called Satan was really the Messiah, or Desire or Energy. 'The reason Milton wrote in fetters when he wrote of angels and God, and at liberty when of the Devil and Hell, is because he was a true poet and of the Devil's party without knowing it.' In bearing these passages in mind, which are of the greatest importance in reading Blake's Prophetic Works, it is also useful to bear in mind Shelley's famous remark that 'The only imaginary being resembling in any degree Prometheus, is Satan'; and Shelley goes on to attribute to Satan,

[1] I may add that I have not tried to tabulate all the myths which Blake sought to incorporate into his work. I have given outstanding examples in order to illustrate his procedure.

as to Prometheus, 'courage, and majesty, and firm and patient opposition to omnipotent force'.[1] Again, in the *Defence of Poetry*, Shelley observes that 'Nothing can exceed the energy and magnificence of the character of Satan in *Paradise Lost* . . . Milton's Devil as a moral being is far superior to his God . . . and this bold neglect of a direct moral purpose is the most decisive proof of the supremacy of Milton's genius'.[2] These remarks at once link Shelley with Blake, and Prometheus with Satan. Orc is the Satan and Urizen the God of *Paradise Lost*.

We must not, however, imagine that Blake gives a consistent and clear version of the story of the fall of Satan and of his temptation of Adam and Eve. In addition, I think there were good reasons why Blake could not follow Milton's story of Satan out closely, just as there were good reasons why he could not follow the Prometheus story closely. Of these we shall speak at a later juncture; my immediate purpose is only to indicate this important component in Blake's confused mythology. In the Seventh Night of *Vala*, in its first version, Orc is represented in his caves in a manner which recalls Satan in the first book of *Paradise Lost*. Orc is in a 'cavern'd universe of flaming fire'; and lines such as the following, spoken by Urizen who visits Orc in his 'hell', directly recall some of Milton's lines—

> Yet thou dost laugh at all these tortures, and this horrible place:
> Yet throw thy limbs these fires abroad that back return upon thee
> While thou reposest, throwing rage on rage, feeding thyself
> With visions of sweet bliss for other than this burning clime.
> (p. 367)

Now there are at least two passages in the first book of *Paradise Lost* which went to the making of these lines. First (l. 53):

> But his doom
> Reserv'd him to more wrath; for now the thought
> Both of lost happiness and lasting pain
> Torments him;

and (l. 220):

> Forthwith upright he rears from off the Pool
> His mighty Stature; in each hand the flames
> Drivn backward slope their pointing spires, and rowld
> In billows, leave i' th' midst a horrid Vale.

Again, the creation of the world by Urizen, in *The First Book of Urizen*, directly recalls the creation of the world in *Paradise Lost*:

[1] Oxford *Shelley*, p. 201.
[2] *Prose Works of Shelley*, Chatto & Windus, 1912, vol. ii, p. 25.

He form'd a line and a plummet
To divide the Abyss beneath;
He form'd a dividing rule;

He formed scales to weigh,
He formed many weights;
He formed a brazen quadrant;
He formed golden compasses,
And began to explore the Abyss;
And he planted a garden of fruits. (p. 255)

In *Paradise Lost* (book VII, l. 218), the Messiah (not indeed God)

On the Wings of Cherubim
Uplifted, in Paternal Glorie rode
Farr into *Chaos*, and the World unborn . . .
Then staid the fervid Wheeles, and in his hand
He took the golden Compasses, prepar'd
In Gods Eternal store, to circumscribe
This Universe, and all created things.

In this way Blake draws directly upon Milton's verse in *Paradise Lost*, identifying Orc with Satan who is cast down, and Urizen with Jehovah. For Orc is also the serpent, the 'eternal viper'; and Urizen made Orc

In serpent form compell'd, stretch out and up the mysterious tree.
He suffered him to cling that he might draw all human forms
Into submission to his will, nor knew the dread result.

So far Blake goes; but it was not easy for him to use the story any further. There were complications; for Orc in the role of the Satan who brought 'death into the world and all our woe' could hardly suit Blake's purposes. Indeed he did not introduce Orc as the serpent until, as we shall see, he had discovered, or thought he had discovered, a way of meeting this difficulty.

To this strand in Blake's mythology I shall refer at greater length at a later point. I indicate now, and briefly, a third body of 'myth' which must be noticed, namely that of the life and death of Christ. In the works which succeed the group which we now study, Blake gives his version of the redemption of the world by Christ; but in these earlier poems we find frequent representations of his crucifixion. I have already referred to *The Everlasting Gospel*, written in 1818, in which Blake exhibits Jesus as acting, as he says in *The Marriage*, 'from impulse and not from rules'. We are not surprised therefore to find in the Prophetic Works that Jesus is Orc; the Messiah is Orc and Satan. The poem *Europe* is of special interest here. The part of it called 'A Prophesy' begins, significantly, with lines directly reminiscent of the language and rhythm of Milton's *Ode on the Nativity*:

The deep of winter came,
What time the secret child
Descended thro' the orient gates of the eternal day:
War ceas'd, and all the troops like shadows fled to their abodes.
(p. 234)

Blake then expounds in his mythological language what he considers to be the significance of the birth of Christ. Los, here the husband of Enitharmon, sings a song of triumph on the event and cries to Orc:

Arise, O Orc, from thy deep den!
First born of Enitharmon, rise!
And we will crown thy head with garlands of the ruddy vine . . .
(p. 235)

The birth of Jesus who 'acted from impulse' is the triumph of Orc. Unfortunately the triumph is short-lived; and Blake goes on to describe the falling away from the perfection of Jesus and the further domination of Orc by Urizen in the growth of Christianity. Eighteen hundred years later, however, with the coming of the French Revolution, Orc emerges again:

Terrible Orc, when he beheld the morning in the east,
Shot from the heights of Enitharmon,
And in the vineyard of red France appear'd the light of his fury.
(p. 241)

Orc then is very closely associated with Jesus, if indeed he is not to be identified with him. But the following facts must be noticed. In *The First Book of Urizen* and in *The Book of Ahania* an apparently new figure makes his appearance. He is Fuzon.[1] He is, so far as can be gathered, Orc with a new name. He plays essentially the same role as Orc as the supreme enemy of Urizen; he is the Prometheus and the Satan. But there is this difference. Ordinarily, Orc is a son of Los and Enitharmon. Orc, under the new name of Fuzon, becomes suddenly and without explanation a son of Urizen. Now this change of name and change of parenthood makes for obscurity. But the obscurity is to some extent done away with when we read that Urizen slays Fuzon and then

The corse of his first begotten
On the accursed Tree of Mystery,
On the topmost stem of this Tree,
Urizen nail'd Fuzon's corse. (p. 262)

Now these lines unmistakably suggest the crucifixion of Christ. And we realize that Blake, now thinking of Orc as Christ, the only begotten of the Father, must make him a son of Urizen, who

1 Fuzon is indeed briefly referred to at the end of *The First Book of Urizen*.

slays and crucifies his son. Fuzon then is Orc in the Christ-role. And Blake irresponsibly and without explanation changes names and genealogies in order to set out another aspect of Orc, his Christ-aspect, so to speak.

I am not at present chiefly concerned to discuss the problem of the obscurity of Blake's Prophetic Works, the problem, I mean, of why these works are so obscure. For the moment I have wished rather only to point out three elements which have gone into the making of Blake's mythology. Also, it is worth remarking here that Blake introduces into his mythology other material which he incorporates into the body of his myths. For example, there is an incident, repeatedly used, in which Orc, the son of Los and Enitharmon, is taken by his parents to the top of a mountain and in the name of Urizen is chained to a rock with the 'Chain of Jealousy'. Now by this incident we cannot fail to be reminded of the intended sacrifice of Isaac by Abraham. This sacrifice which Abraham was willing to make, so profound and important in the history of religion, was to Blake anathema, just as the crucifixion, as ordinarily seen by Christians, was anathema to him. He uses this Old Testament narrative as he uses the narrative of the crucifixion for his own irreligious purposes. I mention Blake's use of this familiar narrative to illustrate his constant use of a wide variety of material, which depends for its effect, to some extent, at least, upon our recognizing its origin. Thus, if what has so far been said is true, Blake's mythology is neither simple nor original. It is a compound of many things, and many narratives, all of which Blake, however, uses for his peculiar purposes and which he does not scruple to adopt or change.

For it would be idle to think that, if it is true that Blake is using the stories of Prometheus, of Satan, and of Christ to compose his mythology, we have thereby a neat clue to the understanding of Blake's writings. Although it is possible to follow Blake's use of these three stories, they are so mixed up and run into each other, as well as suffering additions from other quarters, that reading Blake is never anything less than laborious. What I have already said and quoted illustrates this constant mixture. The lines

> The corse of his first begotten
> On the accursed Tree of Mystery,
> On the topmost stem of this Tree,
> Urizen nail'd Fuzon's corse,

illustrate the running together of the Satan myth and the Christ myth—the Cross is also the forbidden Tree in Eden. Or again, in the incident which I have suggested is (and was probably intended by Blake to be) reminiscent of Abraham's sacrifice, the

Prometheus myth is also present; for Los does not propose to sacrifice Orc in the Old Testament manner; instead he binds him to the rock. And by the colloquies of Orc with Urizen in these poems from which I have quoted we cannot fail to be reminded of Prometheus. We see therefore the complexity, and as it were discern the very obscurity, of these poems.

§ 5

I have now described the very broad outlines of Blake's mythology. In the present sections, I shall try to expound this mythology, as it appears in this group of poems, in greater detail. I shall proceed primarily by trying to expound Blake's beliefs as they appear here; but to do this is also, of course, to try to follow the mythology. I cannot, however, hope to do this with any completeness, for the good reason that there is in these poems a good deal which I do not apprehend at all clearly. But I venture to think that so far as the exposition goes, it can claim as much certainty as is possible in anything which has to do with Blake. In the course of making this exposition, I hope that some at least of the reasons for the confusion and difficulty of these Prophetic Works may become clear. I have therefore three purposes: to expound Blake's thought, to follow his mythology, and to explain why the latter is so confused.

Now we have a tyrannical Urizen and a rebellious Orc. Urizen is 'religion', the moral law, thought; Orc is desire, and he is also imagination. As I have said, Urizen has the mastery of Orc; we see Orc either chained Prometheus-like to a mountain or lying, Satan-like, in the fires of Hell. Now Los and Enitharmon are the parents of Orc, and they symbolize humanity. They are the Adam and Eve of Blake's mythology. In *Vala* Los is called the spectre of Urthona, where Urthona is the name of innocent man before he fell into the false conflict of duty with desire. To call Los the spectre of Urthona is to say of him that, as fallen man, he is but the shadow of what he 'really' is, namely Urthona. Los is also called, for reasons which are not clear, the 'Eternal Prophet'. Now Los and Enitharmon, standing for 'fallen' humanity, acknowledge Urizen, as we would expect, as God. In the Fourth Night of *Vala* Los says:

> Our God is Urizen the King, King of the Heavenly hosts;
> We have no other God but he. . . .

and it is Los and Enitharmon who bind their child Orc to the rock with the 'Chain of Jealousy'.

They took Orc to the top of a mountain.
O how Enitharmon wept!
They chain'd his young limbs to the rock
With the Chain of Jealousy
Beneath Urizen's deathful shadow. (p. 255)

So far, we might think we have a fairly clear mythology. Urizen, the God; Los and Enitharmon, humanity, who bring forth Orc, who will be a rebel against the jealous and overbearing God of his parents. In fact, what I have just recounted is very much a simplification and a selection, although it is certainly a very important element in Blake's myth-making. The following is the major complication which we must carefully notice.

In *The First Book of Urizen* we find the following lines:

Los wept, howling around the dark Demon,
And cursing his lot; for in anguish
Urizen was rent from his side,
And a fathomless void for his feet,
And intense fires for his dwelling.

But Urizen laid in a stony sleep,
Unorganiz'd, rent from Eternity.

The Eternals said: 'What is this? Death.
'Urizen is a clod of clay.' (p. 247)

In these lines Blake is describing the birth of Urizen; he was 'rent from the side' of Los, and rent therefore from 'Eternity'. By this we may take Blake to mean that Los originally enjoyed an 'eternal' existence, that is to say, one of innocence, without the anguish of 'before' and 'after' which belongs to moral man; and that Urizen, the tyrannical God, was formed by and out of the 'fall' from innocence. He is, in this sense, derived from Los; so that Los might be said to be the Creator, Urizen the Created. For it was part of Blake's belief, as we have seen, that there is no God; that God is but the creation of man in his conflict of duty and desire. We see therefore the inevitable complication which Blake's mythology must undergo. If Urizen, his God, must be both a God for the human Los and Enitharmon, and an offshoot of Los, Los and Enitharmon must be creatures of Urizen but also the source of his life.

Now after Urizen has been rent from the side of Los he is, we are told, 'unorganiz'd, rent from Eternity'. He has been born from Los, but is shapeless, a mere death. Then, in Blake's myth, Los proceeds to give Urizen shape. Los with his hammer and anvils forms Urizen, 'cold, featureless', into human shape. Chapter IV (*b*) of *The First Book of Urizen*, describing the slow formation of Urizen's body, is a piece of typical Blakish nightmare:

In a horrible, dreamful slumber,
Like the linked infernal chain,
A vast Spine writh'd in torment
Upon the winds, shooting pain'd
Ribs, like a bending cavern;
And bones of solidness froze
Over all his nerves of joy. . . . (p. 249)

Not only does Los thus beat Urizen into human shape; he also binds him with innumerable fetters:

Los beat on his fetters of iron,
And heated his furnaces, and poured
Iron sodor and sodor of brass.

By thus representing Los as hammering Urizen into human shape, Blake probably intends two things. First, the creation of an anthropomorphic God by man, a God anathema to Blake; secondly, the notion that Urizen has in him no life, that he is deathly and that what form he has is mechanically contrived, something superficial and unreal, something not at all his own. But we emphasize here that if in Blake's mythology Urizen is God, the creator of the world and of men, he is also a mere creation of man and of a very mechanical kind. We can understand why Blake should thus complicate his mythology. For he wishes, first, to represent the traditional God of Christianity (as he saw him) as a tyrant and impostor; but he also wishes to make it clear that no such being exists and that he is a pure creation of the human mind. But the result is that his mythology becomes difficult and unreasonably complicated. In this mythology Los, it is to be noted, enchains both Urizen, casting 'nets and gins about him', and Orc, whom, in the name of Urizen, he later binds to the rock with the 'Chain of Jealousy'. For both Urizen and Orc spring from Los. Urizen, his God, is in some sense created by him; Orc is his son. Thus Urizen, symbolizing morality and thought, and Orc, symbolizing desire and imagination, are, so to speak, parts of Los, disrupted from him; and their disruption from him is the fall of Los from 'Eternity' and innocence. The temporal history of Los, so to speak, is the history of the conflict between these two elements, symbolized by Urizen and Orc, which have become separated off from him.

§ 6

We must now inquire further into Urizen as one who 'has been rent from the side of Los'. Thus 'rent', 'hammered into human shape', and after the birth of Orc, Urizen begins to create the world:

He formed golden compasses
And began to explore the Abyss,

in the manner of Christ in *Paradise Lost*. But it is important to understand what Blake has in mind when he thus makes Urizen create the world. We must remember that Blake does not believe in Milton's God who brings a world into being. What Blake means when he describes the creation of the world by Urizen is the habit, which arises from the separation of Urizen from Los and the consequent pre-eminence of Reason, of apprehending the world as dead and mechanical. Hence the weights, quadrants, and compasses, the instruments of science. Urizen is not a maker of a world like Milton's God; but he does, in a sense, bring a new world into being, that is to say, a world represented by thought as 'dead' and unlike the 'living' world of the imagination. Urizen *is* Newton, who is one of Blake's favourite symbols for science; and he *is* Locke, who is said to be the type of sensationalist philosopher. Hence in Blake's mythology, the world as it is seen by thought and science, the world, that is to say, of Urizen, is 'hard', 'solid', 'petrific', 'iron', 'brass', 'forg'd in mills', 'rock', 'mountain', 'ice':

Coldness, darkness, obstruction, a Solid
Without fluctuation, hard as adamant,
Black as marble of Egypt, impenetrable . . . (p. 268)

these are the qualities of Urizen and his world. Hence the world which Urizen makes is unreal and artificial, machine-made, so to speak. His world is what *he* is, tool-made. He has himself been hammered into shape, mechanically contrived, and what he is, thus does he himself make. In the Second Night of *Vala* we have another account of the creation of Urizen's world. Urizen is described as 'standing in the human brain':

He saw the indefinite space beneath and his soul shrunk with horror,
His feet upon the verge of Non Existence. (p. 303)

And then:

The Bands of Heaven flew thro' the air singing and shouting to Urizen.
Some fix'd the anvil, some the loom erected, some the plow
And harrow form'd and fram'd the harness of silver and ivory,
The golden compasses, the quadrant, and the rule and balance.
They erected the furnaces, they form'd the anvils of gold beaten in mills
Where winter beats incessant, fixing them firm on their base.
The bellows began to blow . . .
The tygers of wrath called the horses of instruction from their mangers,
They unloos'd them and put on the harness of gold and silver and ivory,

In human forms distinct they stood round Urizen, prince of Light,
Petrifying all the Human Imagination into rock and sand. (p. 303)

This passage makes Blake's intention clear enough. The 'tyger' gives way to the 'horse' ('the tygers of wrath are wiser than the horses of instruction' he had said in *The Marriage*); life, movement, energy, give way to petrifaction, rock, sand. Imagination yields to science. Thus does Urizen create a 'mundane shell'.

On clouds the Sons of Urizen beheld Heaven walled round;
They weigh'd and order'd all . . .
Travelling in silent majesty along their order'd ways
In right lined paths outmeasur'd by proportions of number, weight,
And measure, mathematic motion wondrous along the deep,
In fiery pyramid, or Cube, or unornamented pillar square
Of fire, far shining, travelling along even to its destin'd end . . .
Such the period of many worlds.
Others triangular, right angled course maintain. Others obtuse,
Acute, Scalene, in simple paths; but others move
In intricate ways, biquadrate, Trapeziums, Rhombs, Rhomboids,
Paralellograms triple and quadruple, polygonic
In their amazing hard subdu'd course in the vast deep. (p. 312)

This is Urizen's mathematical universe; and in Blake's judgement it is a universe of death. This is the universe as it is apprehended by Reason. This 'change' in the universe goes along with, or results from, a 'contraction' of the mind and senses, which results from Urizen and his domination.

All the vast of Nature shrunk
Before their shrunken eyes. (p. 274)

We read of Urizen in *The First Book of Urizen* that he is 'self-clos'd'; and in *The Marriage of Heaven and Hell* we read that

'If the doors of perception were cleansed every thing would appear to man as it is, infinite.

'For man has closed himself up, till he sees all things thro' narrow chinks of his cavern.'

In the reign of Urizen our senses serve only to close us within ourselves. In contrast to us, 'ev'ry Bird that cuts the airy way is an immense world of delight' (p. 192), where the significant word is 'world'; the bird *is* the world from which *it* is not cut off. Again, he says of mankind that 'they wander moping', and that 'beyond the bounds of their own self their senses cannot penetrate'. In contrast, once more, the natural world does not suffer this enclosure within a cavern of self:

The tree knows not what is outside of its leaves and bark
And yet it drinks the summer joy and fears the winter sorrow.

That is to say, we have knowledge which is yet not knowledge; and as we have seen, Blake regards our so-called knowledge as something to be got rid of. Urizen must somehow be overcome. The senses have become the instruments of reason; and life to the reason is death to the senses and the imagination. The 'minute particulars' are lost sight of in this deathly condition.

We must, however, remember that if Urizen is the enemy, he sprang forth from Los. He is, in some form, a part of the original constitution of Los, humanity. His separation from him was a disaster; it was, indeed, the Fall. In worshipping Urizen we worship but a debased portion of ourselves. But Urizen was not always thus. In the original perfection of humanity he was not Reason and therefore also Doubt; he was Faith and Certainty. In the Second Night of *Vala*, Luvah (who is another form of the Orc of earlier poems) says:

> I suffer affliction
> Because I love, for I was love, but hatred awakes in me
> And Urizen, who was Faith and certainty, is chang'd to Doubt.
> (p. 306)

Originally, then, Urizen was not reason and mediated knowledge, but intuitive and unmediated knowledge. He has become divorced from Luvah or Orc who for his part was, in the beginning, Love; with this divorce, certainty and perception become thought and scepticism, and love turns into hatred, envy, and jealousy. Then thought, with which go morality, conscience, and duty, seeks, in perpetual enmity, to control and deny feeling and impulse. Both Urizen and Orc (Luvah) are sprung from Los. They are his constituent elements, having allegorical form; and in terms of their conflict and separation, Blake sets out the tragedy of human nature.

§ 7

We are now perhaps in a position to consider the nature of Blake's attempts at mythology. I have said that Blake uses a number of myths for his purposes: some fragments at least of Greek mythology, the Miltonic myth as we may call it, and the Christ myth. Some of his later use of these myths we shall observe at another stage. But we have already seen that he uses none of these myths with care; he runs pieces of them into an original synthesis in which none of them is retained with any clearness of outline. They run into each other and are mingled quite bewilderingly; and if their outlines, singly, are lost sight of, Blake's synthesis equally has no sharp outline. That this is so, no reader of Blake takes long to discover. I have illustrated

Blake's irresponsibility by speaking of his arbitrariness in giving substantially the same figures different names when it pleases him to do so. And it would not be at all difficult to show his disregard for elementary rules of communication in several other respects.

Our immediate purpose, however, is to notice Blake's use of mythology in the light of what we may think his purpose was in writing these poems. The preceding paragraphs represent, I believe, a substantially correct record, so far as it goes, of Blake's doctrine. If so, it may be of some value to consider his mythology as an expression of his beliefs. So far, I have spoken of Blake's *mythology*. The point I wish to make in this section is that Blake's Prophetic Books can with equal justice be said to be allegorical; and that at least a part of his failure is due to his having fallen between the two stools of mythology and allegory.

Now a myth is not a thing which springs, fully formed, from the head of any man; it grows up as part of the culture of a people or peoples. Now Blake, setting out to create a mythology, however original he may intend it to be, in fact draws upon the mythology and symbols of the past. He takes pieces of them, uses them very much as he wishes, joins them together, acts in no loyalty to any one. Also, because a myth is not a quick creation but a slow development, it has a richness and a depth which are inexhaustible. In it the symbol and what is symbolized are wellnigh inseparable; the symbol is apprehended with a singleness of mind in which thoughts are, as it were, more perceived and felt than explicitly grasped as thoughts. No philosophy of religion is a substitute for symbolic figures and events; in the last resort a theology is barren in comparison with the contemplation of the story. Now an allegory on the other hand may well spring, neat and fully grown, from the mind of an individual. But it differs from a myth in a very important respect. In allegory, thought and its figurative expression run, so to speak, side by side. We must have both a narrative and a clear conceptual scheme; we are aware of the story as illustrative of the reality which it treats of. These two things cannot become one in allegory, by its very nature; they remain apart. Certainly, they illuminate each other; but our minds are kept moving back and fore between narrative and meaning. It may be said that the difference between myth and allegory is primarily one of degree; and this may be allowed. A successful allegorist will certainly exert himself to reduce the gap between what is thought and what is perceived; but it remains part of the idea of allegory that the gap be not wholly obliterated.

Curiously enough, Blake has himself some illuminating remarks to make on this topic. Speaking probably of *Vala*, possibly of

Milton, he says in a letter written to Butts in July 1803, that 'it is the Grandest Poem that this World Contains. Allegory addressed to the Intellectual powers, while it is altogether hidden from the Corporeal Understanding, is my Definition of the Most Sublime Poetry. . . .' But he says elsewhere, in the note called *A Vision of the Last Judgment*, 'Fable or Allegory are a totally distinct and inferior kind of Poetry. Vision or Imagination is a Representation of what Eternally Exists, Really and Unchangeably. Fable or Allegory is Form'd by the Daughters of Memory. . . . Note here that Fable or Allegory is seldom without some Vision. Pilgrim's Progress is full of it . . . but Allegory and Vision ought to be known as Two Distinct Things.' (p. 828) Blake's prose is rarely more easy than his verse; and the difference between what Blake calls the 'Intellectual Powers' and what he calls the 'Corporeal Understanding' is by no means clear to me. The significant matter in these remarks is, however, his conclusion that 'Allegory' is inferior to 'Vision'; and we may perhaps take Blake to mean substantially what I tried to express above. Myth, we may say, partakes of 'vision'; allegory partakes of 'vision' only partially, and involves constant appeal to memory and to explicit intellectual processes. In this sense, it is not only myth which may appeal to 'vision'. The highest forms of literature, whether using myth or not, may do so. The difference between *King Lear* and *The Faerie Queene* is not far to seek. This difference between myth and allegory is cardinal.

We may add, though with less confidence, that myth is most frequently cosmological and represents deities in their creations of worlds or their dealings with men; allegory is psychological, setting forth states and powers in the human mind in their reaction upon and conflict with one another. Myth is born of speculation, allegory of introspection; the former is outward-looking, metaphysical, and springing from wonder, the latter inward-looking, moral, and springing from mental conflict and suffering. Mr. C. S. Lewis has observed in *The Allegory of Love* that allegory took its rise from the Christian experience of the difficulties and stress of the inner life in its combat with evil; and that the allegorist must be in earnest with the creation of good character; he has a moral purpose and indulges no mere taste for speculation. Mr. Lewis says of the allegorist that 'character is what he has to produce; within he finds only the raw material, the passions and emotions which contend for mastery. That unitary "soul" or personality which interests the novelist is for him merely the arena in which the combatants meet . . .'; and he adds, in a footnote, 'The obvious parallel is modern psycho-analysis and its shadowy personages such as the "censor". At a different level, it might be argued that the application of psychological terms *at all* to the unconscious is itself a species of allegory.' (p. 61) Now if this is so, allegory may be distinguished from myth in its matter as well as in its procedure.

When, in the light of these remarks, we turn to Blake's Prophetic Works, we discern some of the causes of the dissatisfaction which they arouse in us. Blake draws upon the great myths of the past—Greek, 'Miltonic', 'Christian'. Now it is hardly necessary to remark that Blake did not believe in the mythologies he used. It might be said that he at least believed that Jesus lived and died. But to believe this is not to accept the Christian doctrine, according to which, among other things, Christ's death effected the redemption by God of a humanity sinful and otherwise utterly lost. This certainly Blake did not believe. Now Aeschylus and Milton, if they could not wholeheartedly believe in the 'reality' of the myths they respectively used, at least lived in societies in which the myths they expressed were 'natural' and no doubt accepted widely. On the other hand, though Blake lived in a country in which very many people, at least, gave credence to the narrative of the life and death of Christ as it is upheld by Christianity, he for his part resolutely denied it. Thus, in using Pagan myths he was indeed *using* something with which he had, through the society in which he was living, no organic connexion, so to speak; but in using Christian 'myth' he was also *using* something, and in a manner which itself cut him off from the society of his time, so far as it was Christian—in so far, that is to say, as his use of the Christian narrative was to convey a set of beliefs very widely removed indeed from those of Christianity. We have therefore a notable and significant situation, the importance of which can hardly be exaggerated: namely, literary genius, standing outside all religious tradition, but using the mythologies of past and then existing religions for its own private purposes. Literature, that is to say, in Blake (and also, as we shall see, in Shelley and Keats) declined religion, but was yet dependent on rejected mythologies for its own expression. And we may well ask whether literature which thus *uses* religious mythology can possibly fail to come to grief? Whether, if a mythology is not 'real' in one and, so to speak, a part of one, it can fail, in its exercise in literature, to be more than a dead hand? Certainly, in Blake, in Shelley, and in Keats such use of mythology comes (however splendidly) to grief.

Now Blake, using the myths of Zeus, of God and Satan, and of God and Christ, is yet not writing as a theist. He is no believer in a transcendent God. From the beginning, therefore, he is placed outside these myths in the act of using them. Not only is Urizen, who is Zeus and the God of Christianity rolled into one, an object of hatred to Blake; Blake levels at him the final insult of not believing in his existence. How then can he manipulate these myths satisfactorily to his purpose? And why does he undertake to use them at all? The answer to the latter question is, in part at least, that Blake's use of them is negative in intention; he wishes to explode them, to use them in order to deny them. But this, after all, could not be the *whole* of his intention. For he had something he wished to say, or show, or both. And he must, while exploding them, also turn them to positive use. They must be the vehicle of both denial and assertion. But how could Blake manage this difficult mental gymnastic so long as he believed what he did? It is true that he managed it somehow; but at the cost of great obscurity and failure of communication. There can be no doubt that we find one of the causes of the extreme difficulty of Blake's writings in the double purpose which animated him in the creation of his mythology.

Even so, the question 'How could Blake proceed?' remains. *The answer is that his work is mythological in its negative intention, allegorical in its positive.* What he denies are certain myths; what he asserts are these myths used (upside-down, so to speak) as allegories. He uses the myths in order that he may make God appear distasteful and altogether to be rejected; he at the same time uses them allegorically in order to express what he himself believes. How he does this will appear clearly if we bear in mind the (partial) exposition of Blake's poems which I attempted in the preceding section (6). We saw there that by the creation of the world by God Blake means a change in the quality of human apprehension. The making of the world is the process of 'contraction' of the mind and senses of man which causes the mind to see the world as solid, hard, and mathematical. The 'world' in Blake's poetry is a world apprehended without imagination, seen in a utilitarian way and scientifically, and without therefore the flowing life and 'fire' of the 'infinite'. Similarly 'God' is not really God; he *is* the human 'Reason' pre-eminent and tyrannizing over mankind. That is to say, he is an allegorical figure, in Blake's positive intention, representing Reason. So with Orc, who is an allegorical representation of human passion and desire; and the struggle of Urizen and Orc is a struggle within the mind of man, of opposing forces. Los represents humanity fallen; and these gigantic and nightmare figures which move around him are powers within himself which have got out of control and are at war with each other. Thus Blake uses the old myths; but as myths proper he will have nothing to do with them, except to express his violent hostility to what they were originally intended to convey. But while doing this he also turns them into an allegory of the human mind. For his own intentions are not cosmological; rather he wishes to give us a map of the human mind. Thus does Blake proceed. But it is clear that the resulting complications must be very great.

For the net result is that what Blake writes is neither mythology nor allegory, but a curious compound of the two. I can illustrate this by quoting once more a passage I used formerly for the purposes of exposition only:

The Bands of Heaven flew thro' the air singing and shouting to Urizen.
Some fix'd the anvil, some the loom erected, some the plow
And harrow form'd and fram'd the harness of silver and ivory,
The golden compasses, the quadrant, and the rule and balance.
They erected the furnaces, they form'd the anvils of gold beaten in mills
Where winter beats incessant, fixing them firm on their base.
The bellows began to blow, and the Lions of Urizen stood round the
anvil
And the leopards cover'd with skins of beasts tended the roaring fires...
The tygers of wrath called the horses of instruction from their mangers,
They unloos'd them and put on the harness of gold and silver and
ivory,
In human forms distinct they stood round Urizen, prince of Light,
Petrifying all the Human Imagination into rock and sand. (p. 303)

In this passage, the lines I have italicized tell their tale. It is as if Blake pauses in his myth-making and his story of the creation to nudge our elbow and explain that really he is talking about the human mind and of how instruction took pre-eminence over passion and the imagination decayed. He has, that is to say, to come away from the level of perception to make his explanation of his intentions and poetic method, and also of his meanings. I say 'intentions' and 'meanings', for Blake has to explain both that his myths are being allegorically employed and what the allegorical meaning is. He indeed is not at great pains throughout the bulk of his work to explain his meaning; but when and where the explanation, however limited and perfunctory, occurs, it comes with a certain incongruity. He will not let us rest in a mythology having fairly clear outlines; he takes over mythologies and hacks them for a purpose which is not mythological at all. And this state of affairs he has to explain to us. But even this explanation he does for the most part with no attempt at thoroughness.

§ 8

Blake then has to explain what he is doing, to make his poetry declare its purpose and method. And to say this is to say that he cannot wholly allegorize the mythological fragments he is using; he cannot so treat them as to make them tractable to an allegorizing purpose. And this is not indeed very surprising. The result is that we have not a mythology nor an allegory; rather we have the uneasy presence of both. What mythological material he derives from the past he changes and mixes up, having a private purpose alien to it; and the result is not clear allegory. He makes the best of neither world.

That Blake does not create clear allegory in the course of his management of old myth is clear enough. For, when all is said, the myths which he uses do not supply sufficient grist to his allegorical mill. The psychology of the human spirit which Blake seeks to expound is a complicated one. We have seen that it is a very unsatisfactory one. But it is as intricate as it is unsatisfactory. Therefore, however much we may discern in Blake's poems the presence of figures derived from story and myth familiar to us all, he has to make considerable and original additions. These personages, original to Blake's imagination, are grafted on to the myths. This must make for obscurity. We feel lost between the (fairly) familiar and the wholly novel; and to adjust them to each other and ourselves to them both is a laborious undertaking. At this juncture I shall not delay by giving examples of Blake's additions; I shall refer to some of them later on. My present concern is to remark that while, as we have seen, Blake could not successfully allegorize what myth he used, he also found the body of myth insufficient, so to speak, in bulk, for the exposition of his beliefs about the mind. He must therefore make his own additions.

Now so long as Blake expressed himself in terms of familiar myths, even though he made certain changes in them and adapted them considerably to one another, he had some basis for communication, something which joined his mind with that of his readers But when he adds new figures and new situations, we are lost. Now even Blake could not fail to be aware, to some extent at least, that this is so; and he is driven therefore to set out in his verse what he means by it all. Now his usual practice is that illustrated in the previously quoted passage from *Vala*; he uses lines in which he tries to run his doctrine, with as little fuss as possible, into a descriptive passage. He is, as it were, surreptitiously providing his gloss as he goes along. And the gloss remains a gloss. His narrative is not, in and by itself, sufficiently significant and self-illuminating. But also, from time to time, he apparently feels compulsion, and to our relief, to embark on fairly extensive passages of pure exposition of doctrine. He is aware that the conceptual scheme of his beliefs is too elaborate and subtle to obtain a clear revelation in his narratives. An example of such a purely expository passage is the following, taken from *Milton*:

Distinguish therefore States from Individuals in those states.
States Change, but Individual Identities never change nor cease.
You cannot go to Eternal Death in that which can never Die.
Satan and Adam are States Created into Twenty-seven Churches,
And thou, O Milton, art a State about to be Created,
Called Eternal Annihilation, that none but the Living shall
Dare to enter, and they shall enter triumphant over Death
And Hell and the Grave: States that are not, but ah! seem to be.

Judge then of thy Own Self; thy Eternal Lineaments explore,
What is Eternal and what Changeable and what Annihilable.
The Imagination is not a State: it is the Human Existence itself.
Affection or Love becomes a State when divided from Imagination.
The Memory is a State always and the Reason is a State
Created to be Annihilated and the new Ratio Created. (p. 529)

Now this passage, barely distinguishable from prose, is typical of what Blake must from time to time resort to. It is a collapse into pure doctrine. That it is exceedingly obscure doctrine is not now the point at issue. In it Blake lays bare (as far as he can) the system of meanings to which he is endeavouring to give allegorical representation. In the first of these two passages he has tried, up to a point, to run his exposition into his imagery. In the latter, he has given up poetry wellnigh altogether and undertakes a solid exposition of the psychology to which he adheres. So far is he from the force and expressiveness of myth proper, so far indeed from what he himself called 'vision' in poetry. Not only does he fail to allegorize myth; he cannot make his allegory self-explanatory.

We have observed that allegory, unlike myth, proceeds through both conceptual scheme and narrative, which must remain in some measure distinguishable and separately apprehended. But this is not to say that satisfactory allegory must be composed of narrative with an accompanying gloss. The greatest English allegorists, Spenser and Bunyan, feel no compulsion to provide explanations parallel with their narratives. By the choice of proper names, by description of the figures introduced, whose physical qualities show and represent the spiritual, and by the course of the narrative itself, such allegorists make clear without great difficulty what they may be said to mean. Now of Spenser and Bunyan we can say that their meanings are comparatively simple; they appeal to familiar enough experience; and they find therefore no overwhelming difficulty in creating figures and narratives adequate to their moral intention and conceptual schemes. Moreover, they wrote as Christians to Christians, enjoying with their readers a unity of belief and outlook. Blake, on the other hand, not only does not write as a Christian, but writes as one expounding an intricate psychology. His allegory has to bear the burden of somehow conveying an inherently difficult set of beliefs; in addition these beliefs were profoundly alien to the society of his time, and were in any case very novel. Therefore, putting on one side the element of familiar myth in Blake's poems (for even this is used as allegory), and regarding the Prophetic Works wholly as allegory (probably the best way of seeing them), we can discern why they are so diffuse, disordered, and difficult. Blake puts upon allegory a burden which it cannot possibly bear—the double burden of intricacy and novelty. The result is that we move back and fore between very disordered narrative and very difficult statements of belief. If allegory is to be successful, it must make it easy for the mind to hold together the conceptual and the imaginative; it must also render easy the passage of the mind from one to the other by rendering that passage as brief and short as possible. This can only be done when the doctrines are at least fairly familiar and not intricate, and when the narrative too is clear and simple. In no sense does Blake satisfy these conditions.

For a detailed exposition of Blake's beliefs the most careful exercise of language and the drawing of many distinctions would be required. We may think it would have been better had Blake written a philosophical treatise. It certainly would have been better, both for Blake's thought and for our comprehension of it. What made this impossible were the habits of his rash and brilliant mind, and his contempt for the labour of the intelligence. The same factors would have prevented his undertaking the writing of a philosophical poem, had it even been conceivable that careful exposition of his beliefs could possibly have lent themselves to such a purpose. As it is, the difficulties which crowd upon him, when he wishes to express apparently important distinctions allegorically, are innumerable. For example, we find in these poems Urthona (sometimes identical, as in *America*, with Urizen), the Spectre of Urthona, Urizen, and the Spectre of Urizen. Now it is likely that all four are Urizen conceived from different points of view, forms corresponding to what in prose would be finely drawn distinctions and requiring careful formulation. Again, Orc appears as now the son, now the lover, and now the destroyer of Enitharmon; he is now called Orc, now Fuzon, now Luvah. We may be sure that Blake had his reasons for these things, changing the name and history of one of his figures as different aspects in him impressed themselves on his mind. But the consequences of this for his narratives are disastrous. His thought and his narrative fail to come together; and this is to say that neither reaches lucidity. At one moment we are trying to follow the story; at another trying to make out what it all means.

It is perhaps worth while returning for a moment to the remarks of Blake on the subject of allegory which I quoted above. In the first of the two remarks he praises allegory as being the 'sublimest poetry'. But in the second he pours contempt on 'allegory'; it is, he says, an inferior kind of poetry. We may suppose that he regards it as too intellectual; at any rate it does not sufficiently partake of 'vision'. He is willing to agree that allegories may contain an amount of 'vision'; *Pilgrim's Progress* he says is full of it, and, having perhaps an eye on his own allegories, he is implying that there is 'vision' in them also. But he is clear that 'allegory' and 'vision' ought to be two distinct things. These two remarks, so different in their respective attitudes, throw light on Blake's poetic practice. He writes allegorical poetry; but he also wants 'vision'. But allegory and 'vision' are really 'two distinct things'. Thus what he writes is, nominally at least, allegory; but his impatience with mere allegory as too intellectual prevents him from taking sufficient trouble with it to make it adequate as allegory; and in his impatience with mere allegory he hurries into 'vision', which in fact serves little other purpose than to obscure the allegory. What we have therefore is a mixture of 'allegory' and 'vision' in which neither is clear. He may be right in saying that allegory is not the highest form of literary creation; it may not have the unity and wholeness of apprehension which belong to myth and to the highest imaginative creation. But if allegory is to be written, it must be written as allegory and not another thing; the allegorist must be content with the limitations imposed by the very idea of allegorical writing, and must not try, in the act of writing allegory, to transform it into what it is not and cannot be. Yet this is what Blake does. He uses his mythological material very much as he wishes; he attempts, as we have seen, to allegorize it. But he is not, even then, faithful to allegory. He will not bow his mind to its demands and ensure clarity to it.

It is important to pay due respect to Blake's difficulties. No man ever more wished to write with that unified sensibility of which Mr. Eliot has spoken; no one, perhaps, of our great writers at least, failed more signally to achieve it. He found himself in a position in which, writing allegory, he yet despised it, and refused to recognize in practice its limitations. His desire to use poetry for the conveyance of 'vision' was natural and proper; and we can imagine his dislike for writing poetic glosses explaining the significance of his narratives. To some extent he forces himself to do so; but so uncongenial is it to him, so remote is it from 'vision', that he does so half-heartedly, perfunctorily, and sporadically, thereby depriving his work of clarity. He should, we may urge, have realized that he was placing on allegory, in trying to make it express such intricate beliefs, a burden which it could not possibly bear. Such an argument has great force. But, to speak in defence of Blake, we can only counter it with a question: If Blake on reflection had abandoned allegory, what poetic form or procedure was left for him to use? This is a crucial question in the study of Romanticism, and a problem always at the centre of Romantic writing. In speaking later of Shelley and Keats we shall observe this difficulty further, and shall see that they failed, as Blake did, to solve it.

§ 9

We shall now pass on to discuss *Vala* in greater detail. Blake went on, in 1795, from the writing of the Lambeth books to the writing of *Vala or The Four Zoas*; and he was engaged in this work from 1795 until 1804. When it was finished he did not proceed to engrave it, but went on at once to the composition of *Milton*, the etching of which was finished by 1808. The fact that Blake did not etch *Vala* shows that he was dissatisfied with it. Now between 1795 and 1801 he wrote the first six 'Nights'; then he revised extensively what he had written, and we have two versions of Night the Seventh. Even so, when he had brought the poem to its conclusion, he did not think it worth etching.

Now before proceeding to consider *Vala* it is worth while to look back for a moment to the Lambeth books. On reading through these poems we can hardly fail to conclude that in them Blake's vitality is flagging. Each poem in its turn appears to be an attempt to do better what the preceding poem has tried and failed to do; there is an amount of repetition which strongly suggests that Blake was aware, however vaguely, that there was something seriously wrong. But he continued to try without any fundamental change in his methods; what changes he does introduce, in the naming, genealogy, and history of his characters, further confuse the work; and even so, he repeats a great deal. The causes of this failure we have now tried to investigate; we have seen that both his thought and his method of expressing it are confused. Also, there are some lines in *The Song of Los* (the poem which immediately precedes *Vala*) which it is interesting and probably important to notice carefully:

Then Oothoon hover'd over Judah and Jerusalem,
And Jesus heard her voice (a man of sorrows) he reciev'd
A Gospel from the wretched Theotormon. (p. 273)

Now Oothoon and Theotormon are figures who made their appearance in an earlier poem, *The Visions of the Daughters of Albion.* There Oothoon is a woman, innocent, in whom sex is not associated with shame; Theotormon is the conventionally minded lover whose attitude to sex is very far from that of the innocent soul. He is one of the 'breeders of pestilence' referred to in *The Marriage of Heaven and Hell.* Now in the lines I have quoted Jesus is said to have received a message from Theotormon; Jesus, that is to say, is now, in Blake's opinion, to be classified as a 'breeder of pestilence', as one whose attitude to sex is wrong and unhealthy, as one who denies sex and desires the strict restraint of sexual desire. Now this is very different from earlier poems in which the cause of Orc is identified with that of Jesus, and indeed from *The Everlasting Gospel* of 1818, where Jesus is said to have been in no sense 'virtuous' but, in the language of *The Marriage of Heaven and Hell*, to have acted 'wholly from impulse'. If this is so, there are grounds for believing that when Blake was writing *The Song of Los* (in 1795) he no longer felt with any confidence that he was a 'real' Christian, in contrast to the hosts of self-styled Christians whom he had previously regarded as altogether removed from the beliefs and practices of the founder of their religion. If so, this may have seriously disturbed his assurance and caused him to doubt the truth of his beliefs.

Now whether or not this was so, he went on, without delay, in spite of the sense of frustration he must have derived from the writing of his earlier poems, to write *Vala*. It is possible that, if he did feel such a sense of frustration, he also felt that a poem on a larger scale might succeed and express more perfectly what was in his mind; and *Vala* is certainly a long poem. But as we have observed, when he had written six of the poem's 'Nights' he turned in dissatisfaction to revise them; and it is plausible to believe that he again felt that he had failed as he had failed in the earlier and shorter poems. Certainly, the early books of *Vala*, even as Blake finally left them, also contain a great deal repeated from the earlier prophetic verse. And that he had by this time reached something like a crisis is shown clearly enough from the evidence of his letters written about this time.

In July 1800, at a time when Blake had been engaged on *Vala* for nearly five years, he wrote to his friend Cumberland: 'I begin to Emerge from a deep pit of Melancholy, Melancholy without any real reason for it, a Disease which God keep you from and all good men.' (p. 1044) Now it is from this time that his revision of *Vala* dates; and it is likely that his decision to revise followed the recovery of his spirits. Now in the August of 1800 the Blakes went to Felpham at Hayley's invitation. Very quickly the last signs of his melancholy seem to have left him; for in September he wrote to Flaxman: 'And Now Begins a New life, because another covering of Earth is shaken off.' (p. 1049) To his friend Butts he wrote in the same month: 'Meat is cheaper than in London, but the sweet air and the voices of winds, trees and birds, and the odours of the happy ground, makes it a dwelling for immortals. Work will go on here with God speed.' (p. 1050) In reply came a letter from Butts in which the following passage occurs:

'Whether you will be a better Painter or a better Poet from your change of ways and means I know not, but this I predict, that you will be a better Man—excuse me, as you have been accustomed from friendship to do, but certain opinions imbibed from reading, nourished by indulgence, and rivetted by a confined Conversation, and which have been equally prejudicial to your Interest and Happiness, will now, I trust, disperse as a Day-break Vapour, and you will henceforth become a Member of that Community of which you are at present, in the opinion of the Archbishop of Canterbury, but a Sign to mark the residence of dim incredulity, haggard suspicion, and bloated philosophy—whatever can be effected by sterling sense, by opinions which harmonize society and beautify creation, will in future be exemplified in you, and the time I trust is not distant, and that because I truly regard you, when you will be a more valorous Champion of Revelation and Humiliation than any of those who now wield the Sword of the Spirit; with your natural and acquired Powers nothing is wanting but a proper direction of them, and altho' the way is both straight and narrow I know you too well to fear your want of resolution to persevere and to pursue it—you have the Plough and the Harrow in full view and the Gate you have been prophetically told is Open; can you then hesitate joyfully to enter into it?[1]

To this letter Blake replied on 2 October:

'I thank you for your very beautiful and encouraging Verses which I account a Crown of Laurels, and I also thank you for your reprehension of follies by me foster'd. Your prediction will, I hope, be fulfilled in me, and in the future I am the determined advocate of Religion and Humility, the two bands of Society. . . ." (p. 1051)

It seems likely that Blake and Butts (who seems to have been a sensible person and a good friend to Blake) have had talks together about Christianity and Blake's beliefs; and that Blake is willing to agree that he has taken a wrong turning in the past. Butts

[1] Quoted in the *Life of William Blake*, by Mona Wilson, Nonesuch Press, 1927, p. 129.

seems to have had no illusions about Blake's beliefs, and was robustly concerned to put him right. There are a number of other letters dating from the early years of the century which are also important in this connexion. In November 1802 he said, again in a letter to Butts:

'And now let me finish by assuring that, Tho' I have been very unhappy, I am so no longer. I am again Emerged into the light of day; I still and shall to Eternity Embrace Christianity and Adore Him who is the Express image of God; but I have travel'd thro' Perils and Darkness not unlike a champion. I have Conquer'd, and shall go on Conquering. Nothing can withstand the fury of my course among the Stars of God and in the Abysses of the Accuser. My Enthusiasm is still what it was, only Enlarg'd and confirm'd.' (p. 1065)

Again, in October 1804, in a letter to Hayley he writes about this new happiness. It is a long passage which I shall quote entire because of its striking importance:

'For now! O Glory! and O Delight! I have entirely reduced that spectrous fiend to his station, whose annoyance has been the ruin of my labours for the last passed twenty years of my life. He is the enemy of conjugal love and is the Jupiter of the Greeks, an iron-hearted tyrant, the ruiner of ancient Greece. I speak with perfect confidence and certainty of the fact which has passed upon me. Nebuchadnezzar had seven times passed over him; I have had twenty; thank God I was not altogether a beast as he was; but I was a slave bound in a mill among beasts and devils; these beasts and these devils are now, together with myself, become children of light and liberty, and my feet and my wife's feet are free from fetters. O lovely Felpham, parent of Immortal Friendship, to thee I am eternally indebted for my three years' rest from perturbation and the strength I now enjoy. Suddenly, on the day after visiting the Truchsessian Gallery of pictures, I was again enlightened with the light I enjoyed in my youth, and which has for exactly twenty years been closed from me as by a door and by window-shutters. Consequently I can, with confidence, promise you ocular demonstration of my altered state on the plates I am now engraving after Romney, whose spiritual aid has not a little conduced to my restoration to the light of Art. O the distress I have undergone, and my poor wife with me: incessantly labouring and incessantly spoiling what I had done well. Every one of my friends was astonished at my faults, and could not assign a reason; they knew my industry and abstinence from every pleasure for the sake of study, and yet—and yet—and yet there wanted the proofs of industry in my works. I thank God with entire confidence that it shall be so no longer—he is become my servant who domineered over me, he is even as a brother who was my enemy. Dear Sir, excuse my enthusiasm or rather madness, for I am really drunk with intellectual vision whenever I take a pencil or graver into my hand, even as I used to be in my youth, and as I have not been for twenty dark, but very profitable, years. I thank God that

I courageously pursued my course through darkness. In a short time I shall make my assertion good that I am become suddenly as I was at first, by producing the Head of Romney and The Ship-wreck quite another thing from what you or I ever expected them to be. In short, I am now satisfied and proud of my work, which I have not been for the above long period.' (p. 1108)

Finally, he wrote a few weeks later:

'I have indeed fought thro' a Hell of terrors and horrors (which none could know but myself) in a divided existence; now no longer divided nor at War with myself, I shall travel on in the strength of the Lord God, as poor Pilgrim says.' (p. 1110)

Taken together these letters seem to show that in these years an important change occurred in Blake's mind. Before returning to *Vala* I shall make a number of observations upon them. In the first place, although he writes as early as August 1800 that 'a new life begins', he is still in October 1804 writing with a strong sense of deliverance from past errors; and we surmise that the recovery of his enthusiasm went on steadily through the first four years of the century, until in 1804 he can speak with extreme confidence of his hopes of future work. It is likely then, that in these years when he was revising and finishing *Vala* he was still in a process of 'recovery'. Then in 1804, with, as he appears to think, complete health of mind, he decides not to trouble himself further with *Vala*, but to go on at once to a new poem. Secondly, we notice that in these letters he says that the follies he has fostered in the past extend back over the previous twenty years of his life; but now (1804) he has reduced a spectrous fiend 'whose annoyance has been the ruin of my labours for the last passed twenty years of my life'. He has been, he says, 'a slave bound in a mill among beasts and devils'; but the years at Felpham, 'lovely Felpham', have released him. Blake then is now prepared to say of his previous work that there was something seriously the matter with it; he says indeed that it had been 'ruined'. Further he says in the same letter that he was 'again enlightened with the light I enjoyed in my youth'. In another sentence he remarks again that his regeneration is a recovery of youthful feelings: 'I am really drunk with intellectual vision whenever I take a pencil or graver into my hand, even as I used to be in my youth, and as I have not been for twenty dark, but very profitable, years.' During these 'dark years' he was, he says, 'incessantly labouring and incessantly spoiling what I had done well'; his 'industry and abstinence' were great and yet 'there wanted the proofs of industry in my work'. Here is certainly Blake's own confirmation of our impression that in the early Prophetic Works he laboured with constant frustration to express what was in his mind.

He speaks of twenty years of 'darkness'. To take the figure as intended accurately we are taken back to 1784 when Blake had published only the *Poetical Sketches* (1783). The *Songs of Innocence* were finished by 1789; the *Songs of Experience* added in 1794. It was in 1789 that he embarked on his symbolical work. If we assume (as we may do without great risk) that he was using a round figure in speaking of 'twenty years', we are tempted to think that the 'dark years' began with the Prophetic Books in the later eighties, and that the *Songs of Innocence* lay in the period of youthful 'light'. This view is natural because the latter Songs are altogether without the anger and bitterness which are present in the *Songs of Experience* and the Lambeth books, and certainly have more 'light' than the later work. If this is so, his re-emergence 'into the light of day', of which he speaks in November 1802, appears to mean that he has recovered something of the spirit of the *Songs of Innocence*. This, along with certain expressions in these letters ('I still and shall to Eternity Embrace Christianity and Adore Him who is the Express Image of God', and, 'in the future I am the determined advocate of Religion and Humility, the two bands of Society'), gives us the strong impression that Blake has undergone a reconversion to Christianity and has now rejected the 'gospel of Hell'.

Yet there is at least one thing which gives us pause before coming to this conclusion. This is the obstinacy and even defiance with which he defends his 'twenty years of darkness'. There is even a note of self-congratulation when he speaks of them. 'I have travel'd thro' Perils and Darkness not unlike a champion.' The mixed modesty and pride of the last phrase is affecting. 'And now', he goes on, 'Nothing can withstand the fury of my course among the Stars of God'. He also speaks of the 'twenty dark, but very profitable, years'. Now we suspect that this is not the accent of a man converted to Christianity. It is all very well to say that he 'Adores Him who is the Express Image of God'; but it is hard to believe that one converted to Christianity could regard twenty years given up to the 'gospel of Hell' as 'profitable'. Blake indeed appears to regret these years of error; but he seems more impressed by his having behaved like a champion than by any sense of having been delivered by God from his errors. It was not thus at least that Augustine after his conversion spoke of Manichaeism and of his sojourn in that doctrine. And if Blake is impressed by his performance even in error, he is also impressed by what his future performance is to be—'Nothing can withstand the fury of my course among the Stars of God'. We surmise, therefore, that if there has been any sort of conversion it has not been a very whole-hearted one. Indeed we suspect that in part at least it is a confirmation of himself, with renewed energy, in old errors. What change there was in Blake we shall see at a later stage. What does seem certain is that he once more feels certain that he is a Christian. If in *The Song of Los* he doubted, with possible dismay, whether he was indeed a 'Christian', he now has reassurance, and appears to feel that he can rightly claim the name.

There is another feature of Blake's life at this time which has a special interest for us. During these early years of the century, when Blake was undergoing or at least recovering from his 'crisis', he wrote not only the concluding 'Nights' of *Vala*, but also a quantity of lyrical verse. That he should, at a time when he was recovering his vitality and the 'light' of his youth, return to lyrical verse is important. Writing to Butts in October 1800 (the letter in which he speaks of himself as 'in future the determined advocate of Religion and Humility'), he inscribes a lyrical poem which is very much in the manner of the *Songs of Innocence*. The following are some lines taken from it:

Soft consum'd in delight
In his bosom Sun bright
I remain'd. Soft he smil'd,
And I heard his voice Mild
Saying: 'This is my Fold,
'O thou Ram horn'd with gold,
'Who awakest from Sleep
'On the Sides of the deep.
'On the Mountains around
'The roarings resound
'Of the lion and wolf,
'The loud Sea and deep gulf.
'These are guards of my Fold,
'O thou Ram horn'd with gold!'
And the voice faded mild.
I remained as a Child;
All I ever had known
Before me bright Shone. (p. 1053)

These lines certainly suggest the *Songs of Innocence*, but without having their ease and certainty. In comparison with the *Songs*, they are wooden and forced; and indeed the remainder of the lyrical poems of these years 1800 to 1804 have more in common with the *Songs of Experience* than with the *Songs of Innocence*. Even so, they show the extraordinary lyrical powers which Blake still possessed; and our concern now is to suggest that it is perhaps significant that he should now have turned back to lyric; for it may be that, dissatisfied with *Vala*, it occurred to him to abandon 'prophetic' writing and to return extensively to the composition of lyrical verse. It is not, probably, extravagant to think that a doubt arose in his mind at this time about the wisdom of proceeding with a kind of poetry in which, on his own admission, he had failed continuously in the past. It is likely that he was in two minds. But it was allegory which won the day. He persevered with *Vala* and went on to *Milton*. Now if I am right in suggesting that Blake's recovery from previous errors was at best a partial one, his decision to continue with his peculiar form of allegory is what we should expect. Had he had a complete liberation from 'darkness', he would not have continued to create the darkness which seems inevitable in his allegorical methods of writing. As it was, he continued to write allegory up to 1820. At the outset we can feel with some confidence that had he been indeed converted to Christianity and put away the confused 'gospel of Hell' he could not have gone on to write poems of such extreme obscurity and difficulty as *Milton* and *Jerusalem*. For not only, had he become converted to Christianity, would his thought have become clearer; probably also, a newly found humility and sense of past tradition would have made him more critical of the methods of communication he was using.

§ 10

We must now consider whether in fact any notable changes manifest themselves in the work of Blake which succeeds this crisis in his mental life. We should expect some signs of his 'deliverance' in the later books of *Vala* as well as in *Milton* and in *Jerusalem*. Certainly, in the first six 'Nights' of *Vala* there is not a great deal that is new, and there is a great deal that is old. Once more we have Blake's version of the Fall, of the consequent disunity in the human mind, of the creation of the world. In the Fourth Night there is repeated, almost word for word, the version of the binding of Urizen and his transformation into human shape which we have in *The First Book of Urizen*; in the Fifth Night Orc is again bound to the mountain in the chain of jealousy by his parents. We certainly obtain the impression that Blake is trying in *Vala* to do better what he had failed to do in the shorter poems which preceded it; and again we have the impression that he fails. It may indeed have been his increasing consciousness of failure in *Vala* which precipitated the melancholy from which he was recovered by his years at Felpham. Certainly, the poem is disorganized and obscure in the greatest degree. There are indeed novelties in *Vala*, figures and situations which have not appeared in earlier poems; but they add to the difficulties instead of lessening them.

We notice that in *Vala* Luvah makes his appearance. Now Luvah is probably intended by Blake for Orc conceived as Jesus. We noticed earlier the figure of Fuzon who appears in *The First Book of Urizen* and in *The Book of Ahania*, who appeared to be Orc in that aspect in which Blake saw him as identical with Christ. In *Vala* Luvah appears to be Fuzon under a new name. Curiously enough, Orc also appears in *Vala*. But one of the great happenings in this poem is the recognition by a terrified Urizen that Luvah *is* Orc. Urizen, it need hardly be said, appears, and is still the supreme enemy of mankind. It is true, as we have said, that these early books were revised by Blake, and when his spirits were reviving. How much they owe to the revision we cannot say. But it is certain that even so, in their revised form, they have the air of frustration, of desperate failure of expression, which the earlier Lambeth books had. The seventh, eighth, and ninth Books are however quite new; and here at least we should expect to see unmistakably the signs of a Blake delivered from 'darkness'. That something new emerges in these books is undeniable. What it is and how important it is we shall now pass on to discuss.

The clue to the understanding of the last three Nights of *Vala* is to be found in the letter from which I have already quoted, written to Hayley on 23 October 1804. Here are the two relevant passages: 'For now! O Glory! and O Delight! I have entirely reduced that spectrous fiend to his station, whose annoyance has been the ruin of my labours for the last passed twenty years of my life. He is the enemy of conjugal love and is the Jupiter of the Greeks. . . . I was a slave bound in a mill among beasts and devils; these beasts and these devils are now, together with myself, become children of light and liberty, and my feet and my wife's feet are free from fetters.' Secondly, having spoken, in the way I described earlier, of the failure of his previous work, he says: 'I thank God with entire confidence that it shall be so no longer—he is become my servant who domineered over me, he is even as a brother who was my enemy.' The reference to Jupiter makes it quite certain that the 'spectrous fiend' to whom Blake has now given his rightful station, and who has become now a brother after being an enemy, is no other than Urizen. Blake, writing of his deliverance from a 'divided condition' in which he was 'at War' with himself, expresses it in terms of his changed attitude towards Urizen; and that this is so is confirmed by the study of the last three Nights of *Vala*.[1] In these and in

[1] There are two versions of the Seventh Night. It is likely that it is that labelled (*a*) which is the later. (*b*) appears to be more of a piece with the preceding Nights, while (*a*) begins the narrative of 'redemption' from the 'Fall'.

still later work, Orc (who is of course very much Blake himself) is somehow reconciled with the 'spectrous fiend', or Urizen, who has troubled him and tyrannized over him for so long. In this reconciliation 'redemption' consists; and man, so long divided against himself and at war with himself, is finally made whole once more. The change in Blake's work may be said to be one which consists in transferring emphasis from the 'Fall' (as Blake understands it) to 'redemption' (again, as Blake understands it).

Now at first sight at least, this change is not as revolutionary and far-reaching as Blake would, judging from his letters, have us believe. For we had gathered from the Lambeth books that Urizen was in some sense a constituent part of the original and perfect humanity who had assumed a wrongful and tyrannical power over the other components. The idea that Urizen in his rightful place might harmonize with the rest of human nature does not strike us as a novel one. I have already quoted some lines from the Second Night of *Vala* in which Luvah says of Urizen that he was originally 'Faith and Certainty' but that he has become 'chang'd to Doubt'. These lines may indeed have come with Blake's revision of *Vala*, after his recovery from melancholy; but, coming in *Vala*, they do not surprise us as embodying an idea quite new in Blake's work. However this may be, it is certain that formerly Blake concentrated his energies on delineating the deep division in human nature which Urizen's tyranny had brought about; that in *Vala*, in *Milton*, and in *Jerusalem* his work is filled with a new hope; and that they portray the coming restoration of humanity to perfection through reconciliation with Urizen. Prometheus and Zeus will become friends.

We may then, briefly, state the nature of the change in Blake's mind and beliefs by saying that up to the year 1800 he appears to have had unbounded confidence in desire and impulse; but that he is now acknowledging the insufficiency of desire and 'energy' which, he now says, in some way requires the guidance of an Urizen, however changed and mitigated. If the notion that Urizen is not intrinsically and necessarily evil seems to us to be implied in the Lambeth books, it seems certain that it came to Blake in the early years of the century with the force of an astounding discovery, and gave him a new lease of vitality and confidence. How Urizen could become a friend and not a foe of humanity we shall try to discover.

I need not say that I do not propose to try to expound the poem *Vala* in any detail. It may be doubted whether exposition of it in detail is possible. However that may be, I shall call attention only to certain situations and events in it in order to throw light upon Blake's new psychology. Urizen is again the chief figure, and is frequently referred to as 'Prince of Light'. Luvah, who is the figure next in importance, is called 'Prince of Love' and he is a son of Urizen. As I have said, Urizen embodies 'Doubt' and therefore reason, intellect, and moral duty; but originally he was 'Faith and Certainty'. Luvah is the 'heart' of man, 'energy', and the emotions; and he too is fallen—into wrath and hate; originally he was love. What is required, according to Blake's new beliefs, is that they be reconciled; and *Vala* is the story of this reconciliation. With certain features of the long and confused narrative I shall deal briefly later. For the present we notice the Ninth Night in which Urizen is changed. Here the 'Eternal Man' who is the ideal humanity, enjoying a perfect and natural innocence, gives judgement on Urizen and Luvah, the leading actors in the drama of disrupted and fallen humanity. He says, calling for Urizen:

> O Prince of Light, where art thou? I behold thee not as once
> In those Eternal fields, in clouds of morning stepping forth
> With harps and songs when bright Ahania sang before thy face
> And all thy sons and daughters gather'd round my ample table.
> See you not all this wracking furious confusion?
> Come forth from slumbers of thy cold abstraction! Come forth,
> Arise to Eternal births! Shake off thy cold repose,
> Schoolmaster of souls, great opposer of change, arise!
> That the Eternal worlds may see thy face in peace and joy,
> That thou, dread form of Certainty, maist sit in town and village
> While little children play around thy feet in gentle awe,
> Fearing thy frown, loving thy smile, O Urizen, Prince of Light.
> (p. 428)

He then goes on, still addressing Urizen:

> But if thou darest obstinate refuse my stern behest,
> Thy crown and scepter I will sieze, and regulate all my members
> In stern severity, and cast thee out into the indefinite
> Where nothing lives, there to wander; and if thou returnest weary,
> Weeping at the threshold of Existence, I will steel my heart
> Against thee to Eternity, and never recieve thee more. (p. 429)

Urizen hears and proceeds in a long speech to acknowledge the error into which he has fallen in the past. Having done so,

> . . . he shook his snows from off his shoulders and arose
> As on a Pyramid of mist, his white robes scattering
> The fleecy white: renew'd, he shook his aged mantles off
> Into the fires. Then, glorious bright, Exulting in his joy,
> He sounding rose into the heavens in naked majesty,
> In radiant Youth.
> (p. 430)

Urizen is no longer the cold and icy tyrant of earlier years; he becomes a bright and glowing figure of youth. We observe indeed that the 'Eternal Man' discriminates sharply against him, placing responsibility for all that has happened more upon him than upon Luvah; and he has to be lectured into repentance. Blake did not forget old feuds too easily. Even so, Urizen is not what he was. When he is thus changed, the Universe rejoices, as it rejoices in *Prometheus Unbound* when Jupiter is destroyed. Earth is renewed and the family of the immortals reunited. The 'Eternal Man' welcomes them to the Feast:

> The feast was spread in the bright South, and the Regenerate Man
> Sat at the feast rejoicing, and the wine of Eternity
> Was serv'd round by the flames of Luvah all day and all the Night.
> (p. 448)

Now if Urizen is transformed, Luvah also is chastised and changed. The following is the reproof he suffers from the 'Eternal Man' or, as Blake sometimes calls him, the 'Regenerate Man'. Henceforth, he says, you are a servant—

> Obey and live.
> You shall forget your former state; return, and Love in peace,
> Into your place, the place of seed, not in the brain or heart.
> If Gods combine against Man, setting their dominion above
> The Human form Divine, Thrown down from their high station
> In the Eternal heavens of Human Imagination, buried beneath
> In dark Oblivion, with incessant pangs, ages on ages,
> In enmity and war first weaken'd, then in stern repentance
> They must renew their brightness, and their disorganiz'd functions
> Again reorganize, till they resume the image of the human,
> Co-operating in the bliss of Man, obeying his Will,
> Servants to the infinite and Eternal of the Human form. (p. 438)

So far then, the position appears to be as follows: Urizen, the Prince of Light, 'comes forth from slumbers of cold abstraction'. Urizen is knowledge, light. In the past his light has been changed in the distorting medium of 'abstraction' and 'science', or of conceptual apprehension; with this went the 'detestable deceit' of religion and the 'stony law'. But now he throws off this kind of knowledge; he is changed from 'Doubt' to certainty, from uncertainty to immediate knowledge and faith; his real light is restored to him. But this is possible only because Luvah also is humbled; his 'function' also has been 'disorganized' and he now 'obeys the will of Man', not arrogating to himself powers not naturally his. This makes possible unity with Urizen; 'energy' now is guided by 'light', and 'light' is no longer an old, withering, and icy thing, but a thing of warmth, energy, and youth. The 'head' and the 'heart' are no longer in conflict; indeed, they are no longer two things, separated from each other. Urizen and

Luvah must now take their places 'not in the brain or heart but in the place of seed'.

The passage I quoted last is important for another reason. It makes quite clear a fundamental feature of Blake's beliefs. If, says the 'Regenerate Man', gods combine against man they must be cast down, repent, and in humility 'resume the image of the human' and 'obey the will of the human'. They are the 'servants of the human form'. That is to say, the gods are but the creation of a disordered human mind; but when the mind is 'regenerate' and 'eternal' they are seen as the servants of the human; that is to say, they are gods no longer, for it is the 'Human form' which is divine. This passage makes clear beyond any possible doubt that however Blake has changed, he has quite certainly not become a Christian. His mind is set upon exalting the human and not the divine. Urizen is no longer, indeed, the evil figure of the earlier poems; for with the old Urizen, the maker of religion and science, Blake still will have nothing to do. The last line of *Vala* is:

> The dark Religions are departed and sweet Science reigns.

By 'science' here he does not of course mean the science of 'Newton'; but the knowledge which belongs to the imagination and not to the intelligence, a knowledge which sees 'all things as infinite', but knows no gods and no worship. The new and regenerate humanity has 'science', not worship, 'understanding', and not holiness.

§ 11

Early in this chapter I discussed some of the issues raised by Blake's beliefs, and I shall return briefly to them at the end. I shall now notice two features in the narrative of *Vala*; first, Blake's use in it of Greek mythology; secondly, his use of Christian 'mythology'. Milton and Satan he reserves for his next poem. I shall briefly recount his use of Greek and Christian mythology partly to illustrate his exceedingly confusing practice in the matter of myth, and partly because to do so may help to show further the nature of the changes which had come about in Blake's beliefs.

Now as we have seen, Urizen in *Vala* is, in an important respect, the Urizen of the earlier poems, the god of thought and of moral duty. In this connexion he is unfavourably contrasted with Prometheus—Luvah—Orc. But Blake's favourite phrase in describing him, namely, Prince of Light, provides a clue not only to a new aspect (which we have already observed) of Urizen's nature but to his employment of another Greek myth which is used to emphasize this novel aspect of Urizen. Urizen is in part the old

Urizen; but in part he is a new Urizen, having at least hitherto unperceived possibilities. To show this in narrative, Blake's story suffers a complication. In it Urizen is both the Jupiter of the Greeks and Helios, Phoebus, Prince of Light. Urizen's double nature has its expression in narrative by his being in effect two figures who are in Greek mythology quite distinct. This of course must make Blake's poem very obscure and difficult. That Urizen is thought of by Blake as Helios is, I think, fairly certain. The description of the Golden Hall of Urizen in the Second Night certainly recalls the Palace of the Sun-God:[1]

> The Golden Hall of Urizen, whose western side glow'd bright
> With ever streaming fires beaming from his awful limbs. (p. 309)

More striking however than this, is the frequent reference in *Vala* to Urizen's having given the 'Horses of Light and Chariot of Day' into the hands of Luvah. In the Third Night Ahania asks Urizen:

> Why didst thou listen to the voice of Luvah that dread morn
> To give the immortal steeds of light to his deceitful hands? (p. 321)

This happening is repeatedly referred to and is of the utmost importance for Blake's purposes in the poem. For, according to his new beliefs, Urizen's having given the Horses of Day into the hands of Luvah *was* the fall of man from 'Eternity' or innocence into intellectuality and the moral state. The function of light-giver was transferred from its true possessor to Luvah who is passion and energy; and it is the assumption by 'energy' and 'impulse' of the right to guide humanity which brings about disaster. In this piece of mythology both Urizen and Luvah are in the wrong, Urizen in allowing Luvah to attempt to guide the horses through the Heavens, Luvah in presuming to try to do so. This new strand of mythology, then, is introduced directly on account of Blake's new beliefs. Formerly Urizen, conceived as Jupiter, was wholly to be deplored, a tyrant over Orc and without any justification. In the new myth, Urizen, conceived as Helios or Phoebus, shares guilt with Orc (here called Luvah) for the fall of humanity. Orc is no longer a champion, but a fellow sinner with Urizen. As I have remarked, Urizen in *Vala* is still Jupiter; but he is also, to our confusion, Phoebus.

Now the myth which Blake is using in delineating this (in part) new Urizen is presumably that of Helios and Phaethon, in which Phaethon asks his father Helios for permission to drive the horses and chariot of the Sun; Helios unwillingly allows him to do so;

[1] It may owe something to the opening lines of the second book of Ovid's *Metamorphoses*. We know that Blake read and liked Ovid. It is possible that the description of Hyperion's palace in *Hyperion* is also indebted to Ovid in translation.

he loses control of the horses, burns up the earth and is cast from the chariot by Zeus who hurls a thunderbolt. Blake by no means follows the story with any scruple, as he follows no other of the myths he uses with scruple. *His* Phaethon is not destroyed; he becomes one who instead of supplying light to the earth as he tried to do, burns up the earth with heat and fire. Now it will be recalled that in the earlier books Orc is constantly described as 'fiery'; in them Orc's 'fire', meaning his energy and passion, is considered wholly desirable in contrast to Urizen's snows. In *Vala*, however, the 'fieriness' of Orc (Luvah) is no longer wholly desirable; on the contrary, his fire withers the earth. That is to say, when 'fire' undertakes to supply not only warmth but light also, the result is fatal. Let Phaethon-Luvah keep his station and office; the function of light-giver belongs to Helios-Urizen, when at least the light he gives is that of the imagination and not of the intellect. If we are left to the guidance of energy merely, we are both scorched and cast into darkness. Thus does Blake rebuke the pride of energy (as he had extolled it in *The Marriage of Heaven and Hell*) in assuming the right to supply knowledge and understanding in addition to passion. Thus does he formally reject the 'Gospel of Hell', according to which impulse may justly order human behaviour. In 'regenerate man' Urizen, Prince of Light, derives warmth from Luvah; and Luvah's 'warmth' is guided by light from Urizen; that is to say, knowledge and passion become a single, undivided thing.

Such was probably Blake's intention in introducing this new myth. But how exasperating is the effect of it so long as he was also using the Zeus-Prometheus myth may be seen clearly from the following passage, which I have already quoted but which will be more fully understood in the light of what is above. When, in Night the Seventh (*a*) in *Vala*, Urizen visits Orc in his fiery dens and offers him mercy, Orc replies:

King of furious hail storms,
Art thou the cold attractive power that holds me in this chain?
I well remember how I stole thy light and it became fire
Consuming. (p. 371)

Here Urizen is Zeus—'King of furious hail storms'; Orc is Prometheus—he has stolen (what at least becomes) fire. But Orc is also Phaethon, for he stole light which *became consuming fire*; and if Orc is also Phaethon, Urizen is also Helios. Thus does Blake confound and confuse his myths and us. To make the confusion thrice confounded, there is a third factor present: the preceding description of Orc as he lies in his fiery dens and is spoken to by Urizen unmistakably recalls Milton's description of Hell.

In the second place, I shall try to say something of Blake's use of Christian 'myth' and symbol in *Vala*. I shall say little, if only for the reason that, of all the strands of story which go to make up the narrative of *Vala*, it is this one which, as Blake handles it, is wrapped in greatest obscurity. But this at least can be said, before going on, that it is interesting and significant that it is precisely at these points where Blake is labouring to give a 'Christian' note to his narrative that it becomes quite peculiarly obscure. Now the renewal of Urizen of which we have spoken, the change in him from age and cold to youth, light, and warmth, and the reproof and correction of Luvah occur at a late point in the narrative (in the Ninth Night) after Blake has recounted his version of the Crucifixion as he understands it. In the Eighth Night the 'Lamb of God' is crucified. He is crucified by Urizen, acting in his role of Zeus, not of Helios—

> Urizen call'd together the Synagogue of Satan in dire Sanhedrim
> To judge the Lamb of God to Death as a murderer and robber:
> As it is written, he was number'd among the transgressors. (p. 409)

What then does Blake intend by the 'Lamb of God'? In certain passages he is identified with Luvah; for after the regeneration of man has taken place we find the following lines:

> 'Attempting to be more than Man We become less', said Luvah
> As he arose from the bright feast, drunk with the wine of ages.
> His crown of thorns fell from his head, he hung his living Lyre
> Behind the seat of the Eternal Man and took his way . . . (p. 454)

The identification of the two, through the mention of the 'crown of thorns', is here certain enough. But this identification raises a difficulty. For Luvah has previously been rebuked by the 'Eternal Man' for having helped to bring about 'disorganization' in the spirit of man. And indeed in the narrative of the crucifixion we read that not Luvah, but the Lamb of God *in the 'Mantle of Luvah'* suffers at the hands of Urizen and the 'dire Sanhedrim'; and throughout *Vala* the 'Lamb of God' is described as being 'in Luvah's robes'. From this we may perhaps judge that if Luvah and Christ are not identical there is at least a close and important connexion between them. The following lines are no doubt the clue to this relation. Having described the creation of the world by Urizen and his sons, Blake goes on to say:

> For the Divine Lamb, Even Jesus who is the Divine Vision,
> Permitted all, lest Man should fall into Eternal Death;
> For when Luvah sunk down, himself put on the robes of blood
> Lest the state call'd Luvah should cease; and the Divine Vision
> Walked in robes of blood till he who slept should awake. (p. 313)

These 'robes of blood' are Luvah's, for on the preceding page we read that

> the Divine Vision appear'd in Luvah's robes of blood.

What these lines are intended to convey I cannot say. But they certainly suggest that while Urizen, who crucifies the 'Lamb of God in the Mantle of Luvah', is utterly alien to Christ, Christ somehow dwells in Luvah; that the principle of Christ is in Luvah and not in Urizen. This would accord with the judgement of 'Regenerate Man' in the Ninth Night which I have already quoted:

> My anger against thee is greater than against this Luvah,
> For war is energy Enslav'd, but thy religion,
> The first author of this war and the distracting of honest minds . . .
> Is a deciet so detestable that I will cast thee out
> If thou repentest not . . . (p. 429)

Thus, the responsibility for the strife between Urizen and Luvah rests upon Urizen. He is, as he stands, beyond redemption and must be completely changed; but Luvah it seems has erred much less seriously and later escapes with a rebuke. In this way is Blake still cleaving, though with less confidence, to his earlier doctrine, that Jesus 'acted wholly from impulse and not from rules'. Change there may have been in Blake's beliefs, but it is not a thorough-going one. Even now 'impulse' and 'energy' are at least far more 'Christ-like' than 'religion'. Luvah is at most only one remove from Christ; indeed after the regeneration of man Blake does not scruple to give his name to the bearer of the crown of thorns. And earlier, Christ wears his garments.

Finally, Orc as well as Luvah appears in *Vala*. By introducing both these figures Blake complicated his narrative greatly, for he appears to intend very much the same thing by each of them; and in the Eighth Night we are told that they are one and the same. Previous to this disclosure, Orc has gone through experiences similar to if not identical with those which he suffered in the Lambeth books; he is, for example, bound by the chain of jealousy to the high mountain rock. Then come the lines in which, despite their very different descent and previous histories, we are told that they are, in reality, one person. Now in the Lambeth books Orc, or the embodiment of fire and impulse, was, as we have seen, identical with Christ in Blake's eyes. And here, in *Vala*, by being finally shown as identical with Luvah, or at least as 'assuming the form of Luvah', he is revealed as being, if not identical with Christ, at least on the side of the angels—or, out of deference to Blake, of the devils.

All this is hardly clear and intelligible. I have thus briefly tried to expound the way in which Blake labours to incorporate the Christian myth into his narratives not because I imagined that I could bring it to lucidity (what I believe cannot be done), but in order to show the (even for Blake) unusually dense obscurity which attaches to his version of what he understands by Christianity. But so far as anything at all clear emerges from his statement of his 'Christianity', it points to Blake's retention in some measure of the old gospel of Hell, and to an at best incomplete conversion from it. If the Greek myth he employs appears to exalt Urizen in his new form and to suggest the emergence of a genuine novelty in Blake's beliefs, the version of Christian 'myth' he employs appears to suggest that a good deal remains over in his mind from earlier days. What I think is also reasonably clear from a reading of the last books of *Vala*, of *Milton*, and of *Jerusalem*, is that any Christianity they contain is of the Marcionite kind, bent, as we have seen, on viewing God as an illusion, and also on erecting Christ into a Saviour-God, the 'Eternal Humanity Divine'.

§ 12

Leaving *Vala* in manuscript, Blake went on to write *Milton*, and then *Jerusalem*. I do not think that these two poems contain any development in Blake's thought or practice which is important, and I do not propose to try to analyse them. My purpose, in drawing this essay on Blake to a conclusion, is to discuss briefly the system of beliefs, if it may be so described, to which Blake appears to have come in these later years, beliefs which remain substantially in *Milton* and *Jerusalem* what they were in *Vala*.

It will, I hope, be clear from what goes before, that Blake has certainly not come to rest in what may with any propriety be called Christianity. But on the other hand, he now perceives the need of the formerly despised Urizen, however changed, and now 'thrown down from his high station in the Eternal Heavens of Human Imagination'. Somehow, Urizen has become incorporated into the imagination and acts in union with the passions. Now Blake identified the soul in its perfection with imagination; and in 'Regenerate Man' both 'knowledge' and 'passion' (which were Urizen and Orc-Luvah) partake of the nature of imagination. Thus much, so far as it is clear at all, is clear from the account of *Vala* which we have given. But there is a further element in Blake's later beliefs of which we have as yet made no mention, which yet is a part of and arises out of the new considerations which we have discussed. So far, I have inclined to minimize the extent and depth of Blake's change of belief. But we shall now be able to see more clearly the genuine novelty of Blake's later doctrines and also the new difficulties in which they involved him.

Now in the Lambeth books, in which Blake preaches the 'Gospel of Hell' with great consistency, evil so far as it has reality at all is a thing of man's own making, and results from his refusal to follow the road of passion. What is called evil by the generality of mankind is not really evil at all; it is only the protest of suppressed mankind against the tyranny of a moral law which has no objective validity whatsoever. We have, he urged, only to be ourselves and to put aside 'ideas of good and evil'. Now this view he could hold so long as the intellect was, in his judgement, antagonistic to 'good' and suppressed man's natural 'goodness'. But in his new scheme of belief the source of man's trouble is in the passions as well as in his knowledge. Formerly he believed that all our distress arose from the opposition of thought to passion, of 'head' to 'heart'. Now that 'head' and 'heart' alike may both be impugned, he must see our situation as one in which knowledge and passion together are opposed to—what? What is that which has brought low both knowledge and feeling, changed faith to doubt, imagination to intellection, and love to hatred? What, in Blake's new scheme, is the new figure of 'evil'? Blake's answer is that it is 'self-hood', by which he apparently means self-seeking and self-aggrandizement in all their forms; and through 'self-hood' came about the fall of man's knowledge and passion alike. Instead then of the 'gospel of Hell' we have a new gospel of 'self-annihilation'—'by self-annihilation back returning to life Eternal'. The return to our natural and primitive innocence, which is also 'life Eternal', is through 'self-annihilation'. And in *Milton* the place formerly occupied by Urizen is now occupied by Satan who is the embodiment of 'self-hood' as it is manifested both in thought and the moral law and in depraved feeling. *He* now is the 'opacity' which formerly was Urizen. In *Milton*, he is represented as the 'self-hood' of Milton; for the latter says:

> I in my self-hood am that Satan: I am that Evil one.

Satan then is the state of 'self-hood'; and Milton is set over against him as a 'state about to be created, called Eternal Annihilation'. Thus, the old 'gospel of Hell' is certainly greatly changed, however much Satan reminds us of the old Urizen and the new Milton of the old Orc-Luvah.

I shall quote a passage from the second book of *Milton*; in it

Blake sets out, more clearly than in any other in the poem, the meaning he is labouring to express. Milton, addressing Satan, says:

> Satan! my Spectre! I know my power thee to annihilate
> And be a greater in thy place and be thy Tabernacle,
> A covering for thee to do thy will, till one greater comes
> And smites me as I smote thee and becomes my covering.
> Such are the Laws of thy false Heav'ns; but Laws of Eternity
> Are not such; know thou, I come to Self Annihilation.
> Such are the Laws of Eternity, that each shall mutually
> Annihilate himself for others' good, as I for thee.
> Thy purpose and the purpose of thy Priests and of thy Churches
> Is to impress on men the fear of death, to teach
> Trembling and fear, terror, constriction, abject selfishness.
> Mine is to teach Men to despise death and to go on
> In fearless majesty annihilating Self, laughing to scorn
> Thy Laws and terrors, shaking down thy Synagogues as webs.
> I come to discover before Heav'n and Hell the Self righteousness
> In all its Hypocritic turpitude, opening to every eye
> These wonders of Satan's holiness, shewing to the Earth
> The Idol Virtues of the Natural Heart, and Satan's Seat
> Explore in all its Selfish Natural Virtue, and put off
> In Self annihilation all that is not of God alone,
> To put off Self and all I have, ever and ever. (p. 541)

In what follows Milton proceeds to 'annihilate' Satan. The result is that knowledge is no longer an affair of 'Bacon, Newton, and Locke', and that the passions are purified. In the past both have been the victims of selfishness and self-seeking; they are now liberated into disinterestedness and return to what originally they were. There is, then, this much novelty in these last beliefs of Blake, that Satan, who formerly was 'God' in Blake's eyes, has now become something apparently evil, with which there can be no reconciliation and which must be utterly cast out. There was reconciliation with Urizen; there is none with Satan. This appears to be an acknowledgement by Blake, at last, that evil is real, that the difference between good and evil is real and absolute, that the formerly despised 'morality' is after all necessary. Also, we might imagine, despite what we have already said, that Blake is moving towards Christianity; for the new gospel of self-annihilation, so different from the old gospel of 'energy', is certainly nearer to Christianity. In fact, it is certain that if, in this respect, his new beliefs approximate to Christianity, he does not become Christian; he also remains the bitter enemy of what he chooses to call 'righteousness' and 'holiness'. This passage, from a speech of Los in *Jerusalem*, shows his enduring hatred of Christianity and its 'righteousness':

Go to these Fiends of Righteousness,
Tell them to obey their Humanities and not pretend Holiness
When they are murderers as far as my Hammer and Anvil permit.
Go tell them that the Worship of God is honouring his gifts
In other men and loving the greatest men best, each according
To his Genius which is the Holy Ghost in Man; there is no other
God than that God who is the intellectual fountain of Humanity.
He who envies or calumniates, which is murder and cruelty,
Murders the Holy-one. Go, tell them this, and overthrow their cup,
Their bread, their altar-table, their incense and their oath,
Their marriage and their baptism, their burial and consecration.
I have tried to make friends by corporeal gifts but have only
Made enemies. I never made friends but by spiritual gifts,
By severe contentions of friendship and the burning fire of thought.
He who would see the Divinity must see him in his Children,
One first, in friendship and love, then a Divine Family, and in the midst
Jesus will appear. (p. 736)

Satan, then, is the new figure of evil in Blake's mythology; he has taken the place of Urizen as the embodiment of evil. Moreover, he is present both in Man's passions and in Man's reason; and he is selfishness, self-centredness, and the desire for power. As such he has been responsible for the science of Newton and for the moral and religious doctrines of the churches.

Now the questions arise, Whence came this evil? and How may it be removed? As to the first, Blake can no longer say that it had its origin wholly in the perversion of the reason (even if that were a satisfactory answer to the question); for in his new scheme of belief he holds the passions equally guilty; and I have not discovered that he attempts to supply an answer to the question. It is, however, worth noticing that in the last passage but one which I have quoted he speaks of the 'Selfish Natural Virtue' of Satan—a curious form, we may surmise, of the doctrine of original sin. He means, presumably, that the 'virtue' of the churches (which is really, he thinks, 'evil') is original or natural to the human heart; and however confused all this may be, it is an acknowledgement that evil is natural to man.

Similarly, in regard to the second question, he appears sometimes to approximate to the Christian belief in salvation through grace. In Night the Seventh (*a*) of *Vala* the process of 'self-annihilation back returning to Life Eternal' is spoken of in a passage in which we hear Los being told that 'of himself he is nothing',

. . . being Created Continually by Mercy and Love Divine. (p. 380)

Of this strain in Blake's writings, in which he makes play with the contrast between the natural and the spiritual, I shall speak at the end of this chapter. But for the present we can ignore it, and say that Blake for the most part will have little to do with the traditional Christian doctrines of original sin and divine grace. For much the greater part, Blake tries his hardest to keep his ethical thought within naturalistic limits.

Let us therefore consider what Blake says about removing evil from man's nature. We have seen (in section 11) that Blake looks forward to a union of Luvah (passion) and Urizen (knowledge). This perfection of them both, in indissoluble union with each other, he now says will come about by 'self-annihilation' and the extinction of Satan (the 'self-hood') in each alike. Passion will act by the light of regenerate knowledge, and knowledge will enjoy the warmth of purified passion. Now how may this two-fold purification and this union come about? In accordance with his discovery (recorded in the letter to Hayley in 1804), that 'he [Urizen] is become my servant who domineered over me, he is even as a brother who was my enemy', the lead in the advance to this regeneration he gives increasingly to the new Urizen. In *Jerusalem*, Los says:

> I care not whether a Man is Good or Evil; all that I care
> Is whether he is a Wise Man or a Fool. Go, put off Holiness
> And put on Intellect, or my thund'rous Hammer shall drive thee
> To wrath which thou condemnest, till thou obey my voice. (p. 738)

Now the implication of these lines is that 'evil' passion is only 'foolishness'; and that therefore it may be purified by a regenerate Urizen (knowledge or 'intellect'). But in fact this is not, on Blake's own showing, satisfactory. For we must remember that if passion is 'foolish', reason is, as Blake has been at great pains to labour, itself the victim, as well as the passions, of the 'self-hood'. If passion is foolish, reason is passionate. If this is so, the reason or 'intellect' cannot undertake to purify the passions from 'self-hood', for it is itself actuated by 'Satan'. So long as it is the victim of these 'evil' passions it cannot be nor become a regenerate reason; it must itself be 'foolish' and be unable to direct the regeneration of the soul. Blake therefore cannot explain how the desired regeneration can come about. Moving within naturalistic limits, his ethic cannot explain the beginnings of the release of the soul from (it matters not whether we call it) foolishness or base passion.

This difficulty, on which Blake's ethic breaks down, is very similar to that which may be brought against Spinoza's ethic. It will be recalled that in the Lambeth books, Blake's ethic had not even the safeguard of Spinoza's; for he refused to acknowledge, as Spinoza acknowledges, the need of wisdom or understanding to free us from unworthy passion. Now, in these later works, he has come near to Spinoza; for he appears to recognize the need for 'wisdom' and 'intellect' whereby passion may be rightly guided. But we ask, How can he appeal to understanding or 'adequate' ideas to release us from the 'bondage' of passion and to give us freedom? For, so long as we are imperfect, and our 'unworthy' passions strong, our understanding (which is only a part of our natural being) must be clouded by passion; it cannot be a master in its own house, still less cleanse the heart. The circle is vicious; and Blake must move within it appealing now for deliverance to passion (as in *Vala* it is Luvah who wears the robes of Christ) and now to wisdom (as in *Jerusalem* he exalts 'wisdom' over 'goodness'). As Blake has said, the 'self-hood' infects both feeling and knowledge; and the blind can hardly lead the blind; nor does Blake at all explain how the blindness of one or the other may be removed. Like Spinoza, Blake looks for a form of knowledge higher than the discursive, in which thought becomes vision; Spinoza believed that reason might become 'scientia intuitiva', and Blake looked for the reign of 'sweet science'. But neither Spinoza nor Blake explains how this may come about. We search in vain in the pages of *Milton* for an account of how Milton overcomes his Satan, of how the self-hood is 'annihilated'. It is true that in *Vala* he tries desperately to use the life and crucifixion of Christ for his purposes; but because his ethic was naturalistic and his religion pantheistic, the version of the narrative which he gives falls into confusion and impenetrable obscurity.

Certainly Blake's later ethic is very much more worthy of respect than that of the 'gospel of Hell'. But he refuses to carry through to its logical end the movement which started in his mind in the early years of the century. He appears, especially in his new doctrine of 'Satan' and the 'self-hood', to have come near to acknowledging the reality of genuine evil; but he halts, and refuses to become in earnest with morality; if he comes to believe in a Devil he will not believe in a God. He has so long, for whatever reason, hated the insistence of Christianity upon morality and all that Christianity believes to be implied in it, that he resorts to what is, in effect, an intellectual subterfuge to avoid, in the last resort, confessing his error. He was so far right as to be able to say that 'there is no natural religion'; but he was always so far wrong as to be unable to see what this denial implies. He lived his life uneasily between this denial of natural religion and a denial of a religion which is founded on the supernatural. He hated the 'boundedness' and 'opacity' of the world of science; but equally he hated the mystery which is part and parcel of true religion. His position therefore was an insecure form of compromise from which he despised both science and religion proper; it was also one which helped to reduce his art to confusion and failure.

§ 13

There is, however, one further observation which calls to be made. I have said that when we survey the entire body of Blake's work, we see it as the writing of one who, in spite of beginning from a mode of Christian sensibility of extraordinary purity and beauty, sets out strenuously to oppose the beliefs in the supernatural and the sense of the mysterious which we may call Christian. Although Blake is equally strenuous in asserting a spiritual principle in life and in opposing all forms of sensationalistic and mechanistic philosophy, he denies much that is quite essential to a Christian philosophy. The exposition I have attempted, along with the quotations I have given, makes this, I hope, abundantly clear. But this has to be added. In his campaign, if we may so call it, against the supernatural, he was not consistent. The reader is frequently baffled and irritated by passages and comments, in his poetry and prose alike, which appear, at least, to cut across the prevailing naturalism of his writings. Such passages reduce the reader to despair of fixing Blake into a clear frame of doctrine. His mind breaks out, sometimes passionately and angrily, into outrageous contradictions, which appear to show a supernaturalistic philosophy breaking through the hard crust of his formal and prevailing beliefs.

I shall give one or two examples of what I mean. Writing in 1788 (the year before that in which the *Songs of Innocence* appeared), in a series of notes, Blake said: 'Observe the distinction here between Natural and Spiritual as seen by man. Man may comprehend, but not the natural or external man.' Now this remark, dating from the time of the *Songs of Innocence*, does not surprise us; it is what we should expect from him at that time, an opinion far removed from the later naturalism of *The Marriage of Heaven and Hell*. Now if we pass to a year very much later in Blake's life, we find him writing in 1826 that he sees 'in Wordsworth the Natural Man rising up against the Spiritual Man Continually and then he is no Poet but a Heathen Philosopher at Enmity against all true Poetry or Inspiration'. (p. 1024) He goes on to quote the lines:

> And I could wish my days to be
> Bound each to each by natural Piety,

and he adds: 'There is no such Thing as Natural Piety Because the Natural Man is at Enmity with God.' He says also that 'Imagination is the Divine Vision not of The World, or of Man, nor from Man as he is Natural man, but only as he is Spiritual Man'. Again, I shall quote some further remarks of Blake's on a passage of Wordsworth's, where the latter remarks: 'How exquisitely the individual mind is fitted to the external world, and how exquisitely too the external world is fitted to the mind.' Blake's remark is: 'You shall not bring me down to believe such fitting and fitted. I know better and please your Lordship.' (p. 1026)

Now it cannot be denied that there is a good deal of justice in these remarks which Blake directs at Wordsworth. But what Blake failed to see, on account of an extreme perversity, was that the bulk of his writing lay open to a similar charge; the distinction he so passionately makes between the natural and spiritual is one which cannot be made, with any show of consistency, in his scheme of belief. Such a blindness may seem to us unbelievable; but we have simply to accept it. G. K. Chesterton believed he could find sufficient evidence in Blake's writings for thinking that the prevailing bent of Blake's mind was towards Christianity in the fullest sense. I believe this to be mistaken. What, however, cannot be denied is that at times there appear in Blake's writings passages which go far beyond any possible naturalism, but which yet run counter to the main stream of his beliefs. If we have any difficulty (and it is natural to have a great deal of difficulty) in believing that so powerful a mind as Blake's could thus fail to clarify his beliefs and could persevere in such confusion, we are helped by remembering two things. First, that Blake was a man of such strong prejudices, and felt such an antipathy to traditional Christianity, that cool and detached reflection on these matters was wellnigh impossible for him. Secondly, confusion in regard to these same matters was widespread in the most remarkable minds of the time. Coleridge, for example, in his earlier days whole-heartedly took over from Hartley both a thorough materialism and a belief in Christian theism, and continued for many years unclear about quite fundamental and, as we would think, obvious conflicts of belief in his mind. Wordsworth, in *The Prelude*, and indeed in the bulk of his earlier work, gives evidence of pantheistic beliefs but equally of beliefs unmistakably not pantheistic. Shelley in his maturest work will be now crudely naturalistic, and now Platonic[1] or Christian. Such confusion and failure to discriminate what appear to be the simplest issues must be accepted as quite general in the rarest minds of the time.

[1] There are bursts of Platonism in Blake also; there are also virulent attacks on Plato.

We shall speak of this again at a later stage. Why it should be so, we need not now inquire. That it was so, is quite certain. It was only in his later years that Coleridge brought, we may say, the Romantic Movement to clarity in spiritual belief. He remarked late in life that he wished he had met Shelley, for he believed he might have helped him greatly. Coleridge indeed met Blake; but only when Blake's work was done.

We shall now go on to study the poetic fortunes and misfortunes of Shelley and Keats.

Part Two

PURGATORY BLIND

§ 1

IT is well at the beginning of this chapter to observe a certain weakness in Shelley's mind which it is impossible to overlook. This weakness was a willingness to obtain emotional satisfaction at the expense of a certain honesty, and along lines which his imagination and thought in strictness forbade him. He was too often the victim of high emotions for their own sake; and to enjoy them he was unwilling to acknowledge that they were incoherent with the general pattern of his sensibility. He was, that is to say, excessively given to 'enthusiasm', and too little critical of the conditions under which alone such enthusiasm may be properly permitted. Of all the great Romantic poets, Shelley most justifies the suspicion felt by a colder age for strong feeling; and in this bad sense Shelley is the most typically Romantic poet. This weakness in Shelley can be illustrated alike from *Queen Mab* and from *Prometheus*; and I shall make the following quotations from these two poems to show not only this general failing in Shelley but also to show how, if it distresses us in *Queen Mab*, it does so with far greater reason in *Prometheus*. I shall give first the lines from *Prometheus* (III. iv):

> The loathsome mask has fallen, the man remains
> Sceptreless, free, uncircumscribed, but man
> Equal, unclassed, tribeless, and nationless,
> Exempt from awe, worship, degree, the king
> Over himself; just, gentle, wise: but man
> Passionless?—no, yet free from guilt or pain,
> Which were, for his will made or suffered them,
> Nor yet exempt, though ruling them like slaves,
> From chance, and death, and mutability,
> The clogs of that which else might oversoar
> The loftiest star of unascended heaven,
> Pinnacled dim in the intense inane.[1]

Now although Shelley describes the ideal man of the future as 'exempt from awe and worship', he has said roundly in a former scene in the play that God is the maker of the world; but passing this by, let us observe how Shelley's mind works in the later lines of this passage. In a state of perfection to come man will be free

[1] Quotations from the poetry of Shelley are made from the Oxford *Shelley*, ed. Hutchinson, 1919.

F

from guilt and pain; these he thinks sprang from man's own will and may therefore be got rid of. But men will not be exempt from 'chance, and death, and mutability'; but these, he says, he will 'rule like slaves'. Now what does Shelley mean when he says that, not exempt from mutability and death, man will yet 'rule them like slaves'?—for this, I take it, is what he says. At the most he can only mean that man will not be afraid of death. But to express this state of affairs, the phrase 'man will rule death like a slave' is very far, to say the least, from precise. A slave is one who does one's bidding and who is wholly under one's control; and death and mutability, even in Shelley's ideal society, will hardly be this. We are aware that a rhetorical imprecision is being exercised to obscure a state of affairs not likely to satisfy all emotional demands. Shelley is trying to obtain an emotional satisfaction through the mere cloudy use of words. Then, in the last lines, chance, death, and mutability are described as

> The clogs of that which else might oversoar
> The loftiest star of unascended heaven,
> Pinnacled dim in the intense inane.

Here we suspect that the position is, that if the soul of man may not end in Heaven, at least Shelley's peroration shall. We are left with the thought of something 'pinnacled dim in the intense inane'; but the real situation is that from a Heaven of perfect fulfilment man is simply shut out. And the language only too readily lends itself to veiling this fact instead of stating it. It is the language of enthusiasm where we might have expected the language of dismay. This is the kind of disingenuousness which frequently mars Shelley's work.

It is just this kind of thing, appearing in one of Shelley's major pieces and when his powers were at their height, which we find also, but with less surprise, in *Queen Mab*. There too we have this same illegitimate emotional satisfaction. Having described what he considers an ideal and perfect human life, Shelley writes of death in this way:

> Mild was the slow necessity of death:
> The tranquil spirit failed beneath its grasp,
> Without a groan, almost without a fear,
> Calm as a voyager to some distant land,
> And full of wonder, full of hope as he. (p. 788)

Now the philosophy of *Queen Mab* is aggressively naturalistic. What then is the 'fullness of hope' which men dying may feel? Hope of what? We are not told. The disparity between this 'hope' and Shelley's humanitarian atheism is merely disregarded; and we suspect that the lines try to unite quite improperly the traditional satisfaction of the Christian hope of an eternal existence with the satisfaction which Shelley obtained from his impassioned atheism.

Now if we are surprised at the emotional and intellectual confusion of *Queen Mab*, we have to recognize that Shelley never overcame a tendency to exaggerate rhetorically because of a lack of order and clarity in the emotional and intellectual economy of his mind. 'Curb your magnanimity,' said Keats to him, 'and load every rift of your subject with ore.' Shelley was generous of excitement and high emotion when he might well have contracted a little, so to speak, to the greater clarity of his experience. His poetry might have been less 'exciting'; but we should have respected it more.

§ 2

Both the illustrations I have given have to do with Shelley's feelings about death. In *Queen Mab*, so aggressively secular in its beliefs, he refuses to face the embarrassment which the thought of death so clearly creates in him. But in the poems which succeed *Queen Mab* the thought of death is clearly uppermost in his mind; and correspondingly, his dreams of a perfected social order fall away. His mind becomes concentrated on this crucial issue; and of this phase in Shelley's growth, *Alastor* is the chief expression. *Queen Mab* was printed in 1813; in the years immediately following, his health was poor, and it was not at all unlikely that he would die soon. It is not surprising therefore if the *Alastor* volume shows Shelley's mind prepossessed, not by dreams of secular happiness, but by the thought of death. By the middle of 1814, also, his marriage with Harriet had become an unhappy one; and soon he left England with Mary Godwin. No doubt the emotional strain of these events, along with serious ill health, turned his mind in directions which he had formerly declined to explore. The poems published with *Alastor* are not indeed the work of one reconciled to death and mutability. The stanzas beginning 'Away! the moor is dark beneath the moon', *Mutability*, and *On Death* are made sombre by the thought of death.

> Thou in the grave shalt rest—yet till the phantoms flee
> Which that house and heath and garden made dear to thee erewhile,
> Thy remembrance, and repentance, and deep musings are not free
> From the music of two voices and the light of one sweet smile.
> (p. 517)

The soft illusions of *Queen Mab* are gone; in the poem *On Death* (p. 520) he says that

. . . the coming of death is a fearful blow
To a brain unencompassed with nerves of steel;

and only in *A Summer Evening Churchyard* does he permit himself, without giving himself false comfort, to entertain hope:

Thus solemnized and softened, death is mild
And terrorless as this serenest night:
Here could I hope, like some inquiring child
Sporting on graves, that death did hide from human sight
Sweet secrets, or beside its breathing sleep
That loveliest dreams perpetual watch did keep. (p. 521)

These poems, with their grave and weighted rhythms, are among Shelley's finest. How much his experience gained in depth in a short time may be seen from the fact that *Away! the moor is dark* was written early in 1814, the year after that in which *Queen Mab* was printed. The feeling of these poems is, for Shelley, quite extraordinarily pure, free that is to say from the emotional incoherence of which I have spoken; and it is for this reason that they are free from the suggestion of rhetoric and the sounding but unnecessary word which mars so much of Shelley's work. The intensity of these poems, though sombre, is real; unlike a good deal of 'intensity' in others of Shelley's poems which is at bottom only a strained and tense condition due to a fundamental unease and disorder. Not infrequently, the very speed and lightness of Shelley's rhythms, in later poems as in *Queen Mab*, are an escape, not an expression. Here in these early poems he is whole enough, though in sadness and dismay, to master slow large rhythms with the greatest accomplishment.

Alastor, too, is a poem of death. But now, death appears differently. Here, it excites Shelley's imagination. It is no longer a source of dismay; nor indeed, a source of hope. Perhaps the most striking feature of *Alastor* is its freedom from belief and doctrine; in it Shelley *says* very little. If only for this reason, it takes a place among his best poems. After the assurance of *Queen Mab*, founded in obscurity and contradiction, we pass, in *Alastor*, to a condition which is beliefless, but of profound spiritual interest and value. Here, he is wholly without assurance, 'moving about in worlds not realised'; and as he is without a pattern of belief, so he is without a pattern of feeling. He is removed from despair and hope alike, exposed, as it were, in a kind of spiritual destitution, to the world. For this reason, the poem takes us to the very bounds of life, to a state of the mind which is at once one of numbness and torpor, and also one pregnant with richest possibility. On this condition death, 'faithless perhaps as sleep', descends; and the poem is withheld from speculation.

Before speaking further of *Alastor* itself, it is important to study Shelley's Preface: 'It represents', says Shelley of *Alastor*,

'a youth of uncorrupted feelings and adventurous genius led forth by an imagination inflamed and purified through familiarity with all that is excellent and majestic, to the contemplation of the universe. He drinks deep of the fountains of knowledge, and is still insatiate. The magnificence and beauty of the external world sinks profoundly into the frame of his conceptions, and affords to their modifications a variety not to be exhausted. So long as it is possible for his desires to point towards objects thus infinite and unmeasured, he is joyous, and tranquil, and self-possessed. But the period arrives when these objects cease to suffice. His mind is at length suddenly awakened and thirsts for intercourse with an intelligence similar to itself. He images to himself the Being whom he loves. Conversant with speculations of the sublimest and most perfect natures, the vision in which he embodies his own imaginations unites all of wonderful, or wise, or beautiful which the poet, the philosopher, or the lover could depicture.' (p. 14)

Later, he proceeds: 'The Poet's self-centred seclusion was avenged by the furies of an irresistible passion pursuing him to speedy ruin.' Shelley condemns Alastor for 'self-centred seclusion', a touch of conscience in the writer of *Queen Mab*; still, he hurries on to defend him in a passage of pathetic compromise:

'But that Power which strikes the luminaries of the world with sudden darkness and extinction, by awakening them to too exquisite a perception of its influences, dooms to a slow and poisonous decay those meaner spirits that dare to abjure its dominion. Their destiny is more abject and inglorious as their delinquency is more contemptible and pernicious. They who, deluded by no generous error, instigated by no sacred thirst of doubtful knowledge, duped by no illustrious superstition, loving nothing on this earth, and cherishing no hopes beyond, yet keep aloof from sympathies with their kind, rejoicing neither in human joy nor mourning with human grief; these, and such as they, have their apportioned curse. They languish, because none feel with them their common nature. They are morally dead. They are neither friends, nor lovers, nor fathers, nor citizens of the world, nor benefactors of their country.'

Then he concludes with a quotation from *The Excursion*:

The good die first,
And those whose hearts are dry as summer dust,
Burn to the socket!

A 'Power' indeed strikes down the 'self-centred' poet; but the poet yet despises those who indulge no 'generous error', desire no knowledge which is 'doubtful', have no 'illustrious superstition', cherish no hopes beyond the grave. The error is however an error; though 'generous' it 'deludes' us; the knowledge is at best 'doubtful', at worst a 'superstition' though 'illustrious'; there is little beyond 'hope'. With what intricacy does Shelley not pass back and fore between defence and condemnation of his poet! And the final defence he puts up for him is that it is such as he who love their fellow-beings; those undeluded by generous error and duped by no illustrious superstitions are without human love and sympathy. Thus, in this extraordinary passage, does Shelley's divine love clash with his humanitarianism and excuse itself before it. He upholds it and apologizes for it. He asserts it and denies it. *Queen Mab* had been prefaced by a celebrated quotation from Voltaire, printed in big type—ECRASEZ L'INFAME! and its notes consisted chiefly of quotations from the French philosopher. *Alastor* is prefaced by a celebrated quotation from St. Augustine—*Nondum amabam, et amare amabam, quaerebam quid amarem, amans amare.*

Alastor is usually marked down as written under the influence of Wordsworth. But it is more illuminating to observe what it has in common with the first long poem of Keats, *Endymion.* But before going on to speak of the likeness between these two poems, let us notice a sonnet of Keats written early in 1819. I shall quote it in full:

Why did I laugh tonight? No voice will tell:
  No God, no Demon of severe response,
Deigns to reply from Heaven or from Hell.
  Then to my human heart I turn at once.
Heart! Thou and I are here sad and alone;
  I say, why did I laugh? O mortal pain!
O Darkness! Darkness! ever must I moan,
  To question Heaven and Hell and Heart in vain.
Why did I laugh? I know this Being's lease,
  My fancy to its utmost blisses spreads;
Yet would I on this very midnight cease,
  And the world's gaudy ensigns see in shreds;
Verse, Fame, and Beauty are intense indeed,
But Death intenser—Death is Life's high meed.[1] (p. 470)

Of this sonnet I think it is true to say that it expresses the very essence of *Alastor*. It has the very mood and feeling of *Alastor*—a poem of human ignorance, of ignorance which is near to scepticism as it is also near to faith. Moreover, if we look at the *Hymn to Intellectual Beauty* (published in Hunt's *Examiner* in 1817), a poem written by Shelley when he was still in the state of mind most extensively embodied in *Alastor*, we find the following lines:

[1] Quotations from the poetry of Keats are made from H. W. Garrod's edition, Oxford, 1939.

Ask why the sunlight not for ever
Weaves rainbows o'er yon mountain-river,
Why aught should fail and fade that once is shown,
Why fear and dream and death and birth
Cast on the daylight of this earth
Such gloom—why man has such a scope
For love and hate, despondency and hope?

No voice from some sublimer world hath ever
To sage or poet these responses given—
Therefore the names of Demon, Ghost, and Heaven,
Remain the records of their vain endeavour. (p. 526)

It is clear from the opening lines of his sonnet that Keats echoes Shelley's *Ode* in its very choice of words.[1]

Now to return to *Alastor* and *Endymion*, how far *Endymion* was influenced by *Alastor* it is idle to speculate. But it is of some value to observe the main resemblances between the two poems. To both Alastor and Endymion there appear in dream visions of what they must then always pursue; and this pursuit of what is disclosed in dream is the theme of both poems, the one cast in a framework of Shelley's invention, the other in a framework of Greek myth. Shelley says that in the figure of his dream is embodied 'all of wonderful, or wise, or beautiful, which the poet, the philosopher, or the lover could depicture'; his imagination reaches out to grasp these absolutes in a single image. He does not desire acquaintance with a set of ideal values; his mind 'thirsts for intercourse with an intelligence similar to itself'—an Eternal Good in which these values live. So does Endymion feel

A hope beyond the shadow of a dream,

which is a dream of the 'completed form of all completeness'. This was Keats's 'mighty abstract Idea of Beauty' which placed an 'awful warmth about his heart like a load of immortality'. And so Shelley in the *Hymn to Intellectual Beauty*:

Man were immortal, and omnipotent,
Didst thou, unknown and awful as thou art,
Keep with thy glorious train firm state within his heart. (p. 527)

Again, both poems express the despair of ever coming to knowledge of what they dimly envisage as the Supreme Good. 'Why', asks Shelley in the *Hymn to Intellectual Beauty*,

. . . has man such a scope
For love and hate, despondency and hope?

[1] Keats quotes from the *Ode* in a letter written in March 1818. (Buxton Forman, Oxford, 1935, p. 112.)

To both Alastor and Endymion the union comes, and is then lost. The greater part of each of the poems is taken up with recounting a state which is not indeed one of despair, but of mingled despair and hope, a condition which is not one of abandonment nor one of possession. 'Whither have fled', says Shelley, after the loss of Alastor's vision,

> The hues of heaven that canopied his bower
> Of yesternight? The sounds that soothed his sleep,
> The mystery and the majesty of Earth,
> The joy, the exultation? His wan eyes
> Gaze on the empty scene as vacantly
> As ocean's moon looks on the moon in heaven. (p. 19)

And Endymion cries:

> A homeward fever parches up my tongue—
> O let me slake it at the running springs!
> O let me hear once more the linnet's note! . . .
> Before mine eyes thick films and shadows float. . . .
> Young goddess! let me see my native bowers!
> Deliver me from this rapacious deep! (p. 105)

Keats describes the state of both Alastor and Endymion in describing one of the regions to which Endymion goes:

> 'Twas far too strange, and wonderful for sadness;
> Sharpening, by degrees, his appetite
> To dive into the deepest. Dark, nor light,
> The region; nor bright, nor sombre wholly,
> But mingled up; a gleaming melancholy . . . (p. 102)

Both visit places of great beauty—'sunny spots of greenery'; but they are also cast into scenes of extreme strangeness, ghastliness, and desolation. These lines, which describe the scene of Alastor's death, are especially interesting:

> The near scene,
> In naked and severe simplicity,
> Made contrast with the universe. A pine,
> Rock-rooted, stretched athwart the vacancy
> Its swinging boughs, to each inconstant blast
> Yielding one only response, at each pause
> In most familiar cadence, with the howl
> The thunder and the hiss of homeless streams
> Mingling its solemn song, whilst the broad river,
> Foaming and hurrying o'er its rugged path,
> Fell into that immeasurable void
> Scattering its waters to the passing winds.

Yet the grey precipice and solemn pine
And torrent, were not all;—one silent nook
Was there. Even on the edge of that vast mountain,
Upheld by knotty roots and fallen rocks,
It overlooked in its serenity
The dark earth, and the bending vault of stars.
It was a tranquil spot, that seemed to smile
Even in the lap of horror. (p. 26)

We observe the serenity, set 'in the lap of horror'. To this scene Alastor alone has penetrated:

One step,
One human step alone, has ever broken
The stillness of its solitude. (p. 27)

Endymion indeed comes into his heaven—he is 'spiritualised from this mortal state'; but Alastor dies:

The brave, the gentle, and the beautiful,
The child of grace and genius;

and Shelley does not break through with a single word of consolation or hope. We follow Alastor to the very limits of life, dying in a 'blind earth and heaven'. Certainly, in *Alastor*, Shelley's imagination was more purely submissive to the 'object' than in any other of his major poems; indeed we may doubt if he ever achieved such restraint and impersonality. He indulges in no consolations and in no prophecies. He looks, to use his own subtle word, 'vacantly' on the object; and just this kind of 'vacancy' is so often lacking in Shelley's work.

If *Alastor* reminds us of *Endymion* it is none the less true that there is enough in *Alastor* to remind us of Wordsworth. No poem was ever so completely one of 'obstinate questionings' (the phrase makes its appearance in *Alastor*):

Of sense and outward things,
Fallings from us, vanishings;
Blank misgivings of a Creature
Moving about in worlds not realised.

But I wish specially to call attention to a quality which *Alastor* shares with much of Wordsworth's work and which is, indeed, perhaps one of the most notable features of the Romantic mind. It is in Keats and in Coleridge also. I mean the fascination exercised on the minds of these poets by strangeness and desolation. We have recognized enough the liking of the Romantic mind for the merely eerie and abnormal; we have not perhaps paid due attention to the way in which, in the greatest Romantic poets, at a level of the most serious perception scenes of the greatest strangeness and desolation come to carry profound significance. Thus in the lines I have already quoted from *Alastor* the spectacle of the single pine 'stretching athwart the vacancy', in a scene 'naked and severe' and exposed to the winds, brings back to mind Wordsworth's

> The single sheep and the one blasted tree,
> And the bleak music from that old stone wall,

on a day 'tempestuous, dark and wild', and the 'visionary dreariness' which invested 'the naked pool and dreary crags'. To spectacles such as these Wordsworth tells us he 'oft repaired and drank as at a fountain'. In this kind of experience the Romantic mind transposes the love of common horrors and eerieness to the level of intensest spiritual experience where bleakness and desolation to the point of ghastliness exhibit the boundaries of mortality. It is so in Keats's *Endymion*; and it is so in *The Ancient Mariner*. Shelley of course could not have read *The Prelude*; yet what brings him so near to Wordsworth in *Alastor* is not his use of Wordsworthian rhythms and phrases but his turning of terror to high imaginative use.

§ 3

The phase in Shelley's experience of which we are now speaking did not close before he wrote two other notable poems: the *Hymn to Intellectual Beauty* and *Mont Blanc*, both written in the summer of 1816, in Switzerland. The *Hymn* is, like *Alastor*, far enough away from *Queen Mab*; and writing in Switzerland Shelley was happily able to free himself from the humanitarian conscience which troubled him in *Alastor*, which he had written in England. It is also significant that its manner and rhythms sometimes recall Wordsworth's *Ode to Duty*, for Wordsworth was the good genius of Shelley's verse in this period. The *Hymn* is filled with a sense of the Divine Beauty which Alastor had sought and whose light alone

> gives grace and truth to life's unquiet dream.

Its humility in its celebration of the 'unknown and awful' and of its 'inconstancy'—

> Like memory of music fled,—
> Like aught that for its grace may be
> Dear, and yet dearer for its mystery;

and its sense of extreme dependency—

> Depart not as thy shadow came,
> Depart not—lest the grave should be,
> Like life and fear, a dark reality—

are qualities the thought of which does not ordinarily arise in our minds when we think of Shelley. This is a Shelley speaking without shrillness, nearer to despair than in *Prometheus* and *Hellas*, and nearer therefore to self-possession and to an assured and not a forced hopefulness.

Mont Blanc is a difficult poem and requires the most careful study. Once again, in reading it, we are aware of the influence of Wordsworth; and I wish to call attention to the way in which, as it seems to me, this influence is shown in Shelley's poem. One of the most interesting qualities of Wordsworth's poetry is what we may call his symbolical apprehension of natural scenery. Ordinarily, in order to convey vivid awareness of something not disclosed in the sensuous, a quality of the mind, or a relation of the mind to what is not sensible, a poet derives a simile or metaphor from the external world whereby to give body and precision to his perception. Most often, in the poetry of Wordsworth, his perceptions of spiritual realities are reached strictly through excited response to natural scenery. In saying this, I have not in mind that he rejoiced as a 'poet of Nature' in the life and features of the natural world, but that his coming to what he believed to be truth about human life was a process which cannot be separated out from his perception of natural scenery; so that the scene beheld becomes an image of spiritual reality hitherto unknown to him. Thus he does not draw upon a store of recollections of past scenes to give body to his imaginative idea; the 'idea' arises in and through awareness of the present scene; nor can Wordsworth convey the 'idea' other than by description of the scene actually beheld. The 'thought' and the 'perception' are inseparable; or rather the spiritual perception and the sensory perception are inseparable; and frequently the former, the 'meaning', is not susceptible of mere statement. This is, I think, a striking characteristic of Wordsworth's imagination; and it is this which makes his imaginative life at once so sublime and so narrow. Hazlitt said truly of him that 'the current of his feelings is deep, but narrow'. When we compare him with Shakespeare and Milton we are most impressed by the slightness of the store of experience, imagery, and reading upon which he draws; his vision of life is most powerfully conveyed through a description of a road crossing

The naked summit of a far-off hill;

of a beggar whose shadow 'moved not'; of a mountain suddenly uprearing its head; of a sudden mountainous landscape disclosed above a mist; of a sheep couching from a storm: all simple, familiar things which yet shock us in Wordsworth's lines with strangeness and wonder, so that what he lacks in range he atones for by a quite peculiar intensity of mystical vision. In his view, the evocation of such sudden and shocking responses to the world was the most important part of what he called the education which 'Nature' gives, a process which proceeds primarily through a 'discipline of fear'.

Now in *Mont Blanc* we are reminded sharply of Wordsworth in this respect. Here, the contrast of the high and quiet impassivity of the mountain to the steep sounding valley below becomes the image of 'the utmost we can know'; it becomes one of what Wordsworth was accustomed to call 'living images' which act by purifying

> The elements of feeling and of thought
> And sanctifying by such discipline,
> Both pain and fear.

How much of 'pain and fear' is in Shelley's lines we see from the following:

> Far, far above, piercing the infinite sky,
> Mont Blanc appears,—still, snowy, and serene—
> Its subject mountains their unearthly forms
> Pile around it, ice and rock; broad vales between
> Of frozen floods, unfathomable deeps,
> Blue as the overhanging heaven, that spread
> And wind among the accumulated steeps;
> A desert peopled by the storms alone,
> Save when the eagle brings some hunter's bone,
> And the wolf tracks her there—how hideously
> Its shapes are heaped around! rude, bare, and high,
> Ghastly, and scarred, and riven. (p. 529)

The last five lines especially bring Shelley near to Wordsworth: 'A desert peopled by the storms alone'; and shapes 'rude, bare, and high, Ghastly, and scarred, and riven'. And he goes on to say of this 'wilderness' that it has

> . . . a mysterious tongue
> Which teaches awful doubt, or faith so mild,
> So solemn, so serene. . . .

This juxtaposition of awful doubt and mild faith is very significant; it expresses the mood and feeling of *Alastor*, an exposure to infinite spaces and to scenes inhuman to the point of ghastliness which produces a trembling solemnity of the spirit, bowed down in humility and fear; it is a frontier line of the mind at which the obvious characters of doubt and faith are no longer sufficiently expressive.

The mountain is the eternal and changeless. It is 'Power' which

. . . dwells apart in its tranquillity,
Remote, serene, and inaccessible. (p. 530)

The ravine of Arve is the Mind and the Life of Man, 'pervaded with a ceaseless motion' and the 'path of an unresting sound'. It is an 'awful scene'

Where Power in likeness of the Arve comes down
From the ice-gulfs that gird his secret throne. (p. 528)

For if the Ravine in its confusion, tumult, and movement seems far from the unchanging mountain, it is the Arve, coming from the 'ice-gulfs' of the mountain, which at once causes and symbolizes the ceaseless change of the Ravine. Somehow the silent and eternal passes into the sound and movement of the deep valley; the Arve has its source in the tranquil mountain. Yet in the sounding ravine the poet seeks to look above and beyond it:

One legion of wild thoughts, whose wandering wings
Now float above thy darkness . . .
Seeking among the shadows that pass by
Ghosts of all things that are. . . . (p. 529)

Above the Ravine

Mont Blanc appears,—still, snowy, and serene.

The fourth section of the poem begins with these lines:

The fields, the lakes, the forests, and the streams,
Ocean, and all the living things that dwell
Within the daedal earth; lightning and rain,
Earthquake, and fiery flood, and hurricane,
The torpor of the year when feeble dreams
Visit the hidden buds, or dreamless sleep
Holds every future leaf and flower;—the bound
With which from that detested trance they leap;
The works and ways of man, their death and birth,
And that of him and all that his may be;
All things that move and breathe with toil and sound
Are born and die; revolve, subside, and swell.
Power dwells apart, in its tranquillity,
Remote, serene, and inaccessible:
And *this*, the naked countenance of earth,
On which I gaze, even these primaeval mountains
Teach the adverting mind.

'Power' is not in the 'daedal earth', in what is born and dies, in what revolves, subsides, and swells. It dwells in tranquillity and serenity, in the still source of all change. Thus Shelley goes on, representing in the mountain the stillness and silence of the Eternal:

Mont Blanc yet gleams on high:—the power is there,
The still and solemn power of many sights,
And many sounds, and much of life and death.
In the calm darkness of the moonless nights,
In the lone glare of day, the snows descend
Upon that Mountain; none beholds them there,
Nor when the flakes burn in the sinking sun,
Or the star-beams dart through them:—Winds contend
Silently there, and heap the snow with breath
Rapid and strong, but silently! Its home
The voiceless lightning in these solitudes
Keeps innocently, and like vapour broods
Over the snow. (p. 531)

But the mountain is no mere sublime consolation. It is a source of terror and destruction:

The glaciers creep
Like snakes that watch their prey, from their far fountains,
Slow rolling on; there, many a precipice,
Frost and the Sun in scorn of mortal power
Have piled: dome, pyramid, and pinnacle,
A city of death, distinct with many a tower
And wall impregnable of beaming ice.
Yet not a city, but a flood of ruin
Is there, that from the boundaries of the sky
Rolls its perpetual stream; vast pines are strewing
Its destined path, or in the mangled soil
Branchless and shattered stand; the rocks, drawn down
From yon remotest waste, have overthrown
The limits of the dead and living world,
Never to be reclaimed. The dwelling-place
Of insects, beasts, and birds, becomes its spoil;
Their food and their retreat for ever gone,
So much of life and joy is lost. The race
Of man flies far in dread; his work and dwelling
Vanish, like smoke before the tempest's stream,
And their place is not known. (p. 530)

It is this 'Power', set in a silent wilderness, which

. . . has a mysterious tongue
Which teaches awful doubt, or faith so mild,
So solemn, so serene.

It is also this Power, so much a source of terror, which has a voice

. . . to repeal
Large codes of fraud and woe; not understood
By all, but which the wise, and great, and good
Interpret, or make felt, or deeply feel. (p. 530)

In its terror are healing, renewal, and righteousness.

In several respects, *Mont Blanc* is an obscure poem. But its chief intention is clear enough. In *Alastor* the Ideal is an object of desire, a living and eternal Good; in *Mont Blanc* the Eternal is seen in its creation and destruction of what is temporal and passing. Seen from out of the temporal and changing, its impassivity, stillness, and silence are terrible: 'remote, serene, and inaccessible', surrounded by inhuman and terrible wastes, removed, unseeing. Before it we have doubt and faith, are terrified and healed. It creates the world of time; yet is for ever beyond it and unapproachable.

§ 4

'The deep truth is imageless' says Demogorgon in *Prometheus Unbound*. Yet in *Mont Blanc* Shelley sees something of an image of it in the mountain and the ravine. But the image necessarily falls short; expressive as it is, it does not succeed in uniting the eternal and the temporal as the imagination desires, or in showing how they may come together. We have said that in this poem Shelley's mind has turned from the contemplation of the Divine as an object of desire, as in *Alastor*, to contemplation of it as 'Power'; as causing the world of time and 'all things that move and breathe with toil and sound'; as a law inhabiting the universe; and as making and overthrowing the life of man. Yet in the poem the unchanging and the changing stand apart. Certainly, the image conveys truth; it is a vision of the life of God, overflowing indeed into a created world, yet complete in itself and transcendent; it communicates to us a sense of the complete sufficiency of God to Himself and of the smallness of the human world which we see as issuing from inexhaustible power which can destroy what is created with no loss to itself. Yet something more is desired than this, whether with justice or not; that is, that we should somehow behold the eternal inhabiting the temporal, or the temporal informed by the stillness and perfection of the eternal.

Now Shelley passed from the thought of the Ideal Good to that of Divine Power; so did Keats. In the third and last book of *Hyperion*, Apollo speaks thus to Mnemosyne:

> Goddess benign, point forth some unknown thing:
> Are there not other regions than this isle?
> What are the stars? There is the sun, the sun!
> And the most patient brilliance of the moon! . . .
> I have heard the cloudy thunder: Where is power?
> Whose hand, whose essence, what divinity
> Makes this alarum in the elements,
> While I here idle listen on these shores
> In fearless yet in aching ignorance? (p. 303)

To these questions, Where is power? and what the essence or divinity which rules the world? Mnemosyne, it will be recalled, gives no reply. Yet Apollo obtains his answer through beholding the face of Mnemosyne; and through his beholding he becomes a god:

> Yet I can read
> A wondrous lesson in thy silent face:
> Knowledge enormous makes a God of me.
> Names, deeds, gray legends, dire events, rebellions,
> Majesties, sovran voices, agonies,
> Creations and destroyings, all at once
> Pour into the wide hollows of my brain,
> And deify me, as if some blithe wine
> Or bright elixir peerless I had drunk,
> And so become immortal. (p. 304)

Now again, these passages are difficult and obscure. What, however, is clear enough is that Apollo becomes a god through coming to knowledge of names, deeds, creations and destroyings, majesties, agonies. He becomes immortal through apprehending the world of time, of creation and destruction. But even so, there is difficulty enough; and we turn to the second version of *Hyperion* for possible help. (I may say here that I do not wish at this stage to anticipate discussion which occurs later, of certain matters which naturally arise from the study of the two *Hyperions*; I am proceeding now with a limited purpose in view.) In the second *Hyperion*, the place of Apollo is taken by Keats himself who is one of those

> . . . to whom the miseries of the world
> Are misery, and will not let them rest.

He feels the 'giant agony of the world'; he seeks to understand the world of 'creations and destroyings', and, in the language of the first *Hyperion*, to know

> Whose hand, whose essence, what divinity
> Makes this alarum in the elements?

For Keats in the second version, like Apollo in the first, stands in 'fearless yet in aching ignorance', and, like Apollo, seeks 'knowledge enormous'. Now in the second *Hyperion* the poet does what he does not do in the first, he describes the face of Moneta (the Mnemosyne of the first version):

> Then saw I a wan face,
> Not pin'd by human sorrows, but bright blanch'd
> By an immortal sickness which kills not;
> It works a constant change, which happy death
> Can put no end to; deathwards progressing

To no death was that visage; it had pass'd
The lily and the snow; and beyond these
I must not think now, though I saw that face—
But for her eyes I should have fled away.
They held me back, with a benignant light,
Soft-mitigated by divinest lids
Half closed, and visionless entire they seem'd
Of all external things—they saw me not,
But in blank splendor beam'd like the mild moon,
Who comforts those she sees not, who knows not
What eyes are upward cast. (p. 514)

These lines we may fairly take as a commentary on and, so far as it goes, an explanation of how, on beholding the face of Mnemosyne, Apollo had become a God.

Now it would be mistaken to pretend that these lines make perfectly clear what we wish to know and what Keats wished to convey. Keats here, like Shelley in *Mont Blanc*, is labouring to convey in image ultimate metaphysical perceptions; and we need not be surprised if they fail in clarity and assurance. The face of Moneta reveals a 'sickness' which is immortal; it is a God's sickness which can come to no end, and by it her face is 'bright blanch'd'. The face is deathly but cannot die. It was so terrible to behold that the poet would have fled away; but he was held from flight by the eyes of the Goddess; benignant and without the sense of external things, they 'in blank splendor beam'd, like the mild moon', and gave comfort. Therefore the chief character of the face is the union of great suffering with a luminous and profound peace. It is both frightening and comforting, exhausted and inexhaustible, agonized and calm, defeated and triumphant. This is the face beholdment of which transformed the young Apollo into deity; it gave him knowledge of creations and destroyings, of dire events and agonies; but with this it also gave him knowledge of those events of time and suffering as held and encompassed by an ineffable peace. So much, at least, in the interpretation of this passage, seems certain enough; it is in such a face, blanched by suffering and bearing the sorrows and sufferings of the world, that 'power' resides, the 'essence of divinity' which upholds sun, moon, and stars. In *Mont Blanc* Shelley images the life of God in its self-completeness and sufficiency, removed from the ravine of men into which its power flows; in *Hyperion* Keats exhibits the eternal informing the finite, and containing the suffering of the world.

§ 5

In speaking in this way of *Hyperion* I have gone ahead into 1819, and in comparing it with *Mont Blanc* have disregarded chronological sequence; and I trust the reader will allow me to refer now to a passage from Wordsworth's *Prelude* which I wish to put alongside the passage from Keats's *Hyperion* of which I have been speaking. In doing this, I am deviating from the main intention of this chapter. But the comparison is interesting and I think valuable in the study of Romanticism. I shall then return to the professed undertaking of this chapter.

The passage from Wordsworth is long; but I shall quote it entire:

> Once, when those summer months
> Were flown, and autumn brought its annual show
> Of oars with oars contending, sails with sails,
> Upon Winander's spacious breast, it chanced
> That—after I had left a flower-decked room
> (Whose in-door pastime, lighted up, survived
> To a late hour), and spirits overwrought
> Were making night do penance for a day
> Spent in a round of strenuous idleness—
> My homeward course led up a long ascent,
> Where the road's watery surface, to the top
> Of that sharp rising, glittered to the moon
> And bore the semblance of another stream
> Stealing with silent lapse to join the brook
> That murmured in the vale. All else was still;
> No living thing appeared in earth or air,
> And, save the flowing water's peaceful voice,
> Sound there was none—but, lo! an uncouth shape,
> Shown by a sudden turning of the road,
> So near that, slipping back into the shade
> Of a thick hawthorn, I could mark him well,
> Myself unseen. He was of stature tall,
> A span above man's common measure, tall,
> Stiff, lank, and upright; a more meagre man
> Was never seen before by night or day.
> Long were his arms, pallid his hands; his mouth
> Looked ghastly in the moonlight: from behind,
> A mile-stone propped him; I could also ken
> That he was clothed in military garb,
> Though faded, yet entire. Companionless,
> No dog attending, by no staff sustained,
> He stood, and in his very dress appeared
> A desolation, a simplicity,
> To which the trappings of a gaudy world
> Make a strange back-ground. From his lips, ere long,
> Issued low muttered sounds, as if of pain

Or some uneasy thought; yet still his form
Kept the same awful steadiness—at his feet
His shadow lay, and moved not. From self-blame
Not wholly free, I watched him thus; at length
Subduing my heart's specious cowardice,
I left the shady nook where I had stood
And hailed him. Slowly from his resting-place
He rose, and with a lean and wasted arm
In measured gesture lifted to his head
Returned my salutation; then resumed
His station as before; and when I asked
His history, the veteran, in reply,
Was neither slow nor eager; but, unmoved,
And with a quiet uncomplaining voice,
A stately air of mild indifference,
He told in few plain words a soldier's tale—
That in the Tropic Islands he had served,
Whence he had landed scarcely three weeks past;
That on his landing he had been dismissed,
And now was travelling towards his native home.
This heard, I said, in pity, 'Come with me.'
He stooped, and straightway from the ground took up
An oaken staff by me yet unobserved—
A staff which must have dropt from his slack hand
And lay till now neglected in the grass.
Though weak his step and cautious, he appeared
To travel without pain, and I beheld,
With an astonishment but ill suppressed,
His ghostly figure moving at my side;
Nor could I, while we journeyed thus, forbear
To turn from present hardships to the past,
And speak of war, battle, and pestilence,
Sprinkling this talk with questions, better spared,
On what he might himself have seen or felt.
He all the while was in demeanour calm,
Concise in answer; solemn and sublime
He might have seemed, but that in all he said
There was a strange half-absence, as of one
Knowing too well the importance of his theme,
But feeling it no longer. Our discourse
Soon ended, and together on we passed
In silence through a wood gloomy and still.
Up-turning, then, along an open field,
We reached a cottage. At the door I knocked,
And earnestly to charitable care
Commended him as a poor friendless man,
Belated and by sickness overcome.
Assured that now the traveller would repose
In comfort, I entreated that henceforth
He would not linger in the public ways,

But ask for timely furtherance and help
Such as his state required. At this reproof,
With the same ghastly mildness in his look,
He said, 'My trust is in the God of Heaven,
And in the eye of him who passes me!'

The cottage door was speedily unbarred,
And now the soldier touched his hat once more
With his lean hand, and in a faltering voice,
Whose tone bespake reviving interests
Till then unfelt, he thanked me; I returned
The farewell blessing of the patient man,
And so we parted. Back I cast a look,
And lingered near the door a little space,
Then sought with quiet heart my distant home.[1]

This passage, perhaps the most remarkable in all Wordsworth's work, not only requires close study of itself, but invites comparison with the famous lines of Keats I have previously quoted. It may seem a far step from Keats's Goddess to Wordsworth's homeless soldier. In some respects it may be so. But there are features which the passages share. Wordsworth sets his scene against a background of youthful pleasure and jollity. (We may recall the wedding which Coleridge employs for the narrative of the Mariner's wanderings.) Wordsworth walked home alone, on a road glittering in moonlight, and everything was still. Suddenly the 'uncouth shape' appears, a tall, upright, and meagre man.

Long were his arms, pallid his hands; his mouth
Looked ghastly in the moonlight.

He was alone, and his form kept an 'awful steadiness'; 'at his feet his shadow lay, and moved not'. Wordsworth needed to overcome his fear, and doing so advanced. Replying to the poet's questions, the old soldier was 'neither slow nor eager'; uncomplainingly, he spoke with a 'stately air of mild indifference'. They spoke of the soldier's past, 'of war, battle, and pestilence'. 'He all the while was in demeanour calm', and he had

. . . a strange half-absence, as of one
Knowing too well the importance of this theme,
But feeling it no longer—

the theme of his past and his soldier's life and fortunes. Coming to a cottage, Wordsworth arranges shelter for him and beseeches him not to wander alone and helplessly, but to seek help. Then, with the same 'ghastly mildness in his look', he replies that he trusts in God and men. And Wordsworth reaches home with a 'quiet heart'.

[1] Oxford *Wordsworth*, ed. Hutchinson, 1932, p. 664.

What this passage has in common with that of Keats will be clear to the reader. The faces of Keats's Goddess and Wordsworth's soldier share a 'ghastliness' and a 'mildness'; and both alike terrify and comfort. Keats speaks of 'names, deeds, gray legends, dire events, rebellions'; Wordsworth of 'war, battle, and pestilence'. In each case, the 'mildness' in their look transcends without obliterating the suffering these events have brought. Keats and Wordsworth alike shrink in fear; but Keats is comforted, and Wordsworth's heart made quiet. Finally, Moneta's eyes seemed 'visionless of all external things', did not see the past; the soldier speaks with a 'strange half-absence' knowing, yet not feeling, the 'importance of his theme'; the gaze of both appears to be away from and beyond the world. I suggest that the two passages convey perceptions of the same order and kind, of a state in which there is manifested an extreme helplessness and submission to suffering and also a plenitude of power; and the old and homeless soldier 'of stature tall',

> A span above man's common measure

has the sublimity and awfulness of a God.

§ 6

To return now to Shelley. His vision in *Mont Blanc*, of the life of God, complete and transcendent, yet overflowing into the ravine of commotion and tumult, a ravine out of which the mind is raised to behold and know the Eternal, is the climax of this phase in Shelley's life. This he discovered as the answer to the question which the nearness of death had compelled him to ask. And we might think that having reached this point he would proceed with assurance to explore the consequences of this perception for the life of man in society. But he was uneasy, to say the least, in making this transition. The sense of that of which he had seen an image in the silent and inexhaustible mountain, which is hidden from us in the 'ravine' of life, did not remain steady in his imagination. The image wavered and became dim; it did not become the centre around which a single widening and inclusive pattern of perception might have grown. He was well educated, widely read, and had great intellectual and imaginative endowment; yet his mind, failing in stability and order, became split into a number of patterns of apprehension which defied unification. When he returned to England, he settled at Great Marlow, where he saw enough evidence of the extreme neediness of the poor at that time. They were years of widespread distress and discontent; and it is probable that the social conditions of the time turned his mind to revolutionary themes and thoughts. Throughout the following summer of 1817 he wrote *The Revolt of Islam*; and study of this poem is of great importance for our purpose.

I have said of *Mont Blanc* that it is typical of Romantic work in its 'symbolical' apprehension of landscape, in which the poet does not so much draw on a store of past impressions as discover significances suddenly and with surprise through the presented spectacle. He does not imagine a landscape to illustrate, or effect vivid conveyance of, an attitude towards the world; he is aware of the idea only as, so to speak, embedded and thus perceived in sensory patterns. Here at least thought and perception are one, for it is the perception of the sensory which is the very occasion of the 'thought'. Now in discussing the nature and difficulties of Romantic sensibility, *The Revolt of Islam* raises some interesting questions not unconnected with these observations. I suggest that it is most useful to see this poem as an attempt, though not a whole-hearted one, at allegory; and this is a convenient point at which to make some remarks on the importance of allegory for the Romantic writers.

We know that in 1816 and 1817 Shelley read *The Faerie Queene*. *The Revolt of Islam* is in Spenserian stanzas; and there are other considerations which make it of some advantage to relate Shelley to Spenser. It is not perhaps altogether fanciful to see some likeness between Laon and Cythna and St. George and Una. That the differences are very great is clear enough. But there is this fundamental similarity: St. George and Una set out to do nothing less than to deliver mankind from the domination of evil. The parents of Una and their subjects were dispossessed of their homeland, their Eden, and the slaying of the Dragon effects their return. Laon and Cythna also attempt nothing less than the deliverance of the entire human race from evil, and the place of the Dragon is taken by the Tyrant. No doubt this does not take us very far; but it takes us far enough by supplying a fundamental identity of theme. Also, it is interesting to compare Spenser's Prefatory letter to Raleigh with Shelley's Preface to *The Revolt of Islam*.

'The generall end therefore of all the booke is to fashion a gentleman or noble person in vertuous and gentle discipline: Which for that I conceiued should be most plausible and pleasing, being coloured with an historicall fiction, the which the most part of men delight to read, rather for variety of matter, then for profite of the ensample: I chose he historye of king Arthure . . .'

writes Spenser. Shelley says that he has written his poem

'in the view of kindling within the bosoms of my readers a virtuous enthusiasm for those doctrines of liberty and justice, that faith and hope in something good, which neither violence nor misrepresentation nor prejudice can ever totally extinguish among mankind. For this purpose I have chosen a story of human passion in its most universal character, diversified with moving and romantic adventures. . . . It is a succession of pictures illustrating the growth and progress of individual mind aspiring after excellence, and devoted to the love of mankind . . .' (p. 32)

These two statements of intention are similar enough—'to fashion a noble person' and 'to kindle virtuous enthusiasm'; 'to colour with an historicall fiction' and to diversify 'with moving and romantic adventures'. It is therefore of interest to compare the two poems and to observe their similarities and differences of poetic method.

Now there is good reason why a Romantic poet should turn to allegory. Blake and Shelley, like Spenser, were concerned to say something which they believed to be of the highest importance for human life; and we have no right to call them lesser poets on account of this. We have been told that allegory arose from a strong sense of the inner life and of its dire conflicts; the men who wrote allegory in the Middle Ages were concerned without disguise to write in a manner which confessed to their sense of the urgency of the spiritual life. So it is with Spenser, Blake, Shelley; of Keats I shall say something later; but Wordsworth chose an alternative to allegory, an alternative which we have partly at least already noticed. Instead of using allegory Wordsworth wrote a great deal of autobiographical poetry; his poetry recounts his experience. Now this is obviously dangerous and difficult. How dangerous and difficult we can see from Wordsworth's work. His poetry, or at least the greater part of it, consists in 'saying'; certainly he made some splendid poetry out of this kind of direct utterance about nature, God, and man, but a great deal of it is hardly poetry at all. His poetry combines greatness and purity in the highest degree when, as we have seen, he beholds men and landscapes in a symbolical way. Here, indeed, there is unification of sensibility; but these passages are comparatively rare. I should be, I think, the last man to wish to minimize Wordsworth's greatness. But no one can deny the extent of Wordsworth's failure and the dangers of what he tried to make poetry do.

Blake and Shelley tried other methods. We have sought to explain Blake's methods and the cause of his failure. Now in *The Revolt of Islam* Laon and Cythna, embodying individually and, through their love, together, a certain kind of spirituality, set out to save the world; they are what in Shelley's view Man and Woman should be and may be. In the course of their attempt they will meet with numerous adventures 'moving and romantic'. I do not wish to press too far the likeness, slight enough, which I have suggested between *The Revolt* and the first book of *The Faerie Queene*; but it is perhaps worth remarking that in the former as in the latter it is the woman who shows the greater force and tenacity of mind. Cythna is clearly stronger than Laon, as Una shows greater force and directiveness than St. George. What is effected in each poem is more due to the heroine than to the hero. Laon and Cythna do not indeed carry any nominal significance as do St. George and Una as embodying Holiness and Truth respectively; yet St. George and Una in Spenser's poem overflow as it were their designation, and Laon and Cythna no doubt may be said to embody for Shelley, each and together, saintliness combined with truth. They are saints, if secular saints; and if Una symbolizes the truth of Protestantism against Rome, Laon and Cythna symbolize the truth as against any kind of church whatsoever. Yet when we have said this, we seem to come to the end of any resemblance between the two poems. We can at most say that the Iberian Priest, symbolizing the church, corresponds to Duessa; that the Tyrant, symbolizing secular power and evil, corresponds to the Dragon; that the old man who restores Laon from his despair and madness corresponds to the good occupants of the House of Holiness who restore St. George after his despair, so that both heroes are restored to make their final effort. Finally, we may say that Shelley is not afraid to introduce a frankly allegorical figure—that of Pestilence—in canto VI; this no doubt is not in itself very much, but it shows, I think, that Shelley felt he was not far away from avowed allegorism. Even so, if all this is allowed, the correspondences between the two poems are general and vague enough; but if they are sufficient to justify us in seeing *The Revolt* as in any degree an allegory, we may go on to see how different is Shelley's manner and method from Spenser's.

Clearly, Shelley's narrative is far more realistic than *The Faerie Queene*. This no doubt is in large measure to be explained by the fact that, little removed from the Middle Ages and its habit of allegory, and with the Italian epic before him, Spenser could have little hesitation in using knightly adventure, monsters, and symbolical figures, though, as Mr. Lewis observes, *The Faerie Queene* was, as an allegorical poem, slightly out of fashion at the time of its appearance; Shelley could not possibly resort to this usage. He was indeed writing, as was Spenser, the drama of the inner life, of the conflict of love and hate within the soul; and he needed his symbols and figures to give body to this conflict. But while Spenser could symbolize a humanity released from evil in the subjects of Una's parents, who are saved by the slaying of a dragon, Shelley has no alternative but to depict a vast social revolution such as had in a measure actually occurred in France. But the inevitable result of this is a huge vagueness in Shelley's narrative outlines contrasting sharply with the clarity of *The Faerie Queene*; for Shelley was forbidden the neat equivalences which were to Spenser's hand. He has to pack a huge canvas and give a sense of multitude and tumult which destroys concision and clarity. Blake, in using allegorical figures, creates for us the difficulty of understanding their respective significances and actions; Shelley's meaning, like Spenser's, is clear enough, but his method and condition of work require so great a measure of realism as to defeat, not clarity of understanding, but clarity and vividness of perception. Shelley does not attempt explicit allegory, nor perhaps could he be expected to have done so. He must try to achieve a measure of realism, while retaining a strong suggestion of allegory. But the two things largely cancel each other out. We can see in greater detail how Shelley fails both in realistic and in allegorical effect.

Dr. Spens, discussing the dramatic and realistic power Spenser is capable of, quotes the following stanzas from the first book of *The Faerie Queene*[1] in which Spenser describes the crowd watching the corpse of the dragon:

> Some feard, and fled; some feard and well it faynd;
> One that would wiser seeme, then all the rest,
> Warnd him not touch, for yet perhaps remaynd
> Some lingring life within his hollow brest,
> Or in his wombe might lurke some hidden nest
> Of many Dragonets, his fruitfull seed;
> Another said, that in his eyes did rest
> Yet sparckling fyre, and bad thereof take heed;
> Another said, he saw him moue his eyes indeed.
>
> One mother, when as her foolehardie chyld
> Did come too neare, and with his talants play,
> Halfe dead through feare, her little babe reuyld,
> And to her gossips gan in counsell say;
> How can I tell, but that his talants may
> Yet scratch my sonne, or rend his tender hand?
> So diuersly themselves in vaine they fray;
> Whiles some more bold, to measure him nigh stand,
> To proue how many acres he did spread of land.[2]

Dr. Spens suggests that these stanzas, fine as they are in themselves, giving so vivid a picture, are in this context a mistake, as

[1] Quotations from Spenser are made from the edition of J. C. Smith, Oxford, 1909.

[2] I. XII. x–xi.

indeed they may be. They depart too far from the manner and method of allegory. But certainly in *The Revolt*, in which such accuracy in human delineation, on account of the greater realism of the poem, would not be so out of place, we get nothing so precise and sharp.

Shelley cannot obtain descriptive effects of a realistic kind; but he also fails to obtain those descriptive effects which are of an allegorical kind. In her book, *Spenser's Faerie Queene*, Dr. Spens says: 'Spenser is essentially an Elizabethan, and the Elizabethans tended to utter their more intense emotions through the imagery of human figures: the men of the nineteenth century through the imagery of inanimate nature'; and again, 'the Elizabethans saw moral qualities and mental experiences steeped in colour and confined by form. They thought and felt in pageants'; but in our days, 'the visions have grown pale in human sensibility. This entanglement of the Elizabethan mind in sensuous detail explains why so much of Spenser's finest figures—the emotional quality—is given through a description of their raiment.' Now in *The Revolt* we have nothing like the stanzas I have just quoted; and we may compare this description of Cythna:

A Form most like the imagined habitant
  Of silver exhalations sprung from dawn,
By winds which feed on sunrise woven, to enchant
  The faiths of men: all mortal eyes were drawn,
  As famished mariners through strange seas gone
Gaze on a burning watch-tower, by the light
  Of those divinest lineaments—alone
  With thoughts which none could share, from that fair sight
I turned in sickness, for a veil shrouded her countenance bright,
(p. 88)

with this description of Una:

A louely Ladie rode him faire beside,
  Vpon a lowly Asse more white then snow,
  Yet she much whiter, but the same did hide
  Vnder a vele, that wimpled was full low,
  And ouer all a blacke stole she did throw,
  As one that inly mournd: so was she sad,
  And heauie sat vpon her palfrey slow:
  Seemed in heart some hidden care she had,
And by her in a line a milke white lambe she lad.[1]

Again, we can contrast Shelley's further delineation of Cythna:

She moved upon this earth a shape of brightness,
  A power, that from its objects scarcely drew
One impulse of her being—in her lightness

[1] I. I. iv.

Most like some radiant cloud of morning dew,
Which wanders through the waste air's pathless blue,
To nourish some far desert: she did seem
Beside me, gathering beauty as she grew,
Like the bright shade of some immortal dream
Which walks, when tempest sleeps, the wave of life's dark stream,
(p. 58)

with the portrait of Belphoebe in the third canto of the second book, of which I shall quote two stanzas:

Vpon her eyelids many Graces sate,
Under the shadow of her euen browes,
Working belgards, and amorous retrate,
And euery one her with a grace endowes:
And euery one with meekenesse to her bowes.
So glorious mirrhour of celestiall grace,
And soueraine moniment of mortall vowes,
How shall fraile pen descriue her heauenly face,
For feare through want of skill her beautie to disgrace?

So faire, and thousand thousand times more faire
She seemd, when she presented was to sight,
And was yclad, for heat of scorching aire,
All in a silken Camus lylly whight,
Purfled vpon with many a folded plight,
Which all aboue besprinckled was throughout
With golden aygulets, that glistred bright,
Like twinckling starres, and all the skirt about
Was hemd with golden fringe.[1]

In each case Shelley tries to express his heroine in terms of something unhuman ('cloud of morning dew'; 'imagined habitant Of silver exhalations sprung from dawn'), a method as much negative as positive, which cannot give more than a vague impression of beauty; in each case Spenser gives us exact image of raiment which conveys spiritual quality. Consider also, in the same context, these lines from the *Purgatorio*, in which Dante sees Beatrice:

Io vidi già nel cominciar del giorno
la parte oriental tutta rosata
e l'altro ciel di bel sereno adorno,

e la faccia del sol nascere ombrata,
sì che per temperanza di vapori,
l'occhio la sostenea lunga fiata:

così dentro una nuvola di fiori,
che dalle mani angeliche saliva
e ricadeva in giù dentro e di fuori

[1] 2. III. xxv–vi.

sopra candido vel cinta d'oliva
    donna m'apparve, sotto verde manto,
    vestita di color di fiamma viva.

(Ere now have I seen, at dawn of day, the eastern part all rosy red, and the rest of heaven adorned with fair clear sky,

and the face of the sun rise shadowed, so that by the tempering of the mists the eye long time endured him:

so within a cloud of flowers, which rose from the angelic hands and fell down again within and without,

olive-crowned over a white veil, a lady appeared to me, clad, under a green mantle, with hue of living flame.)[1]

Here Dante resorts to imagery of nature, and then portrays Beatrice directly. We cannot fail to notice the greater sobriety and clarity of Dante (as of Spenser also); and the colours have their effect, at least in part (like those Spenser employs), because of the allegorical significance they possess.[2] Comparing Shelley and Spenser we may, of course, be content to say that the difference is that between two imaginations; but the imagination of a poet is not something absolute, fixed in and by itself; its natural powers necessarily depend on the conditions and tradition of the time. Spenser was working within a tradition of allegory, practised over a long period, though it was then dying. Shelley, anxious to do something very similar to Spenser, and, denied the form which Spenser found natural, has not at his disposal nor has succeeded in fashioning, a clear method of procedure, or set of conventions capable of fusing, in the greatest degree possible, perception and thought.

There is another way in which what is fundamentally the same feature of Shelley's work can be illustrated. Shelley knew that for a long narrative poem 'moving and romantic adventures' were necessary. But in fact they are woefully lacking in *The Revolt*. If the figures moving in it want precise delineation, the narrative recounts huge events which are not reduced to a size and form which our imaginations can master. Now Spenser could draw on medieval chivalry and romance, on Boiardo and Ariosto; Shelley, pushed in the direction of realism, was forbidden, by the moral ideal he was urging, to use even the symbol of war and fighting. St. George, no less idealistic than Laon, can fight Sansjoy and the Dragon, thereby supplying incident and excitement to the narrative. Laon, seeking the liberation of mankind by the

[1] Tr. Okey, canto XXX, ll. 22–33.

[2] I have the less hesitation in quoting Dante because the marks of the *Commedia* are upon *The Revolt of Islam*; cf., for example, *The Revolt*, XII. xx with the *Purgatorio*, canto II.

exercise of purely spiritual force, fails to provide lively incident for us. Unable to use symbol, above all the symbol of fight, Shelley is at a loss to create 'moving adventure'. Further, for the sake of his narrative, Shelley has to be disloyal to his doctrine of non-resistance; when the Tyrant's hordes descend on the camp in canto VI Shelley has no other alternative than to make Laon and his comrades fight. There was a limit to Shelley's surrender of incident and violent excitement. Spenser, as an allegorist, treats spiritual issues universally; he tells, like Shelley, 'a story of human passion in its most universal character', and is not limited to the particular in the manner of the dramatist or writer of 'straight' narrative. Shelley, on the other hand, neither exposes the universal in the particular like the dramatist or 'straight' narrator, nor uses the particular for the sake of the explicit universal, like the allegorist. He has neither significant 'realism' nor significant symbol.

I would not have made these rather obvious remarks about *The Revolt of Islam* were it not that the poem shows us the difficulties with which the Romantic poets were beset, in particular the difficulties besetting their attempt to do something similar to what a poet at the end of the sixteenth century could do with conspicuous success. Blake's failure in the use of allegory was on account of what he was trying to do, the nature of his intention; Shelley's failure arises from no fault of his own; it arises from the impossibility of using full allegory for a purpose which, unlike Blake's, is wholly legitimate. Now if Shelley fails here, what other forms will he attempt? But before we go further, we must notice certain other characteristics of *The Revolt of Islam*.

§ 7

At first sight at least, *The Revolt of Islam* seems very far removed from *Alastor* and the Switzerland poetry, and to be much nearer *Queen Mab* in tone, however superior to it in technical control. Shelley's mind appears now to have withdrawn itself, as it were, from beyond the world and passed to the hope of drastic changes within it. He leaps back into the imaginative and emotional pattern of his first poem; he is at considerable pains to imbue us with a secular and revolutionary outlook, however noble its ideals. The revolution he urges is indeed a spiritual one which shall not resort to the use of violence; and his theme is love 'which endureth unto the end'. Yet, for the greater part of the poem at least, he excludes the sense, which was so strong in his preceding poetry, of the ideal and eternal. The pattern which was emerging in *Alastor* and *Mont Blanc* is not enlarged to include an attitude towards moral and social change, as it well might have been; it appears to have become forgotten. We are in another world here, apparently unrelated to the weird and terrifying landscapes of *Alastor*. He is, if only half-consciously, repressing his former experience, and trying to effect a false simplification; he is so aggressively secular that we suspect that his very emphasis betrays an uneasiness, and that he is trying to persuade himself out of the way into which his former poetry had led him. In this sense *The Revolt of Islam* is an essay in self-deception.

I have already observed how Shelley carries over into so late a work as *Prometheus Unbound* his habit of temporizing with momentous issues which we find in *Queen Mab*. In *The Revolt of Islam* also we are back to the uncritical disingenuousness of that early poem. In the Preface to *The Revolt* Lucretius is proclaimed the master philosopher; and he had quoted Lucretius at the head of *Queen Mab*. Here again 'Necessity' is proclaimed. Cythna (who is far more Shelley's mouthpiece than the milder Laon) tells her followers with great assurance that the tomb is 'devouring', and she tells Laon that the grave is 'passionless'. Yet we warm to her a little when she acquires something of the humility of ignorance; for after the defeat of their cause she tells Laon that reason and sense, which teach us that death is a 'ruin dark and steep', may be only 'blind fancies':

> There is delusion in the world—and woe,
> And fear, and pain—we know not whence we live,
> Or why, or how, or what mute Power may give
> Their being to each plant, and star, and beast,
> Or even these thoughts. (p. 127)

This is nearer to wisdom, although we think that Shelley has forced this utterance on her to spare her something of the embarrassment she must feel when, after her death, she is translated into a Paradise. Not that this Paradise is likely, we feel, to be satisfying. It is 'intoxicating' no doubt; but it is also likely to become dull.

For the outstanding feature of *The Revolt* is a clash between Shelley's beliefs and Shelley's perceptions. This is seen from a brief summary of the narrative. Acknowledging the failure of the French Revolution, Shelley undertakes to portray in his narrative the revolution which he hopes will occur in the nineteenth century (in its first version the poem was called *Laon and Cythna—A Vision of the Nineteenth Century*). Universal love such as animates his hero and heroine can alone bring the bloodless revolution he desires. Under Cythna's leadership the revolution occurs; but the Tyrant leads a counter-revolution which is successful.

Laon and Cythna, their cause defeated, are pursued. Laon gives himself up on condition Cythna is allowed to go free. Laon, about to be burnt at the stake as an appeasement of what the Iberian Priest, symbolizing the Church, believes to be an outraged God, is joined by Cythna who also suffers martyrdom. After their death they are carried to a 'Temple of the Spirit'—a spirit who is called the Morning Star, the spirit of good in the world whom Shelley opposes to the cruel and tyrannical God whom Humanity now worships. Not only then is the story tragic in its outcome; it is throughout far more a poem of suffering than of achievement. Previous to Cythna's revolution both Laon and she have suffered extreme tortures which bring them to temporary insanity. After a brief success their hopes are overthrown and there ensues throughout the world a state of famine and death on the description of which Shelley lavishes his powers. Then comes the martyrdom of Laon and Cythna, and humanity is returned utterly to the rule of Tyrant and Priest.

Now whatever Shelley's hopes and theories may have been, the narrative is one of gloom relieved only for a short time. What Shelley *believed*, or professed to believe, was a secular humanitarianism animated by love and sanguinely proceeding to revolution without violence. What Shelley *saw* was failure, misery, treachery, wickedness, and a world in which good is tragically defeated. The poem is full of innumerable illusions and an optimism which outruns all reason; it is also a poem which has no illusions and no optimism. It is true that in accordance with his doctrine he rests responsibility upon secular and ecclesiastical institutions. Even so, his poetry rises to its highest quality in that part of the poem in which, after defeat, Cythna embraces martyrdom. The poem, after all, is predominantly a celebration of love which no secular scheme can possibly explain. Therefore Shelley is unable to close his poem without carrying his martyrs to a 'Temple of the Spirit' in which the 'Morning Star' shines. In his obstinate and half-ashamed way he brings his poem to a conclusion which makes nonsense of three-quarters of Cythna's speeches, of which the following is typical:

> To feel the peace of self-contentment's lot,
> To own all sympathies, and outrage none,
> And in the inmost bowers of sense and thought,
> Until life's sunny day is quite gone down,
> To sit and smile with Joy, or, not alone,
> To kiss salt tears from the worn cheek of Woe;
> To live, as if to love and live were one,—
> This is not faith or law, nor those who bow
> To thrones on Heaven or Earth, such destiny may know. (p. 116)

The simple fact is that Shelley's story belies his doctrine; and in strictness, he cannot have both this narrative and this doctrine. But he tries, to the ruin of his poem, to bring them together. Thus we complain chiefly, not that he does not show us what he thinks, but that what he shows and what he thinks cannot be reconciled. Doctrine was the curse of the Romantics, not because doctrine must necessarily be excluded from poetry and a poet forbidden a philosophy, but because, when the Romantics held a doctrine, it was quite frequently a very poor affair. Moreover, it clashed with their perceptions and threw their work into incoherence. Fortunately for them, their imaginations outran their doctrines and saved their work from the extinction to which their doubtful beliefs would have brought it. Now this clash between perception and belief is a striking feature of Romantic work. Wordsworth's work illustrates it, for when he was, so far as he had clear thought, pantheistic in belief, his imagination constantly swept him beyond the confines of his intellectual pattern. There are many passages in the first (1805) version of *The Prelude* which show his imagination belying his nominal beliefs. What he wanted to believe and what his imagination compelled him to see were frequently very different things. Because this is so, it is at best only half true to say that Wordsworth was ever a pantheist; as it is only half true to say that Shelley was ever secular in his attitude to the world. No doubt this shows a curious lack of self-criticism, of 'dry light' in the Romantic mind; and it is one of the things which merit for them some of Arnold's drastic criticism. So often, in the writings of the Romantic poets, we observe a curious and even strenuous reluctance to formulate belief in accordance with what was perceived and felt; and it is Shelley who excels in this perversity. His state of mind is one in which his intelligence strives to demolish any theoretical grounds for modes of imaginative perception which happily he never succeeds in throwing off.

§ 8

Shelley's next work on a considerable scale was *Prometheus Unbound*; and I propose to write of it in comparison with Keats's *Hyperion*. At an earlier point I remarked that it is of some value to compare *Alastor* with *Endymion*. In fact Keats and Shelley were engaged on *Endymion* and *The Revolt of Islam* at the same time; they had undertaken to each other to compose a long poem. Now in *Endymion* Keats plunged into Greek mythology, Shelley in *The Revolt* into what may perhaps be called allegory. That both these poems failed to a considerable extent cannot be denied; and no doubt both poets recognized their failure. In August 1820, after the publication of *Prometheus*, Keats wrote to Shelley:

'You, I am sure, will forgive me for sincerely remarking that you might curb your magnanimity, and be more of an artist, and load every rift of your subject with ore. The thought of such discipline must fall like cold chains upon you, who perhaps never sat with your wings furled for six months together. And is not this extraordinary talk for the writer of *Endymion*, whose mind was like a pack of scattered cards? . . . I am in expectation of *Prometheus* every day. Could I have my own wish effected, you would have it still in manuscript, or be but now putting an end to the second act.' (p. 507)[1]

This was in August 1820. The previous year, 1819, had been remarkable enough in the lives of both poets. Shelley wrote *Prometheus* and *The Cenci*, each remarkable in itself and differing very greatly from the other. Keats had written *Lamia*, *St. Agnes*, the great odes, and the two versions of *Hyperion*.[2] Shelley had turned to Greek mythology and used it to create a kind of drama; Keats had reverted to Greek mythology, and had attempted a long narrative poem, *Hyperion*.

Before going on to speak of *Prometheus* and *Hyperion*, I wish to make some observations on Keats's work in 1819. The first thing we observe is that from September 1818 up to September 1819 Keats worked, on and off, on *Hyperion*; up to April 1819 on the first version, in the summer of 1819 on the second. In a statement dated April 1819 Woodhouse said that he had seen a copy of *Hyperion* which consisted, he said, of two and a half books and ran to about 900 lines. This is a sufficiently close description of the first version, which in fact runs to 883 lines. Woodhouse also said that Keats 'said he was dissatisfied with it; and should not complete it'. But in August, Keats, in a letter to Bailey, said: 'I have also been writing parts of my *Hyperion*.' This was the second *Hyperion*. But this, too, was to be unfinished; on 21 September, in a letter to Reynolds, he says: 'I have given up *Hyperion*.' From this it is clear that *Hyperion* was never far from his mind throughout a whole twelve-month; it is also clear that it gave him a great deal of trouble.

We must notice some other dates. He wrote *St. Agnes* in the January of 1819. *Lamia*, the other great narrative poem of the year (leaving *Hyperion* aside for the moment), he was engaged on in June and July. But between the writing of these two narrative poems, he wrote his most celebrated lyrical poems, chiefly in April and May. Then he went on to *Lamia* and to the second *Hyperion*.

[1] All quotations from Keats's letters are made from Buxton Forman's edition, Oxford, 1935.

[2] Strictly, Book III of the first *Hyperion* and the second *Hyperion*. The first two books of the first version were written late in 1818.

I shall consider *The Eve of St. Agnes* and *Lamia* only briefly. It is clear, I think, that the most serious side of Keats does not emerge in either of them. This is certainly the impression we obtain from them, greatly as Keats expended the force of his gorgeous imagination in both; and here are two quotations from his letters which show his attitude to them. This is a remark of his about *Lamia*, written to George Keats on 18 September 1819: 'I have been reading over a part of a short poem I have composed lately call'd Lamia—and I am certain there is that sort of fire in it which must take hold of people in some way—give them either pleasant or unpleasant sensation. What they want is a sensation of some sort.' We observe the half-contemptuous tone of this remark—'let them have sensation'.[1] Here is the other quotation, from a letter written to Taylor in November 1819:

> 'I have come to a determination not to publish any thing I have now ready written, but for all that to publish a Poem before long and that I hope to make a fine one—As the marvellous is the most enticing, and the surest guarantee of harmonious numbers I have been endeavouring to persuade myself to untether Fancy and let her manage for herself. I and myself cannot agree about this at all. Wonders are no wonders to me. I am more at home amongst Men and Women. I would rather read Chaucer than Ariosto. The little dramatic skill I may as yet have however badly it might shew in a Drama would I think be sufficient for a Poem. I wish to diffuse the colouring of St. Agnes Eve throughout a poem in which Character and Sentiment would be figures to such drapery. Two or three such Poems if God should spare me, written in the course of the next six years, would be a famous Gradus ad Parnassum altissimum. I mean they would nerve me up to the writing of a few fine plays—my greatest ambition when I do feel ambitious.'

These sentences show Keats undecided as to what he shall do. On the one hand is the temptation to 'untether Fancy' and to write on themes that are 'marvellous'; such themes, he says, are the 'most enticing, and the surest guarantee of harmonious numbers'. But, he says, 'I and myself cannot agree about this at all. Wonders are no wonders to me. I am more at home amongst Men and Women. I would rather read Chaucer than Ariosto.' He thinks (and this is the alternative road his poetry may take) that he may write good dramatic poems which might lead on to the writing of good plays. In comparison with such dramatic poems, *The Eve of St. Agnes* has no 'character and sentiment'. From the marvels of *St. Agnes* (and of *Lamia*) he would turn to 'men and

[1] It is possible to see *Lamia* as a poem setting out the claims of 'philosophy' and 'poetry' respectively. But we have the impression that Keats is only half-serious in this; and here, no doubt, is the weakness of the poem. 'Philosophy' and 'poetry' are certainly not represented in the poem as Keats represented them in his letters.

women'. The 'sensation' of the first quotation and the 'marvellous' and 'wonders' of the second, he feels disposed to leave behind. I think Keats's attitude to *Lamia* and *St. Agnes* is clear from these letters. We can add, what is significant here, that he seems to have had little trouble with the writing of either poem, in striking contrast to *Hyperion*.

There is another passage from Keats's writings which I think may be applied to these poems. Writing in a copy of *Paradise Lost*, he said:

'The genius of Milton, more particularly in respect to its span in immensity, calculated him, by a sort of birthright, for such an "argument" as the *Paradise Lost*: he had an exquisite passion for what is properly, in the sense of ease and pleasure, poetical Luxury; and with that it appears to me he would fain have been content, if he could, so doing, have preserved his self-respect and feel of duty performed; but there was working in him as it were that same sort of thing as operates in the great world to the end of a Prophecy's being accomplish'd: therefore he devoted himself rather to the ardours than the pleasures of Song, solacing himself at intervals with cups of old wine; and those are with some exceptions the finest parts of the poem. With some exceptions—for the spirit of mounting and adventure can never be unfruitful or unrewarded: had he not broken through the clouds which envelope so deliciously the Elysian field of verse, and committed himself to the Extreme, we should never have seen Satan as described—

"But his face
Deep scars of thunder had entrench'd," etc.'[1]

Keats also had 'an exquisite passion for what is properly, in the sense of ease and pleasure, poetical Luxury'; and it comes out in *Lamia* and *St. Agnes*. But he could not be content with that. He must preserve his 'self-respect and feel of duty performed'. He might solace himself 'at intervals with cups of old wine'; but he must also, like Milton, 'commit himself to the Extreme'.

Before going on to speak of *Hyperion*, I wish to look back to the great lyrical verse of this year. I shall not speak at any length of it; but I shall try to point out its place in Keats's poetic life. He had written *St. Agnes* in January; he began *Lamia* in June. In the spring months he wrote the great Odes, *La Belle Dame Sans Merci*, the sonnets *Why did I laugh?* and *How fevered is the man*. The outstanding fact here then is that Keats gives up writing narrative verse on the failure of *Hyperion* early in the year and turns to writing lyrical verse before, in June, July, and August, coming back to narrative, first in *Lamia* and then in another attempt at making a job of *Hyperion*. Failing in narrative, he turns to lyric; and no doubt we have to thank the failure of *Hyperion* for the creation of the Odes. To this we must add the

[1] *Complete Works of Keats*, ed. Buxton Forman, Glasgow, 1901, vol. iii, p. 256.

consideration I have mentioned, namely, that *Hyperion* is Keats at his most serious. That being so, his failure to go on with it might well lead us to expect that there would flow into the Odes something at least of what he had tried to put into *Hyperion*; certainly, the Odes are serious enough. And when he thinks again of narrative, he drinks a cup of old wine in the form of *Lamia*, but his mind also turns again on *Hyperion*.

§ 9

When we consider the great lyrics of the spring months, it is clear that they have for their main theme the sorrow of the temporal and its longing for the Ideal. In the *Ode to Psyche* he again employs a Greek story which, like *Endymion*, tells of the visitation of the Divine to the human and he sees Psyche, like Endymion, win a celestial immortality. It is the other side he sees in *La Belle Dame*, reminiscent enough of *Alastor* and *Endymion* despite its vastly different context of association; and there is a good deal of the ghastly despair and disillusion of *La Belle Dame* in the course of the narratives of *Alastor* and *Endymion*. The *Nightingale* and the *Urn* can be taken together; they are very different and very similar. In accordance with the symbols which the two poems severally employ, the one is 'romantic', personal, and (despite its close and subtle architecture) diffuse; the other is 'classical', composed, restrained, and objective. In the *Nightingale* there is a note of hysteria; the *Urn* is quieter, more self-possessed and mature.

Moreover, the *Nightingale* as Keats employs it has not, as a symbol, the purity of the *Urn*. We see this if we trace the movement of the poem. Keats begins with himself in his dismay and unhappiness; and then passes (by a not too happy transition—the syntax of the fifth, sixth, and seventh lines of the first stanza is extremely difficult) to the thought of the nightingale singing of summer. The mention of 'summer' takes his mind far from the nightingale, to warm Mediterranean lands and the pleasures of wine. There is here a crisis in the structure of the poem; somehow we must get back to the nightingale. Keats manages this with great adroitness; by the intoxication of wine he can forget the world and pass into the 'tranced' world of the nightingale, away from a world filled with sorrow, short-lived beauty, and dying love. From this world he will flee—and here he conveniently and cleverly drops the intoxication of wine for the wings of poesy. Fancy, not wine, will bear him. The 'dull brain perplexes and retards', it is true; but for the present, the fancy can cheat well enough. So he passes in the fourth and fifth stanzas into a luxury of darkness and odour. In the second stanza we had a heaven of light and taste; here we have a heaven of verdurous glooms and the soft incense of the flowers. (The nightingale can symbolize these luxuries more suitably than the former.) Even so, there is a yet greater luxury, the luxury of death; and the death he imagines is certainly luxurious. It is 'on the midnight', without pain, and with the nightingale singing a requiem over him. 'The dull brain' may make its protest; but 'the fancy' is still strong. The nightingale has served (however loosely) as a symbol of the luxury of death; but now, through a deft turn, it serves for a symbol of immortality. Keats has died, but the nightingale sings on, 'not born for death', and into the imagined immortality of the nightingale Keats brilliantly packs three worlds of differing association: 'emperor and clown', 'Ruth', and 'magic casements'. Thus the nightingale comes to include these, too, in its covering symbolism. But the poet must come back, somehow, to himself; in its immortality the nightingale has left him. The return is cleverly effected through the word 'forlorn'; and he hears the bird as it flies away into deep valley-glades. The fancy cannot cheat for ever.

From this brief analysis of the poem, it will be clear in what sense the nightingale, as a symbol, is not pure, or single. It symbolizes an immortality of beauty, but also luxurious death; and if it symbolizes what is eternal it also symbolizes the delights of the several senses. Thus the poem is, at least in a measure, an utterance of the 'luxurious' Keats, and a 'fanciful' escape from what the poem begins and ends with, the poet's own despair. The 'dull brain' is repressed and 'the fancy' given rein. In its mention of these things, the poem acknowledges that it falls short of the wholly serious, however real Keats's sorrow and dismay.

But the *Ode on a Grecian Urn* is different. Its beginning, in contrast to the *Nightingale*, is filled with a sense of the object, not of the poet:

> Thou still unravish'd bride of quietness.

The urn is the bride of quietness and the child of silence and of a time which is unhurrying. It can tell a tale, but does not. Hence the first and fourth stanzas are questions addressed to the urn. But the urn does not speak; it is silent. We can only ask questions which will not be answered. That is why the urn 'teases us out of thought as doth eternity'. Our thoughts and questions are baffled and we are 'teased' out of them, and made helpless by that which we cannot master. In passing I shall quote lines from the *Epistle to Reynolds*, which was written in March 1818, in which this expression occurs:

O that our dreamings all of sleep or wake,
Would all their colours from the Sunset take:
From something of material sublime,
Rather than shadow our own Soul's daytime
In the dark void of Night. For in the world
We jostle—but my flag is not unfurl'd
On the Admiral staff—and to philosophize
I dare not yet! Oh, never will the prize,
High reason, and the lore of good and ill
Be my reward. Things cannot to the will
Be settled, but they tease us out of thought.
Or is it that Imagination brought
Beyond its proper bound, yet still confined,—
Lost in a sort of Purgatory blind,
Cannot refer to any standard law
Of either earth or heaven?—It is a flaw
In happiness to see beyond our bourn—
It forces us in Summer skies to mourn:
It spoils the singing of the Nightingale. (p. 485)

It is clear that these lines have a striking relevance to the *Ode on a Grecian Urn* and illumine its symbolism. Seeing 'beyond our bourn' we become lost; and then things cannot 'to the will be settled', but 'tease us out of thought'.

But in the second and third stanzas, and set in between the two stanzas of unanswered questions, we see love and beauty which never fade, a spring which is enduring. These things the *Nightingale* also symbolized, but less happily; and as Keats fled with the nightingale from a world

Where Beauty cannot keep her lustrous eyes,
Or new Love pine at them beyond tomorrow,

the figures of the urn are far above 'all breathing human passion' . . .

That leaves a heart high-sorrowful and cloy'd,
A burning forehead, and a parching tongue.

The song of the nightingale is immortal; the songs of the melodist are 'for ever new'. But although the *Urn* and the *Nightingale* are to this extent identical in their symbolism, the former is for obvious reasons the apter symbol; and also, it is single, symbolizing what is enduring only and not at all the worlds of the senses, like the *Nightingale*. Hence it is fitting that the nightingale should flee away, but that the urn should 'remain, a friend to man, in midst of other woe than ours'. Moreover, it does after all break its silence; it tells us all that on earth we need to know, that Beauty is Truth, and Truth Beauty. The *Nightingale* ends with a question:

> Was it a vision, or a waking dream?
> Fled is that music:—Do I wake or sleep?

The *Urn* ends with a statement:

> Beauty is truth, truth beauty,—that is all
> Ye know on earth, and all ye need to know.

This is the 'conviction' of which he speaks in the letter to Bailey which he wrote in November 1817, that 'Beauty must be truth'. 'Adam's dream will do here'—on earth, as the Ode says; we shall 'awake and find it truth'. 'On earth' we can have only a 'conviction'; hereafter, vision—or so we must hope. The *Urn* speaks Keats's favourite 'speculation', as he liked to call it, and his earliest. As early as 1814 he wrote:

> Can death be sleep, when life is but a dream,
> And scenes of bliss pass as a phantom by?
> The transient pleasures as a vision seem,
> And yet we think the greatest pain's to die.
>
> How strange it is that man on earth should roam,
> And lead a life of woe, but not forsake
> His rugged path; nor dare he view alone
> His future doom which is but to awake. (p. 537)

This same speculation also upheld him in his last days. Writing after he had left England in 1820, he said to Brown: 'Is there another Life? Shall I awake and find all this a dream? There must be we cannot be created for this sort of suffering.' Thus, as we have said, the *Nightingale* is uncertain in its aim, where the *Urn* is clear; the former has the note of escape and a note of self-pity, the latter the notes of faith and courage.

§ 10

The poems of the springtime of 1819 which we have now studied have had, in their different ways, one theme. But two other Odes now require mention, those *On Melancholy* and *To Autumn*, which were written in the September of the year. The lyrics of which we have already spoken show the desire for the Ideal; these Odes reveal another side of Keats in which he shows his disillusioned sense of this world. The former are the cry of his spirit, and of Endymion's, for the Moon; the latter show his rich apprehension of the real. The former pursue the unknown, the latter show the known. This is therefore a convenient place at which to make some observations, which will effect the required transition from the one group of lyrics to the other, on Keats's attitude to what he called his 'speculation' about the Ideal. The *Urn*, we have said, utters one of his chief speculations; and it came to him, he says, in the letter to Bailey, as 'auxiliary to another favorite Speculation' of his, namely, 'that we shall enjoy ourselves here after by having what we called happiness on Earth repeated in a finer tone'. His 'speculations' have to do with the Ideal and the hoped-for knowledge of it after 'awaking' from life. Here he is 'speculating' again in a letter to his brother and sister-in-law (1818–19):

'There you are with Birkbeck—here I am with Brown—sometimes I fancy an immense separation and sometimes, as at present, a direct communication of Spirit with you. That will be one of the grandeurs of immortality—There will be no space, and consequently the only commerce between spirits will be by their intelligence of each other—when they will completely understand each other, while we in this world merely comprehend each other in different degrees—the higher the degree of good so higher is our Love and friendship.' (p. 246)

These then are his 'speculations', or some of them.

But of equal interest with his 'speculations' is his attitude towards them. Here is an important passage from one of his letters in which he expounds this attitude. The letter was written to Bailey in March 1818. Bailey was at Oxford, a candidate for holy orders and deeply respected by Keats,[1] who had unfolded himself readily in his letters to him. 'You know my ideas about Religion. I do not think myself more in the right than other people, and that nothing in this world is proveable.' (It is, I think, certain that Keats means that he does not think himself more in the right than other people, and thinks that nothing in the world is provable. That this is so is made abundantly clear by what follows.)

'I wish I could enter into all your feelings on the subject, merely for one short 10 minutes and give you a Page or two to your liking. I am sometimes so very sceptical as to think Poetry itself a mere Jack a lanthen to amuse whoever may chance to be struck with its brilliance. As Tradesmen say every thing is worth what it will fetch, so probably every mental pursuit takes its reality and worth from the ardour of the pursuer—being in itself a nothing—Ethereal things may at least be thus real, divided under three heads—Things real—things semireal—and no things. Things real—such as existences of Sun Moon and Stars and passages of Shakspeare. Things semireal such as Love, the Clouds, &c. which require a greeting of the Spirit to make them wholly exist—and Nothings which are made Great and dignified by an ardent pursuit—which, by the by, stamp the burgundy mark on the bottles of our Minds, insomuch as they are able to "*consecrate whate'er they look*

[1] See the letter to George and Tom Keats, 13 January 1818.

upon". I have written a Sonnet here of a somewhat collateral nature—so don't imagine it an a propos des bottes.

> 'Four Seasons fill the Measure of the year;
> Four Seasons are there in the mind of Man.
> He hath his lusty spring when fancy clear
> Takes in all beauty with an easy span:
> He has his Summer, when luxuriously
> He chews the honied cud of fair spring thoughts,
> Till, in his Soul dissolv'd they come to be
> Part of himself. He hath his Autumn ports
> And Havens of repose, when his tired wings
> Are folded up, and he content to look
> On Mists in idleness: to let fair things
> Pass by unheeded as a threshold brook.
> He has his Winter too of pale Misfeature,
> Or else he would forget his mortal nature.

'Aye this may be carried—but what am I talking of—it is an old maxim of mine and of course must be well known that every point of thought is the centre of an intellectual world—the two uppermost thoughts in a Man's mind are the two poles of his World—he revolves on them, and every thing is southward or northward to him through their means. We take but three steps from feathers to iron. Now my dear fellow I must once for all tell you I have not one Idea of the truth of any of my speculations—I shall never be a Reasoner because I care not to be in the right, when retired from bickering and in a proper philosophical temper.' (pp. 111–12)

We see here the play of a deep scepticism upon his 'speculations'. He is 'so very sceptical as to think Poetry itself a mere' Jack o' Lantern. The ethereal things which he pursues, for which he longs, and about which he speculates may be 'Nothings'. (I shall speak of the sonnet at a later juncture.) Then he goes on, 'Every point of thought is the centre of an intellectual world' in which north and south are determined by the individual. Therefore he can say, 'I have not one Idea of the truth of any of my speculations'. Unlike Bailey, he will not try to argue things out and try to arrive at 'Truth' by reasoning; and this, he adds, is 'a proper philosophical temper'. The relevance of this to a passage in another letter to Bailey is clear—that in which he pronounces his chief speculation concerning the truth of imagination and Adam's Dream—'Can it be that even the greatest Philosopher ever arrived at his goal without putting aside numerous objections? However it may be, O for a Life of Sensations rather than of Thoughts.' (p. 68) He will cleave to his 'sensations', intuitions, dreams; yet *now* he will say, 'I am certain of nothing but the holiness of the Heart's affections and the truth of Imagination'; and *now* he will say, 'I must once for all tell you I have not one

Idea of the truth of any of my speculations.' 'Sensations', the Imagination, 'speculations' may be only Jack o' Lanterns; and at that he can leave it.

The kind of perception out of which this scepticism takes its rise can be shown by other quotations from the letters. 'Every point of thought is the centre of an intellectual world', he says in the letter I have just quoted. 'The two uppermost thoughts in a Man's mind are the two poles of his World—he revolves on them and every thing is southward or northward to him through their means.' This way of expressing what is in his mind arises from a sense of man's nature as animal and instinctive, an instinctive and animal nature which shows itself in *all* man's activities. In the long journal letter to his brother and sister-in-law which he wrote in the spring months of 1819, he speaks of disinterestedness and says that we can hardly hope to come to it, and he goes on:

'For in wild nature the Hawk [if disinterested] would lose his Breakfast of Robins and the Robin his of Worms—the Lion must starve as well as the swallow. The greater part of Men make their way with the same instinctiveness, the same unwandering eye from their purposes, the same animal eagerness as the Hawk. The Hawk wants a Mate, so does the Man—look at them both they set about it and procure one in the same manner. They want both a nest and they both set about one in the same manner—they get their food in the same manner—The noble animal Man for his amusement smokes his pipe—the Hawk balances about the Clouds—that is the only difference of their leisures. This it is that makes the Amusement of Life—to a speculative Mind. I go among the Fields and catch a glimpse of a Stoat or a fieldmouse peeping out of the withered grass—the creature hath a purpose and its eyes are bright with it. I go amongst the buildings of a city and I see a Man hurrying along—to what? the Creature has a purpose and his eyes are bright with it.' (p. 316)

Later, he goes on:

'May there not be superior beings amused with any graceful, though instinctive attitude my mind may fall into, as I am entertained with the alertness of the Stoat or the anxiety of a Deer? Though a quarrel in the Streets is a thing to be hated, the energies displayed in it are fine; the commonest Man shows a grace in his quarrel—By a superior Being our reasonings may take the same tone—though erroneous they may be fine.'

And here is another quotation from a letter written to the same correspondents (1818–19):

'We with our bodily eyes see but the fashion and Manners of one country for one age—and then we die. Now to me manners and customs long since passed whether among the Babylonians or the Bactrians are as real, or even more real than those among which I now live

—My thoughts have turned lately this way—The more we know the more inadequacy we discover in the world to satisfy us—this is an old observation; but I have made up my Mind never to take anything for granted—but even to examine the truth of the commonest proverbs —This however is true—Mrs. Tighe and Beattie once delighted me—now I see through them and can find nothing in them—or weakness—and yet how many they still delight! Perhaps a superior being may look upon Shakespeare in the same light—is it possible?' (p. 259)

All three quotations throw light, from different angles, on the remark that 'every point of thought is the centre of an intellectual world'. This strong sense of the extreme individuality of truth which makes even proverbs suspect and makes what we each call truth something animal, is then what plays, like a subtle scepticism, about Keats's 'speculations'. To assert the truth of the imagination may be only 'fine'. And we may regret, in passing, that Keats has not evoked an essay from the pen of Mr. Santayana (who curiously enough has written about Shelley), who also combines the passion for the Ideal of transcendent essences with a sharp but curiously undestroying scepticism.

This is not to say, and we must carefully avoid saying, that Keats held this as a doctrine and as true; it is another 'speculation' which he sets over against the rest. His scepticism is all-pervading; and if he gently directs his scepticism, born of his sense of development, against his 'speculations', he also upholds his 'speculations' against this naturalism. He says that he has 'seen through' Mrs. Tighe and Beattie and 'can find nothing in them' (while yet 'how many they still delight!'); 'perhaps a superior being may look upon Shakespeare in the same light—is it possible?' Then comes the answer: 'No—This same inadequacy is discovered . . . in Women with few exceptions. . . .' It is possible, and it is not. The idea is entertained; then put away from him rather than denied. Again: 'I have never yet been able to perceive how anything can be known for truth by consecutive reasoning'; and then: 'and yet it must be'. It cannot, and it can. Again: 'May there not be superior beings amused with any graceful, though instinctive attitude my mind may fall into, as I am entertained with the alertness of the Stoat of the anxiety of a Deer? Though a quarrel in the Streets is a thing to be hated, the energies displayed in it are fine; the commonest Man shows a grace in his quarrel—By a superior being our reasonings may take the same tone—though erroneous they may be fine.' Here is the 'superior' scepticism, cutting like acid into human values. But then comes: 'This is the very thing in which consists poetry; and if so it is not so fine a thing as philosophy—For the same reason that an eagle is not so fine a thing as a truth.' (p. 317)

There is no end to the exquisite play of this scepticism. Against his 'speculations' he leads in his 'superior being'; against his superior being he leads in philosophy. It may be, after all, the angel who is saddled with the 'Jack o' Lantern' of poetry, and Keats's speculations which have philosophy (whose reasonings may *not* be erroneous) on their side. Keats's naturalism is much more worthy of respect than any of the other forms of naturalism which broke out among the Romantic writers; but, what is more important, he was also armed against it. He held and did not hold his 'superior' naturalism. We are trying to show the complex play of Keats's mind in his last years; and there is no one formula in which it can be caught. It is not that Keats's mind was disordered or confused, but it was too rich and fecund to settle with comfort into a rigid scheme of belief and perception; it moved forward with great delicacy, sensitiveness, and openness, which is another way of saying that it moved forward courageously. Such openness of mind as Keats showed is an unwillingness to adopt easily 'speculations' which may be judged to arise naturally and quickly from the heart's desire; he refused, quite properly, to rest with speedy assurance in them, and tried to look around and beyond them. The 'ignorance' of Apollo in the first *Hyperion* is 'fearless', and the adjective does not occur haphazardly. But also, Keats refused to move impulsively into denial of his 'speculations'; in respect of any such denial, too, his mind remained open, for such denial also is a 'speculation'.

Thus it is that Keats's scepticism does not destroy the impulse towards the Ideal, which can no more be denied than breathing. He can entertain the thought that a superior being may see Shakespeare as he, Keats, sees Mrs. Tighe; he can hold it before his mind as possible. But Shakespeare remains a devouring passion to him. The dreams and sensations may be untrue, but he cannot cease to act and live as if they were true. No doubt so complex a state of mind makes life more difficult, but it also makes it more honest. There is no claim to know what we cannot know. 'I have scarce a doubt of immortality of some nature or other' he writes after Tom's death—the qualification is there. And in July 1820, in one of the agonized letters to Fanny, he can only say, 'I long to believe in immortality'. This is the human situation, a 'straining at particles of light in the midst of a great darkness'.

§ 11

We can now see something of the chief difference between Keats and Shelley. Shelley had nothing of the tender play of scepticism which distinguishes Keats, a scepticism which is also a humility. Scepticism of this kind neither kills nor debauches; it is completely free of any hardness of mind and heart; it deepens, steadies, enriches, and makes wise. Shelley might move from a dogmatic atheism to a dogmatic Platonism; he could not pursue his life acknowledging ignorance and submitting to uncertainty. Keats was aware that his mind was maturer and rounder than Shelley's; and his criticism of Shelley, in letters to him, is frank, modest, and assured. Here also we can see what Keats had in mind when he spoke, in a celebrated phrase, of 'negative capability'. Coleridge would not rest in 'sensation'; he must press on, through reasoning, to the truth, and in this is much nearer to Shelley than to Keats. Keats profoundly revered Wordsworth; but he broke out once into speaking of his 'egotism, vanity and bigotry'. (p. 107) 'Every man', he says, again speaking of Wordsworth, 'has his speculations, but every man does not brood and peacock over them till he makes a false coinage and deceives himself. Many a man can travel to the very bourne of Heaven, and yet want confidence to put down his half-seeing.' (p. 96) Keats shrinks alike from Coleridge's refusal to rest content with 'half-seeing' and from Wordsworth's erection of 'half-seeing' into what is claimed as knowledge. Shelley, Coleridge, and Wordsworth are all, in varying degrees, men of 'power', 'identity', and doctrine. 'One thing . . . has pressed upon me lately', he remarks to Bailey, again in the letter in which he speaks of the 'truth of the imagination', 'and encreased my Humility and capability of submission and that is this truth—Men of Genius are great as certain ethereal Chemicals operating on the Mass of neutral intellect—but they have not any individuality, any determined Character—I would call the top and head of those who have a proper self Men of Power.' (p. 67) This is, of course, an exaggeration, for certainly Keats would never deny the genius of Wordsworth; but the highest form of poetical genius is exhibited in Shakespeare (and Keats frankly believed that he possessed it himself), where it has 'no character' but is 'everything and nothing' and has as much delight 'in conceiving an Iago as an Imogen' (p. 228). And certainly it is just to distinguish in this way between Shakespeare and the doctrine-ridden Shelley, Wordsworth, and Coleridge. Shakespeare's imagination advanced in an exploratory movement, never in accordance with any preconceived schemes of belief; yet it also, as it moved, evolved a pattern, proceeding by unanticipated discoveries and by 'fine surprises'. It is in the Romances alone, the final phase of his work, that we become aware that exploration is finished and that his mind is at last resting, however lightly, on beliefs which, however, he shrinks from making explicit. Now this 'negative capability', humility, and openness of mind to experience is part and parcel of the play of Keats's scepticism upon his dearest 'speculations'.

§ 12

Thus, we see Keats advancing without dogmatism and with two sets of perceptions. The one is embodied in the *Nightingale* and more fully and clearly in the *Urn*; it is the sense of the Ideal for the knowledge of which in another world he ardently hopes, and in which, sometimes, he has strong faith. The other is naturalistic; it brings man near to the natural world and sees him, even in his dreams and hopes, as 'animal' and 'instinctive' and 'fine'; and this is embodied in *Autumn*, in a number of sonnets I wish to associate with it, and to some extent perhaps in *Melancholy*. Before going on to study these poems, there are three things I wish to observe.

First, Keats's capacity for ignorance and powers of scepticism gave him, paradoxically as we might think at first sight, great balance of mind and ability to suffer disillusion without strain. So far as doctrine went he quickly saw through the hocus-pocus of perfectibility; and in practice he could achieve a certain stability and 'capability of submission' to what he thought were inevitable aspects of human experience. He could rest, as Shelley could not, in acceptance of and belief in suffering; so that whether he saw the world in the light of what is eternal or naturalistically, he did not see it as a world from which suffering could be removed. In April 1818 he wrote to Taylor (he was twenty-two at the time): 'Young Men for some time have an idea that such a thing as happiness is to be had and therefore are extremely impatient under any unpleasant restraining—in time however, of such stuff is the world around them, they know better and instead of striving from Uneasiness greet it as an habitual sensation, a pannier which is to weigh upon them through life.' (p. 134) Again, to Bailey: 'You perhaps at one time thought there was such a thing as Worldly Happiness to be arrived at, at certain periods of time marked out. . . . I scarcely remember counting upon any Happiness—I look not for it if it be not in the present hour. . . . The first thing that strikes me on hearing a Misfortune having befallen another is this. "Well it cannot be helped—he will have the pleasure of trying the resources of his spirit" . . .' (p. 69)

In the second place, and having in mind his naturalistic vein, his perception of all 'truth' as 'animal' went along with a sense of the individual life as an organism which grows, comes to maturity, and dies. We see the life of the stoat or the deer as something which grows, matures, and decays; thus does the 'superior' imagination of the poet see the life of a man and grasp it as development and decline. In this way the patterns of perception through which we apprehend the life of the natural world are those through which we should apprehend human life.

Thirdly, and closely bound up with this, is Keats's doctrine (if what is put out tentatively in a letter may be so called) of 'disinterestedness'. To show this, I shall quote again from the Journal-letter of the spring of 1819 the passage in which he speaks of the 'noble animal Man', giving it in its context; this context will be seen to be very significant:

'Very few men have ever arrived at a complete disinterestedness of Mind: very few have been influenced by a pure desire of the benefit of others—in the greater part of the Benefactors of Humanity some meretricious motive has sullied their greatness—some melodramatic scenery has fascinated them—From the manner in which I feel Haslam's misfortune I perceive how far I am from any humble standard of disinterestedness. Yet this feeling ought to be carried to its highest pitch, as there is no fear of its ever injuring Society—which it would do I fear pushed to an extremity—For in wild nature the Hawk would lose his Breakfast of Robins and the Robin his of Worms—the Lion must starve as well as the swallow. The greater part of Men make their way with the same instinctiveness, the same unwandering eye from their purposes, the same animal eagerness as the Hawk. The Hawk wants a Mate, so does the Man—look at them both, they set about it and procure one in the same manner. They want both a nest and they both set about one in the same manner—they get their food in the same manner—The noble animal Man for his amusement smokes his pipe—the Hawk balances about the Clouds—that is the only difference of their leisures. This it is that makes the Amusement of Life—to a speculative Mind. I go among the Fields and catch a glimpse of a Stoat or a fieldmouse peeping out of the withered grass—the creature hath a purpose and its eyes are bright with it. I go amongst the buildings of a city and I see a man hurrying along—to what? the Creature has a purpose and his eyes are bright with it. But then, as Wordsworth says, "we have all one human heart"—there is an ellectric fire in human nature tending to purify—so that among these human creatures there is continually some birth of new heroism. The pity is that we must wonder at it: as we should at finding a pearl in rubbish. I have no doubt that thousands of people never heard of have had hearts completely disinterested: I can remember but two—Socrates and Jesus—their histories evince it. What I heard a little time ago, Taylor observe with respect to Socrates may be said of Jesus—That he was so great a man that though he transmitted no writing of his own to posterity, we have his Mind and his sayings and his greatness handed to us by others. It is to be lamented that the history of the latter was written and revised by Men interested in the pious frauds of Religion. Yet through all this I see his splendour. Even here though I myself am pursueing the same instinctive course as the veriest human animal you can think of—I am however young writing at random straining at particles of light in the midst of a great darkness—without knowing the bearing of any one assertion, of any one opinion. Yet may I not in this be free from sin?' (p. 316)

It will be seen now that the chief burden of this passage is not the perception of man's life as 'instinctive' but the achievement of 'disinterestedness'. Or it might perhaps be true to say that Keats is balancing 'instinctiveness' and 'disinterestedness' against each other. On the one hand, man's nature is 'instinctive': 'the greater part of Men make their way with the same instinctiveness . . . as the Hawk'. But this is not, after all, the whole of the story. For, on the other hand, we can become 'disinterested', so that instead of seeking our purpose with 'animal eagerness', we rise completely above the animal and natural—'there is an ellectric fire in human nature tending to purify . . . there is continually some birth of new heroism', so that we are surprised 'at finding a pearl in rubbish'. On the one hand, 'the greater part of Men make their way with instinctiveness'; on the other, Keats has no doubt that thousands of people have reached disinterestedness, though he can recall but two. The majority may act on 'instinct'; a minority on 'disinterestedness'.

But what is the relationship of 'instinctiveness' to 'disinterestedness'? Clearly they are very different from each other, the one blind and naturally self-seeking, the other seeing and self-transcending. Yet we suspect that, because the two things come together under discussion in Keats's letter, there is, somehow, a significant and close relation between them. And how does the 'pearl' emerge out of the 'rubbish'? Now in this I may be wrong, but I suggest that the relationship between the 'instinctive' and the 'disinterested' as Keats saw it consists, at least in part, in this: that 'disinterestedness' occurs through the perception of human nature as 'instinctive'; that this perception is a detachment whereby the individual becomes a 'superior being'; that this perception is creative and gives release from 'instinct'; and that, perceiving itself without illusion for what it is, instinctive human nature becomes changed into disinterested human nature. I cannot indeed quote a passage from the letters as authority for saying with certainty that Keats thought this; but I cannot help thinking that this was in his mind when he wrote the passage I have quoted. By perceiving ourselves after the manner of the 'superior being' we become ourselves superior and shed the 'animal'. Similarly, to perceive ourselves as human animals undergoing the great natural phases of growth, maturity, and decline, is to transcend these temporal processes and to give them a kind of eternity. Now if this is indeed what Keats had in mind, it is natural, once more, for Spinoza to come to mind. Blake's naturalism, while it offers a certain parallel to Spinoza's, is very inferior to it; that of Keats is much nearer to it, and is worthy of it, if only because it has so few illusions and is not infected with the notion of perfectibility but looks for the eternal in the present. To this we shall return again. We can now turn to the poems which we can relate fairly conclusively to this naturalistic vein in Keats's mind.

§ 13

It was, it will be remembered, in the letter to Bailey in which Keats speaks of 'ethereal' things which are, he says, 'Nothings', that he writes out the sonnet (which, he says, is of 'collateral interest to the preceding remarks')

> Four Seasons fill the Measure of the year;
> Four Seasons are there in the mind of Man.

This was in March 1818. He expresses the life of man in terms of the seasons, and goes straight on to state his 'old maxim' that 'every point of thought is the centre of an intellectual world'. In April 1819, in the Journal-letter to George and Georgiana Keats, he writes out the sonnet *On Fame*:

> How fever'd is the man, who cannot look
> Upon his mortal days with temperate blood,
> Who vexes all the leaves of his life's book,
> And robs his fair name of its maidenhood;
> It is as if the rose should pluck herself,
> Or the ripe plum finger its misty bloom,
> As if a Naiad, like a meddling elf,
> Should darken her pure grot with muddy gloom:
> But the rose leaves herself upon the briar,
> For winds to kiss and grateful bees to feed,
> And the ripe plum still wears its dim attire,
> The undisturbed lake has crystal space;
> Why then should man, teasing the world for grace,
> Spoil his salvation for a fierce miscreed?

This was in April 1819, the month in which he gave up the first *Hyperion*; and he was soon to write the *Nightingale* and the *Urn*. Once more, in this sonnet, he represents human life, at least as he thinks it should be, in terms of the natural—in this case, the flower and the fruit; moreover, in the last two lines he turns sharply upon religion which he says with its 'fierce miscreed teasing the world for grace' spoils man's salvation which must consist in his accepting himself for natural. In these lines Keats appears to be in conscious reaction against that other side of him which submitted to the 'teasing' of eternity, as in the *Epistle to Reynolds* (which we have noticed when speaking of the *Ode on a Grecian Urn*), or as in *Sleep and Poetry* where he had written:

> Then the events of this wide world I'd seize
> Like a strong giant, and my spirit teaze
> Till at its shoulders it should proudly see
> Wings to find out an immortality.

In the *Ode to Autumn* he again employs the seasons through which to convey what is in his mind; and he does so, as everyone has agreed, with flawless beauty. The *Nightingale* looks beyond the passage of time to an eternal summer; the *Urn* to a world which never bids the spring adieu. Time is transcended in them; their origin is the desire to deny time. But *Autumn* is saturated with the sense of and acquiescence in the passing. The *Nightingale* and the *Urn* look to eternal joy; *Autumn* rests in a poignant fusion of joy and sorrow.

Where are the songs of spring? Ay, where are they? The first two stanzas are loaded with images of harvest in the full sun. The last stanza brings in the dying day; we see no longer the harvest but the stubble-fields from which the harvest is gathered and gleaned, and it is upon them that the hues of heaven rest. The gnats mourn; the lambs of spring are gone; the swallows of summer are departing; the redbreast of winter remains. Thus we glance back through the year and look on to winter; yet here, in this passage from life to death, we rest and are quiet. The *Ode to Autumn* has its eternity also; different indeed from the eternities of the *Nightingale* and the *Urn*, and at once embracing and transcending time.

Keats finds in autumn his adequate 'objective correlative'; it requires no explication in terms of feeling, as the calm objectivity of the poem shows. His 'capability of submission' is here at its fullest. Shelley's *Ode to the West Wind* is also an ode to autumn. But Shelley was a 'Man of Power', and his poem is filled with images of swift movement in earth, sea, and sky. Moreover, it looks to the succeeding spring, as Keats's poem nowhere does; the *Ode to Autumn* looks only backwards to the spring which has gone. The mingled joy and sadness of autumn, it is true, is in Shelley's Ode:

> Make me thy lyre, even as the forest is:
> What if my leaves are falling like its own!
> The tumult of thy mighty harmonies

Will take from both a deep, autumnal tone,
Sweet though in sadness.

But Shelley passes quickly from this to the hope of a world regenerated through his words; and the poem ends with prophecy and anticipation, where Keats ends with the spectacle of the swallows gathering for their flight. Throughout the *Ode to the West Wind* we feel the pressure of Shelley's suffering, passion, and 'magnanimity'; but in the *Ode to Autumn* we have only quiet images of harvest and approaching death.

In the *Ode on Melancholy* Keats speaks, and with less effect, what the *Ode to Autumn* shows. It lacks the solemnity of the former poem and risks a certain artificiality. But it continues the theme of *Autumn*; and it is a theme which cannot fail to make us think of *King Lear*, and also of passages and scenes in the Romances. It is always important, and indeed inevitable, in reading Keats, to have *Lear* in mind. The references to the play in the letters are numerous; and in January 1818 he had written:

O Golden tongued Romance, with serene lute!
  Fair plumed Syren, Queen of far-away!
  Leave melodizing on this wintry day,
Shut up thine olden pages, and be mute:
Adieu! for, once again, the fierce dispute
  Betwixt damnation and impassion'd clay
  Must I burn through: once more humbly assay
The bitter-sweet of this Shakespearian fruit:
Chief poet! and ye clouds of Albion,
  Begetters of our deep eternal theme!
When through the old oak Forest I am gone,
  Let me not wander in a barren dream,
But, when I am consumed in the fire,
Give me new Phoenix wings to fly at my desire.

Here, the line,

The bitter-sweet of this Shakespearian fruit,

relates directly to what was in his mind in *Autumn* and *Melancholy*. Again, lines like these, describing Cordelia after she has returned to England and has heard from Kent:

. . . patience and sorrow strove
Who should express her goodliest. You have seen
Sunshine and rain at once: her smiles and tears
Were like a better way: those happy smilets
That play'd on her ripe lip seem'd not to know
What guests were in her eyes, which parted thence,
As pearls from diamonds dropp'd. In brief,
Sorrow would be a rarity most belov'd,
If all could so become it;

or like these, describing the death of Gloucester:

> But his flaw'd heart
> Alack! too weak the conflict to support!
> 'Twixt two extremes of passion, joy and grief,
> Burst smilingly;

or like these, spoken by Edgar, who certainly endured more unmerited suffering than any in the play and did so in a quiet endurance:

> What! in ill thoughts again? Men must endure
> Their going hence, even as their coming hither;
> Ripeness is all.

The last quotation is of especial importance, as Mr. Murry has emphasized. I do not wish to suggest that either these lines or Keats's sonnet on *Fame* and the *Ode to Autumn* express the total attitude which is embodied in *Lear*; I do not think they do. But certainly the mode of feeling which animates Keats in these poems has a very great deal in common with what Shakespeare was putting into his conception of the character and bearing of Edgar. Edgar is indeed a study in 'disinterestedness'. Not only is his suffering quite unmerited, but it continues steadily throughout the play; he has to witness the sufferings of Lear and Gloucester throughout, as Cordelia does not; and throughout he shows a union of unselfishness and detachment (the latter most strikingly shown in his care of his father) which makes him the most remarkable moral study in the play, and which also makes it no accident that it is he, and not Kent (as unselfish, but not so detached) nor Albany, who comes to the throne.

We can therefore see that the three features of Keats's feeling and thought which we spoke of in the preceding section are embodied in this group of poems—his 'capability of submission' to suffering, his apprehension of human life in terms of the phases of animal and natural existence, and the disinterestedness, which comes from this apprehension and which exists ''twixt two extremes of passion, joy and grief'.

§ 14

The question must arise, How adequate to experience is this apprehension of life? That it is superior to the naturalistic attitudes of Blake and Shelley there is little doubt; it is profound where the others are shallow. Yet, concerning its ethic, if I have at all interpreted rightly what was in Keats's mind when he indulged, in his letters and in his poetry, this naturalistic 'speculation', we see that it cannot in strictness be contained within naturalistic limits. For the appearance of the 'pearl' of disinterestedness and detachment among the 'rubbish' of instinct can be no natural phenomenon, occurring wholly within the confines of what is 'animal'. To form a 'clear idea' of the passions which animate us is, according to Spinoza, to find release from them and detachment; but we have seen that this does not explain what happens in such a case. In viewing ourselves as instinctive and animal, and thereby becoming disinterested, we are carrying through a process which is not itself instinctive and animal. The 'superiority' of which Keats speaks is not possible to the 'animal'; and the disinterestedness of which we are all capable according to this belief, however few of us realize it, belongs to the order of what is rational and universal, not of what is impulsive and particular. The gap between the two is too wide and deep to be bridged by a naturalistic scheme. So far, what we said of Blake's later ethic applies to Keats when he writes in this way.

But it is another aspect of this attitude (which we can express either as a set of beliefs or as a set of perceptions) which I wish to emphasize. From the time when Keats began to write he desired to perceive how suffering may be justified; to 'seize the events of the wide world' so as to see the 'miseries of the world' in such a way as to reconcile them with beauty. To relieve mankind, somehow, of the 'burden of the mystery' was in his eyes a great part of the task of the poet. This he asserts in *Sleep and Poetry*, in his first volume of poems; he asserts it in the letters; and he asserts it in the second version of *Hyperion*. Now so long as Keats followed that track of 'speculation' in which the end of life is a disinterestedness which occurs through what is, by paradox, both an acceptance of and release from our 'animal' nature, he was naturally disposed to believe that the entirety of human experience is an individual whole which, could we see it *sub specie aeternitatis*, would be perceived as a unity in which all suffering and evil took their place and contributed to a perfection which satisfied the demands of the imagination. To accept and to love such an individual order becomes then the ultimate end of our life, and so far Keats is near enough to philosophers such as Spinoza and Bradley. To accept what is set up for a naturalistic ethic of the kind of which we have spoken, while not at all looking for perfectibility and 'earthly' happiness, is, by an understandable process, to accept also a universe in which moral values are not ultimate, but which is justified to the imagination by its beauty. So long as this was in Keats's mind he was able to suggest an identification of beauty and truth along lines different from those he explores in what he says of 'Adam's dream'. There, an Ideal and Eternal Beauty is asserted by an act of faith, to be real; here, Beauty may be said to be Truth in the sense that, if the world of time could be seen truly, it would be seen to be beautiful, despite all its suffering and evil. That something like this last interpretation was present in Keats's mind can be shown by the remark in a letter (to George and Thomas Keats, December 1817) that 'the excellence of every art is its intensity, capable of making all disagreeables evaporate, from their being in close relationship with Beauty and Truth'; and he adds, 'Examine *King Lear* and you will find this exemplified throughout . . .' If this is so, the *Ode to Autumn* expresses not only the excellence of the disinterested life which endures its passing hence even as its coming hither, and in so doing masters, in its way, the passingness of the world, but also the perfection of a universe which, as Bradley said of his Absolute, 'has all its seasons at once'.

We must, then, keep in mind the two interpretations of 'Beauty is Truth'; it seems certain that they were present in Keats's mind at different times, according as his 'speculation' was set upon an eternity into which we shall 'awake' at death, and for which we are prepared by the 'vale of soul-making', or upon an apprehension of the temporal as somehow contained in a timeless and perfect whole. Such was his mind that we cannot say it was committed to the one or the other; he was only 'speculating', though by no means speculating lightly or unseriously; we have seen that his scepticism did not issue from triviality but from 'aching and fearless ignorance'. But it is with the second of these 'speculations' we are now concerned. Keats thought that possibly it was well founded and able to satisfy the desire of the imagination. But he also found good reason to believe it was not well-founded and could not satisfy the desire of the imagination.

Now, in this matter, I wish to speak of the *Epistle to John Hamilton Reynolds* which Keats wrote in March 1818. Reynolds is ill, and Keats writes to him 'in hopes of cheering' him. He begins by writing fancifully of the 'shapes and shadows and remembrances' which come before the eyes before sleep finally comes:

> Two witch's eyes above a Cherub's mouth,
> Voltaire with casque and shield and Habergeon,
> And Alexander with his night-cap on—
> Old Socrates a tying his cravat;
> And Hazlitt playing with Miss Edgeworth's cat. . . . (p. 125)

He goes on from playful fancy to the pleasures of romance, and evokes for Reynolds an image of a castle:

. . . it doth stand
Upon a Rock on the Border of a Lake
Nested in Trees, which all do seem to shake
From some old Magic like Urganda's Sword.

He goes on further to describe the castle, painting it with all the colours and associations of 'antique romance'. Then he passes suddenly to say:

O that our dreamings all of sleep or wake
Would all their colours from the Sunset take:
From something of material sublime,
Rather than shadow our own Soul's daytime
In the dark void of Night. For in the world
We jostle—but my flag is not unfurl'd
On the Admiral staff—and to philosophize
I dare not yet! Oh never will the prize,
High reason, and the lore of good and ill
Be my award. Things cannot to the will
Be settled, but they tease us out of thought.
Or is it that Imagination brought
Beyond its proper bound, yet still confined,—
Lost in a sort of Purgatory blind,
Cannot refer to any standard law
Of either earth or heaven?—It is a flaw
In happiness to see beyond our bourn,—
It forces us in Summer skies to mourn:
It spoils the singing of the Nightingale.

Keats is describing the progress of the imagination from the trivial and fanciful to its most serious occupation. All our dreams do not take their colours from the sunset, and the imagination must enter a 'dark void of night', a 'sort of purgatory blind'; it seeks to pass beyond its 'proper bound' within the world, to try to see the world from outside the world, to see, as Keats says in *Hyperion*, as a God sees. But it cannot succeed; for if the imagination is 'brought beyond its proper bound' it is 'yet still confined, lost in a sort of purgatory', in which it cannot see. It seeks to see the world's 'ill' somehow justified to itself and reconciled to its desire; but this also is defeated.

Then the *Epistle* continues:

Dear Reynolds. I have a mysterious tale,
And cannot speak it. The first page I read
Upon a Lampit Rock of green sea weed
Among the breakers—'Twas a quiet Eve;
The rocks were silent—the wide sea did weave
An untumultous fringe of silver foam
Along the flat brown sand. I was at home,

And should have been most happy—but I saw
Too far into the sea; where every maw
The greater on the less feeds evermore:—
But I saw too distinct into the core
Of an eternal fierce destruction,
And so from Happiness I far was gone.
Still am I sick of it: and though to-day
I've gathered young spring-leaves, and flowers gay
Of Periwinkle and wild strawberry,
Still do I that most fierce destruction see,
The Shark at savage prey—the hawk at pounce,
The gentle Robin, like a pard or ounce,
Ravening a worm—Away ye horrid moods,
Moods of one's mind! You know I hate them well,
You know I'd sooner be a clapping bell
To some Kamschatkan missionary church,
Than with these horrid moods be left in lurch . . .

He is not able to speak his 'mysterious tale', a tale brought back from beyond the 'proper bound', for the reason that he is dismayed because he sees 'an eternal fierce destruction' in the world:

The Shark at savage prey—the hawk at pounce,
The gentle Robin, like a pard or ounce,
Ravening a worm.

His poem has become too serious and grave to be of much use in cheering the sick Reynolds; and Keats tries his best to end playfully: better a Kamschatkan missionary church than be left in the lurch with such moods. But here, in his perception of the senseless suffering in the natural world, his imagination is baulked. In the sonnet *On Fame* he was to write:

But the rose leaves herself upon the briar,
  For winds to kiss and grateful bees to feed,
And the ripe plum still wears its dim attire,
  The undisturbed lake has crystal space;
  Why then should man, teasing the world for grace,
Spoil his salvation for a fierce miscreed?

But it is not as simple as this.

. . . the rose leaves herself upon the briar
For winds to kiss and grateful bees to feed;

but (it is Keats himself who says so in the Journal-letter of Spring (1819) 'suppose a rose to have sensation, it blooms on a beautiful morning, it enjoys itself—but there comes a cold wind, a hot sun—it cannot escape it, it cannot destroy its annoyances—they are as native to the world as itself . . .' In the sonnet, he says:

> Why then should man, teasing the world for grace,
> Spoil his salvation for a fierce miscreed?

But in the *Epistle*, in which he has no soft illusions about the natural world and sees the 'annoyances' which beset the animals, he says,

> You know I'd sooner be a clapping bell
> To some Kamschatkan missionary church,
> Than with these horrid moods be left in lurch—

the 'fierce miscreed' of the sonnet is no longer so distasteful, and may be necessary for salvation, instead of 'spoiling' it. It is not, after all, easy to see how the suffering of the world can be fused into a harmony acceptable to the imagination. Nor, as Keats's own suffering became so terrible in his last days, could his wretchedness be seen, by him or by anyone else, as 'evaporating' in a universal beauty. 'It surprises me', he wrote, 'that the human heart is capable of containing and bearing so much misery. Was I born for this end?' (p. 524) He himself gives the answer, which has been previously quoted, in the letter to Brown written during his journey to Italy: 'Is there another Life? Shall I awake and find all this a dream? There must be, we cannot be created for this sort of suffering.' (p. 520) When we consider the ills of the world, whether animal or human, we see evil and suffering which cannot be counted unreal and imagined as dissolved in any fine universal synthesis. If by the love of God we mean loving the world as we know and see it in all its aspects, the love of God can only be withered in bitterness and rebellion against what contains such hideous suffering and wickedness.

'The excellence of every art is its intensity, capable of making all disagreeables evaporate, from being in close relationship with Beauty and Truth. Examine *King Lear* and you will find this exemplified throughout.' (p. 71) But does *King Lear* exemplify this? No one, indeed, can afford to treat any judgement of Keats on Shakespeare lightly; but we can do no other than follow our own perception and judgement, such as it is. And when we consider *Lear*, *do* the 'disagreeables evaporate'—the wickedness of Goneril, Regan, and Edmund, the blinding of Gloucester, the terrible deaths of Cordelia and Lear? And is not *King Lear* much less an 'evaporation' of the terrible than a question thrown out into the heavens by a mind speculating and baffled, in 'aching but in fearless ignorance'? *Lear* is not a vision of a sublime harmony, but a sublime question to which no answer is supplied by the play.

Let us return for a moment to the letter in which Keats speaks with less illusion than in the sonnet *On Fame*, of the rose and its life. He speaks of its annoyances, as we have seen. And he goes on at once to say that man also has his inevitable annoyances 'as native to the world as himself'; then he proceeds:

'The common cognomen of this world among the misguided and superstitious is "a vale of tears" from which we are to be redeemed by a certain arbitrary interposition of God and taken to Heaven—What a little circumscribed straightened notion! Call the world if you Please "The vale of Soul-making". Then you will find out the use of the world (I am speaking now in the highest terms for human nature admitting it to be immortal which I will here take for granted for the purpose of showing a thought which has struck me concerning it). I say "*Soul making*" Soul as distinguished from an Intelligence. There may be intelligences or sparks of the divinity in millions—but they are not Souls till they acquire identities, till each one is personally itself. Intelligences are atoms of perception—they know and they see and they are pure, in short they are God.—How then are Souls to be made? How then are these sparks which are God to have identity given them—so as ever to possess a bliss peculiar to each one's individual existence? How, but by the medium of a world like this? This point I sincerely wish to consider because I think it a grander system of salvation than the chrystiain religion—or rather it is a system of Spirit-creation.' (p. 335)

Thus, when Keats contemplates the 'annoyances', he goes on to 'speculate' on a scheme of 'Spirit-creation', admitting the soul to be immortal. The scheme of salvation which he outlines may not, indeed, be called a 'fierce miscreed', and he thinks it superior to Christianity which it yet, say what he will, resembles. He may, rightly enough perhaps, poke fun at Kamschatkan missionary churches, but he acknowledges, in this speculation, something which is not, after all, so far removed from them. The whole story is not told by speaking of the rose leaving

. . . herself upon the briar,
For winds to kiss and grateful bees to feed,

nor even by uttering the name and images of autumn in their traditional loveliness. There are also, what Keats was too open and too honest to overlook, the annoyances, the fierce destruction, the taint and misery of the world; and then his mind turns from any thought of the completeness of the world in itself, to the thought of it as a vale through which we pass, in discipline, to what is beyond it. In such an apprehension of the world the peculiar and moving union of joy and sorrow which marks *King Lear* and *Autumn* may keep its place and significance.

§ 15

We can now pass, after long delay, to speak of *Prometheus Unbound* and *Hyperion*. I shall first make some general observations on what seems to me to be the significance of the extensive use of Greek mythology by Shelley and Keats; secondly, I shall briefly compare the purposes of Shelley and Keats in their manipulation of narrative material which in each case has to do with the conflict of Jupiter and the Titans; thirdly, I shall treat of the two works separately.

Of the Romantic poets we may say that they were concerned with nothing less than the ultimate questions of human destiny, the relation of man and his life to the universe. Now in this concern, they resemble the great writers of the sixteenth and seventeenth centuries in a way that no writer of the eighteenth century does. Though, significantly enough, the phrase is Johnson's, the 'hunger of the imagination which preys upon life' is not a characteristic of the eighteenth century; it was predominantly interested in the life of man set against a social and not a cosmic background. Generalizations such as these are no doubt dangerous; and no doubt objections might well be raised against them. Yet we may say that the Romantic poets take their place, whatever their differences and inferiority, with Spenser, Marlowe, Shakespeare, and Milton in the scope and grandeur of their imaginative aims; however we may explain it, the fact seems beyond question. Now, if we have in mind the three greatest writers of the sixteenth and seventeenth centuries, Spenser, Shakespeare, and Milton, we see the advantages they enjoyed which were not shared by the Romantic writers, advantages in respect of form or substance or both. Spenser wrote at a time when allegory was to his hand; when Shakespeare wrote, the drama was living; Milton was able to use a narrative very near to the minds of men, though he himself was content to regard it as perhaps mythical, willing to treat the entire story as no less valuable if it possessed only allegorical significance, as indeed he was willing to believe. Yet, though Milton probably believed in Copernican astronomy, and certainly had no fanatical attachment to the historicity of the creation story (or indeed perhaps even to that of the life and death of Christ), he was using a narrative and machinery accepted by the majority of men in his time. Spenser's poem had an immediate and great popularity; in presenting his Romances, Shakespeare at least provided exquisite story and poetry, even if his profound intentions were unclear; and *Paradise Lost*, published after the Restoration, was greeted as a world's masterpiece by Dryden, a man of very different mind from Milton, who was yet enough a man of the seventeenth century to enter with joy and passion into the biblical epic.

Now when the Romantic poets wrote there were no literary forms having general acceptance; there was far less agreement in religion and philosophy; society was incomparably more unstable. In this sense they were traditionless and standing alone and isolated. They did not work, and could not work, within a framework of established convention, literary, religious, and social. They were necessarily innovators. They had not a certain homogeneity of culture, the sense of working in a tradition, of writing for their fellow men on a basis of community of experience, whether social or religious. Wordsworth saw the poet as a 'man speaking to men'; but to do this, at such a time, was exceedingly difficult, if not impossible; and it has become increasingly difficult ever since. It is easy to feel exasperated by the Romantic poets, and to utter harsh judgements at their expense. But it is only charitable to remember their difficulties and what they lacked. If we do this we shall be far more impressed than dismayed by what they did.

To return to Shelley and Keats, through what medium and by the use of what material could they express the imaginative patterns to which in these years they were coming? The advantages possessed by Spenser, Shakespeare, and Milton were not theirs. Being what they were, they could not write Christian poetry, as Spenser and Milton did; and Spenser's poetic method and Milton's material were denied them. They were both attracted to drama; Keats aspired to write a 'few fine plays' and Shelley tried his hand at *Charles I* and *The Cenci*. But in fact, not only were the prevailing conditions against them, but it may very well be doubted if the drama could ever be a suitable vehicle for what they wished to convey. Philosophical dramatic poetry they might perhaps have written in greater maturity; what they wished to do would have overflowed the limits of drama proper: 'objective correlatives' deriving from the world of human action could not be forthcoming, for the mind of both Shelley and Keats alike rested, in the last resort, on certain metaphysical perceptions; and properly dramatic material could not be manipulated so as both to exhibit their deepest perceptions and to make effective drama. Of Shelley's dramatic work we shall speak later. Of Keats we can say that, while he greatly desired to write plays (as we have seen), his most ambitious piece, though a fragment, is *Hyperion*.

Both alike required to write what may be called philosophical poetry. But naturally, they did not wish to write explicitly philosophical poetry, but poetry in which their apprehension of the world would be shown forth through situation, event, and figure, so far as was possible. But also, they were both of them poets enough to wish to avoid symbolical use of wholly human narrative; for unless allegory is used, such a method inevitably makes for the difficulty (as *The Revolt* shows) of reconciling the demands of interesting and living human narrative with those of clear spiritual signification. Such work presents great difficulties, as they well knew, and tends to fall between two stools. Thus, shut out from the use of allegory, open or disguised, and in reaction against Christian dogma and idiom, they turned, naturally, to Greek mythology.

The advantages this gave them were obvious enough. In the first place, there was abundant material and narrative which could easily be manipulated and changed for their purposes; in addition, through the use of mythological figures, they could give a philosophical and meditative heightening to their work which would place little or no unfair strain upon the reader, who might be presumed to have some knowledge at least of Greek myth. That is to say: denied, or denying themselves, the use of Christian thought, imagery, and myth, they retired to the religious narrative of a previous and quite different civilization. Placing themselves, as it were, outside Christendom, they sought to turn the rich legacy of pagan imagination and thought to their uses; and this they were able to do, to any degree, because, if Christianity was breaking down as a commonly possessed framework within which the poet might write, Greek mythology supplied an alternative framework within which, up to a point at least, all readers, who would indeed be educated readers and therefore constituted a limited public, might fairly happily move. Blake had fallen back on a crude mythological mixture to the vast confusion of himself and his readers. Shelley and Keats, properly avoiding this path, fell back on the religious myths of one great civilization, which was not, however, strange to the small public which they must now be content to reach.

Now this was a desperate expedient; and it was one doomed to failure. That they should have thought it necessary to take this course has the greatest significance and interest; that they should have thought they could possibly succeed in it is even more interesting. For, whether they knew it or not, and whether they liked it or not, Shelley and Keats had a great deal in them that was certainly not Greek; and to try to use Greek mythology for the purposes they had in mind was at the worst a misjudgement and at the best a gamble. Here again, they must fall between two stools. *Prometheus* shows that Shelley failed to sustain his sensitiveness to Greek feeling and forms; Keats, a man of greater sensitiveness to the Greek imagination, gave up *Hyperion*, recast it, and gave it up again. This, the feeling that so long as he wrote in a manner loyal to the consciousness which bodied forth Greek myths, he could not satisfy the demands on his own expressiveness, was not, probably, the only reason for the abandonment of *Hyperion*; but we may be sure it was one of the factors which caused Keats's dissatisfaction. It was all very well for Shelley to say of Keats that 'he *was* a Greek'; he could play the Greek to perfection, but for Keats or anyone else living at thousands of years' remove from Greek civilization and after thousands of years of Christian culture to *be* Greek is simply impossible. And indeed what Keats wished to convey in *Hyperion* must inevitably have shattered, indeed did shatter, the loyalty he conscientiously felt to the imagination of Greece which gave him his material. Shelley, cruder in feeling and weaker in criticism, rushed at his myth, and mutilated it without compunction; he gave us, in its place, neither clarity of form nor content, a kind of confused compromise from which Keats shrank. Mr. Santayana once remarked (in *Poetry and Religion*) that 'the more cultivated a period has been, the more wholly it has reverted to antiquity for its inspiration. The existence of that completer world has haunted all minds struggling for self-expression, and interfered, perhaps, with the natural development of their genius. The old art which they could not disregard distracted them from the new ideal, and prevented them from embodying this ideal outwardly; while the same ideal, retaining their inward allegiance, made their revivals of ancient forms artificial and incomplete. . . .'

Yet if we are tempted to deplore *Prometheus*, we must remember that its failings are the price paid by Shelley, who after all gives us plenty of great poetry in the play, for attempting the impossible; and that he should attempt the impossible is more a symptom of the great perplexity in which the poetic imagination was at this time than of his own failings. Keats also tried; and possessing a more sensitive mind, he gave it up. Keats's abandonment of *Hyperion* was, in one sense, the final defeat of Romanticism; the greatest artist of them all despaired of his work and left it alone. In another sense his abandonment of the poem was the greatest achievement of Romanticism; in it the Romantic mind beheld its perplexity and condemned itself.

§ 16

Let us now notice the narratives of *Prometheus Unbound* and *Hyperion* respectively. In *Prometheus* a Titan is in rebellion against the ruling Divinity who is represented as wholly evil. He is at once a symbol of ideal humanity and a Divinity protecting and aiding man. Jupiter was preceded by Saturn who previously with his brother Titans had overthrown Uranus and Ge.

> There was the Heaven and Earth at first,
> And Light and Love; then Saturn, from whose throne
> Time fell, an envious shadow: such the state
> Of the earth's primal spirits beneath his sway,
> As the calm joy of flowers and living leaves
> Before the wind or sun has withered them
> And semivital worms; but he refused
> The birthright of their being, knowledge, power,
> The skill which wields the elements, the thought
> Which pierces this dim universe like light,
> Self-empire, and the majesty of love;
> For thirst of which they fainted. (p. 233)

Jupiter then overthrows Saturn. Prometheus, though one of the Titans, nevertheless, according to Aeschylus, sided with Jupiter, afterwards rebelling against the injustice of Jupiter's treatment of mankind. Then, in Shelley's play, Jupiter becomes the embodiment of evil and tyranny, Prometheus of good; they represent the warfare of good and evil which sprang up in humanity after the decay of the Saturnian order in which Man had enjoyed an innocent life. In Shelley's play Prometheus is delivered and overcome through the agency of Asia (Love) who induces Demogorgon, the real ruler of the Universe, to overthrow Jupiter.

In *Hyperion* we read of the fall of Saturn and his fellow Titans, and of how they are superseded by Jupiter. But in Keats's version the new order is not to be deplored but to be accepted and welcomed. Oceanus and Clymene voice this attitude:

> Say, doth the dull soil
> Quarrel with the proud forests it hath fed,
> And feedeth still, more comely than itself? (p. 295)

The new sovereignty embodied in Apollo is superior; and in the third book we see Apollo achieving deity through the contemplation of

> Names, deeds, gray legends, dire events, rebellions,
> Majesties, sovran voices, agonies,
> Creations and destroyings.

It is this contemplation which 'makes a God' of him; 'with fierce convulse', he 'dies into life'. At this point the narrative is broken off.

It is clear that Shelley and Keats are manipulating their material for different purposes and with very different ends in view. Shelley's purpose is to malign Jupiter, to see in him nothing but evil; Keats's poem is a celebration of his advent to power. Yet the new sovereignty, in Keats's poem no less than in Shelley's, is sovereignty over a tragic world of evil and suffering. And indeed, it is a sovereignty which becomes sovereignty precisely because in some way it is responsible for this suffering and evil. Its deity, we gather, is superior to that of Saturn and the Titans, and more beautiful, on account of the drastic changes which its accession to power brings about in the world. The beauty of the new Gods is a more difficult and terrible beauty than that of the old; yet it is none the less greater. The Godhead of *Hyperion* is that which acknowledges for its own the world in which Lear suffered and Cordelia was hanged, and is yet no less a principle of Beauty and Order; in *Prometheus* the deity of a world in which there are evil and suffering is itself evil. These are the manifest points of contrast between the uses to which Shelley and Keats put their narratives.

§ 17

To attempt a detailed analysis of *Prometheus Unbound* is beyond the scope of this essay. I wish only to remark on some features of the play which appear to be of special importance. Now we could not have required of Shelley that he should provide a close and exact imitation of the Greek manner in tragedy; nor that he should refrain entirely from changing his mythological material. All that we could have the right to expect is a rough approximation in both respects. We might ask, first, that he should maintain a reasonable regard for Greek tragic forms and myth; and secondly that, so far as he was writing what could properly be called drama at all, he should supply firm plot and clear situation.

We know that Shelley did not satisfy these modest requirements. At least, he did so in the first Act, which is as clear in outline and as near to the Greek manner, so far as it goes, as we could fairly expect. Afterwards, however, it is not so. The first Act we can imagine, without undue difficulty, being performed upon a stage; what comes later, we certainly cannot. Now when we consider the development of *Prometheus*, it is not, I think, hard to discover where Shelley's difficulty and failure lay. In the original story Jupiter will be destroyed if he marries Thetis; and this secret Prometheus knows and will not disclose. His continued punishment is a consequence. Now Shelley retains this part of the myth. But such are his intentions that, while retaining it, he must diminish its importance in the plot to the greatest possible degree. The significances which he wishes to show in his play and the introduction of Demogorgon are sharply at odds with the story of the secret. We can express it thus. Whatever may have been Shelley's nominal intention in using his material, the 'secret' with which Shelley is alone seriously concerned is the efficacy of suffering; of love which

> . . . from its awful throne of patient power
> In the wise heart, from the last giddy hour
> Of dread endurance, from the slippery, steep,
> And narrow verge of crag-like agony, springs
> And folds over the world its healing wings; (p. 263)

and of hope, which creates

> From its own wreck the thing it contemplates.

This is the 'secret' of Prometheus as Shelley sees him. But the plot, since after all it is a story of Prometheus, Jupiter, and Thetis, must retain, with however little emphasis, the secret of the myth; and this secret Prometheus withholds from Jupiter. What, therefore, was in Shelley's mind, as a nineteenth-century poet, clashed with the form of the myth he was using; and Shelley found it difficult to combine them. He must retain the story of the secret of Prometheus, and of the marriage of Jupiter and Thetis as the occasion of Jupiter's downfall; he must also retain Hercules as a deliverer. But these occur in the play as incongruous and crude pieces of machinery. The soul of the play cannot enter into these mythological events and make them live. The spirit of the play and what it is seeking to employ in narrative are never really united.

Moreover, there is Demogorgon. What is he doing in a world inhabited also by Jupiter, Thetis, and Prometheus? He is certainly no Greek mythological figure. 'The deep truth is imageless', says Demogorgon himself, and thereby shows himself no true member of the Pantheon. He is

> . . . a mighty darkness
> Filling the seat of power, and rays of gloom
> Dart round, as light from the meridian sun.
> —Ungazed upon and shapeless; neither limb,
> Nor form, nor outline; (p. 232)

and being that, he would have made a Greek jump out of his skin. Why then is he introduced? Partly, we presume, because the plot required him, or something like him. For Prometheus must be released; and, because Prometheus will not yield his secret and Hercules cannot therefore be dispatched by Jupiter (as in the *Prometheus Bound* of Aeschylus), Hercules must be dispatched by another god. Shelley can hardly employ another of the Greek gods; he must create a new one, and when he appears (so far as he can be said to appear) he would have been horrible to the Greek mind. What could conceivably be more different from the radiant clarity of the Greek gods than one 'ungazed upon and shapeless', having 'neither limb, nor form, nor outline', a terrible unknown and 'other'? Yet the initiative and power of Demogorgon is central to Shelley's plot; and by him the Greek mythology which Shelley is employing is condemned and indeed broken. It is true that Shelley shows enough signs of being thoroughly uncomfortable about Demogorgon; but if so, this is not because Demogorgon is hardly Greek; it is because Shelley is somehow anxious both to deliver mankind from 'awe and worship' and to believe that the source of all existence is an almighty God who places suffering and love upon the throne of the world.

Also, it is Demogorgon who undermines *Prometheus Unbound* as drama. The first Act, we said, is reasonably clear and firm; and in it, we hear nothing of Demogorgon—the issue lies between Prometheus and Jupiter. But the second Act is very different. We see nothing of Prometheus and Jupiter; and Demogorgon stands at its centre. We see Asia and Panthea taking, as Bridges said of them, the 'path of spiritual desire' where

> . . . those enchanted eddies play
> Of echoes, music-tongued, which draw,
> By Demogorgon's mighty law,
> With melting rapture, or sweet awe,
> All spirits on that secret way. (p. 229)

We are carried into a world which is beyond the delineation of anything that can be called dramatic, where Hercules and Thetis and the rest do not and could not appear. We soar into a mystical heaven which has no place in drama, and which acts, in respect of spirit and plot, against the success of Shelley's work.

But if Demogorgon caused Shelley some trouble, he was also a convenience. For at least, through him, Shelley was able to fill up his second Act. The second Act was bound to give difficulty; and Demogorgon, though at a cost, solved the problem. For the story of Prometheus, or at least that part of it with which Shelley was concerned, is mostly a story of helpless and inactive suffering; and while a Greek tragedian using this story was aided by the solemn, religious atmosphere and associations of tragic performance as well as by the limits within which Greek tragedy was content to move, a modern tragedian must find such continued and unrelieved suffering a great difficulty. The first Act of Shelley's play shows the tragic situation in which Prometheus finds himself; the third Act would naturally show his release. But something must come between, and it could hardly consist of another version of Act I. Hence the usefulness of Demogorgon. Undramatic as he is, he is also vital to the play. He ruins the play and saves it.

§ 18

No doubt Shelley thought a good deal about the difficulties involved in treating a tragic hero such as Prometheus, whose most significant and powerful attribute is that he can bear persecution calmly and without hate. It was such heroes he wished to represent in drama; but drama unhappily seemed to require something different. I do not propose to speak of *The Cenci* itself; I wish, however, to call attention to an illuminating passage in the preface to that play.

'This national and universal interest which the story [of the Cenci] produces and has produced for two centuries and among all ranks of people in a great City, where the imagination is kept for ever active and awake, first suggested to me the conception of its fitness for a dramatic purpose. In fact it is a tragedy which has already received, from its capacity of awakening and sustaining the sympathy of men, approbation and success. Nothing remained as I imagined, but to clothe it to the apprehensions of my countrymen in such language and action as would bring it home to their hearts. The deepest and the sublimest tragic compositions, *King Lear* and the two plays in which the tale of Oedipus is told, were stories which already existed in tradition, as matters of popular belief and interest, before Shakespeare and Sophocles made them familiar to the sympathy of all succeeding generations of mankind. . . .

'The highest moral purpose aimed at in the highest species of the drama, is the teaching the human heart through its sympathies and antipathies, the knowledge of itself; in proportion to the possession of which knowledge, every human being is wise, just, sincere, tolerant and kind. If dogmas can do more, it is well: but a drama is no fit place for the enforcement of them. Undoubtedly, no person can be truly dishonoured by the act of another; and the fit return to make to the most enormous injuries is kindness and forbearance, and a resolution to convert the injurer from his dark passions by peace and love. Revenge, retaliation, atonement, are pernicious mistakes. If Beatrice had thought in this manner she would have been wiser and better; but she would never have been a tragic character: the few whom such an exhibition would have interested, could never have been sufficiently interested for a dramatic purpose, from the want of finding sympathy in their interest among the mass who surround them. It is in the restless and anatomizing casuistry with which men seek the justification of Beatrice, yet feel that she has done what needs justification; it is in the superstitious horror with which they contemplate alike her wrongs and their revenge, that the dramatic character of what she did and suffered, consists.

'I have endeavoured as nearly as possible to represent the characters as they probably were, and have sought to avoid the error of making them actuated by my own conceptions of right or wrong, false or true: thus under a thin veil converting names and actions of the sixteenth century into cold impersonations of my own mind.' (p. 272)

No doubt, in writing the concluding paragraph of what I have here quoted, Shelley was aware that he was setting out in *The Cenci* to do something quite different from what he had done both in *The Revolt of Islam* and in *Prometheus*, which alike show the impersonations of his own mind under a 'thin veil' of 'names and actions'. The allegory, as we have seen, shows through in *The Revolt*, and the personages of the *Prometheus* are apprehensible only as personifications. Earlier in the passage, Shelley observes that Shakespeare in *King Lear* and Sophocles treated themes already familiar; and he then goes on to point out the dramatic unsuitability of a character who refuses, as Prometheus had, and as Beatrice might have, revenge and retaliation. Such characters, he says, are not tragic; and then goes on: 'the few whom such an exhibition [of a character declining hate and revenge] would have interested, could never have been sufficiently interested for *a dramatic purpose, from the want of finding sympathy in their interest among the mass who surround them*'. Thus, in effect, the character who makes 'the fit return to the most enormous injuries' is not necessarily undramatic; if he is undramatic he is so not on his own account but on account of an audience having insufficient sympathy with his motives and actions. In *The Cenci* Shelley accepted this limitation and was determined to try his hand at what he no doubt felt to be a fundamentally inferior form of drama. Shelley's inclination, we may be sure, which he had followed in *Prometheus*, was for drama exhibiting what he judged to be the highest form of character; but he now denied this inclination through lack of a suitable public, and attempted drama ordinarily judged to be 'tragic', in which retaliation takes the place of passive suffering. This descent of Shelley, so to speak, from the intention of *Prometheus* to the intention of *The Cenci*, and his refusal to make of Beatrice one who did not resort to retaliation is illuminating and, in its way, tragic. For he refuses to condemn as themes for drama of the most proper kind a Prometheus or a Beatrice 'persisting in forbearance'; he observes only that such themes are not suitable for the public for which he writes. What Shelley called for was a homogeneous society united in belief, in which the imagination of the dramatist will be controlled by a predominant pattern which is not private to him. Only under such circumstances could drama such as Shelley wished to write truly flourish, in a society in which the function of the artist would be the humble one of reducing or focusing a generally shared experience of life into the particularity of plot. How much Shelley longed for such a community of interest is shown by what he says of *Lear* and the plays of Sophocles; they were, he said, written on subjects already familiar to the audience; and he gives himself the pathetic and deceptive consolation that the story of the Cenci had been familiar to the Italian people for generations; pathetic, because he was writing for an English audience to whom the story of the Cenci would be strange and revolting. Certainly Shelley, like the other poets of the time, lacked advantages, as we have seen, possessed by Spenser, Shakespeare, and Milton, either in respect of theme or of literary form or both. Yet it is clear that what Shelley desired was something more than familiarity in his audience with the story treated or an accepted literary form. He desired a society having spiritual unity.

Now Shelley did not desire what, with any respect for words, can be called a Christian society; the Church, in any form, violently repelled him. Yet it is abundantly true, as we have seen, that there was a great deal that was Christian in Shelley's imagination, in spite of himself; and this comes out in *The Revolt of Islam* as much as in *Prometheus*. No doubt it is true that to the end his belief in suffering and unresistance was derived in some measure from secular and humanitarian origins; but there were other influences at work and the sense of other possibilities which no secular scheme of life can allow for, as the conclusion of *The Revolt* and the second Act of *Prometheus* show. The confusion in his own beliefs and the abhorrence he felt for the Church and for Christian dogma made it quite impossible for Shelley to speculate on the possibility of a desirable Christian society; but I remark here that Coleridge (who 'could have helped Shelley') was in later years to think a good deal about the possibility of a Christian order in society. At a later stage, I shall outline what Coleridge had to say. Whether, had he lived, Shelley might have become interested in what Coleridge had to say, it is idle to ask. Yet in such a society as Coleridge described (which may or may not be possible and which may or may not be desirable), there would exist a set of social conditions and a common imaginative life which the dramatic artist might serve; there, his function would be to crystallize into personage and event already familiar an experience held in solution, so to speak, in the mind of society. He would be neither prophet nor heaven-sent discoverer of truth; and he would have no novelty. But he could assume interest and sympathy, and his material would be to his hand, in the rich records of the Christian past. To be what Shelley would have him be, the dramatist cannot do his work alone; he must write not as an individual but as a member of a society from which he has derived his experience and sense of life. He must be not unique, and a 'genius', but a servant of society and its church. He must show not what is new but what is familiar; in a Christian society he would be relieved of the task of creating new personages and situations; and what success he might have in treating of saint, martyr, and prophet would issue from and depend upon habitual contemplation, by his audience, of the life and death of Christ.

§ 19

We must now turn to *Hyperion*, which presents a more complicated critical problem than *Prometheus*. At an earlier stage I explained that it occupied Keats's thoughts, on and off, in one version or another, from September 1818 to September 1819. I think we can fairly assume that he set his hopes and ambitions upon making a good job of it; and he was anxious to write a good long poem. In October 1817 he wrote to Bailey that 'a long Poem is a test of Invention, which I take to be the Polar Star of Poetry, as Fancy is the Sails, and Imagination the Rudder.—Did our great Poets ever write short Pieces? I mean in the shape of Tales. This same invention seems indeed of late Years to have been forgotten as a Poetical excellence.' At this time he was busy on *Endymion*. We know what he thought of *Endymion*—or came to think of it. When he criticized *Prometheus* in advance to Shelley, he said that the author of *Endymion* had little right to speak in that vein. And now, in writing *Hyperion*, he again wished to show his powers of invention, but in a poem which would be ordered, lucid, and disciplined. But as early as January 1819 he has temporarily turned aside to write a 'short piece'—*St. Agnes*; and later, by the spring, no longer working at *Hyperion*, he is again writing short poems. The Odes, great as they were, were not the kind of thing he chiefly desired to write. In the summer he is back at *Hyperion*, in its second form; but he soon gives it up—apparently for good.

Now I have said that there can be little doubt that in *Hyperion* Keats was at his most serious. If we should doubt this on reading the first version, and incline to think that in writing it Keats was composing merely a tale of wonders, we have only to look at the second version. For in the second version he says quite explicitly what his interest in the narrative of Hyperion's fate is. In it Keats is himself confronted with Moneta (Mnemosyne), and this experience befalls him only as one of those

> . . . to whom the miseries of the world
> Are misery, and will not let them rest.

Unlike good men who are content to 'labour for mortal good' in the world and also to accept joy when it comes, the poet is not able to take

The pain alone; the joy alone; distinct.

He 'venoms all his days', a metaphysical pain clouding his enjoyment of simple and beautiful things. This is the 'purgatory blind' of the *Epistle* to John Hamilton Reynolds which

. . . forces us in Summer skies to mourn:
It spoils the singing of the Nightingale.

Moneta and what she can show the poet will ease the poet's pain, explain or show to him a true vision of things and thereby lift the burden of the mystery of the world's suffering. So much appears to be clear; and we can safely assume that what Keats explains to us with such care in the second version he also intended in the first version, though there he makes no such explanation. No doubt Keats felt that such an explanation was called for if the story of *Hyperion* was to have its full weight; and therefore he proceeded to a second version, in which he might set it out. But with this matter we shall be concerned later.

When we study the first version, we see that Keats, attempting his highest flight of invention, roughly follows the early books of *Paradise Lost* which also is a story of the wars of deities. That Keats should have *Paradise Lost* in mind was natural, if only because of his passionate admiration for Milton. He was indeed to find that he had to be 'on his guard against Milton', as the Miltonic inversions in *Hyperion* show. But they also show how Milton pressed upon his imagination. In the first book we see the fallen deities, as in the first book of Milton's poem we see the fallen angels; in the second we have the gods in council, as in book II of *Paradise Lost* the fallen angels debate; in the third book we leave the fallen deities to behold Apollo, the new deity, a parallel to the passage, in the third book of *Paradise Lost*, to Heaven, and God and Christ.

It is to the second book of the first version that I wish now to call attention. It represents the fallen deities in council. Saturn and Thea have joined the dismayed Titans; and they must now debate what they shall do. Saturn himself is in despair.

Then Thea spread abroad her trembling arms
Upon the precincts of this nest of pain,
And sidelong fix'd her eye on Saturn's face:
There saw she direst strife; the supreme God
At war with all the frailty of grief,
Of rage, of fear, anxiety, revenge,
Remorse, spleen, hope, but most of all despair.

Against these plagues he strove in vain; for Fate
Had pour'd a mortal oil upon his head,
A disanointing poison: so that Thea,
Affrighted, kept her still, and let him pass
First onwards in, among the fallen tribe. (p. 291)

From Saturn then, the chief God of the old order, we can expect little in leadership. He presents no parallel to the passionate and indomitable hero of Milton's epic. He speaks first; and his speech expresses stupefaction and perplexity merely. There follow three speeches—by Oceanus, Clymene, and Enceladus. Hyperion, who is clearly cast for the role of leader of the Titans against the usurping deities in the wars which we presume are intended to follow (see book II, ll. 69–72), makes his appearance late in the book and does not speak. Of the three who speak after Saturn the first two offer impassioned defences *of the new gods*. Only Enceladus is for conflict and war. Now if we think of *Paradise Lost*, we see that the fallen angels not only showed much more spirit; but also they were certainly not tempted to present arguments in favour of their eternal foe. Of course, we must not press the rough parallel with *Paradise Lost* too far. For, after all, the fallen angels had been rebels against established power; the fallen deities in *Hyperion* had seen their thrones usurped. But the fact remains that at the end of book II of *Hyperion* nothing has been done or decided by the Titans, in striking contrast to the fruitful discussion of the Devils in Hell. It is true that the appearance of Hyperion rouses some enthusiasm; but how this is to show itself in action, we are not told. Saturn is downcast; and we have had abundant and glowing defence by the Titans themselves of their supersession by Jove and Apollo.

But this is not the whole of the story. In the second book, we have heard accounts of the new God of the Sea (from his predecessor) and of the young Apollo (from Clymene). When, in the third book, we see Apollo he is about to become a god. It must be noticed that he achieves the power and office of a god through the ministrations of Mnemosyne, who is a goddess *of the old order*,

Who hath forsaken old and sacred thrones

'for prophecies of' Apollo,

. . . and for the sake
Of loveliness new born.

It is Mnemosyne who gives him the 'knowledge enormous' by which he achieves divinity; and the position is therefore that, not only do the Titans show little sign of regaining their thrones and not only do they argue in favour of the new order; but one at least of their number is an instrument by which Hyperion's successor comes to power. Not only is there little enough spirit in the ranks of the Titans; there is also, as it were, treachery, far-reaching in its consequences.

There is a conclusion which can plausibly be drawn from this. It is, that Keats is loading the dice too heavily in favour of the new gods, too heavily, that is to say, for the health of his narrative. No doubt there is a war to follow, and Hyperion will rally the forces of the Titans. How Keats might have developed his narrative, we do not know. Probably, he did not know himself. But arguing on the basis of what we have and indulging no flights of speculation concerning what we have not, the poem as it stands is too biased, both in eloquence and circumstance, in favour of the usurpers. Out of things as they stand when Keats leaves off, we cannot discern many possibilities of combat in which Saturn and Hyperion have a lively chance of victory. Saturn is 'disanointed'; and we feel that he is likely to remain so.

We must next ask, What is the reason for this heavy loading of the dice? What is happening, in view of Keats's unquestionable desire to write good and vigorous narrative? Why does he thus apparently diminish the chances of his story's coming to any great liveliness? Rightly or wrongly, we think that this question is crucial in the study of *Hyperion*. We know that Keats abandoned this version of the story, and it is natural to think that the circumstances I have outlined have something to do with his abandonment of it. Now we must remember, as I have said, that Keats is telling no mere pretty story. He is attempting his greatest creation, and putting into it his highest resolves as a poet. Wonders are no wonders to him; he is concerned with the world of men and women in their joys and sufferings; and he will seek, through this story of warring deities, to reveal his profoundest perceptions and understanding of human life. (Precisely what these perceptions are, we need not now discuss, though something of their nature will have been disclosed by what has gone before.) But Keats requires that his narrative material, while supplying good and exciting story, should also become a vehicle of his lofty and far-reaching apprehension of human life and destiny. These two things require to be brought together. Yet, at an early stage, his narrative weakens and then ceases.

To the questions we have asked, I suggest the following answer: *Like the Titans, Keats has no heart to struggle with the new Divinities, for he is himself committed to them.* It is he who speaks through the lips of Oceanus and Clymene in defence of the usurpers; and it is he who creates, through Mnemosyne, the 'loveliness new born' of Apollo. Saturn cannot create, Apollo can. We all know that in *Paradise Lost* a considerable piece of Milton's mind was embodied in Satan; and if Milton was on God's side, he was also on the Devil's. He was Satan; and he was also the God who hounded Satan from Heaven into Hell and through the universe. God and Satan wrestled in Milton's mind; and Milton could thus match the adversaries nicely. But in Keats's mind there was no live issue; so far as he was concerned, the issue was decided. It is this which enfeebles his narrative and loads the dice unfairly. This discrimination in favour of the younger gods occurs because they embody an idea, a meaning, or, if we will, a philosophy which Keats finds creative, in contrast to the uncreativeness of the older gods; and he is above all anxious to communicate and defend this idea. This idea, as it is, and so far as it is, embodied in the young gods, he pushes forward in a manner which affects the vigour of his narrative. For the older gods in the persons of Oceanus and Clymene actively defend the younger gods, and in the person of Mnemosyne actively create them. The older gods are too much involved in the occurrence of the new; and the issue between them loses definition. Hyperion himself makes his appearance and splutters his annoyance, and no more.

The place of Mnemosyne in the narrative requires special notice. Oceanus and Clymene merely voice the wonder and admiration they feel for the younger gods they have seen. But Mnemosyne belongs to the world both of the conquered and the conquering; she was a Titan, but is become the foster-mother of Apollo; she is both orders of deity and the transition from one to the other; she is the womb in the old order out of which the new order has been born. It is she who is at the centre of Keats's poem. Without her, Saturn and the Titans must have remained the gods of a world in perpetual infancy; and without her Apollo could not have become divine. In her the childhood of the first gods passes into the maturity of the new, the springtime of the world into its high summer and autumn. Thus, it is precisely Mnemosyne who weakens Keats's narrative and paralyses his invention. If *Hyperion* is the story of the war of the Spring with the autumn, Mnemosyne strides the two worlds; she is not in time but encloses an eternity which has its spring and autumn at once. She cannot therefore appear, with any propriety, in the records of time, one figure among others; she is the totality and negation of time which includes the earlier and the later gods, and therefore stands above and over them all. Keats's main idea in writing *Hyperion* was to communicate some sense of what he had in mind in conceiving Mnemosyne; and he had also to write story. But so long as Mnemosyne occurs *in* the story, she saps away the reality of the clash of old and new gods, and the narrative fades and ceases. The idea wrecks the narrative, for the reason that the eternal as Keats appears to be conceiving it cannot occur within the temporal.

But Keats wished to write a long narrative poem; and he could do so only if the events composing his narrative formed a whole which *showed* the eternal through the representation of the temporal after the fashion of *King Lear*, as he perceived it, in which there is an 'intensity, capable of making all disagreeables evaporate, from their being in close relationship with Beauty and Truth'. *King Lear* is great and exciting drama and also, Keats believed, fulfils the highest aim of poetry, which is to make beautiful and acceptable what is terrible and tragic. To show the eternal through the creative apprehension of the temporal was what Keats wished to do and this is what he believed Shakespeare had done in *Lear*. Let his narrative in *Hyperion* then be content to represent the temporal. But if it was to do this, one thing was necessary: *he must get Mnemosyne out of the story*. Yet, such is his difficulty, that if he does so, his prime symbol and the chief means through which he is conveying the idea which animates the poem is lost to him.

There are two other points of view, very near to the last, from which it is convenient to study *Hyperion*. First, in studying the first version, we need to bear in mind that we have the advantage, not only of knowing Keats's other poetry, but of having read his letters and also, most important of all, the second version. We are able by this means to understand what was in Keats's mind, and to understand the first version in a degree not afforded by the poem itself. Few, I think, would deny that *Hyperion* is an obscure and difficult poem. We might enjoy it for its 'poetry'; but if it was all we had of Keats, it would leave a great deal unanswered. The great speech of Oceanus in the second book would necessarily arouse in us a lively curiosity to know more clearly what was in the poet's mind; and this curiosity would extend to trying to perceive how in the third book Mnemosyne is able to endow Apollo with godhead and just what is the 'knowledge enormous' to which Apollo comes by gazing on her face. Wonderful as *Hyperion* is, it is, as it stands, a baffling poem; and Keats must have known that it did not half express what was exciting his imagination.

Now we may, in the light of all we know of Keats, feel some confidence in saying that Keats desired to show what he believed was the tragic beauty of the world, and to reconcile the imagination to the suffering of the world. This suffering he seems to have believed, when seen 'under the aspect of eternity', to be 'evaporated' in a universal harmony. To see the temporal thus, in the form of eternity, and to behold the wonder of it, is godhead, the godhead of the younger gods, whose world is tragic, but because tragic, more beautiful than the world of Saturnian innocence. Mnemosyne possesses this vision and this godhead, and is able to impart it to Apollo. But all this is something which the poem at best only obscurely reveals; and the last forty lines of the third book, vital to the entire conception of the poem, which describe Apollo becoming a god through gazing on the face of Mnemosyne, not only carry us (or try to carry us) far from the excitement and pressure of narrative to a level of remote contemplative interest; they are also certainly not intelligible either in themselves or in the light of what has preceded them. Just why Apollo, on seeing in the face of Mnemosyne

> Names, deeds, gray legends, dire events, rebellions,
> Majesties, sovran voices, agonies,
> Creations and destroyings,

should become a god is not at all clear; and that Keats recognizes this, I think there can be little doubt. If this is so, Mnemosyne not only arrests Keats's narrative, in the way I tried to show in the previous section, but in the enfeebled narrative which we have, she is too obscure and mysterious a figure to be a substitute for the narrative she impairs.

Secondly, it is significant that of the new gods it is Apollo who is chosen by Keats for the hero of his poem; for if Hyperion was in one sense to be the hero, he must yet, we suppose, be conclusively superseded by Apollo. Hyperion was the sun god, and so is Apollo. But Apollo is also the god of music and poetry. Equally important is the fact that Mnemosyne in Greek mythology is the mother of the Muses. Now before Apollo is made into a god, Mnemosyne says to him:

> Thou hast dream'd of me; and awaking up
> Didst find a lyre all golden by thy side,
> Whose strings touch'd by thy fingers, all the vast
> Unwearied ear of the whole universe
> Listen'd in pain and pleasure at the birth
> Of such new tuneful wonder. Is't not strange
> That thou shouldst weep, so gifted? (p. 302)

Apollo has a new music, to which the whole universe listens in astonishment. It is also a sad music. The music of the spring is over. Yet

> . . . not for this
> Faint I, nor mourn nor murmur; other gifts

Have followed; for such loss, I would believe,
Abundant recompense. For I have learned
To look on nature, not as in the hour
Of thoughtless youth; but hearing oftentimes
The still, sad music of humanity,
Nor harsh nor grating, though of ample power
To chasten and subdue.

The lines of Wordsworth come naturally to the mind. This is the 'new tunefulness' of Apollo. His imagination can hear and his art catch that sad music of humanity and find it neither harsh nor grating.

Apollo then is at once god and poet. His godhead is also his poethood. He comes to see as a god sees, as it is the high and final achievement of the poet to see, as Shakespeare (so Keats believed) came to see, and as Keats wished to see. The poet may come to the divine vision such as a god has. If this is so, *Hyperion* is by way of being an exposition of what poetry, in its highest reaches, consists in; Keats is trying to tell us the aim and object of the poet. But what place, we ask, has this intention in a narrative poem? Can a narrative poem suitably undertake such a purpose? A narrative poem, or, it may be, a play, should in Keats's view so present plot and situation as to show human life 'as a God sees' it, to show 'the disagreeables evaporating from their being in close relationship with Beauty and Truth'. But instead of doing this, Keats is using his poetry to explain that this is what poetry ought to do. He is writing about the aim of poetry, instead of executing it. It is not enough for him to speak of actions and events shown to Apollo in the face of Mnemosyne; he should show, to his readers, the face of Mnemosyne in action and event. It is not enough for him to speak of the new sad tunefulness of Apollo; he must make that music sound in the ears of his readers.

Now if the analysis I have attempted is near the mark, we can sum up the position in this way. *Hyperion* is a poem in which narrative and contemplation, story and symbol, myth and meaning clash with and annul each other.

§ 20

In a famous letter to Reynolds written on the 21st of September 1819, Keats speaks of the beauty of the autumn and remarks that he has 'composed upon it'. Then he goes on to say that he has 'given up Hyperion'—'there were too many Miltonic inversions in it—Miltonic verse cannot be written but in an artful or rather artist's humour'. Now no doubt there are too many Miltonic inversions in *Hyperion* and Milton will break into it—

Nearest him
Asia, born of most enormous Caf,
Who cost her mother Tellus keener pangs,
Though feminine, than any of her sons. (p. 290)

But it is hardly true that *Hyperion* consists of 'Miltonic verse'; for much the greatest part, the manner and rhythms of the poem are peculiar to Keats. No doubt, in the despair he felt of making a job of the poem, he was too willing to underrate it and make extravagant charges against it. The Miltonic inversions could, in any case, be removed without any great labour; and we cannot help thinking that Keats is making a scapegoat of Milton's stylistic influence on him. It seems, at least, more reasonable to see in the inversions a symptom of Keats's uneasiness in the handling of his theme than a cause of his failure in treating it. If Keats found his material intractable to his purpose, as we have suggested, he would naturally become to some extent a prey to earlier influences and manners. That the chief of these influences should be Milton was also natural; for if Keats was not writing in the full epic manner, his style was an approach to it, and he was certainly writing on an epic theme. We may feel justified then in looking, as we have tried to do, for reasons other than 'Miltonic inversions' for the failure of *Hyperion*.

Now in the summer he had collaborated with Brown in writing *Otho the Great*. Neither Keats nor Brown thought of it very seriously. It was an amusing job, in which Brown dictated the plot, scene by scene as they came along, and Keats wrote it up. In the end Keats thought well enough of it and imagined Kean playing Ludolph. Certainly, it is well worth the reading and clearly shows Keats's great facility and power in writing dramatic blank verse. It was in November that he wrote to Taylor, what I have previously quoted, that he wished 'to diffuse the colouring of St. Agnes Eve throughout a Poem in which Character and Sentiment would be figures to such drapery. Two or three such Poems, if God should spare me, written in the course of the next six years, would be a famous Gradus ad Parnassum altissimum. I mean they would nerve me up to the writing of a few fine plays—my greatest ambition when I do feel ambitious.' He is thinking very seriously about play-writing. That play-writing was not something he was content to think of doing six years hence, but something he was thinking of doing at this time, we know from this same letter in which he says he is looking over the Earl of Leicester's history, and also from a beginning of a play he made in this month of November—*King Stephen*. Brown suggested the subject and suggested also that he supply the events of the play and their ordering. Brown started to tell him how it was to go.

Keats shouted 'Stop! I have been too long in leading-strings; I will do all this myself.' So Brown tells us, and Keats went on to write some 190 lines of *King Stephen*. Had Keats required a reason for not going on with it, he might have said, 'There were too many Shakespearean rhythms in it—Shakespearean verse cannot be written but in an artful or rather artist's humour'; if Keats could not write high narrative without Milton breaking in, one might be sure he could not write high tragedy without Shakespeare breaking in, and on a still larger scale:

> Now may we lift our bruised vizors up,
> And take the flattering freshness of the air.

§ 21

We must now consider the second *Hyperion*, which he had composed in the summer. Once again we have to discuss a fragment, and a shorter fragment than the last. In the first version, Keats had failed to unite idea and narrative. In the second version, he plays boldly and simply *sunders* them. He was aware that in the first version he had not been able to make the narrative bear the load of his meaning; and he now begins by telling us what it is all about and why he wants to tell this narrative. He will explain to us. In the first version, the speech of Oceanus leaves us cloudy and uncertain, and the transformation of Apollo into a god through gazing on the face of Mnemosyne is much too mysterious. He must now in his second version make these things clear—if he can. But how can he explain? How can he make the narrative, as it were, speak to us and explain itself? Even if he is determined to sunder, as I have said, idea and narrative, the exposition of the idea on the one hand, and the narrative on the other, must be formally related to each other. He solves this problem by taking Mnemosyne out of the narrative and by introducing himself into the poem. Mnemosyne will show the story of the warring gods in a vision, and will act as chorus and commentary upon it; Keats will be the audience. But even so, how are Keats and Mnemosyne to come together? There is only one way: in a dream of the poet's mind. Mnemosyne will be a figure in his dream; and the story, shown in vision by Mnemosyne, will be a vision within a dream. This scheme is pretty complicated and does not augur well for the success of the poem.

But at the outset it gives Keats a great advantage. He can now both tell the story (however he may work it out) and explain it. But this advantage is, in another way, a dead loss. For it is

Keats's acknowledgement of his failure to make the story self-luminous, to fuse thought and image, the universal and the particular.

It will be recalled that I said three things of the first *Hyperion*: (1) that it was necessary to remove Mnemosyne from the narrative; (2) that Mnemosyne is, in any case, too mysterious and unexplained; (3) that Apollo is a disguise for Keats in particular and poetry in general. In the second version, Keats has tried to do something in respect of all three, which are closely bound up with one another. In the first place, Mnemosyne is taken out of the narrative and is now shown for what she is, a figure out of time. She is now the Eternal Mother of the Muses, to whom Keats can go in this version, as Apollo went in the former. Then, having regard to the third point before speaking of the second, the Apollo of the first version has become the Keats of the second; so that if Mnemosyne has stepped out from the narrative of the gods, so has Apollo, now in the form of Keats. But in this case, were Mnemosyne and Apollo to appear in the story which Mnemosyne will show in vision to Keats? To this question, so far as Apollo is concerned, we cannot give a reply; so far as the second version extends, Apollo is not introduced and we have no means of ascertaining what Keats thought to do. Certainly, this must have presented him with a difficulty, since the poet of the first canto has, it seems, taken on the role of Apollo, as the one who derives 'knowledge enormous' from the vision of the face of Mnemosyne. But so far as the question relates to Mnemosyne, we are in a better position to make reply; and the answer reveals with great clearness, I think, one at least of the difficulties which confronted Keats in the making of the second version.

In the first canto the poet finds himself in dream confronted by Mnemosyne (usually in this version, but not always, called Moneta—she is sometimes called Mnemosyne, as in canto I, l. 331); he is weighed down by the world's pain and speaks to the goddess who uncovers her face. Her face is described in a passage which is famous and which we have already studied. Keats asks to see and understand the 'high tragedy' which

> . . . could give so dread a stress
> To her cold lips, and fill with such a light
> Her planetary eyes; and touch her voice
> With such a sorrow?

The reply to this is a vision of Saturn and Thea, as we see them in the beginning of the first version. Mnemosyne explains who they are (ll. 332–5). Then the poem goes on to further description of Saturn and Thea in their despair. Then, at l. 384, we come to:

A long awful time
I look'd upon them: still they were the same;
The frozen God still bending to the Earth,
And the sad Goddess weeping at his feet.
Moneta silent. Without stay or prop
But my own weak mortality, I bore
The load of this eternal quietude,
The unchanging gloom and the three fixed shapes
Ponderous upon my senses a whole moon.

We have here an uncomfortable feeling that Moneta-Mnemosyne is vaguely a part of the vision as well as a figure outside it who is showing and explaining it to the poet. And in another part (canto I, l. 226) she describes herself as

. . . left supreme
Sole priestess of his [Saturn's] desolation;

so that, even in the second version, she belongs, vaguely, to the narrative of the gods. But she is also an eternal figure, the mother of poets, here conversing with Keats. Now this is clearly a clumsy arrangement, and again, is bound to make Keats's progress in this second version very difficult. And if he was in this difficulty with Mnemosyne, how would the poet who converses with Mnemosyne be connected with Apollo—if Apollo was to appear at all? Thus it is, that if Mnemosyne in the narrative was an embarrassment to Keats, she is also an embarrassment out of it.

To come now to the second of the three points around which this discussion is turning, we see that the second version at least gives Keats the chance of showing us more clearly what he intended by Mnemosyne. The subjective framework of the second version makes possible what the epic and high objective manner of the first rendered very difficult, if not impossible. Released, by his new procedure, from the pressure of the demands of narrative, he can in favourable and leisured circumstances describe at length the face of Mnemosyne, which he did not do in the first version. This passage, in the first version, would have been too remote from action, too rarefied and mystical. Here it is more natural, after the converse Keats and the goddess have had together. Moreover, Keats does not regard the face of Mnemosyne, as he has described it, as satisfying his burning curiosity; and he leads on to the narrative of the wars of the gods by offering the coming story as an explanation of the stress of her lips, the sorrow of her words, and the light of her planetary eyes. The whole story to come will serve the purpose of providing fuller apprehension of the face of Mnemosyne; for it is she, in the second as in the first version, who is central, though in the first she is set in the story and in the second outside it. For in both versions she is the mother of all poets, in her sorrow and suffering and luminous serenity.

Something of the difficulties with which Keats was confronted in the second version will have become clear by this time. He was using now, in order to avoid his former difficulties, a complicated machinery, which must destroy the ease and straightness required of narrative. What we have of the second canto illustrates well enough the awkwardness of his present procedure. It consists of sixty-one lines. The first fifty consist of a speech of Mnemosyne's addressed to the poet, and describing the angry Hyperion in his palace. From this narration, made to the poet of events which he does not see, we pass in ll. 49–56 to a brief description of Keats and Mnemosyne, whereupon Hyperion breaks upon their vision journeying to the Titans in council. Thus has Keats to proceed partly by indirect narration, and partly by direct narration; but also he has from time to time to speak of himself and of Mnemosyne, and of their converse. It seems fairly obvious that the attempt could not continue long.

When we compare the two versions, the outstanding point of contrast is this. The first version is an attempt at high narrative, in a more or less epic manner. Keats was setting out to use his powers of invention. He desired a long, objective poem. In this he fails. He falls back on something less ambitious, reduces his style from anything approaching the epic level, and writes in 'cantos' instead of 'books'; but above all, he writes something professedly subjective, which is a dream in his own mind, and which is indeed frankly about himself and about poetry. 'Invention' has been defeated; and this not only in the first version, but even in the lesser degree required in the second. In adopting the second mode of procedure, Keats obtained, as we have seen, certain advantages; but these advantages also brought complications. In any case, Keats was aware that in the second version he was attempting something intrinsically inferior; for in large measure he had sacrificed objective invention, and his heart could not be in what he was doing in the same degree. This is all the more to be regretted because more than any other member of the Romantic group, Keats saw that what was required was the flowing out of the imagination to apprehend event and circumstance and to show them creatively. He wished to get beyond lyric and subjectivity. He did not wish to talk, but to reveal; not to say, but to show. In *Hyperion*, we may say that the Romantic movement made its greatest effort to create, to go beyond itself into the world. But tragically, like his own Saturn, Keats could not create; Mnemosyne, the mother of the great poets, of whom Keats is one, had failed him. He might, no doubt, have gone on to a finish, as Shelley had done in *Prometheus*. But he chose not to; and his choice was an act of high criticism. The Keats of *Isabella* may, as Arnold said, have lacked criticism. But *Isabella* is no criterion by which to judge Keats. He died in his twenty-sixth year; and his last year was filled with ill health and bitter unhappiness. Yet his mind, in its quality and range, in its passionate desire for what is Ideal, in its exquisite and balanced scepticism, in its acceptance, in serenity, of sorrow and suffering, is wonderful to contemplate; and not least wonderful is his failure in what was to be his greatest and most ambitious work. He set himself high standards, in a plenitude of critical power; and he knew what was failure and what was not.

§ 22

In the course of this long discussion of *Hyperion*, I have left to the end for fuller treatment a crucial consideration to which I have briefly referred at earlier stages. The reader will recall that I suggested that the second Act of *Prometheus*, built around Demogorgon, conflicts with Shelley's use of Greek mythology; and I also suggested that Mnemosyne presents a parallel to Demogorgon in this respect. So far, in speaking of *Hyperion*, I have emphasized the difficulty Keats found in conveying what was in his mind in conceiving her, while also having regard to the demands of narrative, a difficulty which constrained him to resort to another method of procedure in a second version. We must now ask whether this difficulty is not part of a wider one, which in another aspect may consist in placing Mnemosyne, as Keats imagined her, in a setting of Greek mythology.

The reader will have noticed that in what I have said of *Hyperion*, I have interpreted Mnemosyne as symbolizing a perfection and harmony in all existence—an interpretation in accordance with that second strain of speculation and with that second interpretation of 'Beauty is Truth' which we have noticed earlier. This interpretation appears, in the light of all we know, to suit the poem most adequately. I need not again comment on the passage in which Keats describes the face of Mnemosyne as it is disclosed to him. It shows a union of extreme suffering with great serenity. As we have seen, on beholding the countenance of the goddess, Keats desires to know what 'high tragedy' lies behind, in the 'dark secret Chambers' of her mind. If the interpretation by which we have proceeded is correct, Keats, using Mnemosyne as a symbol, sees the world of human experience as a 'high tragedy' which is somehow serene and beautiful. Our imagination of Mnemosyne is, I think, best helped by the thought of Cordelia. Indeed it is exceedingly likely that Keats's own imagination was thus helped.

> Patience and sorrow strove
> Who should express her goodliest. You have seen
> Sunshine and rain at once; her smiles and tears,
> Were like a better way; those happy smilets
> That play'd on her ripe lip seem'd not to know
> What guests were in her eyes; which parted thence,
> As pearls from diamonds dropp'd. In brief,
> Sorrow would be a rarity most belov'd,
> If all could so become it.

In lines which follow, Shakespeare appears almost to endow Cordelia with divine attributes:

> . . . there she shook
> The holy water from her heavenly eyes.

Then, after she and Lear have been defeated and captured, these are the words (they are the only words) she speaks:

> We are not the first
> Who, with best meaning, have incurr'd the worst.
> For thee, oppressed King, I am cast down;
> Myself could else out-frown false fortune's frown.

(In passing, we remark that in his first volume of poems Keats had asked, in the opening lines of *Sleep and Poetry*, what can be

> More serene than Cordelia's countenance?)

Now Cordelia, it is true, is set within a tragedy; unlike Mnemosyne, she is a suffering mortal. But it is precisely by the achievement of serenity within the tragic sequence that she rises above it and partakes of what Keats symbolizes in Mnemosyne. Moreover, what Mnemosyne was and symbolized, Keats wished to be, as a poet and as a man. Mnemosyne is indeed a goddess, but in one respect she stands for what Keats hoped the human soul might come to, acceptance of a tragic lot and the attainment of serenity in it, through which what is tragic is also seen as beautiful.

Now I have already said that this 'speculation' of Keats is one which the facts of our experience press against with great force. We may, and perhaps ought to, be able to come to the serenity in suffering of which Keats speaks; but we cannot come to the reconciliation with this world of which he speaks. I think it very probable that when Shakespeare was writing *Lear* some such 'speculation' as animated Keats animated him also, at least to some extent. But Shakespeare gave his 'speculation' no mercy. He did not seek to spare it; and he loaded the play with suffering, both physical and mental, which goes beyond anything in his other plays. And we see, in *Lear*, seeping in unobserved, obscurely determining the choice of phrase and incident, a mode of perception which cannot spring from *this* 'speculation', but which arises from another. Lear comes out of the storm into the redeeming love of Cordelia in her superhuman beauty; she receives back the Prodigal, who has fallen from and rejected her, with words that echo the familiar story:

> And wast thou fain, poor father,
> To hovel thee with swine and rogues forlorn,
> In short and musty straw?

Then she is hanged from a beam, and darkness descends on us; but being what we are, it cannot fail to be a darkness of waiting and expectation.

Now when we read the lines in *Hyperion*—

> But for her eyes I should have fled away.
> They held me back, with a benignant light,
> Soft-mitigated by divinest lids
> Half closed, and visionless entire they seem'd
> Of all external things—they saw me not,
> But in blank splendor beam'd like the mild moon,
> Who comforts those she sees not, who knows not
> What eyes are upward cast—

we cannot fail to ask, Who is Mnemosyne,[1] thus suffering and serene, benignant and comforting? If she is benignant she is no mere cosmic tragedy, however harmonious and sublime; and if she gives comfort, she cannot do so as a high impersonal order in which our sorry lives are but contributions to a grand synthesis. We might well curse such a world beyond Good and Evil in place of loving it. But as Keats sees Mnemosyne, as a symbol of the world, there are in her face values of the spirit which no naturalistic scheme can place at the centre of its universe. To be benignant is to be kind and gracious to inferiors; and the benignancy of Mnemosyne is such as is not warranted by Keats's naturalistic speculation, however noble. The awe and worship which Keats extends to her is no mere love of an impersonal order; it is warmed with a love which is saturated by our values. There is then, another 'speculation' present in this passage; and it is a 'speculation' by no means foreign to Keats and which we have studied in his letters. In *Lear*, Albany says that if

1 She is, of course, for the greater part, called Moneta in the second version.

. . . the heavens do not their visible spirits
Send quickly down to tame these vile offences,
It will come,
Humanity must perforce prey on itself,
Like monsters of the deep.

No doubt in this Shakespeare was 'speculating'. And through Keats's apprehension of Mnemosyne there ran, not explicitly perhaps, a 'speculation' or perception of the Divine as bearing the woes of the world, and through its labour of vicarious suffering, giving comfort and light to perplexed humanity. We can hardly read the lines which portray the countenance of Mnemosyne without seeing the face of the agonized Christ. Christianity has never said that our hearts can be reconciled to the suffering of the world—it must always remain mysterious to us; it has never said that it may be justified by an 'Absolute' to which it is callously condemned to contribute. Instead, Christianity has said that our imaginations can endure the huge reality of evil and pain only when we see it freely endured and borne by God himself. I suggest that something of the sense of this has passed into Keats's lines. At an earlier stage I placed these lines alongside a passage from *The Prelude* in which Wordsworth saw the old soldier as a figure of the utmost religious significance. And when Apollo, in the first version, is shown in his passage into deity after beholding the face of Mnemosyne, Keats can only describe what he undergoes as 'dying into life', a phrase in which, better perhaps than in any other, the Christian life is expressed.

It would be as absurd to call Keats a Christian as to use the word for Shelley. He was repelled by Christian dogma as greatly as Shelley. 'It is to be lamented', he said of Christ, that his history '. . . was written and revised by Men interested in the pious frauds of Religion.' Then he adds that 'through all this I see his splendour' (using a word he employs in describing Mnemosyne). Later on, the Romantic movement (if we can allow ourselves to speak thus loosely) will see Christian dogma very differently. But to Shelley and Keats it was anathema. But this did not mean and could not mean that their imaginations were not shot through with ways of feeling and perceiving which could not have been possible to them had they not been reared in a civilization which owed its existence to Christianity. Thus, when they turned to Greek mythology as material through which they could convey what they perceived, it was precisely their unacknowledged Christianity which shattered their antique myths. For if what we have said is true, Mnemosyne is no Greek goddess, and is no more a natural companion for Saturn and Apollo than Demogorgon is for Jove. In the second version she is brought out from this company into that of Keats himself. But this, if in one sense Mnemosyne belongs more to Keats than to Saturn and Apollo, is also a strained situation, so far as Mnemosyne remains at all, if only in name, a Greek goddess. The fact was that it was Greek mythology and not 'Miltonic verse' that could only be written 'in an artful or rather artist's humour'. Keats had an abundance of 'artist's humour', as *Lamia* and *The Eve of St. Agnes* in their different ways show. He could *play* the Greek to perfection; but his intentions in *Hyperion* were higher and better than this.

§ 23

I have only one further observation to make before we leave Keats and Shelley to speak of that phase of the Romantic movement which is Christian. It is right, I think, to remark on the force exerted by the idea of death upon the imaginations of Keats and Shelley. I have borrowed the phrase of Keats, 'Purgatory blind', for a title to this chapter, with the idea of conveying something of the impression left on us by the study of Shelley and Keats. Their Purgatory was *blind*. In it they were ignorant, and could not see. I shall take leave to quote once again the following sonnet of Keats:

> Why did I laugh tonight? No voice will tell:
> No God, no Demon of severe response,
> Deigns to reply from heaven or from Hell.
> Then to my human heart I turn at once.
> Heart! Thou and I are here sad and alone;
> I say, why did I laugh? O mortal pain!
> O Darkness! Darkness! ever must I moan,
> To question Heaven and Hell and Heart in vain.
> Why did I laugh? I know this Being's lease,
> My fancy to its utmost blisses spreads;
> Yet would I on this very midnight cease,
> And the world's gaudy ensigns see in shreds;
> Verse, Fame, and Beauty are intense indeed,
> *But Death intenser—Death is Life's high meed.*

Death is intense and the high meed of life. This longing for death is the recognition of the insurmountable walls by which human life is encompassed, of the boundary beyond which we cannot see, still less, tread. From this encompassment death is at least a liberation; 'to cease upon the midnight' is a glad acknowledgement of the victory of life. Sometimes, as in the *Ode to a Nightingale*, the desire for death is indulged, to some extent at least, at the level of luxurious longing. But this is not the note of the sonnet I have quoted, in which we cannot doubt the sincerity of Keats's desire for death.

In one of the last letters he wrote (to Brown, 28 September 1820), when he was on board ship for Italy, had seen Fanny for the last time—and could not bring himself to write to her, he said:

'I could not leave my lungs or stomach or other worse things behind me. I wish to write on subjects that will not agitate me much—there is one I must mention and have done with it. Even if my body would recover of itself, this would prevent it. The very thing which I want to live most for will be a great occasion of my death. I cannot help it. Who can help it? Were I in health it would make me ill, and how can I bear it in my state? I dare say you will be able to guess on what subject I am harping—you know what was my greatest pain during the first part of my illness at your house. I wish for death every day and night to deliver me from these pains, and then I wish death away, for death would destroy even those pains which are better than nothing. Land and Sea, weakness and decline, are great separators, but death is the great divorcer for ever. When the pang of this thought has passed through my mind, I may say the bitterness of death is passed.' (p. 520)

This Keats writes on his last journey and, in all truth, hopelessly in love. From the defeat of his love for Fanny, he can turn to the thought of death without bitterness. This is the thought of his last sonnet, also written on board ship:

Bright star! would I were steadfast as thou art—
  Not in lone splendour hung aloft the night
And watching, with eternal lids apart,
  Like nature's patient, sleepless Eremite,
The moving waters at their priestlike task
  Of pure ablution round earth's human shores,
Or gazing on the new soft fallen mask
  Of snow upon the mountains and the moors—
No—yet still steadfast, still unchangeable,
  Pillow'd upon my fair love's ripening breast,
To feel for ever its soft fall and swell,
  Awake for ever in a sweet unrest,
Still, still to hear her tender-taken breath,
And so live ever—or else swoon to death.

Now this sonnet and that I previously quoted may properly be taken together. In the second his love for Fanny—and its strength, and the anguish it caused him can hardly be exaggerated, as the last letters abundantly show—in its frustration and despair gives place in his mind to the thought of death, 'the great divorcer for ever'; in the first sonnet his desire, not for anything in the world, but for the Ideal, whether a transcendent Principle of Beauty or a Beauty which somehow encloses and fills the world of time, also makes him long for death. In each case there is both uncertainty and defeat; he is sure neither of the object of his human nor of his divine love, and neither the one nor the other can he have and hold. Out of this mingled ignorance and dismay, and from the baffled hope of a Beauty which may also be Truth, there arises the thought of the only absolute peace left to man, the completeness of death.

The same ignorance and dismay drives Alastor forward to his death. He sees a swan flying homewards, and he says:

> And what am I that I should linger here,
> With voice far sweeter than thy dying notes,
> Spirit more vast than thine frame more attuned
> To beauty, wasting these surpassing powers
> *In the deaf air, to the blind earth, and heaven*
> *That echoes not my thoughts*? (p. 21)

If the swan flies to its home, Shelley is lost in a 'blind earth'. In the Preface to the poem Shelley says that the 'Poet's self-centred seclusion was avenged by the furies of an irresistible passion pursuing him to speedy ruin'. In part, this is a wilful misrepresentation of his hero and of himself, arising out of the lofty fatuity of his humanitarian morals. But it also contains some truth. There were indeed furies set within his passion which urged him to find death:

> A restless impulse urged him to embark
> And meet lone Death on the drear ocean's waste;

what he desires is for ever beyond him; and he bows himself down in what Keats called the 'quietness of death'. Both Keats and Shelley beat themselves against the imprisoning gates of the world—'ineffectually', no doubt, and necessarily so, being only human. But this is not the whole of the story. There is another word concerning 'blind Purgatory', spoken by Keats himself, in noble verse. It is the sonnet *To Homer*, which may be placed over against the sonnet *Why did I laugh tonight?* (of which last he said that it was written 'with no Agony but that of ignorance; with no thirst of anything but Knowledge'):

> Standing aloof in giant ignorance,
> Of thee I hear and of the Cyclades,
> As one who sits ashore and longs perchance
> To visit dolphin-coral in deep seas.
> So thou wast *blind*!—but then the veil was rent,
> For Jove uncurtain'd Heaven to let thee live,
> And Neptune made for thee a spumy tent,
> And Pan made sing for thee his forest-hive;

Aye, on the shores of darkness there is light,
  And precipices show untrodden green;
There is a budding morrow in midnight;
  There is a triple sight in blindness keen;
Such seeing hadst thou, as it once befel
To Dian, Queen of Earth, and Heaven, and Hell.

Part Three

THE GOSPEL OF HEAVEN

CHAPTER I

KNOWLEDGE AND FAITH

§ 1

IN what follows, I shall speak of Coleridge and Newman. In this chapter I wish to explain their views on human knowledge and imagination; and then to relate these views to ideas we have already encountered in Blake, Shelley, and Keats. I shall begin with Coleridge and shall try to point out certain features of his poetry which throw light on his later development.

In the first place, we observe in his poetry what great pleasure he found in times and places of quiet seclusion and retreat. He liked softness of sound and light, and shrank both from the brilliance of full sunshine and from the dark of night. He especially liked the time of evening. Many illustrations could be given of this. I shall give only a few. These lines from *The Eolian Harp* show nearly all these preferences:

> . . . sweet it is
> To sit beside our Cot, our Cot o'ergrown
> With white-flowered Jasmin, and the broad-leaved Myrtle . . .
> And watch the clouds, that late were rich with light,
> Slow saddening round, and mark the star of eve . . .
> The stilly murmur of the distant Sea
> Tells us of silence.[1]

He is at home and the time is evening; what sound there is serves to emphasize the silence; *and the sea is distant.*

In *Frost at Midnight* he writes of silence in moonlight. *Fears in Solitude* expresses his enjoyment of silence in 'a green and silent spot amid the hills'; and the sense of seclusion is heightened by the coming of evening:

> But the dell,
> Bathed by the mist, is fresh and delicate
> As vernal corn-field, or the unripe flax,
> When, through its half-transparent stalks, at eve,
> The level sunshine glimmers with green light.

[1] Except where stated to the contrary, quotations from Coleridge are made from the convenient Nonesuch selection of his works, ed. Potter, London, 1938.

The Nightingale rejoices in starlight. In the *Dejection: An Ode* he laments the passing of his imaginative power; but it is his failure to respond to evening which especially dismays him:

> It were a vain endeavour,
> Though I should gaze for ever
> On that green light that lingers in the west:
> I may not hope from outward forms to win
> The passion and the life, whose fountains are within.

During daytime Coleridge takes pleasure in a place of seclusion where the sunlight falls brokenly, its heat and intensity diminished by foliage. In the *Lime-tree Bower* he watches

> Some broad and sunny leaf, and loved to see
> The shadow of the leaf and stem above
> Dappling its sunshine.

Only once do we find any enjoyment, in the manner of Wordsworth, in what is bleak, bare, exposed, and windswept; but in the poem in which this occurs (*Reflections on having left a Place of Retirement*) the feeling gathers for the most part around the 'pretty Cot' in a 'Valley of Seclusion' from which the excursion to the mountain was made; the 'bare bleak mountain' would, we surmise, be hardly tolerable to Coleridge were it not for the nearness of a secluded headquarters for such excursion. The poem *To a Young Friend* begins:

> A Mount, not wearisome and bare and steep,
>   But a green mountain variously up-piled,
> Where . . .
>   . . . 'mid the summer torrent's gentle dash
> Dance brightened the red clusters of the ash;
>   Beneath whose boughs, by those still sounds beguiled,
> Calm Pensiveness might muse herself to sleep.

There is little advantage in increasing the number of examples of this kind. It is natural to see in these passages evidence of a certain insecurity in Coleridge's mind, a desire to retreat from the world and, no less, from himself. The first part of *Fears in Solitude* celebrates the 'silent dell', the 'quiet nook'; but preventing his full enjoyment of it is the thought, set out at length later in the poem, of the suffering and cruelty of human life as it goes on beyond the confines of his retreat. This poem was, indeed, written during a time of war and 'during the alarm of an invasion'. But it shows something permanent in Coleridge's mind. Into the paradisal retreat of *Kubla Khan* 'with walls and towers girdled round' and with its 'sunny spots of greenery', there penetrated 'ancestral voices prophesying war'. *Dejection* is written at the time of quiet evening. But a storm is threatening; and into the quiet there is projected the thought of 'the hell within':

> Hence, viper thoughts, that coil around my mind,
> Reality's dark dream;

from them he turns, but only to envisage

> The rushing of an host in rout,
> With groans of trampled men, with smarting wounds,

and a 'little child'

> Upon a lonesome wild,
> Not far from home, but she hath lost her way:
> And now moans low in bitter grief and fear,
> And now screams loud, and hopes to make her mother hear.

In so much of his poetry it is thoughts like these which are set over against his pathetic enjoyment of his retreats.

It is not difficult to relate both *The Ancient Mariner* and *Kubla Khan* to the poems from which I have quoted by seeing them as issuing from the same insecurity of mind. For *The Ancient Mariner* is a study in *exposure*, in the *denial* of seclusion, to a human soul. The mariner is set upon a wide sea, exposed without refuge, beneath a hot and copper sky; and it is in this situation that the ship is *becalmed*. Clearly, if what I have suggested above has any truth, this was for Coleridge a nightmare situation. There can be here no dell, no bower, nor foliage to break the sunlight; also, *there is no twilight—'at one stride comes the dark'*. There is nothing to do but await the coming of wind and rain. Against the background of the wedding, with its goodly and jolly company, the narrative quickly plunges the mariner into the first of his two infernos, the extreme cold of desolate seas, with brilliant ice and fearful noises. Then, after the speed and terror of

> The ice was here, the ice was there,
> The ice was all around:
> It cracked and growled, and roared and howled,
> Like noises in a swound,

the stresses of the verses are thrown backward and deepened, creating a kind of stillness which overcomes the movement and sound of the ice:

> At length did cross an Albatross,
> Thorough the fog it came;
> As if it had been a Christian soul,
> We hailed it in God's name.

The bird flies, we are made to imagine, into this terrible world, slowly and with a wonderful and mild self-containment, evoking deep emotion and bearing a kind of vast sanctity. The mariner slays the Albatross quite motivelessly. In Shelvocke, from whom Coleridge took the story, the bird was slain by a sailor who thought, in view of 'contrary tempestuous winds' then prevailing, that it was a bird of ill-omen. In Coleridge's poem, the bird is received hospitably; and then, with favourable winds blowing, it is slain through an act of purest evil. The mariner can offer no explanation. The result is the second incomparably greater suffering of the calm beneath a copper sun.

'Laudanum gave me repose', wrote Coleridge to his brother in April 1798, 'not sleep; but you, I believe, know how divine that repose is, what a spot of enchantment, a green spot of fountains and flowers and trees in the very heart of a waste of sands!' (p. 575) *The Ancient Mariner* is the story of a man in a waste of sea which offered no refuge, and in which therefore the soul is quite helpless. There is a totality of exposure and, later, seizure by life-in-death. The deathly and decaying stillness of the universe in the calm is matched only by the dryness of the mariner's heart:

I looked to heaven, and tried to pray;
But or ever a prayer had gusht,
A wicked whisper came, and made
My heart as dry as dust.

Thus, life-in-death secures the command of the mariner's life. Yet his suffering is relieved by the gift of love by his 'kind saint'; and thereupon the universe breaks into life and movement:

The upper air burst into life!
And a hundred fire-flags sheen,
To and fro they were hurried about!
And to and fro, and in and out,
The wan stars danced between.

As the 'spring' breaks through in the mariner's heart, come rain, wind, and life. The lines in *Dejection*:

O Lady! we receive but what we give
And in our life alone does Nature live:
Ours is her wedding garment, ours her shroud,

are frequently read as a statement of neo-Kantian theory of the imagination. It is perhaps better to read them in the sense which connects *Dejection* with *The Ancient Mariner*.

Yet, with the deliverance of the mariner from life-in-death, he comes to no final rest, no absoluteness of possession of a new life. The terror remains behind; the mariner has vision, but no secure possession:

> And now this spell was snapt: once more
> I viewed the ocean green,
> And looked far forth, yet little saw
> Of what had else been seen—
>
> Like one, that on a lonesome road
> Doth walk in fear and dread,
> And having once turned round walks on,
> And turns no more his head;
> Because he knows, a frightful fiend
> Doth close behind him tread.

The 'frightful fiend' without, and the frightful fiend within, which had prompted him to the killing of the Albatross, is not himself killed; he still stalks the seas. The refuge which the mariner seeks—his homeland and the 'kirk'—remains a refuge; the terror is still abroad, and within. He does not come to the possession of that mild mastery in the face of desolate seas which the Albatross possessed:

> Since then, at an uncertain hour,
> That agony returns:
> And till my ghastly tale is told,
> This heart within me burns.

An 'agony', he says, 'constraineth' him: the 'unfathomable hell' within, the 'thunder and the shout' without.

So in *Kubla Khan* he cannot come to the music which might create such a garden as he describes in the opening lines; he is without the joy and imagination which might create what in *Dejection* he calls

> A new Earth and new Heaven,
> Undreamt of by the sensual and the proud.

For *Kubla Khan*, like *Dejection*, is elegiac; it is a song of failure.

> Could I revive within me
> Her symphony and song,
> To such a deep delight 'twould win me,
> That with music loud and long,
> I would build that dome in air,
> That sunny dome! those caves of ice!

For, as he says, again in *Dejection*,

> From the soul itself must there be sent
> A sweet and potent voice.

Instead, the fountain of his imagination falls away into a lifeless ocean:

> A grief without a pang, void, dark, and drear,
> A stifled, drowsy, unimpassioned grief;

and beneath the brightness of the garden is a sunless sea.

If we except those poems which have, in varying degree, something of a dream quality—*The Ancient Mariner*, *Kubla Khan*, *Christabel*, we see that nearly all Coleridge's poems have a conversational tone. Even *Dejection*, his finest poem after the three great ones, illustrates this. In this connexion, it is instructive to notice that the poem which is now called *Reflections on having left a Place of Retirement* was originally called *Reflections on entering into Active Life: A Poem which affects not to be Poetry*. And again, Coleridge writes of *Fears in Solitude*: 'The above is perhaps not Poetry,—but rather a sort of middle thing between Poetry and Oratory—*sermoni propriora*.—Some parts are, I am conscious, too tame even for animated prose.' (p. 728) Now of all Coleridge's poems (excepting the three), we can say that they have the air of 'affecting not to be poetry'; they are a 'sort of middle thing'. He introduces into them all an almost informal element, a conversational tone. The reason for this is not far to seek. Coleridge felt the impulse to creation; he was also aware, as he states at its extreme in *Dejection*, of a certain failure of imagination, of something negative arresting the flow of his energies. The result was a 'sort of middle thing'—a poetry conversational, made thereby unpretentious, and yet revealing its author's unease by lapsing from time to time into a false grandeur, an oratorical manner; poetry written almost apologetically, yet also, too frequently, absurdly grandiose. Thus he is either 'affecting' not to write poetry or being excessively 'poetical'.

This imaginative failure is stated in *Dejection*; but it is also set out and explored, however unknowingly, in the *Mariner* and *Kubla Khan*. When Coleridge rose to great poetry, as in these last poems, his theme was still, though possibly he did not know it, his own mind, and the insecurity of his asylums. 'I must think', wrote Keats, 'that difficulties nerve the spirit of a man—they make our Prime Objects a Refuge as well as a passion.' We do not, indeed, ordinarily think of Coleridge in his earlier or later days as greatly 'nerved' to meet the difficulties and demands of life. Yet who would say that Coleridge would have achieved as much as he did in later years, or even, we may add, maintained his sanity, had he not sought 'our Prime Objects' for a refuge? The beneficence and grace of God became increasingly Coleridge's only hope of strength in a world to which he seemed helplessly exposed. We must remember, then, in all that follows, that Coleridge felt himself exposed in a world which was terrible to him.

§ 2

To trace Coleridge's intellectual development is to show in what way Romanticism, after setting out with a strong antipathy to Christianity, came to acknowledge what Coleridge believed to be its necessity. Romanticism was bound, in the course of its history, to come to this acknowledgement. Whatever the faults of the movement as a whole and of its individual writers, it was actuated by so high a degree of passion and was manifested in minds of such great seriousness and power, that perception of the depth and scope of the Christian religion was sooner or later inevitable; and it was fitting and natural that this perception should occur in the mind of the Romantic writer who, in addition to great poetic and critical powers, possessed a vast intellectual and philosophical curiosity. We may doubt, however, if Coleridge would have come to be the originator of the resurgence of interest in the Christian religion which marked the first half of the nineteenth century, had he not, in addition to his natural powers, suffered in a degree considerably greater than any other of the great Romantic writers. Whatever we may say of Coleridge, there was that in his make-up which made life extremely difficult for him; and it was apparently necessary that this, the most richly endowed man of his time, should come near to a dissolution of his personality (in the first decade of the century) in order that he, and therewith, in large measure, his times and generation, should come to perceive the riches and strength which are contained in Christianity. It has become regrettably customary to discern in the Coleridge who came to believe in the reality of God's redemption and in prayer as a vehicle of Divine grace, only a feeble fugitive from life, feeding on fond illusions. It is regrettable that even Mr. Muirhead, who showed in his book so fine a regard for Coleridge's powers and sincerity, should lend some countenance to this view. It is all the more regrettable because in lesser writers than Mr. Muirhead, who have not, like him, a philosophy worthy of respect, and who use Coleridge as an occasion for journalistic jauntiness, should take encouragement to smile condescendingly on the Coleridge who believed that a universe without prayer would be 'petrified'.

For it is a curious mental process which regards the compulsion of experience as something that must necessarily drive us into error. To be driven, through the stress of prolonged and acute suffering, to belief in the doctrines and practices of Christianity, is no occasion for superior pity. I have quoted Keats, who was a manly person, as saying that difficulties make our Prime Objects a refuge; and religion itself has never been ashamed to call God by that name. I have tried elsewhere to suggest that we go wrong if we regard the 'later' Wordsworth as one who came to Christianity from any other motive than a perception of its adequacy and power; and we go equally wrong if we see the 'later' Coleridge as anything other than the real Coleridge who had come, through Christianity, to a measure of security and serenity greater than any he had formerly known. In what follows, therefore, I shall treat the Coleridge of the later years, upholding to the best of his power what he believed to be the truth of Christianity, not as an aberration from what he might have been, but as one who had come to clearer perception of truth through ceaseless suffering and thought. Blake tried to create a private mythology, and that with a philosophy both contradictory in itself and a distortion of Christianity; Shelley and Keats used ancient mythology for expression of modes of sensibility which were largely Christian, whatever their formal beliefs; Coleridge was brought face to face with Christianity under circumstances which made him more willing to learn, and to adopt modes of expression not his own.

§ 3

It is convenient to divide Coleridge's life into three periods, the first extending up to 1801; the second to 1816; the third to his death. By 1801 the influence of Hartley upon him had ceased; Mr. Muirhead judged that by 1817 Coleridge was finally disillusioned so far as Schelling was concerned, and we can say that by 1816 Coleridge was set fair upon the road of Christian belief. From this time on, his chief preoccupation was Christian philosophy and theology.

The first period, that up to 1801, is the least important for our purposes. There is that in it, however, which unites Coleridge with Shelley in an interesting respect; for Coleridge shows at this time very much the confusion of mind which Shelley was to show in his early years as a writer and which indeed he was never wholly to cast off. The confusion shown by each of these writers is a sign of the times in which they lived: a period of transition, of changes in thought and feeling so great that those who lived the transition not unnaturally failed to realize the contradictions, palpable enough to us, in which their minds were caught. Mr. Muirhead in the first chapter of his essay on Coleridge as a philosopher, has discussed the intellectual changes of the time; and has observed that in Hartley, Coleridge's master during his early period, the contradictoriness of men's opinions at the time was present to an even grotesque degree. In the change from the philosophy of the English eighteenth century, whose greatest thinker was Hume, to that of the nineteenth, which reached its most accomplished and thorough expression in F. H. Bradley, Coleridge was to occupy a position of great interest. It is not of course true that neo-Hegelianism, even when informed by the fine sensibility and judgement of Bradley, would have satisfied Coleridge; and we may fairly regret that Coleridge in his efforts to erect a Christian philosophy had not a greater application and orderliness, which might have saved English thought from the influence of Hegelianism and given it, in the course of the nineteenth century, a theistic philosophy having the merits of Bradley's catholicity of mind but also free from that certain lack of humility, that subtle exaltation of the human which underlies the apparent high impersonality informing all Hegelian philosophy. This, however, is by the way. What is relevant here is that Coleridge's lifetime spanned a crucial change in intellectual climate. He was himself to play a vital part in effecting the change. And we must not therefore be surprised if in his early years his ideas show striking disorder and contradictoriness.

But he came out of this confusion. In the course of the second decade of the century it was largely dissipated and by 1820 his path was clear. But if he was coming out of the wood during these years, Shelley was still within it. Coleridge was therefore well placed to understand Shelley's intellectual disorder. He said to J. H. Frere in 1830:

> 'Shelley was a man of great power as a poet, and could he only have had some notion of order, could you only have given him some plane whereon to stand, and look down upon his own mind, he would have succeeded . . . it is a pity, I often think, that I never met with him. I could have done him good. He went to Keswick in order to see me, and unfortunately fell in with Southey instead. . . . I should have laughed at his Atheism. I could have sympathised with him and shown him that I did so. I could have shown him that I had once been in the same state myself, and I could have guided him through it. I have often bitterly regretted in my heart of hearts that I did never meet with Shelley.' (p. 481)

There is no need to question the great sincerity of the 'bitterly regretted'; Coleridge understood Shelley's confusion and difficulty, and rightly thought he could have dissolved it. We may feel some inclination to smile when we read 'Could he only have had some notion of order . . .'; yet it is true that Coleridge had every right to speak in that way. For although Coleridge no doubt lacked ability to live and work in an orderly and systematic way, it cannot be doubted that his mind came to a clarity, power, and depth in religious and philosophical matters which places him far above any Englishman of the early nineteenth century in philosophy. Coleridge's philosophy is indeed fragmentary, but it cannot be said to be confused in any essential.

No doubt we say this with all the more confidence because we know the tradition within which Coleridge came increasingly to think and work, and can therefore draw out what he leaves obscure and incomplete; but it is certain that as we read Coleridge's work we see abundant evidence of a mind more and more sure of itself and of its direction. His rediscovery of a great tradition went hand in hand with steady rejection of writers of inferior quality, Hartley, Fichte, Schelling; also he came, as time passed, to have no illusions about Spinoza, and to refuse to extract from Spinozistic philosophy a vague and deceptive religiosity. Kant, indeed, he never ceased to honour, discerning in him a philosophical power of absolutely the first order. Yet he felt toward him no subservience. He owed him a great deal; he saw in Kant's 'critical' work something which satisfied elements which had always been present, as we shall see, in his own experience; but he reached a position from which he was able to see Kant's position with great clearness and to criticize it with independence. As we read Coleridge's writings of the second and third decades of the century we see him ridding himself at once of the influence of inferior writers (thereby belying, as time passed, one of Arnold's charges against him), and of the confusions of his earlier years. Consciousness of this growth, of the sureness and steadiness of his direction, is in the remarks he made about Shelley; remarks not at all condescending and patronizing, but filled with a natural and proper regret that a wisdom of which he was not boastful had not been able to be communicated to a younger man whose genius he admired and who was stumbling where he himself had stumbled twenty years earlier.

Yet the early period of confusion in Coleridge's beliefs may not have been without its value. His early addiction to materialism and to elements belonging to the Enlightenment at least ensured that when he came to Christianity, it would be to him no mere affair of bright, sweet, and comfortable reasonableness. For Coleridge to have been so caught up, and with such great enthusiasm, in associationism and materialism may well have helped him in later years to perceive that religious belief is not as easy as it may appear. The imaginations of the Romantic writers had been held by the spectacle of a universe empty of any God. In the very year in which *Alastor* was written, Newman copied out in his boyish note-book 'Some French verses, perhaps Voltaire's, against the immortality of the soul', and said, 'How dreadful but how plausible!' It is no far cry, we think, from the *philosophes* of the eighteenth century to Shelley; but it was also no far cry from those same writers to the boy Newman. Now the openness and flexibility of imagination of these men secured that if they came, as Coleridge and Newman did, to a professed life of faith, they must shrink from treating religion as something lightly or comfortably come by. I shall speak later of both Coleridge and Newman in their formulation of what they believed to be the foundations of religion; I remark now only in a general way that what seems to be the absence of God from his universe impressed the imaginations of both with the greatest force and that the sense of it was a kind of scepticism which they never lost. ' "Verily Thou art a hidden God, the God of Israel, the Saviour", is the very law of His dealings with us,' says Newman in *The Grammar of Assent*. We cannot understand the narrow ways into which, in Coleridge and Newman, Romanticism came, nor apprehend the force with which it was carried into these ways, if we do not first discern the scope and range of the Romantic imagination in its original exposure to the world. It makes little difference whether materialism was acclaimed, as by Shelley and Coleridge, or found dreadful, as by Newman; the acclamation and the dread alike arose out of the similar and vivid impressions of a godless world made on the imaginations of men who, however different, were ultimately to be united in their exaltation of the spiritual; they had all felt the 'plausibility' of atheism.

To return to Coleridge, if he had been able enthusiastically to envisage a materialistic universe, he also sought at an early stage the consolations of religious belief. As we have said, he contrived, following Hartley, to combine materialism and necessitarianism with some sort of belief in God. But the letters of these years show a Coleridge never far away from Christianity; and in 1798, when he was still a disciple of Hartley (and enthusiastic about Spinoza), he writes to his brother George of his steadfast belief in original sin and of our 'inherent depravity'; he declares that he 'wishes to be a good man and a Christian' and that he is no 'Whig, no Reformist, no Republican'. (p. 576) In the December of 1796 he had written a long letter in which he passionately defends Christianity from the charge of 'meanness'; and he asserts that there is 'no resting place for morality'[1] (he was at this time a declared 'Berkleyan'). Even before 1795, the year of his marriage, when he may be said to have entered upon adult life, he showed in his letters a quite definite attachment to Christianity.

[1] *Letters*, ed. E. H. Coleridge, London, 1895, vol. i, p. 199 sq.

Certainly from this time on there was always, beneath the succeeding enthusiasms for Hartley, Berkeley, and Spinoza, a core of religious sensibility which had undisguised expression, and which was to expand and stabilize as the years succeeded. In this he was different from all the other great Romantic poets.

§ 4

If it is important in this way to emphasize Coleridge's continuing Christianity beneath the passing phases of speculation, it is important also to emphasize two aspects of his attitude to religion. There occurs the following sentence in one of the letters written when he was still in the army: 'I have little faith, yet am wonderfully fond of speculating on mystical schemes.'[1] This was as early as 1794. As he became increasingly Christian, his lack of faith, together with his vast intellectual curiosity, led him, not unnaturally, to a strong anti-intellectualism; in the interests of a stronger faith, he deprecated a curious and restless intelligence. In the same year, 1794, and in distress of mind (a few days before his release from the army), he wrote to the same brother: 'I long ago theoretically and in a less degree experimentally knew the necessity of faith in order to regulate virtue, nor did I ever seriously disbelieve the existence of a future state. In short, my religious creed bore and, perhaps, bears a correspondence with my mind and heart.'[2] Coleridge's difficulty was not chiefly in reconciling 'heart' and 'head'; despite flirtations with Hartley and Spinoza, Coleridge was never very far from Christianity. What took him to Hartley, to Spinoza, to Berkeley and numerous other philosophers was an intellectual passion, delighting in speculation, as he says, and likely to become, as he realized, little more than an intellectual dilettantism, however impassioned, which passed breathlessly and indefinitely from one grand philosophical possibility to another. In this he discerned, rightly, great danger. Faith, he seemed obscurely to realize from the beginning, was the first necessity, and without it philosophy was vain; only through a faith which flourished in him could he at once think truly, and order the intelligence and its curiosity in the economy of the spirit. 'Well', he writes to Wade in 1796, 'did St. Paul say: Ye have an evil *heart* of unbelief.'[3] In a letter to Benjamin Flower in the same year he says:

'My philosophical refinements, and metaphysical Theories lay by me in the hour of anguish, as toys by the bedside of a child deadly

[1] *Letters*, ed. E. H. Coleridge, vol. i, p. 64.
[2] Ibid., vol. i, p. 69.
[3] Ibid., vol. i, p. 153.

sick. May God continue his visitations to my soul, bowing it down, till the pride and Laodicean self-confidence of human Reason be utterly done away.'[1]

And much later, in a chapter in *Biographia Literaria*, in which he could still say that the *Ethics* of Spinoza is not '*in itself* and *essentially* incompatible with religion, natural or revealed',[2] he also says that the reading of the mystics had

'... contributed to keep alive the *heart* in the *head*; gave me an indistinct, yet stirring and working presentiment, that all the products of the mere *reflective* faculty partook of DEATH, and were as the rattling twigs and sprays in winter, into which a sap was yet to be propelled from some root to which I had not penetrated, if they were to afford my soul either food or shelter.'[3]

In 1801 he writes that 'deep thinking is attainable only by a man of deep feeling'; and that 'all truth is a species of revelation'. (p. 590)

We can discern, in Coleridge's early insistence on faith as the necessary condition of any thought which is to be of worth, a motive for his attraction to the most signal outcome of the *Critique of Pure Reason*. The sharp limits which Kant set to the operations of the understanding were welcomed by one who was acutely aware of the severe limits of the value of thought in the conduct of life. Coleridge's own sense of sin and of himself as a fallen creature, promoting in him a hunger for a continuous life of religious discipline and faith, together with his strong intellectual passion, issued, by way of compromise, into pursuit of a philosophy which while satisfying his speculative interest would also manifest the poverty of the powers of the intelligence. What he held fast to out of his reading in German philosophy was Kant's drastic review of the powers of the understanding. That he let his delight in mere philosophical speculation carry him, for a period, far afield, in temporary enthusiasm for Fichte and Schelling and Spinoza, is undeniable. Yet what was to remain with him was a doctrine which came to him, in Keats's famous words, as a kind of echo to his own deepest thoughts and experience. In the *Biographia Literaria* he says:

'... there had dawned upon me, even before I had met with *The Critique of Pure Reason*, a certain guiding light. If the mere intellect could make no certain discovery of a holy and intelligent first cause, it might yet supply a demonstration, that no legitimate argument could be drawn from the intellect *against* its truth. And what is this

[1] *Unpublished Letters of S. T. Coleridge*, ed. E. L. Griggs, London, 1932, vol. i, p. 64.

[2] *Biographia Literaria*, ed. J. Shawcross, vol. i, p. 99. All quotations from this work are made from this edition. The italics in this and the next quotation are Coleridge's.

[3] Ibid., vol. i, p. 98.

more than St. Paul's assertion, that by wisdom, (more properly translated by the powers of reasoning) no man ever arrived at the knowledge of God?'[1]

We shall return later to Coleridge's maturest formulation of his beliefs in these matters; we observe now that it was present in his earliest reflections.

Secondly, it is important to bear in mind, what goes along naturally with his anti-intellectualism, his enduring sense of the vast and the strange. In one of the biographical letters written to Poole during the years 1797 and 1798 he says that his father explained to him when he was eight years of age the movements of the planets and the magnitude of the universe; he listened, he says, with profound delight but without incredulity.

'For from my early reading of fairy tales and genii, etc., etc., my mind had been habituated *to the Vast*, and I never regarded *my senses* in any way as the criteria of my belief. I regulated all my creeds by my conceptions, not by my *sight*, even at that age. Should children be permitted to read romances, and relations of giants and magicians and genii? I know all that has been said against it; but I have formed my faith in the affirmative. I know no other way of giving the mind a love of the Great and the Whole. Those who have been led to the same truths step by step, through the constant testimony of their senses, seem to me to want a sense which I possess. They contemplate nothing but *parts*, and all *parts* are necessarily little. And the universe to them is but a mass of *little things*. It is true, that the mind *may* become credulous and prone to superstition by the former method; but are not the experimentalists credulous even to madness in believing any absurdity, rather than believe the grandest truths, if they have not the testimony of their own senses in their favour? I have known some who have been *rationally* educated, as it is styled. They were marked by a microscopic acuteness, but when they looked at great things, all became blank and they saw nothing, and denied (very illogically) that anything could be seen, and uniformly put the negation of a power for the possession of a power, and called the want of imagination judgment and the never being moved to rapture philosophy!'[2]

To this we may add that we see perhaps the Romantic movement most adequately as a protest against the habit of calling want of imagination judgement. To possess a mind open to the envisagement of the strange and different, to contemplate unknown modes of being, divine and otherwise, whether God or genii, or demons or angels or a metamorphosed humanity, to refuse to be buckled down to the evidence of the senses, this is the essential Romanticism which is no mere phenomenon that appeared towards the end of the eighteenth century and died out after fifty years. Coleridge urges credulity; and the creator of *Christabel*, caught up

[1] *Biographia Literaria*, ed. Shawcross, vol. i, p. 134.
[2] *Letters*, ed. Coleridge, vol. i, p. 16. Coleridge's italics.

in the credulity of magic and witchcraft, is also the maturing Coleridge, caught up in the credulity of faith. For the 'shadows of imagination' which he created in *The Ancient Mariner* and *Christabel* there is required, he said, a 'willing suspension of disbelief' which constitutes poetic faith; what he longed for in himself and desired for others was a religious faith which would be, not a suspension of doubt, but, in the supernatural shadows of imagination, an unbroken habit of belief. Therefore the Romantic poet of *Kubla Khan*, the *Mariner*, and *Christabel*, and the theologian and Christian philosopher of *Aids to Reflection* are not two, and disparate, people. Those who see the Christian writer as one who has escaped from the Romantic poet fail to discern the true nature both of Romanticism and of Christianity.

'I used to wish', says Newman of himself in his school-days, 'the *Arabian Nights* were true: my imagination ran on unknown influences, on magical powers, and talismans . . . I thought life might be a dream, or I an Angel, and all this world a deception, my fellow-angels by a playful device concealing themselves from me, and deceiving me with the semblance of a material world.'[1] In recording this in the *Apologia* Newman was of course aware that he was saying something very relevant to the story he was telling. He read Mrs. Radcliffe and Miss Porter; and he took a lifelong delight in Southey's *Thalaba* (a great favourite of Shelley's also). 'I never regarded my *senses* as in any way the criteria of my belief' is a sentence which might as well have occurred in the *Apologia* as in a letter of Coleridge's. A little later in the *Apologia* Newman tells us that during his adolescence God became, if only for a time, 'luminously self-evident'; he always doubted the reality of material phenomena; and later he says that he came to view angels 'not only as the ministers employed by the Creator in the Jewish and Christian dispensations, as we find on the face of scripture, but as carrying on, as Scripture also implies, the Economy of the Visible World. I considered them as the real causes of motion, light, and life, and of those elementary principles of the physical universe, which, when offered in their developments to our senses, suggest to us the notion of cause and effect, and of what are called the laws of nature.' We may think of Kant, Coleridge's master; we may also think of (what above all Wordsworth gave thanks for) Wordsworth's obstinate questionings . . .

Of sense and outward things,
Fallings from us, vanishings;
Blank misgivings of a Creature
Moving about in worlds not realised.

[1] *Apologia*, London, 1864, p. 56.

Now to return to Coleridge, I have suggested that these two things, his belief that 'the speculative intellect' must acknowledge 'a higher or deeper ground than it can itself supply', and his denial that 'want of imagination' is 'judgment', go together and issue from a single sensibility. They are manifested abundantly in his writings and letters in the last decade of the eighteenth century; and together they compose a thread which we can follow through his later books and fragments. The Romantic poet of the great years 1797 and 1798 will indeed change as the years pass and under the stress of difficult experience; but there will be not discontinuity but development. There is no ground for believing that the passage from the poetry of *Christabel* to the difficult prose of the later writings is in any sense a sign of decay. That indeed the contrary is true becomes clear when we bear in mind the great intellectual confusion of the time and the need for good philosophy. That Coleridge's poetic powers declined is undeniable. Without resources of joy, and having to struggle too desperately for any degree of mastery over life to make poetic creation possible, he naturally sought to give foundation and stability to his life by what systematic reflection he could achieve. But, as he followed the philosophical road, most powerful in his mind was still, as in his poetry, the sense of the supernatural and of what at once transcends and breaks through the natural order. Thus, to assert the transcendent and mysterious, and to arrest the claims of the intelligence, were desires which occurred naturally together in his mind.

There is another important respect in which the Romantic poet and the Anglican theologian are at one. In speaking of *Kubla Khan* and *The Ancient Mariner* I observed the contrast which occurs in both poems between a longed-for seclusion and exposure to terror and evil. In *Christabel* also there is terror and the extremity of evil. The tumultuous voices of *Kubla Khan* threatening the paradisal happiness of the Garden, the terror of the becalmed and burning seas with the figures of Death-in-Life and Life-in-Death, are matched in *Christabel* by the embodiment, in Geraldine, of the very essence of evil, which is set over against the perfection and beauty of Christabel. What also Coleridge carries over into his years of religious reflection is the same quality of terror, the same vision of the overwhelming reality of evil. *Christabel* above all affords a sense of evil as something vast, as supernatural in its power and efficacy, creating in our minds revulsion as well as a feeling of helplessness. Now we may doubt if the human mind can come to the highest reaches of spirituality without such perception and such terror. At least we know that widespread through the Middle Ages, the period in which, if we are to judge by its greatest men, the human spirit achieved a finer spirituality than ever before or since, was the fear of unfriendly and evil agencies at work in the world. Forest, sea, mountain, valley, and remote places were sinister; they frightened men as they do not now. In Coleridge's dislike of the wild places of nature, of forest, mountain, and sea, we may discern a certain medieval quality of imagination and, we may believe, a condition and possibility of high religious perception. Similarly, what he conveys in *Christabel*, a vision of pure and supernatural evil, he carries over into his years of Christian experience; he was deeply aware of the sin from which we are rescued, by a mystery which matches the mystery of evil, by a supernatural grace. We are not surprised to find him remarking in a later manuscript, when speculating on the origin of evil, that it may be represented 'in a fearful sense, as αὐτομήτηρ αὐτούσιος'.

§ 5

We repeat, therefore, that it is foolish to sneer at Coleridge's philosophical labours. Coleridge was bemused and befogged, we are told, by philosophy and especially by German transcendentalism (as if anyone of any worth philosophizing at that time could fail to be deeply concerned about the achievement of Kant). Coleridge met with sneers enough in his own time; but also, he answered them conclusively enough. His answer consisted in the view of philosophy which was Plato's. He certainly did not behold the reason (which it was the special purpose of his philosophy to discuss) as the peculiar possession of philosophers, Romantic poets, and Anglican theologians; it is the possession of all men, and equally so, at least in the possibility of its employment. And philosophy, in reflecting on truths implicit in human experience, rescues them from comparative impotence and erects them into sources of power, life, and growth. It was, he tells us in *The Friend*,[1] 'long after the completion of what is called a learned education' that he 'discovered a new world of intellectual profit' opening upon him—'not from any new opinions, but lying, as it were, at the roots of those which I had been taught in childhood in my catechism and spelling-book'. (p. 6) Philosophy, he can therefore say in *Biographia Literaria*, is vain in any man whose spirit is not filled by 'the consciousness of freedom (were it only from its restlessness, as of one struggling in bondage)'; such a man can only 'weary himself out with empty words, to which no friendly echo answers, either from his own heart, or the

[1] Quotations from *The Friend* are made from the Bohn edition, 1890.

heart of a fellow-being';[1] and bewilderment can be the only result. In *The Friend* also he says of Plato that

'... the education of the intellect by awakening the principle and method of self-development, was his proposed object, not any specific information that can be conveyed into it from without; not to assist in storing the passive mind with the various sorts of knowledge most in request, as if the human soul were a mere repository or banqueting-room, but to place it in such relations of circumstance as should gradually excite the germinal power that craves no knowledge but what it can take up into itself, what it can appropriate, and reproduce in fruits of its own. To shape, to dye, to paint over, and to mechanize the mind, he resigned, as their proper trade, to the Sophists, against whom he waged open and unremitting war.' (p. 314)

The imaginative labours of the poet have freedom for their end, the achievement, so far as is possible, of patterns of perception which shall supply order and stability; and so it is with the activity of philosophy. That the way of the one is primarily imaginative and the way of the other primarily intellectual need not obscure the fact that poetry and philosophy alike issue from restlessness of the spirit, 'as of one still struggling in bondage'. It is therefore the merest prejudice to deplore Coleridge's passage from the writing of poetry to the writing of philosophy.

§ 6

In 1801 Coleridge rejected associationism and asserted that the mind can be truly regarded only as an 'active agency' in knowledge. The view he came to take of associationism he expressed with unusual succinctness when he said, in the *Bristol Journal* in 1814, that 'associationism in philosophy is like the term stimulus in medicine; explaining everything, it explains nothing; and above all, leaves itself unexplained. It is an excellent charm to enable a man to talk about anything he likes, and to make himself and his hearers as wise as before.' This is a true judgement and one from which Coleridge never turned back. From this time on Coleridge reiterated in his work two distinctions: that between the imagination and the fancy and that between the understanding and the reason. It was the first of these which occupied a considerable portion of his most important writings up to 1816; after this date he becomes especially concerned with the second. The two distinctions are, however, closely bound up with each other.

Of the difference between the imagination and the fancy as Coleridge expounded it I have written at length elsewhere. But

[1] Vol. i, p. 168.

in order that I may relate, at a later point, Coleridge's view of the relation of imagination to 'reason', and of the ways in which they may be said to come together, I shall give here a brief statement of his doctrine of the imagination which is set out chiefly in the *Biographia Literaria*. He followed Kant in thinking of the imagination as indispensable to all perception of objects. The mind in knowledge is receptive of sense impressions, and also possesses an 'understanding' which supplies categories and rules in terms of which objects may be conceptually apprehended in themselves and in relation to other things. But another and distinct activity is also necessary, to mediate between the receptiveness of sense and the conceptual activity of the intelligence; this is so because in perception we are aware of individual objects which we apprehend directly and which never lose, in perception, their particularity. This activity is the imagination. It, as it were, bodies forth individual objects out of the data of sense; these objects must indeed be apprehended in accordance with the fundamental concepts of the understanding; but the latter must fail to operate without the assistance of an activity more direct than itself. It is, however, of the utmost importance to observe that, while we must distinguish between imagination and understanding, the two activities cannot act in independence of each other.

Upholding the doctrine that imagination is present in the simplest act of perception, Coleridge goes on to distinguish between the perception of everyday life and the perception of the artist. The imagination present in the former he calls 'primary', that in the latter 'secondary'. The 'secondary' imagination is a dissolvent of the utilitarian world of the 'primary', and a re-creation at a level of contemplative interest; it is always a struggle to 'idealize and to unify'. The fancy, however, is not serious; it is trivial (though, it may be, in a good sense); it is, whether it recognizes it or not, playful. But through the imagination, on the other hand, the mind seeks power by the ordered apprehension of reality. In its 'secondary' life, no less than in its 'primary', the imagination cannot act in independence of the understanding; but it yet strives to apprehend a unity beyond the discursive. It must also seek to pass, in its apprehension of the world, beyond the level at which the mind and understanding may rest in apprehension of the wholly organized, and must struggle, as best it can, to find symbol and myth to body forth what at best it feebly apprehends. And here, in its pursuit of symbol for what is transcendent, it becomes one with the reason which seeks the aid of the imagination for the expression of its 'ideas'.

Now the imagination is not sharply separated from the understanding though it may seek to pass beyond it; similarly, the reason and the understanding, though they may be distinguished, must by no means be thought to act in complete independence of each other. Moreover, the understanding may be regarded as a branch (though an inferior branch) of the reason. In making this distinction Coleridge believed he was following closely the usage, as he says in the Appendix to *The Friend*, of 'the great men of Europe from the middle of the fifteenth till towards the close of the seventeenth century'; and he was especially fond of the lines in *Paradise Lost* in which Raphael describes the creation of life and speaks of the soul receiving reason from God—

> . . . and reason is her being,
> Discursive, or Intuitive.

Reason may be discursive; but it also rises above the discursive to vision and immediacy.

Now 'objects' are apprehended by the understanding; or, recalling what we have said of the activity of the imagination in perception, the understanding is necessary for the awareness of objects and of objects in their relation to each other. The understanding with its categories makes possible knowledge of a world of related objects; if the understanding were not active through concepts in interpretation, comparing, and contrasting, the world could not be present to our minds which we must certainly not think of as passive in knowledge. The understanding then is the conceptual intelligence; through it we have knowledge of physical objects which, so far as it goes, is distinct and clear; we may therefore live our lives duly manipulating objects in accordance with our purposes; it is the intelligence in its knowledge of the physical world, whether in common sense or in science. 'The understanding', says Coleridge in the third appendix to the first *Lay Sermon*,[1] 'concerns itself exclusively with the quantities, qualities and relations of particulars in time and space' (p. 339); it 'has no appropriate object but the material world in relation to our worldly interests' (p. 342); at its level we may have distinct knowledge, scientific discovery, and utilitarian ethics, the ethics of prudence. But if the understanding has clearness, it has not depth; 'it entangles itself in contradictions, in the very effort of comprehending the idea of substance' (p. 343)—one of its own essential categories. 'It contemplates the unity of things in their limits only, and is consequently a knowledge of superficies without substance.' (p. 343) It organizes the world for us, but is helpless to explain it. In the language of one of the biographical letters from which I quoted earlier, it 'can contemplate nothing but *parts*; and all *parts* are necessarily little'. It can move only

[1] Quotations from the *Lay Sermons* are made from the Bohn edition, 1894.

within the world and then, so to speak, only upon its surface. In the first *Lay Sermon* Coleridge does not hesitate to use Kantian language, and says that the understanding is 'the science of phenomena. . . . Its functions supply the rules and constitute the possibility of experience; but remain mere logical forms, except as far as materials are given by the senses or sensations.' (p. 339) It is possessed in various degrees by animals, uncivilized people, and by civilized people accomplished in science. But it is the reason and not the understanding which is man's peculiar endowment; it alone makes possible the life of art, of morality which transcends prudence and animal considerations, and of religion.

To what extent, so far, Coleridge is a disciple of Kant is clear. The understanding dictates organization and form to the materials of sense and can therefore supply nothing more than a 'science of phenomena'. And I wish now to pass for a moment from Coleridge to Newman and observe this very doctrine as it comes from the pen of Newman. As Coleridge propounds it, the doctrine is clothed, inevitably, in the heavy technicalities of Kant's language; however important or true, it is second-hand, the utterance of a disciple only. But if we wish to know what the doctrine meant to the 'living intelligence' of Coleridge, we cannot do better than to read Newman who utters it, not as something derived from Kant (whom he never read), a body of doctrine adopted from another mind, but as an expression of a religious sensibility strikingly similar in certain respects to that of Coleridge. The passage is a long one, but justifies its length.

'What if the whole series of impressions, made on us through the senses, be, as I have already hinted, but a Divine economy suited to our need, and the token of realities distinct from themselves, and such as might be revealed to us, nay, more perfectly, by other senses, different from our existing ones as they from each other? What if the properties of matter, as we conceive of them, are merely relative to us, so that facts and events, which seem impossible when predicated concerning it in terms of those impressions, are impossible only in those terms, not in themselves,—impossible only because of the imperfection of the idea, which, in consequence of those impressions, we have conceived of material substances? If so, it would follow that the laws of physics, as we consider them, are themselves but generalizations of economical exhibitions, inferences from figure and shadow, and not more real than the phenomena from which they are drawn. Scripture, for instance, says that the sun moves and the earth is stationary; and science, that the earth moves, and the sun is comparatively at rest. How can we determine which of these opposite statements is the very truth, till we know what motion is? If our idea of motion be but an accidental result of our present senses, neither proposition is true, and both are true; neither true philosophically, both true for certain practical purposes in the system in which they are respectively found; and physical science will have no better meaning when it says that the earth moves, than plane astronomy when it says that the earth is still.

'And should any one fear lest thoughts such as these should tend to a dreary and hopeless scepticism, let him take into account the Being and Providence of God, the Merciful and True; and he will at once be relieved of his anxiety. All is dreary till we believe, what our hearts tell us, that we are subjects of His Governance; nothing is dreary, all inspires hope and trust, directly we understand that we are under His hand, and that whatever comes to us is from Him, as a method of discipline and guidance. What is it to us whether the knowledge He gives us be greater or less, if it be He who gives it? What is it to us whether it be exact or vague, if He bids us trust it? What have we to care whether we are or are not given to divide substance from shadow, if He is training us heavenwards by means of either? Why should we vex ourselves to find whether our deductions are philosophical or no, provided they are religious? If our senses supply the media by which we are put on trial, by which we are all brought together, and hold intercourse with each other, and are disciplined and are taught, and enabled to benefit others, it is enough. We have an instinct within us, impelling us, we have external necessity forcing us, to trust our senses, and we may leave the question of their substantial truth for another world, "till the day break, and the shadows flee away".'[1]

I do not wish to suggest that this passage conforms to the letter of Kant's teaching; but in its scepticism at least it is very near to it, however much it is part and parcel of a sensibility which (like that of Coleridge) was in many respects profoundly different from Kant's. Newman never tires of letting his sceptical mind play upon our knowledge; he never exercises it, indeed, in any petty or vainglorious spirit, but apologetically, making the ground crumble under our feet as he gently presses us on to a vantage-point in faith from which all scepticism is seen to be unimportant. He is content to withhold his judgement on its truth or otherwise; but, like Kant, he makes us blind that we may walk by faith.

It is then of value to consider Coleridge and Newman together in this respect. It is of extraordinary interest for the history of philosophy to observe the result of the philosophy of Kant in Coleridge and of the philosophies of Locke and Hume in Newman. As surely as Coleridge was a disciple of Kant, Newman's epistemology is derived from Locke and Hume. It is only necessary to read the sermon from which I have quoted to see how true is this statement concerning Newman. That Kant should have given us Coleridge, and Hume Newman, is not only wonderful in itself; it also throws a penetrating light on Kant and Hume in their relation to each other and on their importance in the history

[1] *Sermons preached before the University of Oxford*, London, 1890, p. 347.

of thought. This, however, is by the way. What is of outstanding importance for our purpose is the unity of Coleridge and Newman in a doctrine which they will employ for the advancement of faith.

§ 7

I shall now pass on to speak of Coleridge's doctrine of the reason, and to see in what way and to what extent he followed Kant in the latter's famous teaching of the primacy of the practical reason. I have previously given a number of quotations from Coleridge's early letters and from the *Biographia Literaria* which make clear that he found Kant's philosophy more an extension of his own thoughts than a surprising revelation.

We can now see what Coleridge means when he says in the *Aids to Reflection*[1] that 'the Judgments of the Understanding are binding only in relation to the objects of the Senses, which we *reflect* under the forms of the Understanding' (p. 208). Now of the reason, he says the following:

'On the contrary, Reason is the Power of Universal and necessary Convictions, the Source and Substance of Truths above Sense, having their evidence in themselves. Its presence is always marked by the *necessity* of the position affirmed: this necessity being *conditional*, when a truth of Reason is applied to Facts of Experience, or to the rules and maxims of the Understanding; but *absolute* when the subject matter is itself the growth or offspring of the Reason. Hence arises a distinction in the Reason itself, derived from the different mode of applying it, and from the objects to which it is directed: accordingly as we consider one and the same gift, now as the ground of formal principles, and now as the origin of *Ideas*. Contemplated distinctively in reference to formal (or abstract) truth, it is the speculative Reason; but in reference to *actual* (or moral) truth, as the fountain of Ideas and the *Light* of the Conscience, we name it the *practical* Reason.' (pp. 206–7)

What needs to be emphasized in this passage is, first, that the reason is the source of '*convictions*' having to do with what is above sense; secondly, that the reason when practical supplies *actual* truth unlike the theoretical reason which supplies only *abstract* truth; thirdly, that the judgements of the practical reason are necessary and *absolute*. Now it is to be observed that in this passage Coleridge allows the use of the word 'reason' to describe the understanding so far as in its procedure with the world of sense-experience it has an *a priori* validity.[2] In this indeed he

1 The page references will be to the edition of 1836.

2 For an exposition of reason in this narrow sense see *The Friend* (p. 97), where Coleridge speaks of it as a 'faculty' to be distinguished from reason as a 'spiritual organ' active in religion.

was following the procedure of Kant in the earlier portions of the *Critique* where reason is the faculty of the *a priori* in all knowledge whatsoever. Thus Coleridge was able to use Kant's authority for Milton's statement that reason may be 'discursive or intuitive'. But generally, by 'reason' Coleridge means the 'practical' reason; and he says, in the Appendix to the *Aids* (p. 406): 'The practical reason alone *is* Reason in the full and substantive sense.'

The practical reason then (or the reason simply as we shall employ the word) supplies 'convictions', 'ideas', 'actual truth' in regard to matters which have not to do with sense. To show what Coleridge meant by the practical reason as productive of ideas, I shall quote the following passage from the first *Lay Sermon* (which was published in 1816):

'Notions, the depthless abstractions of fleeting phenomena, the shadows of sailing vapours, the colourless repetitions of rainbows, have effected their utmost when they have added to the distinctness of our knowledge. For this very cause they are of themselves adverse to lofty emotion, and it requires the influence of a light and warmth, not their own, to make them crystallize into a semblance of growth. But every principle is actualized by an idea; and every idea is living, productive, partaketh of infinity. . . . Hence too it is, that notions, linked arguments, reference to particular facts and calculations of prudence, influence only the comparatively few, the men of leisurely minds who have been trained up to them: and even these few they influence but faintly. But for the reverse, I appeal to the general character of the doctrines which have collected the most numerous sects, and acted upon the moral being of the converts, with a force that might well seem supernatural! The great principles of our religion, the sublime ideas spoken out everywhere in the Old and New Testament, resemble the fixed stars, which appear of the same size to the naked as to the armed eye; the magnitude of which the telescope may rather seem to diminish than to increase. At the annunciation of principles, of ideas, the soul of man awakes, and starts up, as an exile in a far distant land at the unexpected sounds of his native language, when after long years of absence, and almost of oblivion, he is suddenly addressed in his own mother-tongue. He weeps for joy, and embraces the speaker as his brother.' (p. 318)

An 'idea' then is not abstract or notional; it is accompanied by strong emotion; it issues into action; it lives and grows. Light, warmth, and growth; these are the properties of 'ideas'; that is to say, they are the possession of the 'soul of man', reverberating, so to speak, through his total personality and possessed by it in feeling and will no less than in knowledge. In contrast to 'ideas', 'notions', and 'linked arguments' are cold, unproductive, and ungrowing. The abstract or speculative reason 'applies a truth of reason to Facts of Experience, or to the rules and maxims of the understanding'; but, when we speak of the practical reason, the 'subject matter is itself the growth or offspring of the Reason'. In describing the action of the practical reason we must use biological terms; an 'idea' 'grows' out of the 'life' of the man; and becomes, as it develops, a source of further life and power to its possessor. Indeed, it is only in terms of its 'ideas' that we can speak of the 'growth' of a personality at all.

It will be clear to the reader that Newman's doctrine, in *The Grammar of Assent*, of notional and real assent is very relevant to the passage I have just quoted from Coleridge. In the first portion of chapter 4 of the *Grammar*, Newman speaks of 'notional assent'; and among 'notional assents' he classifies what he calls 'presumption'. In speaking of 'presumption' he has in mind chiefly those 'first principles or notions' which Kant called 'categories' and which, following Kant, Coleridge attributed to the understanding, in its organization of sense-experience. And, as Coleridge in the *Aids to Reflection* passes from speaking of the understanding to the idea of the practical reason, so does Newman pass in his next chapter to speak of real assents. I shall, however, find it convenient to quote immediately, not from *The Grammar of Assent* but from the *Essay on Development* in which Newman, in expounding the meaning of 'idea', is also expounding what in later years he was to call 'real assent'. It will be clear that what he says is close to the teaching of Coleridge.

'When an idea, whether real or not, is of a nature to arrest and possess the mind, it may be said to have life, that is, to live in the mind which is its recipient. Thus mathematical ideas, real as they are, can hardly properly be called living, at least ordinarily. But when some great enunciation, whether true or false, about human nature, or present good, or government, or duty, or religion, is carried forward into the public throng of men and draws attention, then it is not merely received passively in this or that form into many minds, but it becomes an active principle within them, leading them to an ever-new contemplation of itself, to an application of it in various directions, and a propagation of it on every side. Such is the doctrine of the divine right of kings, or of the rights of man, or of the anti-social bearings of a priesthood, or utilitarianism . . . doctrines which are of a nature to attract and influence, and have so far a *primâ facie* reality, that they may be looked at on many sides and strike various minds very variously. . . . It will, in proportion to its native vigour and subtlety, introduce itself into the framework and details of social life, changing public opinion, and strengthening or undermining the foundations of established order. Thus in time it will have grown into an ethical code, or into a system of government, or into a theology, or into a ritual, according to its capabilities: and this body of thought, thus laboriously gained, will after all be little more than the proper representative of one idea, being in substance what that idea meant from the first, its complete image as seen in a combination of diversified aspects, with the suggestions and corrections of many minds, and the illustration of many experiences.

'This process, whether it be longer or shorter in point of time, by which the aspects of an idea are brought into consistency and form, I call its development, being the germination and maturation of some truth or apparent truth on a large mental field. . . . The development then of an idea is not like an investigation worked out on paper, in which each successive advance is a pure evolution from a foregoing, but it is carried on through and by means of communities of men and their leaders and guides; and it employs their minds as its instruments, and depends upon them, while it uses them. And so, as regards existing opinions, principles, measures, and institutions of the community which it has invaded; it develops by establishing relations between itself and them; it employs itself, in giving them a new meaning and direction, in creating what may be called a jurisdiction over them, in throwing off whatever in them it cannot assimilate. It grows when it incorporates, and ts identity is found, not in isolation, but in continuity and sovereignty.'[1]

It will be seen that Newman emphasizes, no less than Coleridge, that growth is the mark of the 'idea' and that this growth is momentous for the whole life of both individual and society.

It follows from this that an 'idea' is highly individual, unlike the generalizations and discoveries of the understanding which are common and wholly shareable, impersonal and colourless and cold. Through the 'understanding' and speculative reason or 'notions', we co-operate, in Newman's words, 'in the establishment of a common measure between mind and mind'; but 'ideas' or 'real apprehension and assent' 'depend on personal experience'; and the experience of one man is not the experience of another. 'Real assent, as the experience which it presupposes, is proper to the individual, and, as such, thwarts rather than promotes the intercourse of man with man.' (*Grammar*, chap. 4, pt. 2.) How the peculiar 'privacy' of ideas may be overcome, as it must be in politics, poetry, and religion, we need not now pause to consider. But the central argument of *The Grammar of Assent*, which turns upon the illative sense, is designed to expand and defend the individuality of all thought which is important, in all but quite extraneous ways, to human life. 'Actual' truth is come to by the illative sense and through no formal process of inference. A man's progress, said Newman again, 'is a living growth, not a mechanism; and its instruments are mental acts, not the formulas and contrivances of language'.

So much, then, for the nature of the 'ideas' to which Coleridge

[1] *Essay on Development of Christian Doctrine* (1891), pp. 36–9.

and Newman attach so much importance. Now in speaking of the practical reason, it will be observed that Coleridge says that it is the source of 'actual (or moral) truth'. It is, he says elsewhere, 'the organ of the supersensuous'; it is also the 'light of the conscience'. The practical reason then is identified with the conscience, or is the light by which the conscience moves and acts. The understanding may provide accurate knowledge in the sensuous order; the practical reason alone provides the truths concerning that which is not sensuous. We would be near enough to Coleridge in calling the practical reason the moral reason. Moreover, the ideas which the practical reason provides are, says Coleridge, 'unconditionally necessary'; the light of the conscience is infallible; the necessity of truths of the reason (when 'the subject matter is itself the growth or offspring of the Reason') is absolute.

§ 8

Now there are at least two important respects in which Coleridge differs, in his doctrine of the reason, from Kant. He has agreed with Kant in his distinction between the speculative and the practical reason and in his belief that the practical reason alone can be said to have any competence in dealing with what lies beyond the sensuous. But there are differences. The first is chiefly perhaps one of feeling, of difference between the temperaments and sensibilities of the two men. The other is a cardinal point of doctrine.

In the first place, the ideas of the reason as Coleridge represents them are apprehended with 'warmth' and 'enthusiasm'; as they are represented by Kant they are and should be apprehended with impersonality and with a forbidding denial of feeling. In the paragraph in the first *Lay Sermon* preceding that from which I have quoted, in which Coleridge contrasts 'notions' and 'ideas', we find the following sentences. Coleridge has been speaking of the 'inadequacy of the mere understanding to the apprehension of moral greatness'; and he goes on to say that

'... histories incomparably more authentic than Mr. Hume's (nay, spite of himself even his own history), confirm by irrefragable evidence the aphorism of ancient wisdom, that nothing great was ever achieved without enthusiasm. For what is enthusiasm but the oblivion and swallowing-up of self in an object dearer than self, or in an idea more vivid?—How this is produced in the enthusiasm of wickedness, I have explained in the third comment annexed to this discourse. But in the genuine enthusiasm of morals, religion, and patriotism, this enlargement and elevation of the soul above its mere self attest the presence, and accompany the intuition of ultimate principles alone. These alone can interest the undegraded human spirit deeply and enduringly, because these alone belong to its essence, and will remain with it permanently.' (p. 318)

Similarly, in the passage from which I quoted earlier, he deplores the adverseness of notions to 'lofty emotion'. Now this is not the language and accent of Kant in speaking of morals. No one indeed will deny the nobility and profundity of Kant's ethic; but certainly he desired to extrude from moral action all that savoured of enthusiasm, love, and passion. This is the manner of Kant's representation of morality; and it is not Coleridge's. For Coleridge says 'what is enthusiasm but the oblivion and swallowing-up of self in an object dearer than self?' He believes that what is ethical issues from vividness of imagination and from love no less than from the rational will; that it is (and in all this Newman is entirely at one with him) intensely personal and not, as in Kant, very impersonal.

Yet, having observed that this is so, it is important also to observe that neither Coleridge nor Newman was an addict to mere 'enthusiasm'. No one, probably, would think of making the charge against Newman. It would be equally groundless if made against Coleridge. In an introductory aphorism in the *Aids to Reflection*, he says:

'If acquiescence without insight; if warmth without light; if an immunity from doubt, given and guaranteed by a resolute ignorance; if the habit of taking for granted the words of a catechism, remembered or forgotten; if a mere sensation of positiveness substituted (I will not say, for the sense of certainty; but) for that calm assurance, the very means and conditions of which it supersedes; if a belief that seeks the darkness, and yet strikes no root, immoveable as the limpet from the rock, and like the limpet, fixed there by mere force of adhesion; if these suffice to make men Christians, in what sense could the apostle affirm that believers receive, not indeed worldly wisdom, that comes to nought, but the wisdom of God, that we might know and comprehend the things that are freely given to us of God?' (p. 9)

And later on in the *Aids* he says that he would commence the theological studies of a

'...young man of Talent, desirous to establish his opinions and belief on solid principles, and in the light of distinct understanding,—I would commence his theological studies, or, at least, that most important part of them respecting the aids which Religion promises in our attempts to realize the ideas of Morality, by bringing together all the passages scattered throughout the Writings of Swift and Butler, that bear on Enthusiasm, Spiritual Operations, and pretences to the Gifts of the

Spirit, with the whole train of New Lights, Raptures, Experiences, and the like.' (p. 68)

It is clear then that Coleridge is by no means anxious to urge mere feeling; and that he was aware that feeling, no less than reason and will, required discipline.

The second important difference lies in Coleridge's unhesitating assertion, in the passage which I quoted, of the unconditional truth of the ideas of the reason. The reason, he says, is a 'source of *actual* truth'. Where 'the subject matter is itself the growth or offspring of the Reason', 'its presence is always marked by the necessity of the position affirmed'. And this necessity is not at all conditional but absolute. Now this again is not Kant's manner of speaking about the ideas of the reason. The necessity which Kant is willing to ascribe to the ideas of the reason is a *practical* necessity; we assert the three leading ideas of the reason, the freedom of the will, the immortality of the soul, and the existence of God in and through our moral action. Belief in freedom, the immortality of the soul, the existence of God, is implicit in morality; in moral action we act as if they were true, and cannot help doing so, whether we acknowledge them or not; and it is the actual life of morality, and neither the understanding nor the speculative reason, which gives us religious knowledge. But Kant, in his suspicion of *Schwärmerei*, viewed religion as something of an appendage, however necessary, to the moral life; and the coldness of Kant's religion is the consequence of his predominant concern with morality; religion becomes an aid and ancillary to morality; morality is not, as it is to the religious soul, the way to the love and vision of God.

Now this places Kant and Coleridge at a great remove from each other. Coleridge agrees that the speculative reason is incompetent to establish the ideas of the reason; but in the matter of the practical reason, which 'alone is reason in a substantial sense', it leads us, in Coleridge's view, to certainty and absolute truth; not to ideas merely necessary for the practice of the moral life, but to ideas which show the moral life its end and goal which are outside itself. This difference is crucial. Kant's ethic is cold, forbidding, impersonal; and so is his representation of God. Coleridge's ethic has 'warmth' as well as 'light', and so also therefore has his religion. To Coleridge morality leads to what its ideas disclose; to Kant what the reason discloses may only reinforce the reason. The difference between the two men, united in their belief in the primacy of the practical reason, becomes clear when we examine the ends to which that primacy leads in their respective doctrines. The practical reason then, for Coleridge, supplies certainty; its strong light discloses what is absolutely true.[1] The 'notions' and 'linked arguments' of the theoretical reason cannot do this.

§ 9

I wish now to speak of Coleridge's attitude to the theoretical or speculative reason. So far, I have spoken of the positive doctrine that it is the practical reason which supplies truth concerning what is beyond the sensible; it is worth while to stress for a moment the negative side of this teaching, the impotence of the speculative reason in matters which lie beyond the range of the distinct knowledge of sense possible to science. We shall then be in a better position to understand all that is involved in Coleridge's positive teaching.

'I look round in vain', he said, 'to discover a vacant place for a science, the result of which is to be the knowledge and ascertainment of God, i.e. of the reality and existence of the Supreme Being in the absence or rejection of the idea as the Datum, and the result anticipated and pre-contained in the premise.'[2] If, that is to say, we come upon the idea of God we come upon it as a 'Datum' or not at all. Now Coleridge has followed Kant in seeing the intelligence with its categories and concepts as the 'faculty judging according to sense'; it makes possible a world of objects, and through that act makes also possible distinct knowledge of that world. It is also to be observed that he will not allow to mathematics anything more than a 'conditional necessity';[3] here he follows Kant once more and breaks with Platonic teaching and with the English Platonists of the seventeenth century. Therefore he has no way, nor does he desire a way, in which he can hope to give demonstration of the truth of religion. Belief in God is something come to by the reason; no science, employing the understanding, may prove that He exists.

[1] The rashness of this doctrine is clear from a use to which Coleridge puts it in the *Aids to Reflection* (p. 105). There he avows his 'conviction that the doctrine of imputed Righteousness, rightly and scripturally interpreted, is so far from being *irrational* or *immoral*, that Reason itself prescribes the idea in order to give a *meaning* and an ultimate Object to Morality; and that the Moral Law in the Conscience demands its reception in order to give reality and substantive existence to the idea presented by the Reason'. Coleridge has no doubt of the truth of the doctrine; it is a necessary idea of the reason. But who, in the event of disagreement, is to adjudicate on its truth? Newman, for example, began as a Calvinist; but he had not been long at Oxford before he ceased to hold any such doctrines as this; and then, like many other people, before, then, and later, he held that the doctrine *is* immoral. Thus, these two men, united in so many respects, especially in their exaltation of the 'practical' reason, differ deeply on what Coleridge alleges to be unmistakably an 'idea of the reason'. It is obvious that Coleridge is on dangerous ground; but what kind of safe ground can he give against the dangers implicit in such a doctrine?

[2] Quoted from a MS. in Muirhead, *Coleridge as Philosopher*, p. 223.

[3] Muirhead, pp. 223–4.

He discerns the origin of the idea of God in the reason, the 'ground of its reality in the conscience and the confirmation and progressive development of it in the order and harmony of the visible world'. He is indeed willing to see confirmation of the idea in the order of the natural world; but nowhere does he with any urgency and confidence make that order a ground for argumentation; if he is ever tempted to do so he also shows that he is aware that any God thus 'proved' would be at best a God suitable for Deists. Also, he does not believe that *demonstration* of the idea of God can be derived from the experience of conscience. This is how he speaks of these matters in the *Aids to Reflection* (p. 61). He says that it is reasonable to believe in a 'Universal Power as the cause and pre-condition of the harmony of all the particular Wholes' in nature. Neither here nor anywhere else does he press this consideration as proof. And he goes on to ask if it is then 'unreasonable . . .. to entertain a similar belief in relation to the System of intelligent and self-conscious Beings, to the moral and personal World?' This much only he will say, that it is 'not unreasonable'; to so much does his natural theology come. He is willing to maintain a natural theology, so far as it goes. But he is aware of its limits. For he says in the following paragraph that though the argument he had advanced is merely 'negative', it is sufficient to render the 'union of Religion and Morality *conceivable*; sufficient to satisfy an unprejudiced Inquirer that the spiritual doctrines of the Christian Religion are not at war with the reasoning Faculty, and that if they do not run on the same Line (or Radius) with the Understanding, yet neither do they cut or cross it'. This is to say that at best religious belief can be shown not to be patently irrational. What, however, he is certain of is that 'from whichever of the two points the reason may start: from the things that are seen to the One Invisible, or from the Idea of the absolute One to the things that are seen, it will find a chasm, which the *moral* being only, which the spirit and religion of man alone can fill up or overbridge'.[1] The gap is bridged, that is to say, not by arguments based on moral experience, but by the 'moral being' itself, by the 'spirit and religion of man'. For the moral being itself to fall back on argument is to be told that it is 'not unreasonable' in its beliefs; on the other hand, the gap is bridged by itself in act. In his *Confessio Fidei* printed in the *Omniana*[2] we find him declaring that it is 'evident to his reason' that 'the existence of God is absolutely and necessarily insusceptible of a scientific demonstration'.

If at best argument can give but a 'negative conception', an assurance of not being irrational, the practical reason alone can

[1] Quoted by Muirhead, p. 108. [2] Oxford, 1917, p. 406.

afford a 'positive insight', for 'spiritual truths can only spiritually be discerned' (*Aids*, p. 62). Now as we have remarked, the practical reason might be called the moral reason; and Coleridge calls 'actual' truth 'moral' truth. It is through obedience to conscience alone that we come to know what is real in the spiritual world. This was Coleridge's cardinal doctrine, as it was also Newman's. Now it is by the conscience that we are distinguished from animals. Coleridge allows to animals a measure of 'understanding' though they have not the understanding 'irradiated', as he says, by the *a priori* faculty of the reason; but we have, in behaviour, 'a fidelity to our own being' which the animals do not possess. In this sense of 'fealty' what is human may be said properly to begin. 'It appears then that even the very first step, that the initiation of the process, the becoming conscious of a conscience, partakes of the nature of an act. It is an act by which we take upon ourselves an allegiance, and consequently the obligation of fealty; and this fealty or fidelity, implying the power of being unfaithful, is the first and fundamental sense of Faith.'[1] Now reason as it operates in the will no longer has to do with the understanding which, in the apprehension of the physical world, it may be said to make fecund through the faculty of the *a priori*; it is removed in its operation from the world of sense and 'irradiates' the will; still a faculty of the universal indeed, but having unconditional validity, operative in act. It stands 'in antagonism to all mere individual interests as so many selves, to the personal will as seeking its objects in the manifestation of itself for itself . . . whether this be realised with adjuncts, as in the lust of the flesh and in the lust of the eye; or without adjuncts as in the thirst and pride of power, despotism, egoistic ambition'.[2] Now as thus active in conscience, irradiating both will and feeling, the reason is identified, in faith, with the will of God; the experience of fealty is to what is superior and outside us. This superior is God, who as perfect reason both acts upon us and is the end of our life. For the reason stands above individual claims whether of the self or of other loved selves:

'. . . he that can permit his emotions [i.e. his love for others] to rise to an equality with universal reason, is in enmity with that reason. Here, then, reason appears as the love of God; and its antagonist is attachment to individuals wherever it exists in diminution of or in competition with, the love which is reason.' (p. 348)

Finally, I shall quote the last paragraph of the *Essay on Faith*.

'Faith subsists in the synthesis of the Reason and the individual Will. By virtue of the latter, therefore, it must be an energy, and, inasmuch

[1] *Essay on Faith*, Bohn edition, London, 1884, p. 343. [2] Ibid., p. 347

as it relates to the whole moral man, it must be exerted in each and all of his constituents or incidents, faculties and tendencies;—it must be a total, not a partial—a continuous, not a desultory or occasional—energy. And by virtue of the former, that is, Reason, Faith must be a Light, a form of knowing, a beholding of Truth. In the incomparable words of the Evangelist, therefore,—*Faith must be a Light originating in the Logos, or the substantial Reason, which is co-eternal and one with the Holy Will, and which Light is at the same time the Life of men.* Now, as *Life* is here the sum or collective of all moral and spiritual acts, in suffering, doing, and being, so is Faith the source and the sum, the energy and the principle of the fidelity of Man to God, by the subordination of his human Will, in all provinces of his nature, to his Reason, as the sum of spiritual Truth, representing and manifesting the Will Divine.'[1]

Therefore the reason as it animates will and feeling is the *life* of man—'all of his constituents or incidents, faculties and tendencies'; it is also a beholdment of truth. But it is not merely a beholdment; it is also the light by which we behold, and is not human in the manner of the understanding but divine, and divinely given. Thus Coleridge enters into a tradition of religious thought which goes far back, in the history of civilization, before Kant. It is true that Kant allows that the reverence we feel for the moral law in its demands on us is indeed the kind of feeling we have for someone superior to and above us; but for the most part it is the action of the reason in the human conscience in itself which holds his attention. Certainly, of religion as love for the Divine and as the love of the Divine for the human there is little enough in Kant's philosophy. This may indeed be due in large part to his fear of anthropomorphism, to his dislike of crude attempts of the understanding to imagine and conceive God; but this fear and this dislike showed themselves, paradoxically, in his crude representation of God only in terms of the effects of his activity, namely in securing a final adjustment of merit and consequence; also, in his anxiety to maintain the autonomy of the ethical, he yet goes on to speak of God in a way which revolts the disinterestedness of the spirit of religion. Certainly it appeared so to Coleridge; and having followed Kant so far in the assertion of the absolute primacy of the practical reason, Coleridge, acting in response to his own experience, passes on to speak of the life of religion in a manner which is certainly not that of Kant. He did not at all go back on his discipleship of Kant in the matter of the primacy of the practical reason. He maintained that primacy; but he beheld in the conscience and its law, first and foremost, certainly not something human by which we may be impressed to the point of reverence, but something divine, the indwelling of

1 p. 349. The italics are Coleridge's.

the Divine Reason which acts upon us, seeking to draw us to knowledge of itself, and which obtains from us not merely reverence but worship. In the philosophy of Coleridge the autonomy of the ethical is collapsed; the ethical occurs through the action of the Divine Reason on the creaturely and animal. Coleridge attempts no uneasy compromise between the ethical and the religious as did Kant. With him it is the energies and initiative of God which are primary, not, as with Kant, an autonomous moral consciousness. And at this point Coleridge linked his thought to Christian theology, seeing in the reason, in the conscience of mankind, the activity of the eternal logos. Here he places himself outside the Kantian manner of thinking and re-enters the Christian-Platonic tradition.

§ 10

How similar were Newman's beliefs on these matters I shall now try briefly to show. Now Coleridge and Newman are united in this; that they rest their religion on the experience of conscience: on a belief in the need for holiness; and in the conscience as that through which, in its development, the spiritual is disclosed and known. Now in the second of the *University Sermons*, preached in 1830, Newman speaks of natural theology in the manner of Coleridge; he remarks, in a footnote, added in a later edition, on the similarity between what he says and what Coleridge had said on these topics. And when we turn to the tenth sermon, we read, 'It is indeed a great question whether Atheism is not as philosophically consistent with the phenomena of the physical world, taken by themselves, as the doctrine of a creative and governing Power. But, however this be, the practical safeguard against Atheism in the case of scientific inquirers is the inward need and desire, the inward experience of that Power, existing in the mind before and independently of their examination of His material world.' He shows little interest in the so-called evidences of religion; they belonged peculiarly, he says, to the eighteenth century, 'a time when love was cold'; and he acknowledges that he shares the contemporary disposition to think lightly of the eighteenth century and its 'boasted demonstrations'.

In the majority of these sermons, which were preached at various dates between 1826 and 1843, Newman discusses the relation of faith to reason, and the nature of both. We must, of course, bear in mind that reason, as Newman ordinarily uses the word, means what Coleridge called the 'understanding', both in its exercise in science and in speculative philosophy; Newman calls reason the 'wisdom of the world' as Coleridge called the understanding 'the mind of the flesh'. (Coleridge would have deplored Newman's employment of the word 'reason' for the purposes the latter had in mind.) Newman, unread in Kant, made no distinction between the understanding along with its philosophical offspring, the speculative reason, on the one hand, and, on the other, the practical reason. This distinction was of course crucial to Coleridge; the corresponding distinction in Newman's writings, expounded both in the *University Sermons* and in *The Grammar of Assent*, and equally crucial to Newman, is between what in the former he calls explicit and implicit reason and between what in the latter he calls formal inference and 'natural' inference or the illative sense.

Now the action of the illative sense may, Newman holds, be illustrated in the discoveries of scientific genius or in the strategy of a great general who comes to decisions and conclusions by a way, apparently mysterious, other than that of formal argumentation. But where genius is not in question, that same power of discernment is at work in the human mind. Not that such a process is irrational or opposed to 'reason'; it is only that it is a mode of reasoning which 'is a living spontaneous energy within us, not an art' (p. 257); and it proceeds on 'grounds which are not fully brought out'. (p. 208) Hence it is that 'clearness in argument certainly is not indispensable to reasoning well. Accuracy in stating doctrines or principles is not essential to feeling and acting upon them.... How a man reasons is as much a mystery as how he remembers.' (p. 259) Reasoning of this sort is the activity of the total personality; or at least, more and more of the whole life of a man is involved in his 'reasoning' as we pass from scientific investigation to morals and religion. And here Newman does not shrink from saying that if 'faith . . . does not demand evidence so strong as is necessary for what is commonly considered a rational conviction', it is because it is swayed by 'antecedent considerations' and by 'previous notices, prepossessions, and (in a good sense of the word) prejudices'. (p. 187) He acknowledges that the 'mind that believes is acted upon by its own hopes, fears and existing opinions'; but he holds none the less that faith is a 'process of the Reason, in which so much of the grounds of inference cannot be exhibited, so much lies in the character of the mind itself . . . that it will ever seem to the world irrational and despicable;—till, that is, the event confirms it'. (p. 218)

Also, faith, in which this mode of reasoning is exhibited in its highest reaches, is 'altogether a practical principle'. Newman says of faith that 'it judges and decides because it cannot help doing so, for the sake of the man himself, who exercises it—not in the way of opinion, not as aiming at abstract truth, not as teaching some theory or view. It is the act of a mind feeling that it is its duty any how, under its particular circumstances, to judge and to act.' (p. 298) Here the illative sense, in the realm of morality and faith, is the 'practical reason'. Faith is 'exercised under a sense of personal responsibility', under the pursuit by the individual himself of the good life.

Newman does not hesitate to call faith 'a presumption about matters of fact, upon principle rather than on knowledge'. And he proceeds to ask, 'Its grounds being thus conditional, what does it issue in?' (p. 297) He replies that it issues in the absolute acceptance of certain things as divine; 'that is, it starts from probabilities, yet it ends in peremptory statements, if so be, mysterious or at least beyond experience'.

Now while he upholds such statements, arrived at by faith acting on 'personal responsibility', as absolutely true, he will not acknowledge that the reason *speculating* merely on what is 'beyond experience' can be anything more than what, using Kant's term without knowing it, he calls dogmatism. He also describes such action of the speculative reason as ending in bigotry. When there is no preceding life, committed earnestly to the pursuit of good and to all it must imply, 'when our presumptions take a wide range, when they affect to be systematical and philosophical, when they are indulged in matters of speculation, not of conduct, not in reference to self, but to others, then it is that they deserve the name of bigotry and dogmatism'. (p. 299) And he adds, using a figure Coleridge would enthusiastically have applauded, 'in such a case we make a wrong use of such light as is given us, and mistake what is "a lantern unto our feet" for the sun in the heavens'.

We observed Newman's remark that 'It is indeed a great question whether Atheism is not as philosophically consistent with the phenomena of the physical world, taken by themselves, as the doctrine of a creative and governing Power'. So speaks 'explicit reason' or the 'mind of the flesh'; and, from the point of view of that mind, Newman would have been willing to rank the latter doctrine as being as much a piece of dogmatism as the former. Now Newman did not deny the possibility of metaphysical philosophy. But he did hold that, if it is to exist, it must proceed on certain conditions. What, he asks, is the 'true office, and what the legitimate bounds, of these abstract exercises of Reason . . . ?' Here is the critical question, cardinal to him as to Coleridge. He replies: 'They are in their highest and most honourable place, when they are employed upon the vast field of Knowledge, not in conjecturing unknown truths, but in comparing, adjusting, connecting, explaining facts and doctrines ascertained.' (p. 294) That is to say, in science, where sense-experience provides us with ascertainable fact. But, he adds, 'where the exercise of Reason much outstrips our Knowledge; where knowledge is limited, and reason active; where ascertained truths are scanty, and courses of thought abound; there indulgence of system is unsafe, and may be dangerous. . . . System, which is the very soul . . . of philosophy when exercised upon adequate knowledge, does but make, or tend to make, theorists, dogmatists, philosophists and sectarians, when or so far as knowledge is limited or incomplete.' (p. 295) Does this then mean that metaphysical philosophy is altogether impossible? He replies that it does, except when philosophy proceeds on 'doctrines ascertained'; and he instances Butler, 'the ancient Catholic Divines, nay, in their measure, those illustrious thinkers of the Middle Ages, who have treated of the Christian Faith on system, Athanasius, Augustine, Aquinas'. In other words, philosophy which proceeds without truths obtained by faith or practical reason is in vain; reason of the systematizing kind can act only in 'comparing, adjusting, connecting, explaining facts and doctrines ascertained'. Where, therefore, what is in dispute are not 'facts and doctrines ascertained' from the sensible world, as in science, but matters relating to what is beyond sense-experience, the reason can act properly only on knowledge provided by faith. So also Coleridge. As we have seen, he allows to the speculative reason the privilege of determining what he calls the 'negative truth' of 'what we are required to believe'; and Coleridge continues, 'but the *duty*, and in some cases and for some persons even the *right*, of thinking on subjects beyond the bounds of sensible experience; the grounds of the *real* truth; the *Life*, the *Substance*, the *Hope*, the *Love*, in one word, the *Faith*: these are the derivatives from the practical, moral and spiritual Nature and Being of Man'. (*Aids*, p. 177)

§ 11

Now all this may, at first sight, appear to be remote from what ordinarily we think of as the 'Romantic movement'. In fact, it is not so; and it will be to some advantage to look back to some of the writers of whom we have already spoken. If we do so, we recall that they had a great deal to say about 'imagination'. Keats, for example, writes in this way. He is writing to Bailey, and says:

'O I wish I was as certain of the end of all your troubles as that of your momentary start about the authenticity of the Imagination. I am certain of nothing but of the holiness of the Heart's affections, and the truth of Imagination—What the Imagination seizes as Beauty must be truth. . . . The Imagination may be compared to Adam's dream—he awoke and found it truth. I am more zealous in this affair, because I have never yet been able to perceive how anything can be known for truth by consecutive reasoning—and yet it must be. Can it be that even the greatest Philosopher ever arrived at his goal without putting aside numerous objections. However it may be, O for a Life of Sensations rather than of Thoughts! It is "a Vision in the form of Youth" a shadow of reality to come—and this consideration has further convinced me for it has come as auxiliary to another favourite Speculation of mine, that we shall enjoy ourselves here after by having what we called happiness on Earth repeated in a finer tone. And yet such a fate can only befall those who delight in Sensation rather than hunger as you do after Truth. Adam's dream will do here, and seems to be a conviction that Imagination and its empyreal reflection, is the same as human Life and its Spiritual repetition.' (p. 67)

Now I wish first to call attention to Keats's question: 'Can it be that even the greatest Philosopher ever arrived at his goal without putting aside numerous objections?'; and to his remark in the same letter that 'I am the more zealous in this affair, because I have never yet been able to perceive how anything can be known for truth by consecutive reasoning'. Now alongside this I wish to place the following sentences from Newman:

'It is not too much to say that there is no one of the greater achievements of the Reason, which would show to advantage, which would be apparently justified and protected from criticism, if thrown into the technical forms which the science of argument requires. . . . Let it be considered how rare and immaterial (if I may use the words) is metaphysical proof: how difficult to embrace, even when presented to us by philosophers in whose clearness of mind and good sense we fully confide; and what a vain system of words without ideas such men seem to be piling up, while perhaps we are obliged to confess that it must be we who are dull, not they who are fanciful; and that, whatever be the character of their investigations, we want the vigour or flexibility of mind to judge of them.' (*University Sermons*, pp. 216–17)

And these remarks are a comment upon a preceding sentence to the effect that 'Divine Truth should be attained by so subtle and indirect a method, a method less tangible than others, less open to analysis, reducible but partially to the forms of Reason, and the ready sport of objection and cavil'.

Keats says that he is 'certain of nothing but the holiness of the Heart's affections and the truth of Imagination'. His language, and the context and mode of sensibility in which we have become habituated to representing Keats, appear to place what he says at a great apparent remove from what Coleridge and Newman spent their lives in teaching; and certainly Keats was not writing as a Christian. But we cannot doubt that it is very near to what Coleridge and Newman, in very different language, sought to convey. The passage which I have quoted from Keats hangs upon his 'speculation' that the soul is immortal. And we observe in Keats, as in Coleridge and Newman, the certainty in the deliverances of the 'heart', in the 'dream of Adam', combined with a certain resignation, that knowledge is not in strictness possible. This union of certainty, of faith, with a certain quality of patience, of waiting upon the event—until, as Newman says, 'the event confirms it', or as Keats says, 'we awake and find it truth'—is something which unites Keats, Coleridge, and Newman in a quite striking way.

Again, Wordsworth was accustomed to speak of 'imagination' as but

> another name for absolute power
> And clearest insight, amplitude of mind,
> And Reason in her most exalted mood.

Out of its progress in himself he has drawn . . .

> The feeling of life endless, the sustaining thought
> Of human Being, Eternity, and God. (p. 749)

Elsewhere he speaks of it as a power 'so called through sad incompetence of human speech', through which the 'invisible world' is revealed; through it we know that

> whether we be young or old,
> Our destiny, our being's heart and home,
> Is with infinitude, and only there;
> With hope it is, hope that can never die,
> Effort, and expectation, and desire,
> And something evermore about to be. (p. 684)

Also, the imagination, as Wordsworth traces its growth from infancy, is nourished in affection; and as it grows in the presence of the objects of nature, it brings with it and is in turn nourished by a certain moral discipline and order, and by a freedom from base passion.

Again, it is instructive to look back also to Blake, especially to the two series of aphorisms, *There is no Natural Religion* and that which he calls *All Religions are One*. These aphorisms were etched about 1788 and the *Songs of Innocence* completed by 1789. I shall first quote a number of these aphorisms.

'Man by his reasoning power can only compare and judge of what he has already perciev'd.'

'None could have other than natural or organic thoughts if he had none but organic perceptions.'

'If it were not for the Poetic or Prophetic character the Philosophic and Experimental would soon be at the ratio of all things, and stand still, unable to do other than repeat the same dull round over again.'

'Man's perceptions are not bounded by organs of perception; he perceives more than sense (tho' ever so acute) can discover.'

'As the true method of knowledge is experiment, the true faculty of knowing must be the faculty which experiences. This faculty I treat of.'

'No man can think, write, or speak from his heart, but he must intend truth. Thus all sects of Philosophy are from the Poetic Genius adapted to the weaknesses of every individual.'

'As none by traveling over known lands can find out the unknown, So from already acquired knowledge Man could not acquire more: therefore an universal Poetic Genius exists.'

'The Religions of all Nations are derived from each Nation's different reception of the Poetic Genius, which is everywhere call'd the Spirit of Prophecy.' (pp. 147–9)

Now these aphorisms were written before Blake adopted the 'gospel of Hell'; and a little reflection shows how much the beliefs which are set out so briefly in them have in common with the doctrines of Coleridge and Newman which we have discussed. First there is Blake's remark that the reasoning power only compares and judges of what has already been perceived. But perception he says, occurs not only through the senses; there is perception of what is not sensible. It is perception which discovers and reveals, which 'travels from known to unknown lands'; reason only acts on, compares, and judges of, what is thus discovered and does not itself disclose what is new. Also, he says, the true faculty of knowing must be the 'faculty which experiences'; and he adds that we cannot 'think from the heart' without 'intending truth'. All kinds of philosophy manifest the 'individual'; each philosophy shows the 'Poetic Genius', the 'faculty which experiences' as it exists in the individual thinker. The same is true of the religions of the world. Now the faculty he treats of, the 'faculty which experiences' he calls the poetic genius; he also calls it the 'Spirit of Prophecy'. And here is the last aphorism of the last series—

> 'The true Man is the source, he being the Poetic Genius.'

The 'Poetic Genius' is the 'true Man'. In later days he by no means cast off all, at any rate, of this teaching, as we have seen. And in *Milton* he says, 'the imagination is the Human Existence itself'.

In speaking of Blake early in this book, I observed of him that in the days of the 'gospel of Hell' he appeared to desire for mankind that it entirely throw off its intellectual faculty and live a wholly 'imaginative' life. And I said that however much we may sympathize with Blake in his belief that our intellectual faculties have developed in a way and to a degree which has seriously impaired the total life of the mind, it is idle to imagine that a life which is human may be independent of the intellectual. Blake himself, as we saw, came to think that this was so, and made friends with his Urizen. For, to use the language of the philosopher so important to Coleridge's reflections, the understanding is involved in a quite necessary way in our apprehension of a world of objects. But it is also true that the understanding requires as a condition of its activity a power prehensive of individuals which may then become the subjects of judgements. Our apprehension of objects is direct and indirect, synthetic as well as analytical. Perception can never be an affair either of sense-intuition or of concepts, or both; and what Kant (and Coleridge) called the imagination mediates between the two. This is not to say that the imagination may be independent of thought; but it does mean that it is logically prior.

To this extent, then, Coleridge would agree with what Blake says in his aphorism that man by his reasoning power can only compare and judge of what has already been perceived. It must work upon what perception discloses. So Newman, when he says that the 'abstract exercises of the reason . . . are in their highest and most honourable place when they are employed upon the vast field of knowledge, not in conjecturing unknown truths but in comparing, adjusting, connecting, explaining' truths already known. Hence, in Newman's eyes, the importance of the 'illative sense' in science; and hence the insistence of Coleridge and Newman on the legitimacy of the speculative reason only when preceded by the discernment of truth by faith. Blake became reconciled to Urizen; and Coleridge and Newman, insisting as emphatically as Blake on the primacy of what we may variously call the 'imagination', the 'Poetic Genius', the 'Spirit of Prophecy', 'Faith', yet defend also the value of the work of the analytical and systematizing reason on what is perceived by faith.

Again, Blake observes that the true faculty of knowing must be the 'faculty which experiences'; and when he says that all 'sects of philosophy' are 'from the Poetic Genius adapted to the weaknesses of every individual', I take him to mean by 'weaknesses' the peculiarities of the individual who, 'thinking from his heart', manifests in his thought something discovered not by wholly rational processes, but by the imagination, poetic genius, or Spirit of Prophecy.

Therefore Keats, Wordsworth, and Blake present in their

different ways aspects of beliefs which were of the first importance to Coleridge and to Newman.

This is not to say that there are not certain striking apparent differences between Blake and Keats on the one hand and Coleridge and Newman on the other. The first is that the latter principally emphasize conscience and obedience to it, a holy will, as the condition of the perception of truth; an explicit moral emphasis which is hardly present in Blake and Keats, though it is present in greater degree in Wordsworth. Also, there goes along with this a difference in terminology which we have noticed. Blake, Keats, and Wordsworth speak of the imagination, or the poetic genius; Coleridge and Newman of faith. The latter do not, of course, disguise the fact that their doctrine cannot be a secular thing; it is religious and Christian; they write in the Christian tradition and draw deliberately upon it. It is not so with Blake, Shelley, and Keats. In their different ways they not only stand outside that tradition, but openly oppose it.

Even so, let us bear in mind for a little longer, what is so typical of the Romantic poets, Keats's statement that he was 'certain of nothing but the holiness of the Heart's affections and the truth of the Imagination'; and let us consider it further in relation to the religious consciousness of Coleridge and Newman. Of course, we read Keats's letters as the utterances of one who was primarily an artist; and the artist feels and believes, however obscurely, that, as F. H. Bradley observed in *Ethical Studies* (p. 320), 'beauty where it is not seen, yet somehow and somewhere is and is real; though not as a mere idea in people's heads, nor yet as anything in the visible world'. The dreams of Alastor and Endymion are of this beauty. Now there is no clear dividing line which may be drawn between the artistic and religious consciousness in these matters. Both must seek to identify themselves with what, as they labour to imagine it, is most real; the artist no less than the religious soul 'goes on to realise what it obscurely fore-knows as real'. The difference no doubt is that Coleridge must stress, more than Keats, the importance of the will in its pursuit of goodness and holiness; and this is the mark of the explicitly religious consciousness in contrast to the artistic. But the artist is a man as well as an artist; and 'so soon as the . . . artist is conscious of his will in relation to the real ideal, as a will which has demands on him, he ceases to be a mere . . . artist as such (which after all no human being is), and becomes also religious or irreligious'. (*Ethical Studies*, p. 321) So it was with Keats, who was certainly no mere sensuous dreamer but a manly person who saw in misfortunes the opportunity of trying the resources of his spirit. 'The heart', he said, 'is the mind's Bible.' What the heart, in the course of experience, imagines and loves, is real, no mere dream, though we be unable to disprove its being such. To say of the heart that it is the mind's Bible is only to say what Coleridge and Newman urged when they said that the proper office of the intelligence is to draw out, compare, explain the deliverances of a mode of knowledge which springs not from speculation but from actual experience of life. And if Keats might exclaim 'Beauty is Truth', Coleridge and Newman might exclaim 'Goodness is Truth'; the one believing that the truth will come to be disclosed through the actual pursuit of beauty in all ways and forms, the others that it will be disclosed through the actual pursuit of goodness. Neither Keats nor Coleridge thought of truth as something separate from being, nor as attainable except through the growth of the soul. It does not lie exposed to capture by any faculty or by the intelligence. It is no abstract scheme or system of categories and concepts, but an ultimate and living beauty and holiness apprehensible only through the living beauty and holiness of the soul. Keats's identification of beauty and truth was no mere easy or sententious formula; it was the strictest truth to Keats as it was indeed to all the writers of whom we are now speaking, however different their emphasis and language.

§ 12

We shall, however, inquire further into this matter, and try to relate the typical Romantic belief in the imagination and in its truth to what Coleridge and Newman call faith. Now the link between the two is to be found in Coleridge; for up to about the year 1817 Coleridge's thought turned on the imagination and afterwards principally on the reason, the life of which is consummated in faith. Up to this year he did not write as a Christian; afterwards he did, and during this later period we hear very little of the imagination but a great deal of the practical reason and of faith.

Now when, in the *Biographia Literaria*, Coleridge was at pains to expound the nature and importance of the imagination, he was writing primarily with an eye to aesthetic experience and to the representation and organization of the sensible world by the imagination. So far, he was able to align himself with the teaching of Kant, in which also the imagination played a crucial role, in alliance with the understanding, in sense-perception. But, as time went on, he became more and more concerned with that other part of Kant's philosophy according to which the practical reason is alone competent to deal with the supra-sensible, in morals and religion. Now in these matters, the understanding, in Kant's view, has no legitimate powers; its function has to do only with the organization of the sensible. But what is true of the understanding applies also to the imagination; the natural and proper sphere of both is the physical world; beyond it only the practical reason has legitimacy. When, therefore, Coleridge followed Kant, more and more, in exalting the practical reason, and in denying the powers of the understanding, what was he to say of the imagination, of which previously, in speaking of aesthetic experience, he had made so much?

When he was writing *Biographia Literaria* Coleridge was at a turning-point in his intellectual development. He wrote under the influence of Kant; he was also greatly attracted to Schelling. Now it seems certain that the kind of doctrine which Schelling taught had occurred quite independently to Coleridge. However that may be, we find him taking whole passages from Schelling and professing a doctrine which in a very short time he was to put away from himself for good. Mr. Muirhead gives 1817 as marking the limit of Schelling's influence; and in 1818 Coleridge declares Schelling's philosophy to be 'gross materialism'.

Now it is worth while pausing for a moment to remark that Coleridge's rejection of Schelling is an event of great significance in the history of English Romanticism. For with the rejection of Schelling went an equally emphatic rejection of Spinoza. In the *Biographia* he says of the *Ethics* what I have already quoted, that at no time could he believe that '*in itself* and *essentially* it was incompatible with religion', and he asserts that he is now 'thoroughly persuaded of the contrary'. But so uncertain was his state of mind at the time of writing the *Biographia*, that we also find there plenty of evidence that he is unhappy enough about Spinozism. Describing his earlier and greatest years, he says in chapter 10:

'I retired to a cottage in Somersetshire at the foot of Quantock, and devoted my thoughts and studies to the foundations of religion and morals. Here I found myself all afloat. . . . The *idea* of the Supreme Being appeared to me to be as necessarily implied in all particular modes of being as the idea of infinite space in all the geometrical figures by which space is limited. I was pleased with the Cartesian opinion, that the idea of God is distinguished from all other ideas by involving its *reality*; but I was not wholly satisfied. . . . Still the existence of a being, the ground of all existence, was not yet the existence of a moral creator, and governor . . .

'For a very long time, indeed, I could not reconcile personality with infinity; and my head was with Spinoza, though my whole heart remained with Paul and John.' (p. 132)

Then, he says, he discovered what were in fact to be, substantially, his maturest beliefs:

'Yet there had dawned upon me, even before I had met with the Critique of the Pure Reason, a certain guiding light. If the mere intellect could make no certain discovery of a holy and intelligent first cause, it might yet supply a demonstration, that no legitimate argument could be drawn from the intellect *against* its truth. . . . I became convinced that religion, as both the corner-stone and the key-stone of morality, must have a *moral* origin; so far at least, that the evidence of its doctrines could not, like the truths of abstract science, be wholly independent of the will. It were therefore to be expected, that its *fundamental* truth would be such as *might* be denied; though only by the fool, and even by the fool from the madness of the *heart* alone!' p. 134)

Now in these passages Coleridge is describing his intellectual condition in the last years of the old century. *But he is also describing, very largely, his state of mind when writing these passages in* '*Biographia Literaria*'.[1] He is still attracted to Spinoza (as well as to Schelling); and his head is still, to no inconsiderable extent, with him. But also, he is not happy about it. His heart is with Paul and John; and he looks for a philosophy which will treat adequately the demands of the moral life. He had not changed very much in the time that elapsed between the Quantock days and the time of writing *Biographia Literaria.* The hold of Spinozistic speculation was strong upon his head, if not upon his heart; and it helped to incline him towards Schelling. But in the years immediately following the *Biographia* he gets Spinozism (and Schelling) out of his system, and, we may add, thereby out of the Romantic movement. We have seen that as early as 1802, he had written in some notes on Sir Thomas Browne that 'strong feeling and an active intellect conjoined, leads almost necessarily, in the first stage of philosophising, to Spinozism'. This may be taken as a comment on Coleridge, and no less on English Romanticism, as we have had occasion to see. But soon after he had written the *Biographia* he was finally to liberate himself both from the intellectualism of Spinoza and from what he calls, in his later *Table Talk*, Spinoza's 'monstrous' conclusion. In 1818 he lumps Spinoza and Schelling together as 'pantheists'; and he says (in the additions made to *The Friend* in that year) that 'the inevitable result of all consequent reasoning in which the intellect refuses to acknowledge a higher or deeper ground than it can itself supply —and weens to possess within itself the centre of its own system —is Pantheism'. The *Lay Sermon* of 1816 shows a Coleridge already far more sure of himself than the Coleridge of the *Biographia Literaria.* He has made his final choice, and the attraction of Spinoza is at an end; and Schelling's doctrine is a 'gross materialism'.

[1] In 1815. See Shawcross, pp. xc–xcii.

We can well imagine the increasing dismay with which he came to look back on chapter 12 of the *Biographia*. For him to say[1] that 'self-consciousness is not a kind of *being*, but a kind of *knowing*, and that too the highest and farthest that exists for *us*', was to set up a principle at odds with the ultimate purpose of Kant's teaching and with all that Coleridge was subsequently to uphold. Now there is a sense in which Schelling's doctrine of the ontological unity of subject and object well suited Coleridge's belief that the imagination is the 'prime agent in all perception' and that it suffers a remarkable development in the artist. A monistic view of knowledge such as Schelling was expounding was attractive enough to one who had emphasized so much the role of imagination in perception and art;[2] but it did not accord with the doctrine of the reason as the organ of the discernment of spiritual truth or with the religious truth Coleridge became increasingly anxious to teach. Coleridge had to choose between Schelling's development of Kant's thought, a development Coleridge was later to call a materialism, and which is certainly a naturalism, of however lofty and emotional a kind, and a Christian development of Kant's thought such as he was in fact to supply. But of the two, Schelling's philosophy was, at first sight at least, much more of a piece with Coleridge's defence of the imagination than the philosophy he in fact undertook later to expound and defend; it was more calculated to exalt the truth and importance of art and to keep them in the foreground. Yet the way in which, in Schelling's doctrine, the truth and importance of art were upheld was bound to be, despite the deep attraction he temporarily felt for it, unpalatable to Coleridge. He undertook to develop Kant's philosophy in a way far more in keeping with Kant's fundamental intention than Schelling offered. If the doctrine of the imagination which he had previously expounded was to be retained at all, it must be retained without any savour of naturalism. But it was certain that, immediately, it seemed that there must be some disharmony between his celebrated doctrine of the imagination and his new-found emphasis upon the primacy of the practical reason.

Soon after the writing of the *Biographia Literaria*, then, Coleridge's reflection passed from a chief concern with art to a chief concern with religion, from doctrine having chiefly to do with the imagination to doctrine having chiefly to do with the practical reason. Now the transition is most clearly observed in the *Lay Sermons*; and here indeed he tries to relate something of what he

[1] Strictly, to quote from Schelling's *Transcendental Idealism*.

[2] Even the *Essay on Poesy or Art* written as late as 1818, after the *Lay Sermons*, shows how he was still attracted to Schelling, though his mind was by that time virtually made up.

has said of the imagination to his belief in the primacy of the practical reason. The following is the substance of what he says. Of the understanding he remarks, quoting from *The Friend*, that 'unirradiated by the reason and the spirit' it has 'no appropriate object but the material world in relation to our worldly interests'. Again, he says, as we have seen:

'... of the discursive understanding, which forms for itself general notions and terms of classification for the purpose of comparing and arranging phenomena, the characteristic is clearness without depth. It contemplates the unity of things in their limits only, and is consequently a knowledge of superficies without substance. So much so indeed, that it entangles itself in contradictions, in the very effort of comprehending the idea of substance.' (pp. 342–3)

Then he goes on to say:

'The completing power which unites clearness with depth, the plenitude of the sense with the comprehensibility of the understanding, is the imagination, impregnated with which the understanding itself becomes intuitive, and a living power. The reason (not the abstract reason, not the reason as the mere organ of science, or as the faculty of scientific principles and schemes *a priori*; but reason), as the integral spirit of the regenerated man, reason substantiated and vital . . . this reason without being either the sense, the understanding, or the imagination, contains all three within itself, even as the mind contains its thoughts and is present in and through them all.' (p. 343)

We notice, before proceeding to comment on this passage, that the reason of which he here speaks is (and to Coleridge it is axiomatic that it is) religious; it is the possession of the 'regenerated man'. We must also recall that the 'reason' as Coleridge upheld it, while being 'practical' in the sense that the truths it discovers are not the discovery, if that were possible, of a curious intellect, but of a life which is being lived and which is seeking increasing fulfilment, is not 'practical' in the sense that its truths have only a practical and pragmatic validity; its truths are absolutely true; it perceives what is real. Hence in the same Appendix to the first *Lay Sermon* Coleridge remarks of the reason as he has expounded it in the passage which I have quoted that it is 'neither merely speculative nor merely practical, but both in one'.

By it Coleridge means, as we have already noticed, that the reason, while never ceasing to be dependent on faith and on the 'practical', may yet, in Newman's words (for in this, as we have seen, the two writers were agreed), 'compare, adjust, connect, explain what has been ascertained by faith'; hence, the legitimacy, in this sense, of Christian philosophy. Now because this is so, the understanding acquires (according to Coleridge and Newman) an importance in religious philosophy (as they understand it) never ascribed to it by Kant, who forbade metaphysics in any sense whatsoever; the reason employs the understanding in erecting a philosophy of religion which begins and ends with what has been dictated by faith.

But not only so. In the passage from the Appendix to the first *Lay Sermon* from which I have quoted, Coleridge asserts that in the activity of the reason (not the 'abstract reason' but the reason which is 'both practical and speculative') the understanding is present and is, indeed, indispensable to it. So also are imaginative and sensible elements. These three, he says, do not act in distinction from one another; the reason is not made up of the sum of them. They are somehow fused; and the reason contains them all 'within itself, even as the mind contains its thoughts and is present in and through them all; or as the expression pervades the different features of an intelligent countenance'. Thus, by giving 'speculative' validity to the practical reason, Coleridge is able to carry over the imagination and the understanding from the realm of the sensible where Kant said they are alone 'justified' into that of the super-sensible; they have their place and right in faith no less than in perception of the physical. In perception of the physical, imagination and understanding rely upon each other; they do so also in the life of the reason. In our awareness of the sensible, indeed, the interdependence of imagination and conceptual analysis is profound and close; and so it must be, said Coleridge, in our awareness of what goes beyond the physical.

But how can they enter into the life of reason? In sense-perception there are the sense-stimuli, the presented 'manifold of sensation', which are the occasion of the action of imagination and the understanding. But in faith, in apprehension of what is not sensible, there is, presumably, no corresponding and given stimulus, nothing on which these faculties may act. Yet in the passage I have quoted, Coleridge speaks of the reason as containing sense as well as imagination and understanding. But in what way, in the discernment of the spiritual, is this possible? What conceivable legitimacy can the images of sense obtain in the life of faith? How can the imagination act in the reason? What foothold can it obtain, moving about in worlds not realized? In earlier years Coleridge had spoken at length of the imagination in perception of objects and in art. What can he say of the imagination in the perception of the spiritual and in religion?

§ 13

Before going on to expound what Coleridge has further to say in reply to this question, I shall turn to Newman to observe what he says, in *The Grammar of Assent*,[1] on the religious imagination.

Newman comes to a discussion of this matter from his exposition of the difference between what he calls notional and real assent. The difference between these two kinds of assent, as he expounds them, is between an assent given to an 'abstract' truth and an assent given to an 'actual' truth, to use Coleridge's adjectives. The former is given to 'notions', the latter to 'ideas'. Notional truth is ineffectual, 'floating on the surface' of the mind of the individual or of society; an 'idea' has dynamic power, affects action and rouses the emotions. A notion is something to which we may extend credence, and leave it at that; an 'idea' is something for which, if needs be, we give up our lives. We have already observed that 'notions' are impersonal, the common possession of many minds and shared between them; that on the other hand an 'idea' is personal, apprehended out of the whole personality, and not easily therefore communicated. But there is another important difference. 'Ideas' become 'operative principles' because they spring out of perception; they are not abstract, but close to the concrete and in association with vivid imagination. 'The iniquity of the slave-trade ought to have been acknowledged by all men from the first; it was acknowledged by many, but it needed an organized agitation, with tracts and speeches innumerable, so to affect the imagination of men as to make their acknowledgment of that iniquitousness operative.' (p. 77) Strength of belief and 'reality' of assent require vividness of imagery, a strong sense of what is individual. Newman does not of course assert that the mere presence of vivid imagery or perception is any guarantee of the truth of the idea. Nor does he maintain that vividness of image producing assent is necessarily 'practical'; instead, the imagination serves to stir the passions through which action results.

Now, that notional assent is possible in matters of religion is clear; and indeed theological formulation and exploration is necessary. But if religion is to be vital and an animating principle, there must be real assent, 'a more vivid assent to the Being of a God, than that which is given merely to the notions of the intellect' (p. 102). 'Can I enter with a personal knowledge into the circle of truths which make up that great thought [of the Being of a God]? Can I rise to wha I have called an imaginative apprehension of it? Can I believe as if I saw? . . . How can I assent as if I saw, unless I have seen? but no one in this life can see God.'

[1] London, 1930.

(p. 102) What is required is not a 'theological act' but an 'act of religion'. A dogma of faith must be 'discerned, rested in, and appropriated as a reality, by the religious imagination' in addition to being 'held as a truth' by the theological intellect. (p. 98)

The fifth chapter of *The Grammar* is the answer Newman supplies to these questions. The substance of it is that because we come to knowledge of God through the conscience, God is necessarily represented as a person, and that the language of religion (of religion that is to say, and not of theology) is ever 'concrete and adapted to excite images'. Religious truth lives in the imagination of men, necessarily represented, in some degree, in human imagery. Coleridge, no less than Newman, insisted on the personal nature of God, as one whom we image as best we may as Father and Judge; and without this imaginative apprehension of God, religion must be a dead thing. Again, in the matter of 'revealed' truth. Of the dogma of the Holy Trinity as it is set out in the Athanasian Creed, Newman observes that each word employed 'in its ordinary use stands for things', not for notions merely; so far as religion is to be real, it cannot transcend our experience. That is not to say, it need hardly be said, that Newman is denying that God's being far transcends what can be caught within our imagination, and that there is a vast region of mystery beyond experience and representation by the imagination; but 'what *is* in some degree a matter of experience, what *is* presented for the imagination, the affections, the devotion, the spiritual life of the Christian to repose upon with a real assent, what stands for things, not for notions only, is each of these propositions [of the creed stating the dogma of the Holy Trinity] taken one by one, and that, not in the case of intellectual and thoughtful minds only, but of all religious minds whatsoever, in the case of a child or peasant, as well as of a philosopher'. (pp. 130–1)

Now in here emphasizing the necessity to religion of imaginative apprehension and in asserting that the gap between the finite and the eternal may be bridged only through imagery familiar to us as men, Newman does not of course deny that 'notions' are present in and through that apprehension. Concepts are as unavoidable and as necessary here as in the perception of the physical. Certainly the intelligence no more exhausts or encompasses the life of God than does the imagination; if both act in spiritual vision, they both also recognize their limits. Yet, so far as they go, they may claim substantial truth. They are both, separately and in unison, finally confronted with mystery; but their being so is no demonstration of their falsity.

Also, Newman insists on the need for theology, or systematic reflection upon the essentials of real assent in religion. This employment of the intelligence is, he says, 'natural, excellent, and necessary'; it is the natural and proper function of the intelligence to systematize what is known through other and more direct channels.

Let us now return to Coleridge and to the third appendix to the first *Lay Sermon.* It will be recalled that he said that the reason 'without being either the sense, the understanding, or the imagination, contains all three within itself'. Each makes its contribution and is caught up in the 'living power' of the reason. The reason is, after all, an activity of beings set in a physical world and responding to it not only through the organs of sense but also with imagination and understanding. Thus, in transcending the sensible, it does not cast off, nor could it cast off, these powers. We begin in sensible experience, in which the imagination and understanding impregnate each other. But in time, and in their turn, they are impregnated by the reason and it by them. He illustrates this by an analogy drawn from plant-life. He says that a plant draws upon the lower inorganic elements in nature to build up its own unity and structure and unites them into itself. It thus becomes a 'natural symbol of that higher life of reason, in which the whole series (known to us in our present state of being) is perfected, in which, therefore, all subordinate gradations recur, and are re-ordained "in more abundant honour". We had seen each in its own cast, and we now recognise them all as co-existing in the unity of a higher form, the crown and completion of the earthly, and the mediator of a new and heavenly series.' (p. 345) This life of reason issues from the will; it is also a life of imagination 'which incorporates the reason in images of sense'. It is, indeed, a personal thing, and individual; but it cannot be called a faculty possessed by a person. 'He, with whom it is present, can as little appropriate it, whether totally or by partition, as he can claim ownership in the breathing air, or make an enclosure in the cope of heaven.' (p. 343)

§ 14

Now according to both Coleridge and Newman, the religious imagination (or as Coleridge would be content to say, reason in religion, for in his eyes, as we have now seen, reason contains imagination) issues into *symbol.* Once again, it is interesting to place their statements side by side; and again I shall quote Newman first because of his greater clarity.

'How should any thing of this world convey ideas which are beyond and above this world? How can teaching and intercourse, how can human words, how can earthly images, convey to the mind an idea of the Invisible? They cannot rise above themselves. They can suggest no idea but what is resolvable into ideas natural and earthly. The words "Person", "Substance", "Consubstantial", "Generation", "Procession", "Incarnation", "Taking of the manhood into God", and the like, have either a very abject and human meaning, or none at all. In other words, there is no such inward view of these doctrines, distinct from the dogmatic language used to express them, as was just now supposed. *The metaphors by which they are signified are not merely symbols of ideas which exist independently of them, but their meaning is coincident and identical with the ideas.*[1] When, indeed, we have knowledge of a thing from other sources, then the metaphors we may apply to it are but accidental appendages to that knowledge; whereas our ideas of Divine things are just co-extensive with the figures by which we express them, neither more nor less, and without them are not; and when we draw inferences from those figures, we are not illustrating one existing idea, but drawing mere logical inferences. We speak, indeed, of material objects freely, because our senses reveal them to us apart from our words; but as to these ideas about heavenly things, we learn them from words, yet (it seems) we are to say what we, without words, conceive of them, as if words could convey what they do not contain. It follows that our anathemas, our controversies, our struggles, our sufferings, are merely about the poor ideas conveyed to us in certain figures of speech.' (*University Sermons*, pp. 338–9)

The dogmas of Christianity, that is to say, are to be distinguished from metaphors, for we have no extrametaphorical apprehension of the truths and realities of which they are the expression. The truths and realities of Christianity are known only through 'certain figures of speech' which thereby become no ordinary 'figures of speech', but *symbols.*[2]

This is Coleridge's statement in the first *Lay Sermon* (p. 322):

'It is among the miseries of the present age that it recognises no medium between literal and metaphorical. Faith is either to be buried in the dead letter, or its name and honours usurped by a counterfeit product of the mechanical understanding, which in the blindness of self-complacency confounds symbols with allegories. Now an allegory is but a translation of abstract notions into a picture-language, which is itself nothing but an abstraction from objects of the senses; the principal being more worthless even than its phantom proxy, both alike unsubstantial, and the former shapeless to boot. On the other hand a symbol . . . is characterized by a translucence of the special in the individual, or of the general in the especial, or of the universal in the general. Above all by the translucence of the eternal through and in

[1] My italics.

[2] See *Aids* (pp. 196–8) for other remarks on analogy, metaphor, and symbol. See also the remarkable Bampton lectures (1858) of H. L. Mansel, Dean of St. Paul's, a religious philosopher distinguished no less for literary than for philosophical power, and in the direct line of Coleridge and Newman in these matters. Mansel, I believe, is little read now.

the temporal. *It always partakes of the reality which it renders intelligible*;[1] and while it enunciates the whole, abides itself as a living part in that unity, of which it is the representative. The other are but empty echoes which the fancy arbitrarily associates with apparitions of matter, less beautiful, but not less shadowy than the sloping orchard or hill-side pasture-field seen in the transparent lake below.'

A symbol is a 'medium between literal and metaphorical'. This was Newman's point also. A symbol is not a mode of expression adopted at will to communicate a known state of affairs; 'it always partakes of the reality which it renders intelligible'; it is a 'living part' of what it expresses, so far as what it expresses is known at all. This, if I understand it rightly, is precisely what Newman intends when he says that 'the metaphors by which [the doctrines of the Creeds] are signified are not mere symbols of ideas which exist independently of them, but their meaning is coincident and identical with the ideas'. Symbol, he says again (p. 348), is not metaphor or allegory; 'it is an actual and essential part of that, the whole of which it represents'. (It should also be noticed that in writing this passage, published in 1816, when he was still much concerned about the difference between imagination and fancy, Coleridge relegates allegory to fancy, on account of its play with explicit universals, and puts down symbol to the activity of the imagination.)

Christian dogma, then, is symbol. Symbol is the highest poetry of which the imagination is capable; into it reason issues 'incorporated in images of sense'. This is not to say, it need hardly be added, that either Newman or Coleridge saw this 'poetry' as something created by the human imagination; it is a poetry given by divine authority, though it is true that it can be actively apprehended only by the soul in which the imaginative reason is living and strong, so that it is, at least in a sense, discovered, though under guidance. Moreover, these symbols, divinely given, are not in strictness modes of expression merely; in Coleridge's phrase, they are 'consubstantial with the truths of which they are the conductors'; the truth (so far as it is apprehensible at all) and the symbol are one. The symbol is not a '*mere* symbol' as Newman says; it *is* truth so far as it is communicable to us.

But symbol and truth, existing thus in conjunction, are united into a trinity in which the third element is history. Not only is the symbol not a 'mere symbol'; it is also event. If the symbol is 'consubstantial with the truth of which it is the conductor', it is also embedded in, or rather is a part of, history. For it might be possible for the truth to be communicable only in certain symbols

[1] My italics.

having an eternal validity; but, because the symbols are set in time, they are given a substantial literality and become fact as well as symbol. Therefore it no longer becomes a question of being either literal or metaphorical (if only in the eyes of men possessed by an 'unenlivened generalizing understanding'). Symbol and event are one and the same thing.

Now in the 'poetry' of dogma, in which metaphor becomes symbol, not only must symbol partake of history (thereby formally and in act denying its metaphorical or 'merely' symbolical character); it must include two other characteristics of great importance. In the first place, Christ is God and Man, and this in no attenuated sense but in what must be held as strictest and most literal truth. Christ must be very Man, as well as very God. Only thus can symbol be incorporated into history and the trinity of truth and symbol and event be sealed. In the second place, the element of the miraculous becomes indispensable. Here, Coleridge can speak.

'Christianity is no less fact than truth. It is spiritual, yet so as to be historical; and between these two poles there must likewise be a mid-point, in which the historical and spiritual meet. Christianity must have its history—a history of itself, and likewise the history of its introduction, its spread and its outward-becoming; and as the mid-point above-mentioned, a portion of these facts must be miraculous, that is, *phenomena* in nature that are beyond nature.'[1]

In miracle, that is to say, the godhead of Him who is also very Man is exhibited, and thus the 'myth' is perfectly rounded off, elaborating itself step by step with a process in which it shows itself not to be mythology. To regard dogma in this way, as a poetry labouring to show itself as not poetry, would have been abhorrent to Newman; to Coleridge also, at least as time went on. But in the first *Lay Sermon* (p. 321) from which I have been quoting, written in 1816, Coleridge gives some ground perhaps for thinking that he sees dogma as issuing from a process of myth-making, as when, for example, he speaks of the Scriptures as the 'living educts of the imagination; of that reconciling and mediatory power, which incorporating the reason in images of sense, and organizing (as it were) the flux of the senses by the permanence and self-circling energies of the reason, gives birth to a system of symbols, harmonious in themselves, and consubstantial with the truths of which they are the conductors'.[2] But if

[1] *Confessions of an Enquiring Spirit*, Bohn edition, 1884, p. 293.

[2] In a letter written to Hurrell Froude in 1836 (Newman first read Coleridge in the spring of 1835), Newman remarks of Sir James Stephen that he could not be satisfied 'that he was not too much of a philosopher, looking (in Coleridge's way) at the church, sacraments, doctrines, etc., rather as symbols of a philosophy than as *truths*—as the mere accidental types of principles'.

some such idea was present to any extent in his mind in 1816, it steadily declined.

The reason, therefore, or the imagination, as we can now indifferently call it, rises to its final task in the incorporation of the super-sensible in the images of sense, in the creation of dogma. We may call the creation of dogma a process of myth-making in which there is working a process of high dialectical subtlety; but this was not (at least, finally) the view of Coleridge. The only mythology in which we can rest is the mythology which is also history, and which therefore is given to the imagination. Concerned with truth and reality beyond sense, the reason of man must operate imaginatively. The reason tries to use the concepts of the understanding, despite their feebleness and contradictoriness, to say in what the transcendent consists; also it must use the images of the imagination in its endeavours, also vacillating and inadequate, to show the eternal. But here, in the face of human failure, God's act intervenes. For the Bible is not a human book; the New Testament is the record of God's act in history; Christ's life and the divine Sacrifice of the Cross hold the imagination as nothing less than God's act could do. Nothing less than the rupture of the historical could serve to raise the imagination to its highest reach; and in Christianity the imagination dwells in contemplation on God himself; and Christ as Man lived, suffered, died. This is not to say that reason, understanding, or imagination exhaust the object of their contemplation; the last word is mystery. For the revealed truths of Christianity are a scandal to the understanding; and the imagination does not encompass the mystery of the Atonement. The scope and reach of our imagination are small enough; to it the Divine mercy stooped, took on flesh and blood for our better discernment, and disclosed so much as our imagination could bear. In this, in acceptance of the mythology which is divinely given as history, the long and difficult history of Romanticism in England comes to its end. After the labour of mighty imaginations in the creation of myth and allegory, we return to the mythology enacted in time through the free act of God.

I shall conclude this section by quoting a passage from Newman's essay, 'The Prospects of the Anglican Church',[1] written in 1838, in which he speaks of Scott, Coleridge, Southey, and Wordsworth. Newman was conscious of his closeness to the Romantic movement, and joins with it in its attitude to the eighteenth century.

'There has been for some years, from whatever cause, a growing tendency towards the character of mind and feeling of which Catholic

[1] In *Essays Critical and Historical*, London, 1897, vol. i, p. 268.

doctrines are the just expression. This manifested itself long before men entered into the truth intellectually, or knew what they ought to believe, and what they ought not; and what the practical duties were, to which a matured knowledge would lead them. During the first quarter of this century a great poet was raised up in the North, who, whatever were his defects, has contributed by his works, in prose and verse, to prepare men for some closer and more practical approximation to Catholic truth. The general need of something deeper and more attractive than what had offered itself elsewhere, may be considered to have led to his popularity; and by means of his popularity he re-acted on his readers, stimulating their mental thirst, feeding their hopes, setting before them visions, which, when once seen, are not easily forgotten, and silently indoctrinating them with nobler ideas, which might afterwards be appealed to as first principles. Doubtless there are things in the poems and romances in question, of which a correct judgment is forced to disapprove; and which must be ever a matter of regret; but contrasted with the popular writers of the last century, with its novelists, and some of its most admired poets, as Pope, they stand almost as oracles of Truth confronting the ministers of error and sin.

'And while history in prose and verse was thus made the instrument of Church feelings and opinions, a philosophical basis for the same was under formation in England by a very original thinker, who, while he indulged a liberty of speculation which no Christian can tolerate, and advocated conclusions which were often heathen rather than Christian, yet after all instilled a higher philosophy into inquiring minds, than they had hitherto been accustomed to accept. In this way he made trial of his age, and found it respond to him, and succeeded in interesting its genius in the cause of Catholic truth. It has indeed been only since the death of Coleridge that these results of his writings have fully shown themselves; but they were very evident when they were once seen, and discovered the tendencies which had been working in his mind from the first. Two living poets may be added, one of whom in the department of fantastic fiction, the other in that of philosophical meditation, have addressed themselves to the same high principles and feelings, and carried forward their readers in the same direction.'

§ 15

Before concluding this chapter it is necessary to give full place to the other side of what Coleridge and Newman said on this topic of the religious imagination in its apprehension of the supersensible. I shall find it convenient once again to begin with Newman, and by referring again to the last of the *University Sermons*, called 'The Theory of Developments in Religious Doctrine'. We have seen how he justifies the exercise of the images of sense in religion. Now when he asked, in the passage I quoted at the beginning of the last section, 'How should anything of this world convey ideas which are beyond and above this world?' he was putting an objection. He had been speaking of the creeds and envisages this comment. But it is unmistakably a point of view he deeply realizes and appreciates. How much he does so is clear enough from the succeeding portions of the sermon, in which he defends the poor words in which religion is driven to express itself. For he says in the paragraph which follows:

'... when it is said that such figures convey no knowledge of the Divine Nature itself, beyond those figures, whatever they are, it should be considered whether our senses can be proved to suggest any real idea of matter. All that we know, strictly speaking, is the existence of the impressions our senses make on us; and yet we scruple not to speak as if they conveyed to us the knowledge of material substances. Let, then, the Catholic dogmas, as such, be freely admitted to convey no true idea of Almighty God, but only an earthly one, gained from earthly figures, provided it be allowed, on the other hand, that the senses do not convey to us any true idea of matter, but only an idea commensurate with sensible impressions.'

Now this analogy, of the authority, so to speak, of sense-perception, would be all the more striking in Newman's hands if we felt that he himself accepted this authority. But he proceeds at once to say, 'Nor is there any reason why this should not be fully granted'; and later comes the passage which I have already quoted in which he speaks of sense-impressions as possibly but the 'token of realities distinct from themselves'. Of religious apprehension, therefore, he will only say that 'there may be a certain correspondence between the idea, though earthly, and its heavenly archetype, such, that that idea belongs to the archetype, in a sense in which no other earthly idea belongs to it, as being the nearest approach to it which our present state allows'. (p. 340) 'There may be,' he says calmly. That there *is* a correspondence Newman must and does maintain. But throughout this sermon he is using the epistemology of Locke, an epistemology of representative perception; and throughout all he writes, whether of sense-perception or awareness of the super-sensible, is an overwhelming sense of the disparity between the idea and image which are in our minds, and, on the other hand, 'what is real'. For to assert their correspondence is to assert their disparity, the sense of what transcends the known, the unattainable, that from which we are shut off. This sense is not merely something negative. Newman is not uttering a pious and comfortable warning against anthropomorphizing our God excessively. The illustrations of his point which he makes, derived from music, from mathematics, and from sense-perception, show how strongly there occurred in his mind a 'dim and undetermined sense' of an 'unknown' in which 'no familiar shapes remained'. The words of Wordsworth occur in a setting in *The Prelude* which seems far enough from Newman's Oxford. But the same sense is at work in the minds of both Wordsworth and Newman. Also, the pre-Kantian doctrine of representative perception and Kant's conceptualism serve, in the hands of Newman and Coleridge respectively, one and the same purpose. For to Coleridge no less than to Newman 'clear and distinct ideas' about God and the end of the moral life cannot be forthcoming; and as the 'practical reason' must be content with ideas admittedly obscure, and with a sense of the inexhaustible and unknown, so the imagination which is integral to the reason must struggle on in the face of defeat. The imagination 'dissolves, diffuses, dissipates, in order to recreate; *or where this process is rendered impossible, yet still at all events it struggles to idealize and to unify*'. Both the elements of understanding and imagination present in the reason must fall short. The reason, which is the light of the soul, serves to reveal a darkness which it is unable to dissipate. Yet the sense of this darkness is also necessary to the health of the soul which can be sustained only through acknowledgement of an enveloping unknown. Thus, at this last stage in the growth of Romanticism, does the 'mystery' of all true religion, which Blake had so passionately (and so perversely) opposed, find a frank and eager acceptance.

§ 16

In this chapter, I have tried to show how much Coleridge and Newman had in common with each other in their beliefs about human knowledge and imagination, and how much also they had in common with the Romantic writers we had previously discussed. But there are also some striking differences between the two men which so far I have contrived to overlook. In the next chapter, we shall look further into their Romanticism, and try to bring out certain qualities in their minds which led them respectively to two very different kinds of Christianity.

THE GOSPEL OF HEAVEN

CHAPTER II

PROTESTANT AND CATHOLIC

§ 1

NEWMAN'S life was quieter than Coleridge's. Certainly, Newman knew periods in his life which were dreary and difficult, and which evoked all his resource in patience and endurance. But he did not undergo the tumultuous and terrible trials of Coleridge. His mind and life were calmer; he came early to Christianity, and did not undergo the intellectual labour which Coleridge found necessary; and he was never ensnared by speculation. For the most part, the troubles which destroyed the peace of Newman's life were the making of his own mind as it grew and changed; and if he lost Oxford and knew the bitterness of the parting of friends, it was through the power of a greater consolation. In Sicily he could tell himself, when all seemed dark, that he had not sinned against the light; and he never needed to charge himself with having sacrificed his integrity. His integrity he never lost, however bleak and dreary some days and months and years might be; therefore he had resources, a power of stillness, a sense of order, which did not fail. Everyone who knew him felt his composure and stillness; as we who read him feel these qualities in his style.

It was very different with Coleridge who for a long time was set in a 'wide sea'. He had no Oxford and no Oratory; he might well upbraid himself in anguish and despair; he came near enough to loss of sanity, racked in day by his conscience, terrified at night by his dreams; he was wretched in his marriage, and suffered the parting of friends in no high spiritual cause, but through circumstances to which at least he had helped to give rise.

It is little wonder then that Newman exalts the Incarnation to a first place amongst the great doctrines of Christianity, Coleridge the Atonement, and that the religion of Coleridge was tumultuous and peremptory where that of Newman had a quality of quietness and waiting. We detect indeed in Newman the note of mourning continuously sounded; but in such minds as Newman mourning is founded in or springs from hope; the two are of a piece with each other, and alike continue with a rare steadiness. It was not so with Coleridge, who passed quickly to and fro between despair and the sublime consolation of imputed righteousness.

Some sense of this fundamental difference between the two men the reader may perhaps have gathered from the previous chapter. For it also shows itself in Newman's greater capacity for scepticism. We pointed out how willing he was to entertain scepticism at the expense of our knowledge of the external world; and he compares the knowledge we have in dogma to knowledge in perception. Now this *entertainment* of scepticism merely was something possible to Coleridge in a far lesser degree. Coleridge did not *doubt* our knowledge of the external world; he asserted its complete relativity to our mind and was only too glad to pour something like contempt on the understanding. In this respect Coleridge's scepticism was dogmatic in contrast to the scepticism which Newman could, as it were, 'enjoy' without asserting. Besides, Coleridge made little of the understanding that he might the more exalt the reason which alone, he said, discloses necessary truth; but the passion with which he made this assertion is as indelicate as that with which he inveighed against the understanding. For the reason carries with it, in fact, no more guarantee of its truth than does the understanding; it may give us conviction, but its truth is not self-evident. What the reason affords us may be only an extension of what the understanding gives us, namely an order in which life is possible for the mind. Newman, on the other hand, in comparing our knowledge in dogma to our knowledge in perception, calmly faces a gulf of scepticism which Coleridge could hardly contemplate. With a greater capacity for scepticism, Newman can sustain a quieter and more assured faith. He makes no absolute claim for any human knowledge, reposing his mind calmly on the beneficent providence of God.

§ 2

In order further to compare Coleridge and Newman, I wish to call attention to *The Arians of the Fourth Century*, one of Newman's earliest works, published in 1833, the year preceding that in which Coleridge died.

The Arians is a study in heresy and therefore also in the nature of dogma; its interest lies chiefly in what Newman says of the relation of dogmatic formulations to the state of faith. Behind the many heresies which arose in the early centuries of the Church he discerns a single spirit and mode of feeling of which the heresies, either taken individually or collectively, are signs and symptoms. Heresy, says Newman, is not due to intellectual incapacity. It must be met and fought with the weapons of the intellect; but the struggle between orthodoxy and heresy is a struggle which, if it appears to occur at the level of the intellect, is in reality fought out at deeper levels, between two men or groups of men manifesting in the dispute the quality and nature of their lives as human beings. In such a conflict it is not primarily, if it is superficially, two intellects which clash; instead, it is two imaginations, two sensibilities, two minds of differing moral quality and discipline. In dogma, truth and spiritual value meet and become one; dogma is a witness to this identity; it is something possessed by the religious life and not at all merely acceded to by the intellect, or something to which credence is extended. Dogma is the very spirit of the religious soul. It is not a dead formulation, but the life of the mind which is healthy. And if dogma *is* the health of the soul, heresy *is* its sickness, a disease the origin of which we may detect far lower than the plane at which speculations are disputed. In the preceding chapter we saw how Newman asserted the individual character of real assent; where truth *lives*, it is highly individual. Now dogma is the supreme and living truth, shadowed forth in words only, but dwelling as light in the soul.

Ideally, therefore, dogma is not uttered at all. It comes to formulation in words through historical necessity. 'Freedom from symbols and articles is abstractedly the highest state of Christian communion, and the peculiar privilege of the primitive Church', says Newman; and he continues, 'When confessions do not exist, the mysteries of divine truth, instead of being exposed to the gaze of the profane and uninstructed, are kept hidden in the bosom of the Church, far more faithfully than is otherwise possible'.[1] To expose dogma to the gaze, profane and mocking, of the world, is at once a source of sorrow and a necessity; a necessity because the spirit of the world corrupting the Church must be fought and can be fought only with uttered truth; a sorrow because of the exposure of the holy and mysterious to what is depraved and not understanding. Newman writes at length on the *Disciplina Arcani* of the Alexandrian Church, the teaching of dogma, confession, and symbol as rewards and gifts to those surely advancing in obedience and faith. Faith is, ideally, silent; if it speaks willingly, it does so in secret; if it publicly formulates itself, it does so reluctantly and under stress.

Dogmatic formulations, therefore, occur and take their form through controversy; they are compelled upon the Church, and are not gratuitous undertakings or offered spontaneously to the world. Few portions of Newman's writings are as revealing as the introduction to the essay on St. Chrysostom, written in 1859. Newman there confesses his delight in tracing what he calls the 'interior' of the 'glorious creations of God' whom we call the

[1] *The Arians of the Fourth Century*, London, 1919, pp. 36–7.

saints; and the third and fourth centuries therefore satisfy him as no other centuries do, because we know so much of the interior lives of the saints of the time through the abundant letters which they wrote. His interest in formal doctrinal treatises was slight enough; they did not give him, what the letters of the saints did, the sense of 'identity, growth, continuity, personality'.[1] Abstract statements left him cold; he required the feeling of the life of the saint as it responded to particular occasions, to letters from men and women, to crises in circumstance, to heresies as they arose and needed to be controverted. Their controversies, therefore, were of the nature of autobiography, as were their letters; they were particular and immediate. After speaking, in the part of the essay on St. Chrysostom to which I have referred, of the letters of the saints of the early centuries, he goes on to say:

'This manifestation of themselves the Ancient Saints carry with them into other kinds of composition, where it was less to be expected. Instead of writing formal doctrinal treatises, they write controversy; and their controversy, again, is correspondence. They mix up their own persons, natural and supernatural, with the didactic or polemical works which engaged them. Their authoritative declarations are written, not on stone tablets, but on what Scripture calls "the fleshly tables of the heart". The line of their discussion traverses a region rich and interesting, and opens on those who follow them in it a succession of instructive views as to the aims, the difficulties, the disappointments, under which they journeyed on heavenward, their care of the brethren, their anxieties about contemporary teachers of error. Dogma and proof are in them at the same time hagiography. They do not write a *summa theologiae*, or draw out a *catena*, or pursue a single thesis through the stages of a scholastic disputation. They wrote for the occasion, and seldom on a carefully-digested plan.'[2]

Here again is an illuminating passage:

'Some of those saints who have written most have told us least. There is St. Thomas; he was called in his youth the Bos Siculus for his silence; it is one of the few personal traits which we have of him, and for that very reason, though it does but record the privation of which I am complaining, it is worth a good deal. It is a great consolation to know that he was the Bos Siculus; it makes us feel a sympathy with him, and leads us to trust that perhaps he will feel some sympathy for us, who for one reason or other are silent at times when we should like to be speaking. But it is the sole consolation for that forlorn silence of his, since, although at length he broke it to some purpose, as regards theology, and became a marvel (according to the proverb in such cases), still he is as silent as before in regard to himself. The Angel of the schools! how overflowing he must have been, I say to myself, in all bright supernatural visions, and beautiful and sublime

[1] *Historical Sketches*, 1885, vol. ii, p. 227. [2] Ibid., p. 223.

thoughts! how serene in his contemplation of them! how winning in his communication! but he has not helped me ever so little in apprehending what I firmly believe about him. He wrote his *Summa* and his *Hymns* under obedience, I suppose; and no obedience was given him to speak of himself. So we are thrown upon his biographers, and but for them, we should speak of him as we speak of the author of the *Imitation* or of the *Veni Creator*, only as of a great unknown benefactor. All honour, then, and gratitude to the writers of Saints' lives. They have done what they could. It would not have improved matters if they had been silent as well as the Saint; still, they cannot make up for their Saint's silence; they do not deprive me of my grievance, that at present I do not really know those to whom I am devout, whom I hope to see in heaven.' (pp. 226–7)

Thus it was that between the controversies of the saints and the *Summa* of St. Thomas, Newman saw a great difference. In the former we feel the pressure and passion of great lives; in the other a gratuitous labour of understanding. In the former he delighted; from the latter he shrank. Let the world indeed compel the grace-illumined soul to shed some of its inner light; but there is no call on saintliness freely to dispense it.

If, then, the great dogmatic structures of the early church arose from the 'health' of the great men of the time, were indeed their health, what was the disease which showed itself as heresy, and thus evoked dogmatic formulation? Newman finds little difficulty in supplying the answer: as health shrinks from utterance, the disease of heresy consists in delight in it. 'If the early Church regarded the very knowledge of the truth as a fearful privilege, much more did it regard that truth itself as glorious and awful; and scarcely conversing about it to her children, shrank from the impiety of subjecting it to the hard gaze of the multitude.' (*Arians*, pp. 136–7) Not so heresy. Heresy *is* a willingness for casual utterance, an ease in speaking of the mysteries of religion, a lack of decorous jealousy of the truth. 'They communicate with all men promiscuously; it being nothing to them in what they differ from them. . . . They are all high-minded; all make pretence of knowledge. Their catechumens are perfect in the faith before they are fully taught. . . .' So Newman quotes from Tertullian on the Gnostics. He goes on to add: 'The heretical spirit is ever one and the same in its various forms: this description of the Gnostics was exactly paralleled, in all those points for which we have here introduced it, in the history of Arianism. Arius began by throwing out his questions as a subject for debate for public consideration. . . .' (p. 139) These qualities, 'skilfulness in reasoning and love of disputation', the 'sophistical turn of mind', the 'gymnastics of the Aristotelic school' rarely issued in stable doctrine. 'In their conduct of the argument', says Newman of the Eusebians, 'they seem to be aiming at nothing beyond "living from hand to mouth" as the saying is; availing themselves of some or other expedient, which would suffice to carry them through existing difficulties . . . statements so faintly precise and so decently ambiguous as to embrace the greatest number of opinions possible, and to deprive religion, in consequence, of its austere and commanding aspect.' (p. 274)

To show what Newman has in mind in thus speaking of the 'austere and commanding aspect' of religion, I shall quote further from *The Arians*:

'. . . there is that in religious mysteries which is ever distasteful to secular minds. The marvellous, which is sure to excite the impatience and resentment of the baffled reason, becomes insupportable when found in those solemn topics, which it would fain look upon, as necessary indeed for the uneducated, but irrelevant when addressed to those who are already skilled in the knowledge and the superficial decencies of virtue. The difficulties of science may be dismissed from the mind, and virtually forgotten; the precepts of morality, imperative as they are, may be received with the condescension, and applied with the modifications, of a self-applauding refinement. But what at once demands attention, yet refuses to satisfy curiosity, places itself above the human mind, imprints on it the thought of Him who is eternal, and enforces the necessity of obedience for its own sake. And thus it becomes to the proud and irreverent, what the consciousness of guilt is to the sinner; a spectre haunting the field, and disturbing the complacency, of their intellectual investigations. In this at least, throughout their changes, the Eusebians are consistent,—in their hatred of the Sacred Mystery.' p. 272)

It is clear, then, that in Newman's view heresy springs in the last resort from nothing less than a secular spirit, though it may not acknowledge itself for secular. It is at once 'proud and irreverent', exulting in its own powers and impatient of mystery. Sooner or later, therefore, its humanitarian and secular nature must emerge clearly. Rash utterance and easy debate show a failure in acknowledgement and worship of what is set above the human mind and enforces obedience—'what at once demands attention, yet refuses to satisfy curiosity, places itself above the human mind, imprints on it the thought of Him who is eternal, and enforces the necessity of obedience for its own sake'. Heresy is insurrection against the defeat of curiosity, and unwillingness to bow before mystery. Authority and mystery alike are swept away. The two things are interlocked; and the spirit of sectarianism is also a spirit which finally rests in naturalism. Hence the conflict between (as it were) growing orthodoxy and developing heresy is a conflict in which secularism compels a distillation of living faith into formulation. In such formulation Newman by no means wishes to depress the importance of the theological intellect; only, as it acts, it is no mere disputative skill defending an entrenched position; it is the life of faith as it suffers crystallization into words, and acknowledges therefore that it is not equal to the 'more philosophical determination' (p. 77) of the issues which arise. The intellect, thus identical with faith, or an aspect of it, will not seek to outstep the limits which the wisdom of God has set to our minds; it will not in its employment so far claim independence of the faith of the soul as to desire, even hope, that its curiosity be satisfied; and its labour must terminate in mystery.

§ 3

Newman is at pains to defend Origen and Clement from the charge of liberalism and of having any responsibility for the growth of Arianism. 'It may unreluctantly be confessed . . . that they indulged a boldness of inquiry, such as innocence prompts, rashness and irreverence corrupts, and experience of its mischievous consequences is alone able to repress. Still all this, and much more than this, were it to be found, weighs as nothing against the mass of testimonies producible from extant documents in favour of the real orthodoxy of their creed.' (p. 96) Now these remarks on the Alexandrian writers may be usefully compared with the comment of Newman on Coleridge to the effect that he was a 'very original thinker, who while he indulged a liberty of speculation which no Christian can tolerate, and advocated conclusions which were often heathen rather than Christian, yet after all instilled a higher philosophy into inquiring minds, than they had hitherto been accustomed to accept. In this way he made trial of the age, and found it respond to him, and succeeded in interesting its genius in the cause of catholic truth'. The two statements are very similar. And it is natural that they should be so, on account of the great interest which Coleridge felt in neo-Platonism. If the remark of Newman on Coleridge is harsher than that on the Alexandrian Platonists, this also is natural, on account of Coleridge's interest in Plotinus, a writer for whom Newman felt no sympathy, whose 'liberty of speculation' indeed he sharply condemned.

Coleridge's impulse to speculation was very much stronger than Newman's. Nowhere in Newman's writings is there shown any inclination to philosophical construction. Even when he refers sympathetically to St. Thomas Aquinas he does so without any great show of interest, and sometimes he unmistakably shows embarrassment. We have seen indeed that in *The Grammar of*

Assent, a late work, he justifies those who have 'treated of the Christian faith on system'; and in his lectures on *The Idea of a University*, speaking as the Rector-elect of a proposed university, he is at pains to praise liberal education and freedom of thought so far as possible. But if he thus came in later years to make such acknowledgement, it is clear enough, if only from the evidences of the passages I have quoted from the fairly late essay on St. Chrysostom, that philosophical system and construction roused little interest in him. With his head he might allow it, but his feelings were little roused; indeed I think we may say that early and late they were repelled. In the essay on St. Augustine in *Historical Sketches* not a word is spoken of Augustine's philosophical interests and his Platonism; Newman saw his historical importance in his foundation of monachism in Africa. It has been suggested by Fr. Przywara[1] that the spirit of Augustine finds a 'perfect reincarnation' in Newman. In one vital respect at least this is not true. Certainly, Newman is in the Augustinian tradition in justifying philosophical speculation at all only as it issues from and is guided by the love of God and in refusing it autonomy to any extent. But we may not overlook the difference between the two men, the one delighting in speculation and in neo-Platonism, the other shrinking from them. In this connexion *The Grammar of Assent* is at one, as we have seen, with the early *University Sermons* in exalting reason as 'implicit' and 'illative' as distinct from reason proceeding by syllogism and 'explicitly'. Newman never doubted that religion requires the strenuous employment of the intellect in theology; he never shows signs of thinking that its employment in philosophy is necessary for religion. On the contrary, he never failed to realize the 'mischievous consequences' to which it may lead. There was always in his mind a dread of the impiety which the intellect must acquire if it raises itself in aspiring curiosity to scrutinize the nature of God. Let the mind content itself with what the wisdom of God has seen right to give in revelation; more is not necessary and to seek it impious. 'The greatest risk will result from attempting to be wiser than God has made us, and to outstep in the least degree the circle which is prescribed as the limit of our range.' (*Arians*, p. 76) It is hardly possible to over-emphasize the importance of this sense in Newman. There is a limit prescribed, a circle within which we are shut. To accept that limit and that circle and to abide in patience within it, this, in Newman's eyes, was the highest wisdom; it is at the core of his religious sensibility and we shall have occasion to return to it again. 'Intellectual ability should do no more than enlighten us in the difficulties of our situation, not in the solutions

[1] In *A Monument to St. Augustine*, p. 279.

of them.' Thus he writes in *The Arians*. He was indeed to speak differently of the intellect, at least to some extent, at a later stage; but I believe that this statement best corresponds with the mode of feeling which was enduring in him.

Now Newman reproved Coleridge for his 'liberty of speculation' while paying tribute to him for having aroused the age to a higher philosophy than any to which it had been accustomed. In the preceding chapter I was at some pains to show the striking similarity between Coleridge and Newman in many of their beliefs; and perhaps the chief of these was their refusal to allow an independence to the intelligence in philosophical thought. But, as we have seen, Coleridge in 1794 was 'wonderfully fond' of 'speculating on mystical themes'; and he was to pass enthusiastically from master to master in philosophy in his early days. And, as time passed, as the unpublished manuscripts show, the philosophy of Plotinus greatly engaged his mind until late in life. The *Table Talk* also shows how his mind never ceased to speculate around interpretations (deriving in considerable degree from Plotinus) of the Doctrine of the Trinity. It was just such anxiety to give broad philosophical significance to the dogmas of Christianity which evoked Newman's criticism; and however much in the *Aids to Reflection* Coleridge reiterated his belief in the practical reason as the only road to knowledge of the super-sensible, there is abundant evidence of the hold which philosophical speculation retained over his mind. Against Newman's lifelong antipathy to metaphysics we may place Coleridge's lifelong delight in it.

It is worth while dwelling a little longer on this significant difference between the two men. In this matter Newman's mind was set from early days; to him speculation smacked of liberalism and impiety, and he turned from it. Coleridge's pleasure in it and his impulse to indulge it was deep, powerful, and lifelong. When, therefore, Coleridge followed Kant in setting bounds to philosophical inquiry, and taught that in the practical reason alone lay the road to truth, he was setting up a doctrine which was at war with a strong natural propensity within him. There was here a unique and striking conflict. Certainly there was that in him which would be satisfied by thus bridling the metaphysical impulse; but he was also bridling himself. His masterful philosophical curiosity, exulting in system after system of metaphysic, could hardly accept with docility the restrictions which the other half of his mind imposed; thus it was that, having so much in common with Newman, he could thus merit Newman's censure that he was too bold in speculation. Where Newman's mind therefore patiently followed its course demurely and humbly, declining the hope of understanding and content with what was given, Coleridge's mind, more brilliant and highly strung, moved restlessly and uneasily, now urging the sufficiency of the truths of the conscience, now drawn away into high metaphysic certainly not required by or disclosed to the conscience. Coleridge's mind was naturally masterly, far-ranging, and ambitious, and impatient at its self-imposed restraints; Newman imposed certain limitations on his mind and vision, and accepted them without complaint as altogether necessary. Newman saw dogma therefore as a datum and as a limit; Coleridge saw it as something about which speculation and explication were possible and which he judged to require philosophical interpretation. He therefore partook, in Newman's eyes, of the heresy of the pride of intellect which does not see and acknowledge 'the circle which is prescribed as the limit of our range'. This was in spite of that strain in him which sought to bind the intellect and to deny it in the interests of faith.

In this respect, as in others, Coleridge was divided where Newman was whole. On the one hand, no less than Newman, he saw the 'ideas' intuitively apprehended by the reason as profoundly mysterious, inexhaustible intellectually, and issuing, when cast in propositional form, into contradiction and paradox. 'By Ideas I mean intuitions not sensuous, which can be expressed only by contradictory conceptions, or, to speak more accurately, are in themselves both inexpressible and inconceivable, but are suggested by two contradictory positions.'[1] On the other hand, he quotes Baxter's description of himself: 'And the use that God made of books, above ministers, to the benefit of my soul, made me somewhat excessively in love with good books; so that I thought I had never enough, but scraped up as great a treasure of them as I could. It made the world seem to me as a carcase that had neither life nor loveliness; and it destroyed those ambitious desires after literate fame which were the sin of my childhood. . . . But in order to the knowledge of divinity, my inclination was most to logic and metaphysics, with that part of physics which treateth of the soul, contenting myself at first with a slighter study of the rest: and there had my labour and delight'; and he adds wistfully, 'What a picture of myself!'[2] Newman was never a bookman in this way and to this degree. His greatest and lifelong preoccupation was with the lives of the early saints. Coleridge's passion was theory; Newman's the routine, bearing, and character of saintly men.

[1] *Notes on the English Divines*, 1853, vol. ii, p. 330.

[2] Ibid., p. 53.

§ 4

Coleridge's, then, was a mind which *ranged* far, despite its own protestations; Newman's mind is *shut in* and *enclosed*. This is a cardinal difference which shows itself in many ways. It is shown by the vast reading, secular and religious, of Coleridge in contrast to the narrower scope of Newman's learning; by Coleridge's continuing interest in metaphysics in contrast to Newman's growing sense of history; by Coleridge's Protestantism in contrast to Newman's exaltation of monachism; by, not least, Coleridge's discursive, wandering, tangential style in contrast to the unbroken restraint and deliberation of Newman's.

It was not that Newman lacked in powers of intellectual analysis. He had considerable acquaintance with mathematics and science; and he was by no means guilty of the charge of scorning powers possessed by others and not by himself. But the *practice* of his belief in the superiority of 'ideas' to 'notions' increased the proper subservience of his mind to dogma, and deepened his sense of history. Removed from metaphysical curiosity, he studied the activities of 'ideas' in history; turning from formal treatises he read the letters of the early saints. His mind did not strain upwards, and was content with what was given, which in its richness was also a limit; it could therefore the more reposefully contemplate the world in which he was set; if he was humble before the mystery of the transcendent, he could therefore be humble in the face of its created world, looking everywhere for a continuing providence. This he found increasingly; increasingly he discerned it unbroken with the passing of the centuries. It is not at all to my purpose to justify his conversion to the church of Rome; what is relevant to our purpose is to see the quality of his mind which looked, in increasing expectation, for the signs of the development in human history of divinely given 'ideas'. He saw metaphysics as a kind of challenge to God, an implicit unbelief and a rebelliousness; to seek to understand was virtually to deny, or at least to question. The world of man is absolutely circumscribed, but divinely circumscribed; it is a world of darkness cut away and removed from the over-arching world of light. It is not for us to try, even if we could hope to be successful, to wrest light from a world from which we are shut out. For light has been given. This world is indeed dark; but so much light has the Divine wisdom seen right to allow to enter into it. And our concern must be, not impiously to seek to transcend our limits, but to ensure that in our contemplation of this world in which we are set our eyes are not shut to any portion of the admitted light.

Humble scrutiny of our world is altogether to be preferred to irreverent straining of our eyes to what is transcendent.

Now the divinely given ideas will develop and unfold. It is inconceivable that the wisdom of God should provide revelation of 'ideas' which may languish. Preservation is involved in the idea of creation. As the Creator rested on the seventh day from the work which He had made, yet He 'worketh hitherto'; so He gave the Creed once for all in the beginning, yet blesses its growth still, and provides for its increase. His word 'shall not return unto him void, but accomplish' His pleasure. As creation argues continual governance, so are Apostles harbingers of Popes.[1] Because God entered into history, it cannot be other than that all history is under the ordinance of God; we must pay homage to the temporal lest, if we scorn it, we fail to discern so much of the eternal as has penetrated into it. We must husband the past of time. For living truth, that which is light and warmth (in Coleridge's phrase) to the soul, is not discovered by the philosophers; it grows in the purest and humblest spirits, is carried on from age to age. Nor does it float above the life of mankind, an object of amazement and admiration; it is in the world as an animating and sustaining power and it will grow and expand with the accumulated experience of mankind. Its very struggle with the pride of the world is a source of life. For 'whatever be the risk of corruption from intercourse with the world around, such a risk must be encountered if a great idea is duly to be understood. . . . It is elicited and expanded by trial, and battles into perfection and supremacy'.[2] Because it is truth which is living, in and as the lives of men, it cannot, being God-given, expire; its growth is assured.

A deep sense of history therefore arose out of Newman's way of apprehending the human world in its relation to what is transcendent. Shut in within this world and shut out therefore from so much, we must scrutinize the course of human history for all that it can yield, carefully avoiding conceit of our own judgement. We may rightly mourn our exclusion; but this is all the more reason that we seek and hold what treasure is placed within our grasp.

It is interesting, in regard to Newman's sense of history, to study his essays on St. Benedict and on the Benedictine schools. The essay, *The Mission of St. Benedict*, was printed in January 1858. He was due to write also on the Dominican Order, but the paper for which he was writing (*The Atlantis*) was temporarily suspended; and the next essay he wrote for the paper (printed in

[1] *Essay on the Development of Christian Doctrine*, pp. 85–6.
[2] Ibid., pp. 39–40.

January 1859) was not on the Dominicans but on the Benedictine schools. So far as we know the promised essay on the Dominicans was never written. We can believe that Newman was not sorry to take the occasion not to write of the Dominican Order. In the essay on the schools of the Benedictines he is at pains to explain how, if the task of educating was indeed a deplorable if inevitable departure from the original rule of St. Benedict, the monks yet succeeded in great measure in suiting the manner and method of their teaching, so far as was possible, to the spirit of St. Benedict; and the purpose of both essays is to show 'how undisputatious was the matter and how unexciting the studies'.

There are aspects of Newman's exposition of the Benedictine idea of which I shall speak later. I wish now only to make two quotations which illustrate the pleasure Newman found in observing the taste of the Benedictines for history and their aversion to speculation and polemic. To test the truth of the view of Benedictine learning which he upholds, he remarks[1] that he

'... cannot do better than appeal as a palmary instance to the congregation of St. Maur, an intellectual school of Benedictines surely. Now what, in matter of fact, is the character of its works? It has no Malebranche, no Thomassin, no Morinus; it has no Bellarmine, no Suarez, no Petavius; it has no Tillemont or Fleury,—all of whom were more or less its contemporaries; but it has a Montfaucon, it has a Mabillon, it has a Sainte Marthe, a Coustant, a Sabbatier, a Martene,—men of immense learning and literary experience; it has collators and publishers of MSS. and of inscriptions, editors of the text and of the versions of Holy Scripture, editors and biographers of the Fathers, antiquarians, annalists, paleographists,—with scholarship indeed, and criticism, and theological knowledge, admirable as often as elicited by the particular subject on which they are directly employed, but conspicuously subordinate to it.'

They are, that is to say, scholars and historians; their theological knowledge emerges only when strictly called for at points in historical and scholarly investigations. Again, speaking of a catalogue of Benedictine authors, he remarks that 'those on Scripture and Positive Theology occupy 110 pages; those on history, 300; those on scholastic theology, 12; those on polemics, 12; those on moral theology, 6'.[2]

Now in these matters, the contrast between Newman and Coleridge is very strong. It is far enough from this quiet, demure, and reverent spirit to the intellectual tumult of Coleridge's life, the ceaseless curiosity of his mind, the endless projects of great and systematic works, the inexhaustible if disorganized reading and talk. In Coleridge's mind countless authors jostled each other,

[1] *Historical Sketches*, vol. ii, p. 424. [2] Ibid., vol. ii, pp. 425–6.

claiming in turn his attention, enthusiasm, and judgement; in Newman's mind the great authors took their place in a past order, set in time, not disputants in ideas, but given in and as history.

§ 5

This leads me to speak of Coleridge's Protestantism. Now Newman and Coleridge were agreed on man's need for grace; but we have observed what I have called the peremptoriness of Coleridge's religion. It may be thought wilful to speak of 'peremptoriness' in this connexion. But if we consider the matter, we cannot help concluding that in the Protestant assertion of complete justification by faith there is a note of impatience, a desire to 'deal with' the transcendent, almost to stake a claim upon it. It appears to lie open perhaps to the charge of wishing to master the ineffable, and while acknowledging an extreme helplessness, to assert and claim a subtle and mastering power. Newman's acceptance of the remove of the human from the divine, his patience and mourning in the face of it, the waiting on grace in a life of quiet hope, place him beyond the possibility of this charge.

That Coleridge was deeply and resolutely Protestant requires all the more to be emphasized because the idea quickly grew up in the nineteenth century, and is still to-day popular, that Coleridge was, if not an Anglo-Catholic, at least an Anglo-Catholic in the making. This notion is quite mistaken. It is true of course that Coleridge prepared the way for Newman on account of all that they certainly did have in common—as we tried to expound in the previous chapter. But it cannot be too much emphasized that the theology of the Oxford Movement would have been abhorrent to Coleridge. His addiction to Kant brought him near to Newman in certain respects; his admiration of Luther as, after Apostolic times, the greatest of all Churchmen, put him at a great remove from Anglo-Catholicism.

I shall be at some pains to labour these reflections. And to assure the reader that I am indulging no capriciousness nor bending Coleridge to my purposes, I shall begin by quoting some remarks of Sara Coleridge in the second edition of *Biographia Literaria* (1847).

'There are some' [she says (pp. lxx–xxiii)], 'among the intelligent readers of Coleridge, who take a different view of the character of his opinions from that which I have expressed: who believe that, during his latter years, he became in the main what High Churchmen consider Catholic and orthodox, whilst any notions he still held of a different character were anomalies, remnants of his early creed, which would have been worked out of his mind had his years been prolonged. There are others amongst the proselytes to the Oxford theology, who see nothing more in his teaching than a stunted Anglo-catholicism; some of these aver that, in the beginning of their course they were conducted for a little way by the writings of Mr. Coleridge; that he first led them out of the dry land of negative Protestantism; but that now, by help of newer guides, they have advanced far beyond him, and can look down on his lower station from a commanding eminence. They view the *Aids to Reflection* as a half-way house to Anglo-catholic orthodoxy, just as others, who have got beyond them, in a certain direction, consider their Anglo-catholic doctrine a half-way house to what they consider the true Catholicism,—namely that of the Church of Rome. My own belief is, that such a view of my Father's theological opinions is radically wrong; that although an unripe High Church theology is all that some readers have found or valued in his writings, it is by no means what is there; and that he who thinks he has gone a little way with Coleridge, and then proceeded with Romanizing teachers further still, has never gone along with Coleridge at all, or entered deeply into any of his expositions of Christian doctrine. . . .'

She adds on a later page:

'To me . . . it is manifest, that his system of belief, intellectually considered, differs materially from "Catholic" doctrine as commonly understood, and that this difference during the latter years of his meditative life, instead of being shaded off, became more definite and boldly developed.'

This is emphatic enough; and no one who reads Coleridge with half an eye can doubt that what she here says is true. To begin with, Coleridge had nothing of Newman's reverence for the early centuries of the Church.

'I would say, once for all,' he remarks in commenting on Jeremy Taylor, 'that it was the fashion of the Arminian court divines of Taylor's age, that is, of the High Church party, headed by Archbishop Laud, to extol, and (in my humble judgment) egregiously to overrate, the example and authority of the first four, nay, of the first six centuries; and at all events to take for granted the Evangelical and Apostolical character of the Church to the death of Athanasius. Now so far am I from conceding this, that before the first Council of Nicaea, I believe myself to find the seeds and seedlings of all the worst corruptions of the Latin Church of the thirteenth century, and not a few of these even before the close of the second.'[1]

And he has, elsewhere, also for comment on Taylor:

'It is characteristic of the man and the age, Taylor's high-strained reverential epithets to the names of the Fathers, and as rare and naked mention of Luther, Melancthon, Calvin—the least of whom was not

[1] *Notes on English Divines*, vol. i, pp. 317–18.

inferior to St. Augustin, and worth a brigade of the Cyprians, Firmilians, and the like.'[1]

If, then, Coleridge felt little of Newman's reverence for the early centuries of Christianity, he felt less for the High Church doctrines of the seventeenth century in England.

'Towards the close of the reign of our first James, and during the period from the accession of Charles I to the restoration of his profligate son, there arose a party of divines, Arminians (and many of them Latitudinarians) in their Creed, but devotees of the throne and the altar, soaring High Churchmen and ultra royalists. Much as I dislike their scheme of doctrine and detest their principles of government both in Church and State, I cannot but allow that they formed a galaxy of learning and talent, and that among them the Church of England finds her stars of the first magnitude. Instead of regarding the Reformation established under Edward VI as imperfect, they accused the Reformers, some of them openly, but all in their private opinions, of having gone too far; and while they were willing to keep down (and if they could not reduce him to a primacy of honour to keep out) the Pope, and to prune away the innovations in doctrine brought in under the Papal domination, they were zealous to restore the hierarchy, and to substitute the authority of the Fathers, Canonists, and Councils of the first six or seven centuries, and the least Papistic of the later Doctors and Schoolmen, for the names of Luther, Melancthon, Bucer, Calvin and the systematic theologians who rejected all testimony but that of their Bible. As far as the principle, on which Archbishop Laud and his followers acted, went to re-actuate the idea of the Church, as a co-ordinate and living Power of right of Christ's institution and express promise, I go along with them; but I soon discover that by the Church they meant the Clergy, the hierarchy exclusively, and then I fly off from them in a tangent. For it is this very interpretation of the Church that, according to my conviction, constituted the first and fundamental apostasy.'[2]

This first and fundamental apostasy he saw arise in the early centuries, the 'pernicious error' of the 'gradual concentration of the church into a priesthood, and the consequent rendering of the reciprocal functions of love and redemption and counsel between Christian and Christian exclusively official, and between disparates, namely, the priest and the layman'.[3]

Again, to read Coleridge's comments (in volume ii of the *Divines*) on an elaborate attack on Methodism by an unknown barrister of the time, is to see how quickly and with what passion he would always come to the defence of the doctrine of Justification by Faith against wilful or ignorant attacks upon it. Everywhere, in his later writings, we observe his exaltation of Luther. For example, in his notes, written between 1830 and 1833, on *The*

[1] *Notes on English Divines*, vol. i, p. 230. [2] Ibid., p. 325. [3] Ibid., p. 318.

Pilgrim's Progress, in speaking of the discretion required in pastoral duties, he says: 'In this, as in what not? Luther is the great model; ever reminding the individual that not he, but Christ, is to redeem him; and that the way to be redeemed is to think with will, mind and affections on Christ, not on himself. I am a sin-laden being, and Christ has promised to loose the whole burden if I but entirely trust in him. To torment myself with the detail of the noisome contents of the fardel will but make it stick the closer, first to my imagination and then to my unwilling will.'

§ 6

In order to confirm further what I have said and in order to show how his Protestant position was part and parcel of a point of view of great balance and catholicity, I shall briefly expound Coleridge's theological beliefs, drawing chiefly upon the *Aids to Reflection*. The reader who feels little interest in theological matters may wish to proceed at once to section 9 in which the main narrative of this chapter is taken up.

I shall find it convenient to speak first, of his attitude to the doctrine of Justification by Faith; secondly, of his view of baptism with which it will be convenient to couple his attitude to authority in religion; thirdly, of his exposition of the dogma of original sin; and lastly, of his view of the relation of Church to State. In trying to expound what Coleridge has to say on these matters, I shall try also to emphasize the state of *tension* in which his theological thought existed. Tension, it has been truly said, is a necessary mark of the religious consciousness when it is healthy; it is the state of feeling, of balance difficult to maintain, which corresponds to the endless paradoxes of religion when we seek to give it intellectual formulation. The paradoxes of religion are numerous, indeed indefinitely so; therefore the maintenance of, or we might way, the submission to, tension, is a continuing necessity. To break the tension, to secure release from the strain it involves is a constant temptation; and to combine this tension with serenity is the endeavour of the religious soul. I think that when we review Coleridge's philosophical and theological writings it is impossible not to be impressed by his achievement.

From what I have already recounted, it is not at all surprising that Coleridge found a great deal to sympathize with in the teachings of the Reformers. Their anti-intellectualist note, along with the doctrine of Justification by Faith alone, all sprang from a motive which was real enough in Coleridge's own mind; and it was one of his complaints against the dissent of his time that it no longer had its roots in the teaching of the Reformers. He, for his part, never ceased to be a man of the Reformation, or to exalt Luther as one of the great heroes of humanity. He is emphatic enough in his assertion of the doctrines of Justification by Faith. 'The doctrine of imputed righteousness, rightly and scripturally interpreted, is so far from being *irrational* or *immoral*, that Reason itself prescribes the idea in order to give a *meaning* and an ultimate Object to morality.' (*Aids*, p. 105) Nothing could be more definite than this; the doctrine states a necessary idea of the practical Reason—'the moral law in the conscience demands its reception in order to give reality and substantive evidence to the idea presented by the Reason'. He defends Luther and Calvin against the charge that in their hands the doctrine gives ground to irrationality or immorality; but he makes no defence of the doctrine as, he held, it came to be used by Jonathan Edwards, and saw with the utmost clearness the objection to the doctrine in its extremest form, namely, that it must issue into what is, in effect, a naturalistic scheme. To subject to the mechanism of a Necessitarian scheme 'the moral world no less than the material or physical' has for its result 'that all is nature'. (p. 150)

Certainly, had Coleridge discerned in the doctrine of Justification by Faith anything which might act against a strenuous moral life and the pursuit of holiness, he would have rejected it without hesitation. That the doctrine does, and must, so act is of course the familiar objection to it. Coleridge did not at all agree with the objection. But how far he was from losing a sense of judgement in regard to it we can make clear by quoting this passage from an earlier portion of the *Aids*. He first quotes from Leighton: 'Although from present unsanctification, a man cannot infer that he is not *elected*; for the decree may, for part of a man's life run (as it were) underground; yet this is sure, that that estate leads to death, and unless it is broken, will prove the black line of reprobation. A man hath no portion amongst the children of God, nor can read one word of comfort in all the promises that belong to them, while he remains unholy.' And Coleridge goes on to comment: 'The moral result, the specific Form and Character in which the Spirit *manifests* its presence, is the only sure pledge and token of its presence; which is to be, and which safely may be, inferred from its practical effects, but of which an *immediate* knowledge or consciousness is impossible; and every pretence to such knowledge is either hypocrisy or fanatical delusion.' (pp. 57–8) That one who found life as difficult as did Coleridge should seek and find the consolations which the doctrine of Justification by Faith may bring was natural and proper; but even so, it certainly did not mean for him any relaxation from the pursuit of holiness, any easy self-deception, or complacency.

Even so, we must be careful not to minimize in Coleridge the power of the Reformation teaching. For the Romanist doctrine of Justification he had nothing but scorn: 'As the encysted venom, or poison-bag, beneath the adder's fang, so does this doctrine lie beneath the tremendous power of the Romish Hierarchy.' (p. 312) On the other hand, how clearly and with what certainty Coleridge could sound the unmistakable note of the Reformation is shown in the following passage, which he adapts from Leighton:

> 'The Apostle says not—stedfast by your own resolutions and purposes; but—*stedfast by faith*. Nor yet stedfast in your Will, but *stedfast in the faith*. We are not to be looking to, or brooding over ourselves, either for accusation or for confidence, or (by a deep yet too frequent self-delusion) to obtain the latter by making a merit to ourselves of the former. But we are to look to Christ and "him crucified". The Law "that is very nigh to thee, even in thy heart"; the Law that condemneth and hath no promise; that stoppeth the guilty Past in its swift flight, and maketh it disown its name; the Law will accuse thee enough. Linger not in the Justice-court, listening to thy indictment! Loiter not in waiting to hear the Sentence! No! Anticipate the verdict! *Appeal to Caesar!* Haste to the King for a Pardon! Struggle thitherward, though in fetters; and cry aloud, and collect the whole remaining strength of thy Will in the Outcry—I believe! Lord! help my unbelief! Disclaim all right of property in thy fetters! Say, that they belong to the Old Man, and that thou dost but carry them to the Grave, to be buried with their Owner! Fix thy thought on what *Christ* did, what *Christ* suffered, what *Christ* is—as if thou wouldst fill the hollowness of thy Soul with Christ! If he emptied himself of glory to become Sin for thy salvation, must not thou be emptied of thy sinful Self to become Righteousness in and through his agony and the effective merits of his Cross? By what other means, in what other form, is it possible for thee to stand in the presence of the Holy One? With *what* mind wouldst thou come before God, if not with the Mind of Him, in whom *alone* God loveth the World? With good advice, perhaps, and a little assistance, thou wouldst rather cleanse and patch up a mind of thy own, and offer it as thy *admission-right*, thy *qualification*, to him who "charged his angels with folly".'

He says again,

> 'That Redemption is an *opus perfectum*, a finished Work, the claim to which is conferred in Baptism; that a Christian cannot speak or think as if his Redemption by the Blood, and his Justification by the Righteousness of Christ alone, were future or contingent events, but must both say and think, I *have been* redeemed, I am justified; lastly, that for as many as are received into his Church by baptism, Christ has condemned Sin in the Flesh, has made it *dead in law*, i.e. no longer

imputable as *Guilt*, has destroyed the *objective reality* of Sin. These are Truths, which all the Reformed Churches, Swedish, Danish, Evangelical, (or Lutheran,) the Reformed, (the Calvinistic in mid-Germany, France, and Geneva, so-called,) lastly, the Church of England, and the Church of Scotland—nay, the best and most learned Divines of the Roman Catholic Church have united in upholding as most certain and necessary Articles of Faith, and the effectual preaching of which Luther declares to be the appropriate criterion, *stantis vel cadentis, ecclesiae*.' (pp. 305–9)

Here is the essence of the Reformation teaching, and Coleridge never lost sight of it; the Church of England was to him, in one of its essential attributes, a Reformed Church. He discerned so surely the essence of the Reformation gospel that he never did injustice to the great Reformers. What is embodied in the passage I have quoted above is his conviction that the experience of religion is precisely the looking away from the human to the Divine, the emptying of the mind in order that it may be filled with the 'mind of Him, in whom alone God loveth the world'. This and this alone is, for the Reformation, religion; and to assert that this is so was its purpose, to keep this truth unclouded by innumerable accretions. Intellectual and doctrinal formulations must inevitably bring difficulty and danger with them; and Coleridge, who saw this clearly enough, sought no easy dialectical victories over Calvin and Luther; he found 'harsh and inconvenient Expressions' in the writings of them both, but he understood how and whence they came. Hence he says, characteristically, in speaking of Leighton's treatment of Election, that Leighton 'avoids all metaphysical views of Election relatively to God, and confines himself to the Doctrine in its relation to man. . . . The following may, I think, be taken as a safe and useful Rule in religious enquiries. Ideas, that derive their origin and substance from the *Moral* Being, and to the reception of which as true *objectively* . . . we are determined by a *practical* interest exclusively, may not, like theoretical or speculative Positions, be pressed onward into all their possible *logical* consequences. The Law of Conscience, and not the Canons of discursive Reasoning, must decide in such cases.' (p. 155) Thus, it is because he did not see the doctrines of the Reformers as 'theoretical or speculative Positions' that he was able to enter with such deep sympathy into the essence of their teaching.

I have said that Coleridge followed Leighton in insisting on sanctification as the necessary sign of justification. Here indeed he safeguards against abuse; without the marks of the indwelling of the spirit, we have, he says, no right to claim justification, if indeed we can speak of claiming justification at all. We therefore see here the tension in which, I said, Coleridge's religious life existed. If he asserts the doctrine of Justification by Faith, he none the less insists on sanctification, if we are not to be led aside into self-deception, emotionalism, and hypocrisy. But if he insists in this way on sanctification, it cannot be said that he recedes at all from his belief in Justification by Faith; for, proceed as far as we may in holiness, religion must count our morality for nothing, and is still a looking away from ourselves to what is transcendent. Thus, he held a balance, without sacrifice either of the religious or the moral life.

§ 7

To pass now to Coleridge's view of baptism, the reader will recall how, in the passage from the *Aids* I quoted in the last section, Coleridge spoke of baptism making sin no longer imputable as guilt; and he said of this doctrine that it is essential to all Christianity properly so called. Coleridge is here taking his stand on the Protestant tradition; but he none the less puts us in mind of the Tractarians and their battle with the Evangelicals. Like the Tractarians after him he was convinced there was more health for the spirit in the doctrine of Baptismal Regeneration than in the 'Evangelical and Arminian Methodist' view, with its accompanying 'conversions', 'states', and 'feelings'. Even so, later on in the *Aids* (lxviii) he denies emphatically that 'Regeneration is only Baptism'; like Pusey, when put to the test (in the Gorham judgement), and as Mozley was later to argue, he will not suppose that a 'spiritual regenerative power and agency [inheres] in or [accompanies] the sprinkling the few drops of water on an infant's face'. For if, he says, we can agree that such power resides in the sprinkling of water, what conceivable grounds of objection have we to the 'insufflation and extreme unction used in the Romish Church'? (pp. 333–4). Thus, although he sees the possibility of greater moral health in the doctrine of Baptismal Regeneration than in its denial, that same concern with the moral life prevents us from asserting the doctrine absolutely.

His attitude then to baptism is not a simple one. In the last portion of the *Aids* he makes a further lengthy statement on the doctrine. He says: 'You remember and admire the saying of an old Divine, that a ceremony duly instituted was a Chain of Gold around the Neck of Faith; but if in the wish to make it co-essential and consubstantial, you draw it closer and closer, it may strangle the Faith it was meant to deck and designate' (pp. 364–5); and he goes on to speak of the danger of a merely superstitious view of the ceremony of baptism. He discerns a check to superstition in the recognition that baptism is not merely something received by the child but, in one aspect, an act of the Church. If we recognize, he says, the 'duty and necessity of checking the superstitious abuse of the baptismal rite', then 'I ask, with confidence, in what way could the Church have exercised a sound discretion more wisely, piously, or effectively, than by affixing, from among the several ends and purposes of Baptism, the outward ceremony to the purposes here mentioned? How could the great body of Christians be more plainly instructed as to the true nature of all outward ordinances? What can be conceived better calculated to prevent the ceremony from being regarded as other and more than a ceremony, if not the administration of the same on an *object*, (yea, a dear and precious *object*) of spiritual duties, though the *conscious* subject of spiritual operations and graces only by anticipation and in hope.' (p. 368) Clearly, his feeling is altogether in favour of the baptismal rite, and he recognizes its great importance. Nevertheless he denies that belief in Baptismal Regeneration is essential; what alone is essential is 'such a faith in Christ as tends to produce a conformity to his holy doctrines and example in heart and life, and which faith is itself a declared mean and condition of our partaking of his spiritual Body, and of being "clothed upon" with his righteousness' (p. 363). So, at least, he writes in the *Aids*. But in later editions Derwent Coleridge added a note written by Coleridge in 1828, three years later. Now in this note Coleridge is clearly anxious not only to avoid possible misunderstanding, but also to bring himself into line with Church doctrine. He still, indeed, asserts that there is no necessity to believe in an act of the Spirit at the moment of baptism; but he is careful to say that he does not deny the 'possibility or the reality of the influence of the Spirit on the soul of an infant'.[1] Still less does he, he says, 'think lightly of the graces which the child receives, as a living part of the Church, and whatever flows from the Communion of Saints and the περιχώρησις of the Spirit'. And he concludes characteristically, with a basis in the practical, by saying that 'in reference to our principles of conduct toward, and judgment concerning, our neighbours, the Church declares, that before the time of the Baptism there is no authority for asserting,—and that since the time there is no authority for denying,—that gift and regenerate presence of the Holy Spirit, promised by an especial covenant to the members of Christ's mystical body: and consequently, no just pretence for expecting or requiring another new initiation or birth into the state of Grace'. From this it is not unreasonable to suppose that in 1828 at least he would hold belief in Baptismal Regeneration as essential to the Church's doctrine,

[1] Edition of 1854, p. 319.

as Pusey continued to do after the Gorham judgement. We see, then, that Coleridge was set against any mitigation of baptismal doctrine; he denies indeed that any time 'can be specified for the Spirit's descent and incoming'; but in *practice* our attitude must be determined by the assumption that the moment of baptism is one of 'birth into a state of grace'. He sees, in the recognition of its spiritual duties by the Church towards the baptized, the only sure check upon superstition. Although it be true that 'right Reason', operating negatively, may deny, indeed must deny, that baptism is automatically regeneration, the practical reason, paramount here as everywhere, none the less asserts the need of the rite for the moral and religious life.

We can now turn to notice briefly Coleridge's attitude to authority. After speaking of the dangers which attach to denial of Baptismal Regeneration, of the 'contagious fever-boils of the Evangelicals and Arminian Methodists of the day' and of 'Pharisaic and fanatical individuals', he observes the difficulty which Luther had in 'exposing the working of the carnal mind', in subtle disguises, in religion. He then says:

'One most mischievous and very popular mis-belief must be cleared away in the first instance—the presumption, I mean, that whatever is not *quite* simple, and what any plain body can understand at the first hearing, cannot be of necessary belief, or among the fundamental Articles or Essentials of Christian Faith. A docile child-like mind, a deference to the authority of the churches, a presumption of the truth of doctrines that have been received and taught as true by the whole Church in all times, reliance on the positive declaration of the Apostle . . . and . . . study, quiet meditation, gradual growth of spiritual knowledge, and earnest prayer for its increase . . . .'

—all these, he says, cannot be superseded in the interest of the 'plainest and dullest understanding'. (p. 308) Now Coleridge is not here urging the possibility of widespread study of theology; nor is he despising the 'plainest and dullest understanding'. 'Too soon', as I have quoted earlier, 'did the Doctors of the Church forget that the heart, the moral nature, was the beginning and the end; and that truth, knowledge and insight were comprehended in its expansion.' Reason in all men is one and equal, unlike the understanding; but its light can grow only through discipline, contemplation, and, Coleridge insists, docility. The question is not one of understanding doctrine; it is of the discernment of spiritual ideas by the reason—ideas embodied in the doctrines 'received and taught as true by the whole church in all times'; it is not a question of instruction primarily, but of spiritual growth through which come humility and reverence for the achievement of generations which have gone before. Docility, in its best sense, therefore, is an obligation; and correspondingly, there is no less an obligation on the Church to exercise authority. 'My fixed principle is: that a Christianity without a Church exercising spiritual authority is vanity and dissolution'; in its essence, it is without humility and, in its effects, only disruption. Coleridge is not of course denying the right to private judgement (though such a right in matters of scriptural interpretation attempted without scholarly knowledge may well be challenged); he is asserting as the condition, both of authority as exercised by the Church and of docility in the individual, the presence of continuous moral growth and therefore of the growing light of the reason. In the democracy of the Church, he said, there should be 'focal points, but no superior'. (*Table Talk*, 18 May 1830) Because this is so, authority must partake of docility, and docility of authority. There cannot fail to be a tension between these two poles of the religious life; but the tension is none the less necessary and healthy. As we have seen, his objection to Evangelicalism and Methodism was that their attitude to baptism was bound up with, and indeed issued from, a failure in humility.

§ 8

In expounding his view of original sin, Coleridge is very near to Kant's exposition in *Religion within the Bounds of Mere Reason*. Like Kant, he refuses in the most categorical manner to mean by original sin anything in the nature of inherited tendencies. The origin of evil must be, in some sense, in the will itself; to put the origin of sin outside the will must be, in Coleridge's view, an immoral doctrine; he is determined to maintain at all costs the dignity and freedom of the will. 'In nature there is no origin. Sin therefore is spiritual evil: but the spiritual in man is the will.' Precisely because moral activity is not a part of nature, any doctrine of inherited evil must be put aside. If sin is original, it is directly original to each individual will, however mysteriously. For the origin of sin is not at all in the temporal and historical and anthropological, but in the inscrutable and noumenal grounds of each individual will. This places the origin of sin beyond the range of the understanding. That evil is common to all is beyond dispute; it is equally beyond dispute that we cannot attribute its origin to the divine will; 'it must therefore be referred to the Will of Man. And this evil Ground we call Original Sin. It is a *mystery*, that is, a Fact, which we see, but cannot explain; and a doctrine, the truth of which we apprehend, but can neither comprehend nor communicate.' (*Aids*, p. 281) Hence the 'Adam' who features in the traditional doctrine is not primarily an individual, but the type and pattern of all individuals whatsoever. And if it be objected that Coleridge's doctrine is in effect an evasion, Coleridge can reply, and with good reason, that morality itself is a mystery, so long at least as we treat it at all as something not to be explained naturalistically. And if man is thus mysterious, so also is God; if man's state baffles our understanding, so also does God's act, our redemption through the effective merits of the Cross. The origin of sin and the divine sacrifice of the Cross are not notionally exhaustible, for none of the ideas of the reason are; we cannot encompass them with our minds. We acknowledge their unmistakable reality in us; we acknowledge our sin, we receive the sacrifice. The sin which is original to each of us eludes psychological and anthropological explanation; so does the redemption of our souls by God through the Cross; we discern, but may not comprehend. We are in nature and grasp nature through the understanding; we are also in supernature and may perceive, however dimly, through the reason, its realities; but we fail to encompass them intellectually. This, then, is the supreme tension, which is due to our double nature; for we are in and also out of the temporal. To reflect on morality is to see that we do not and cannot live wholly in the natural; 'it is most true that morality, *as* morality . . . is either absorbed and lost in the quicksands of Prudential Calculus, or it is taken up and transfigured into the duties and mysteries of religion. And no wonder: since Morality (including the personal being, the *I am*, as its subject) is itself a mystery, and the ground and *suppositum* of all other Mysteries, relatively to Man.' (p. 287) But if morality carries us beyond the confines of nature, it cannot carry us to where we can see clearly; and in this acquiescence in what must remain mysterious we must somehow rest, acknowledging to it a fealty which is none the less absolute.

Now it is against the background of this theology, which elevates the doctrine of the Atonement to a first place, and of Coleridge's addiction to Luther and the Reformation, that we must read the essay *On the Constitution of Church and State*. The essence of it lies in the absolute separation which Coleridge makes between the Spiritual Church and the National Church. Now, the first, as spiritual, cannot be English, nor Established; for her 'paramount aim and object is another world, not a world to come exclusively, but likewise another world that now is, and to the concerns of which alone the epithet *spiritual* can, without a mischievous abuse of the word, be applied';[1] but the second, as the learned and teaching body, is secular and has its being in the

[1] Edition of 1839, p. 127.

State, as an estate of the realm. In Coleridge's opinion, it is precisely the failure to realize the spiritual nature of the Church proper, which is not of the world, and the failure sharply to separate the spiritual and the visible, the sacred and the secular, which had brought the Church to its condition of weakness and ineptitude. It is true that the two functions, of the 'Church of Christ' and of the national clerisy, can and should exist together in the same men; still, without a continuous acknowledgement of itself as utterly distinct in essence from the clerisy, the Church's association with it must be, by an insoluble paradox, to the ill health and ultimate extinction of both. Coleridge saw such an ill health in England; it despiritualized the true Church and reduced education to the service of purely worldly ends. Also, the true Church, which alone can be a democracy, under its one invisible Head, loses its touch with the people, and through a false identification with the State becomes aristocratic; for secular position and authority carries no weight in the true Church, which is not and cannot be an institution in this world or in any land. In every respect it is precisely by acknowledging tension and inevitable antagonism between themselves that the Church and State may come together; and the tension must be continuously created by the clerisy, in which religion and culture cohabit without being diminished by each other; for in the persons of the clerisy, religion at once rejects culture and enriches it. In such a society as this, the artist would have his place in the universal Church and in the national clerisy; on him also would fall the labour of a creative tension in his life and work as an artist in a society with which he is at one. This is the answer, drawing its essence from the Protestant Reformation, which later Romanticism offered to the half-formulated questions of Shelley in the Preface to *The Cenci*.

Of course, this answer is very different from Newman's. I am speaking with much brevity of matters which take on great importance in the minds of Coleridge and Newman; but it will be obvious how sharply the latter as a Catholic must differ here from the former as a Protestant. For Coleridge could not have tolerated Newman's incorporation of the visible into the invisible Church. So far as Newman, in the Augustinian tradition, insists on the transcendence and invisibility of the City of God, Coleridge would heartily accord with him. But Coleridge would have drawn back from words such as these: 'The unseen world through God's secret power and mercy, encroaches upon this world; and the Church that is seen is just that portion of it by which it encroaches; and thus though the visible Churches of the Saints in this world seem rare, and scattered to and fro, like islands in the sea, they are in truth but the tops of the everlasting hills, high and vast and deeply-rooted, which a deluge covers.'[1] Such a doctrine of 'encroachment' was not to Coleridge's taste; it must naturally lead to a respect for an authoritative hierarchical Church which it was his special purpose to oppose. Coleridge would agree with Newman that the 'supremacy of conscience is the essence of natural religion'; he would emphatically deny, what Newman goes on to say, that 'the supremacy of Apostle, or Pope, or Church, or Bishop, is the essence of revealed' religion.[2]

§ 9

Now Coleridge's Protestantism is not unrelated to his point of view as a writer about European literature. I shall now consider what Coleridge says in his lectures on literature (delivered in the course of the second decade of the century) about Romanticism; and then about the relation of Romanticism to classical art, to Gothic art, and to Protestantism. We shall then be in a position to go further in our comparative study of Coleridge and Newman.

In an essay in *The Friend*, Coleridge discusses and emphasizes the place of knowledge in morals and religion; and he ends by saying that 'to connect with the objects of our senses the obscure notions and consequent vivid feelings, which are due only to immaterial and permanent things, is profanation relatively to the heart, and superstition in the understanding'. (p. 63) He declares that the intellect must be habituated 'to clear, distinct and adequate conceptions concerning all things that are possible objects of clear conception'; but the 'deep feelings which belong, as by a natural right to those obscure ideas that are necessary to the moral perfection of the human being, notwithstanding, yea, even in consequence of, their obscurity'—these feelings must be 'reserved for objects which their very sublimity renders indefinite'. (p. 63) These objects are of course those apprehended, though inadequately, by the reason; and he is so far at one with Kant in the matter of the practical reason that he asserts that these ideas are and must be wrapped in contradiction as well as obscurity. This obscurity and the inability of the intellect to form clear and distinct ideas in regard to the super-sensible, are necessary, he says, 'for the moral perfection of the human being'. It is through the reason, he says, 'that man knows intuitively the sublimity, and the infinite hopes, fears and capabilities of his nature'.

I quote here Wordsworth's famous lines in the sixth book of *The Prelude*, in which he recalls his crossing of the Alps. He says of the imagination (which in the conclusion of the poem he says is

[1] *Parochial and Plain Sermons* (1900), vol. iv, p. 178.

[2] *Essay on Development*, p. 86.

> . . . but another name for absolute power
> And clearest insight, amplitude of mind,
> And Reason in her most exalted mood),

that, 'like an awful Power', it

> . . . rose from the mind's abyss
> Like an unfathered vapour that enwraps,
> At once, some lonely traveller. I was lost;
> Halted without an effort to break through;
> But to my conscious soul I now can say—
> 'I recognise thy glory:' in such strength
> Of usurpation, when the light of sense
> Goes out, but with a flash that has revealed
> The invisible world, doth greatness make abode,
> There harbours; whether we be young or old,
> Our destiny, our being's heart and home,
> Is with infinitude, and only there;
> With hope it is, hope that can never die,
> Effort, and expectation, and desire,
> And something ever more about to be.
> Under such banners militant, the soul
> Seeks for no trophies, struggles for no spoils
> That may attest her prowess, blest in thoughts
> That are their own perfection and reward,
> Strong in herself and in beatitude
> That hides her, like the mighty flood of Nile
> Poured from his fount of Abyssinian clouds
> To fertilise the whole Egyptian plain. (p. 684)

Here indeed is the recognition of 'the sublimity, and the infinite hopes, fears and capabilities of his nature' which reason, says Coleridge, affords to the spirit of man.

It will be noticed that the passage from *The Prelude*, though it records an unmistakably mystical experience, is especially concerned to exalt the human spirit. It is a sense of the power and glory of the soul which Wordsworth above all conveys. He recognizes the 'glory' of the soul and its 'greatness' which abides and harbours in infinitude. The soul advances under 'banners militant', inexhaustible in hope, effort, expectation, and desire; and there is 'something ever more about to be'. He speaks of the 'prowess' of the soul; she is 'strong in herself'. So that if (continuing the military imagery) she

> Seeks for no trophies, struggles for no spoils,

and obtains beatitude, we are left in no doubt of the power and glory of the human spirit. Now the core of the passage is the paradox of the union of the 'militancy' of the soul with its rest in a beatitude in which trophies and spoils are not looked for, of infinite aspiration with rest, of the unlimited with quietness.

In the course of his lectures on Shakespeare in 1818,[1] expounding the nature of Gothic, Coleridge spoke the following words:

'The Greeks idolized the finite, and therefore were the masters of all grace, elegance, proportion, fancy, dignity, majesty—of whatever, in short, is capable of being definitely conveyed by defined forms or thoughts: the moderns revere the infinite, and affect the indefinite as a vehicle of the infinite;—hence their passions, their obscure hopes and fears, their wandering through the unknown, their grander moral feelings, their more august conception of man as man, their future rather than their past—in a word, their sublimity.' (pp. 194–5)

Coleridge is here contrasting what he has (in *The Friend*) called the gifts of reason and the mode of feeling typified in the lines quoted above from Wordsworth with classical feeling. Also in 1818 he said:

'The Greeks were remarkable for complacency and completion; they delighted in whatever pleased the eye; to them it was not enough to have merely the idea of a divinity, they must have it placed before them, shaped in the most perfect symmetry, and presented with the nicest judgment; and if we look upon any Greek production of art, the beauty of its parts, and the harmony of their union, the complete and complacent effect of the whole are the striking characteristics. . . . The worship of statues in Greece had, in a civil sense, its advantage and disadvantage; advantage, in promoting statuary and the arts; disadvantage, in bringing their Gods too much on a level with human beings, and thence depriving them of their dignity, and gradually giving rise to scepticism and ridicule. But no statue, no artificial emblem, could satisfy the Northman's mind; the dark, wild imagery of nature which surrounded him, and the freedom of his life, gave his mind a tendency to the infinite, so that he found rest in that which presented no end, and derived satisfaction from that which was indistinct.'[2]

Here certainly, in these last sentences, is the essence of the lines of Wordsworth which I have quoted.

Again, in the same lecture, he remarks on the sublimity of Gothic architecture, and then goes on to say that it reveals a kind of religion which,

'while it tended to soften the manners of the Northern tribes, was at the same time highly congenial to their nature. The Goths are free from the stain of hero worship. Gazing on their rugged mountains, surrounded by impassable forests, accustomed to gloomy seasons, they lived in the bosom of nature, and worshipped an invisible and unknown

[1] *Lectures on Shakespeare*, Bohn edition, London, 1904.

[2] *Miscellanies Aesthetic and Literary*, Bohn edition, 1885, pp. 92–3.

deity. Firm in his faith, domestic in his habits, the life of the Goth was simple and dignified, yet tender and affectionate.' (p. 92)

The contrast between Greek and Gothic therefore is between what is 'statuesque', 'what pleases the eye', what is encompassable by the imagination, and what, on the other hand, baffles eye, understanding, and imagination. This is also, he says, the difference between the beautiful and the sublime. The supreme genius of the Greeks is in their statuary. The supreme gift of the 'modern' is in painting, drama, and music. Coleridge liked especially to dwell on the difference between modern and classical music, and he expressed the difference between ancient and modern drama in terms of it. 'The general characteristic of the ancient and modern drama might be illustrated by a parallel of the ancient and modern music; the one consisting of melody arising from a succession only of pleasing sounds,—the modern embracing harmony also, the result of combination and the effect of the whole.'[1] The Organ, he said, is peculiarly Gothic.[2] Coleridge paid due homage to the Greek; but he can hardly disguise what he felt as an overwhelming sense of its limitation. It is not too much to say that he felt, as he seems to think all modern men must feel, and as Renan felt, to judge by a famous passage in the *Souvenirs*, a certain revulsion from the classical. And here is a passage which best sums up Coleridge's judgement on Classical and Romantic:

'The Greeks reared a structure which, in its parts and as a whole, filled the mind with the calm and elevated impression of perfect beauty and symmetrical proportion. The moderns, blending materials, produced one striking whole. This may be illustrated by comparing the Pantheon with York Minster or Westminster Abbey. Upon the same scale we may compare Sophocles with Shakespeare;—in the one there is a completeness, a satisfying, an excellence, on which the mind can rest; in the other we see a blended multitude of materials, great and little, magnificent and mean, mingled, if we may say so, with a dissatisfying, or falling short of perfection; yet so promising of our progression, that we would not exchange it for that repose of the mind which dwells on the forms of symmetry in acquiescent admiration of grace.'[3]

Modern or Romantic art therefore must fall short because of the immensity of the attempted range of its imagination. 'Modern' art can supply no calm catharsis; and its 'faults' are necessary, and manifest the clash between what is human and that which transcends it and cannot be encompassed or exhausted by the imagination. The imagination, he had said in *Biographia Literaria*, 'dissolves, diffuses, dissipates in order to recreate; or where this process is rendered impossible, yet still at all events it

[1] *Lectures*, p. 234. [2] *Miscellanies*, p. 91. [3] *Lectures*, p. 461.

struggles to idealize and unify'; and earlier in the 1811–12 course of lectures he had said, 'The grandest efforts of poetry are where the imagination is called forth, not to produce a distinct form, but a strong working of the mind, still offering what is still repelled, and again creating what is again rejected; the result being what the poet wishes to impress, namely, the substitution of a sublime feeling of the unimaginable for a mere image'.[1] Such 'efforts of poetry' may occur in regard to the merely horrible, or eerie, or marvellous (he had previously quoted the famous description of the figure of Death in book II of *Paradise Lost*); they may also occur at the level at which Wordsworth's imagination is working in the passage I have quoted from *The Prelude*, as it rises in militancy to seek out the infinite.

§ 10

Such is Coleridge's general argument concerning what he vaguely calls 'modern' poetry. Before going on, I wish to refer briefly to an illustration of his general thesis, which occurs in what he has to say in the *Lectures on Shakespeare*, of Elizabethan and Jacobean drama in contrast with Greek drama. The impulse of the Greek mind in drama, Coleridge argues, was to enclose itself within a neat temporal and spatial ordering and 'sensuous unity'. The unities of time and space were, indeed, made necessary by the use of the chorus; but also, the practice of them arose from an instinct deep in the Greek mind. The modern mind, on the other hand, can obtain 'a power over space and time' and 'shake off' their iron bondage. (pp. 122–3) Where the Greeks sought to impose limits, the moderns seek to transcend them. The following is the crucial passage in which Coleridge expounds this application of his general doctrine of Classical and Romantic:

> 'A deviation from the simple forms and unities of the ancient stage is an essential principle, and, of course, an appropriate excellence, of the romantic drama. For these unities were to a great extent the natural form of that which in its elements was homogeneous, and the representation of which was addressed pre-eminently to the outward senses; —and though the fable, the language and the characters appealed to the reason rather than to the mere understanding, inasmuch as they supposed an ideal state rather than referred to an existing reality,—yet it was a reason which was obliged to accommodate itself to the senses, and so far became a sort of more elevated understanding. On the other hand, the romantic poetry—the Shakespearian drama—appealed to the imagination rather than to the senses, and to the reason as contemplating our inward nature, and the workings of the passions in their most retired recesses. But the reason, as reason, is independent of time

[1] *Lectures*, p. 91.

and space; it has nothing to do with them; and hence the certainties of reason have been called eternal truths. As for example—the endless properties of the circle:—what connection have they with this or that age, with this or that country?—The reason is aloof from time and space;—the imagination is an arbitrary controller over both;—and if only the poet have such power of exciting our internal emotions as to make us present to the scene in imagination chiefly, he acquires the right and privilege of using time and space as they exist in imagination, and obedient only to the laws by which the imagination itself acts.' (pp. 204–5)

Here, the reader will see, Coleridge does not hesitate to link the distinction he is making with the distinction between the understanding and the reason; in modern art, the reason refuses to come to terms with the senses. Coleridge can with difficulty withhold something of the scorn he feels for the classical practice. The modern dramatist, he says,

'appeals to that which we most wish to be, when we are most worthy of being, while the ancient dramatist binds us down to the meanest part of our nature, and the chief compensation is a simple acquiescence of the mind in the position, that what is represented might possibly have occurred in the time and place required by the unities. It is a poor compliment to a poet to tell him, that he has only the qualifications of a historian.' (p. 123)

We shall not pause further in this matter than to remark that in addition to his defence of the Elizabethan treatment of time and space, Coleridge applauds the 'improbability' of parts of the plays of the time; he defends it as being permissible and even desirable in what he defines as dramatic illusion. It will be recalled how William Archer complained[1] of the Elizabethan drama because of its treatment of time and space and of verisimilitude. In regard to the former, Archer's complaint was not of course that Shakespeare and his contemporaries did not employ the unities, but that they showed a shocking indifference to temporal and spatial continuity; not only did they range widely in the course of one play through time and space, but they seemed to possess little sense of their due ordering and would not 'buckle themselves down' to their reasonable dictates. Archer's anger was equally sharp against the vast improbabilities of the drama of the time. He put down these features to carelessness, or to laziness, or to sheer incompetence. But if it was carelessness, the carelessness is significant. When Mr. T. S. Eliot replied to Archer, his reply was a complaint that the Elizabethans were at best half-hearted in their use of what conventions they possessed, and fell between the two stools of realism and convention. But these

[1] In *The Old Drama and the New.*

writers, however much we may deplore it, could proceed neither by a set of conventions nor wholly realistically. If Coleridge is right, there was that in these dramatic writers which must outrage the demands of realism; and in doing this, they did not trouble to devise any agreed rules. 'High poetry', Coleridge said, 'is the translation of reality into the ideal under the predicament of succession of time only.' (p. 523) Again, 'A friend of mine well remarked of Spenser, that he is out of space: the reader never knows where he is, but still he knows, from the consciousness within him, that all is as natural and proper, as if the country where the action is laid were distinctly pointed out, and marked down in a map. Shakespeare is as much out of time, as Spenser is out of space; yet we feel conscious, though we never knew that such characters existed, that they might exist, and are satisfied with the belief in their existence.' (p. 67) Speaking of Spenser, he remarks on the 'marvellous independence and true imaginative absence of all particular space and time in the *Faerie Queene* (p. 514). Space and time therefore are yokes to which 'modern' 'romantic' literature will not bend. In this respect also, 'poetry rejects all control, all confinement'. (p. 92)

§ 11

It is clear from the lectures of Coleridge that the contrast he constantly draws between Classical and Gothic is identical in his eyes with the difference between 'ancient' and 'modern'. 'The moderns' he constantly refers to are 'Gothic' in spirit, and 'modern' art begins with the coming of Gothic. It is of great importance to realize this: by 'modern' he does not mean the period dating from the Renaissance. 'The Greeks idolized the finite. . . . The moderns revere the infinite.'[1] This is the core of the distinction which he says shows itself in a variety of ways in all the arts and in religion. The Gothic cathedral is 'modern'; it is, he says, the 'petrefaction of our religion'. Coleridge will make his point by referring indifferently to the contrast between the Pantheon and Westminster Abbey and to that between Sophocles and Shakespeare.

Now sometimes, in speaking of the difference between ancient and modern, he is content to speak of the 'opposition of *Christianity*[2] to the spirit of pagan Greece'; and the following passage is interesting:

'The Greeks changed the ideas into finites, and these finites into *anthropomorphi*, or forms of men. Hence their religion, their poetry,

[1] *Lectures*, p. 195. [2] My italics.

nay their very pictures, became statuesque. With them the form was the end. The reverse of this was the natural effect of Christianity; in which finites, even the human form, must, in order to satisfy the mind, be brought into connexion with, and be in fact symbolical of, the infinite; and must be considered in some enduring, however shadowy and indistinct, point of view, as the vehicle or representative of moral truth.'[1]

Here we see a simple opposition of the classical to the Christian. Yet, allowing, as we must, that the 'natural effect of Christianity' was inevitably to oppose the classical, Coleridge is more often concerned to oppose a specifically Gothic Christianity to classical paganism. The quotations I have already given in preceding sections of this chapter are sufficient to show this.

In Coleridge's view, it was Gothic which introduced 'sublimity'. Greek art satisfies the demands of the senses and of the understanding; it is Gothic which is pre-eminently the art of the reason and is therefore sublime. 'The conquest of the Romans gave to the Goths the Christian religion as it was then existing in Italy; and the light and graceful building of Grecian, or Roman-Greek order, became singularly combined with the massy architecture of the Goths, as wild and varied as the forest vegetation which it resembled.'[2] Then he goes on: 'The Greek art is beautiful. When I enter a Greek Church, my eye is charmed, and my mind elated; I feel exalted, and proud that I am a man.' But the Gothic art is sublime, filling the soul with devotion, awe, and a sense of its littleness. Now in this passage Coleridge is still contrasting Gothic and classical; he is almost entirely overlooking Byzantine and Romanesque and seems curiously unaware of them as possessing any uniqueness in style and idea. In Coleridge, therefore, we see an insensitiveness to what is not Gothic in Christianity.

We have seen that the outstanding characteristic of the 'Northman's mind' is that it finds 'rest in that which presents no end and derives satisfaction from that which is indistinct'. Hence the sublimity of its expressions in religion and in poetry. The senses and the understanding are defied. But this is not all. Coleridge has in another lecture listed the peculiarities of the Northmen—'the love of the marvellous, the deeper sensibility, the higher reverence for womanhood, the characteristic spirit of sentiment and courtesy',[3] these, he says, are the 'heir-looms of nature' to the Goths. Of the love of the 'marvellous' and the 'deeper sensibility' we need say no more; what we notice now is that Coleridge derives the new attitude towards woman, and the practice of chivalry, from traits in the Northern mind. His 'Goth',

[1] *Miscellanies*, p. 140. [2] Ibid., p. 92. [3] Ibid., p. 98.

in addition to his sense of the marvellous and unknown, is naturally 'tender and affectionate'; and this gives rise to the new love-interest and chivalry of the Middle Ages; also, 'the deference to woman, so characteristic of the Gothic races, combined itself with devotion in the idea of the Virgin Mother, and gave rise to many beautiful associations'.[1] Thus, through his fictitious Goth, does Coleridge explain the profound changes and new institutions which mark the later Middle Ages. The period, therefore, which begins at approximately A.D. 1100 is labelled 'Modern' and 'Gothic'; and this period is also the 'Romantic' period. The three words, in Coleridge's use of them, come to the same thing. All three pre-eminently indicate a spirit which in poetry and religion alike 'throws the object of deepest interest to a distance from us', which carries mind and imagination 'beyond the distance which his hand can touch or even his eye reach'; and which points out to us the 'indefinite improvement of our nature',[2] the spirit in short which fills Wordsworth's lines on crossing the Alps.

There is another aspect of Coleridge's exposition of modernity and Romanticism which we must remark. It is the suggestion, never fully and explicitly made, that Gothic is Protestant in its essential character. That this notion was present in Coleridge's mind, I have little doubt; but it is perhaps unlikely that he openly formulated it to himself. That it is what he would have liked to believe, we may fairly assume; but the apparent difficulties in the way of such a doctrine forbade him to make it a part of the general argument of his lectures. I shall call attention to a few passages which appear to confirm what I have said. In a lecture delivered in 1818 he says[3] of Plato that his 'philosophy and religion were but exotic at home and a mere opposition to the finite in all things, genuine prophet and anticipator as he was of the Protestant æra'. (The point which he goes on to make is that Plato in the *Symposium* 'gave a justification of our Shakespeare' by urging that 'one and the same genius should excel in tragic and comic poetry or that the tragic poet ought, at the same time, to contain within himself the powers of comedy'. Plato is thus so far 'romantic'.) Plato, as one who opposes the finite in all things, is therefore, so far, 'Gothic', and anticipates the *Protestant* era. This remark is made in parenthesis and we ought not perhaps to labour it; yet,

1 The reader will observe that I have not undertaken to put Coleridge right concerning his 'Goth'; and here, where Coleridge appears to attribute the romantic love of the Middle Ages to Northern influences, I have not thought it necessary for my purpose to point out that modern scholars give him little, if any, support in the matter. Even so, since scholars continue to be quite perplexed by the question of the origin of romantic love, Coleridge *may* be right, after all. I may add here that while, in regard to the Greek mind, what Coleridge says has great truth, it is not, as we know, the whole of the truth.

2 *Lectures*, pp. 103–4.

3 Ibid., p. 187.

though coming only in an aside, we may properly assume that it throws some light on what was in Coleridge's mind. Again, I think that his representation of the 'Northman's mind' as one that no 'statue, no artificial emblem could satisfy' is significant. For while Coleridge is ostensibly contrasting the Gothic with the classical, it is not fantastic to see in the remark the implication that Gothic is fundamentally opposed to the use of images as in Catholic practice. Finally, I shall quote a passage from what he says of Boccaccio in one of the lectures of 1818:

'To him we owe the more doubtful merit of having introduced into the Italian prose, and by the authority of his name and the influence of his example, more or less throughout Europe, the long inter-woven periods, and architectural structure which arose from the very nature of their language in the Greek writers, but which already, in the Latin orators and historians, had betrayed a species of effort, a foreign something, which had been superinduced on the language, instead of growing out of it; and which was far too alien from that individualizing and confederating, yet not blending, character of the North, to become permanent, although its magnificence and stateliness were objects of admiration and occasional imitation. This style diminished the control of the writer over the inner feelings of men, and created too great a charm between the body and the life; and hence especially it was abandoned by Luther.'[1]

It will be noticed that the last sentence implies that Luther represents the 'character of the North' in its completeness, standing right over against the classical and its influence. He above all dissipated the 'too great charm between the body and the life'.

From these and other hints which the reader will find distributed through the lectures and notes, it is reasonable to uphold, what I have suggested, that Coleridge saw a very close relationship between Gothic and Protestantism. Now any such view, had he formally stated it, would have certain obvious difficulties. Gothic cathedrals were no product of Protestantism; and the Reformation was one phenomenon in the total period which Coleridge labels 'modern', occurring after centuries in which Latin Christendom had held unbroken sway in Europe. Yet he seems to see in the Reformation a purification of and a return to the original characteristics of a Gothic culture.

I do not propose (what in any case I have not knowledge enough to do) to attempt to defend this doctrine. But I have little doubt that the entire trend of Coleridge's argument is towards belief in it. Thus, having in mind the second quotation given immediately above, that the mind of the 'Northman' was repelled by 'statues and artificial emblems', we have only to read Hui-

[1] *Miscellanies*, p. 100.

zinga's admirable essay on the later centuries of the Middle Ages to see how this doctrine might have its application. Huizinga speaks of the fourteenth and fifteenth centuries, and remarks that 'all that was thinkable had taken image-shape: conception had become almost entirely dependent on the imagination'. And he says also, 'symbolism was a defective translation into images of secret connections dimly felt, such as music reveals to us. *Videmus nunc per speculum in aenigmate*. The human mind felt that it was face to face with an enigma, but none the less it kept on trying to discern the figures in the glass, explaining images by yet other images. Symbolism was like a second mirror held up to that of the phenomenal world itself.'[1] The relevance of this to what I am suggesting was in Coleridge's mind is unmistakable. What animated Coleridge, as he says it animates the entire 'Northern mind', is the sense of the limits of the imagination, of their inevitability, and of what the mighty thrust of the Gothic mind cannot encompass. He might have argued that Luther, in sweeping away the universal attempt of the later Middle Ages to achieve a reduction of the transcendent into the finite and sensuous, showed himself the quintessence of Gothic; and that the resistance of the Reformation to the worship of the Virgin and to belief in the saints, on account of the elaborate use of images, however crude, in connexion with them, was of a piece with the same spirit. By dispelling the spiritual hierarchies thus familiar to vulgar imagination,[2] Luther left the soul with an 'invisible and unknown deity' only.

I observe also that Huizinga's remark that 'symbolism was like a second mirror held up to that of the phenomenal world itself' brings the suggestion that Gothic is essentially Protestant into line with one of the most celebrated of Plato's doctrines, and thereby suggests the line by which the first and the second of my quotations from Coleridge in this section[3] might be thought to be connected.

§ 12

Before returning to Newman, we must go back to observe further the paradox which, as we noticed earlier, exists in the lines of Wordsworth which describe his feelings on crossing the Alps. The effect of the contemplation of the sublime is to convey into the mind a sense of its littleness, says Coleridge. 'The Greek art is beautiful . . . my eye is charmed, and my mind elated; I feel exalted, and proud that I am a man. But the Gothic art is sublime.

1 Huizinga, *The Waning of the Middle Ages*, London, 1937, pp. 194–5.
2 See Huizinga, chap. 12.
3 Those on pp. 245–6 and 248.

On entering a cathedral, I am filled with devotion and with awe; I am lost to the actualities that surround me, and my whole being expands into the infinite; earth and air, nature and art, all swell up into eternity, and the only sensible impression left is, "that I am nothing".'[1] Again, the effect of Greek art is a certain 'complacency'. 'If we look upon any Greek production of art, the beauty of its parts, and the harmony of their union, the complete and complacent effect of the whole are the striking characteristics . . . [we] are indeed gratified.'[2] This complacency Gothic shatters; and its effect is at once to 'expand' the soul into the infinite and to impress it with a sense of its littleness. Indefinite expansion of the soul goes along with a sense of its infinitesimal smallness. Wordsworth's lines indeed emphasize more the active and mastering side of this experience; the soul is indefinitely militant and aspiring; yet it also 'struggles for no spoils'. It is clear then that the 'Gothic' experience is more complicated than the classical; it is somehow a restlessness between two opposed movements of the soul and has therefore an instability and unrest which classical art does not know.

Now when we read the lines,

> . . . whether we be young or old,
> Our destiny, our being's heart and home,
> Is with infinitude and only there;
> With hope it is, hope that can never die,
> Effort and expectation and desire,
> And something ever more about to be.
> Under such banners militant, the soul
> Seeks for no trophies, struggles for no spoils
> That may attest her prowess . . .

it is natural to think of the militant banners, flown by the infinite aspiration of Marlowe's Tamburlaine. Tamburlaine, as we know, liked banners, the symbol of *his* inexhaustible militancy, which would

> . . . confute those blind Geographers
> That make a triple region in the world,
> Excluding Regions which I meane to trace,
> And with this pen reduce them to a Map. (I. *Tamb.* iv. 4)

Certainly Tamburlaine, his banners marching, not only to dominate unknown continents, but against the very gods, sought for abundant trophies and spoils. Still, we can connect him with Wordsworth; as we can connect him in the other direction with medieval chivalry and its endless quest of glory (and for that matter, Tamburlaine's Zenocrate may be a kind of distant cousin

[1] *Miscellanies*, p. 92. [2] Ibid., pp. 92–3.

to the female form in which Shelley embodied his ideal in *Alastor*; to read Tamburlaine's most famous speech may incline us to think so). Tamburlaine tried drastically to resolve the paradox of Gothic which vividly recurs in Wordsworth's romanticism. As we have remarked, it is a sense of glory and of the soul's glory which is predominant in Wordsworth's lines; but Coleridge is more careful equally to emphasize the two aspects of Gothic, expansion and mastery along with diminution and defeat; and in Wordsworth there is 'something evermore about to be', however militant the banners.

Now because this is so, and in the light of what has gone before, the reader will see that what I have called the restlessness and unease of Gothic, the Gothic paradox, lived and worked in Coleridge. I have said, and I think truly, that when we contemplate his theology, we see that it is one worthy of respect, in which due tensions are maintained. But if we consider the mental life of Coleridge as a whole, we can see the sources of its distress.

I was at some pains at an earlier stage to observe Coleridge's need of shelter, his love of retreat. How much he needed it, we can see well enough from some lines he wrote in 1803. Here they are:

But yester-night I prayed aloud
In anguish and in agony,
Up-starting from the fiendish crowd
Of shapes and thoughts that tortured me:
A lurid light, a trampling throng,
Sense of intolerable wrong,
And whom I scorned, those only strong!
Thirst of revenge, the powerless will
Still baffled, and yet burning still!
Desire with loathing strangely mixed
On wild or hateful objects fixed.
Fantastic passions! maddening brawl!
And shame and terror over all!
Deeds to be hid which were not hid,
Which all confused I could not know
Whether I suffered, or I did:
For all seemed guilt, remorse or woe,
My own or others still the same
Life-stifling fear, soul-stifling shame.

So two nights passed: the night's dismay
Saddened and stunned the coming day.
Sleep, the wide blessing, seemed to me
Distemper's worst calamity.
The third night, when my own loud scream
Had waked me from the fiendish dream,

O'ercome with sufferings strange and wild,
I wept as I had been a child;
And having thus by tears subdued
My anguish to a milder mood,
Such punishments, I said, were due
To nature's deepliest stained with sin,—
For aye entempesting anew
The unfathomable hell within,
The horror of their deeds to view,
To know and loathe, yet wish and do!
Such griefs with such men well agree,
But wherefore, wherefore fall on me?
To be beloved is all I need,
And whom I love, I love indeed. (p. 115)

Such was, at times at least, his life in this world; and when he thought of what might come after this world, he could be filled with what he calls, in his notes on Baxter, 'the terror of immortality as ingenerate in man'. How is it possible, he says, 'not to run mad at the horrid thought of an innumerable multitude of self-conscious spirits everlastingly excluded from God?'[1]

From all this, only Christianity, the suffering of Christ, and the righteousness of Christ freely imputed to him, could give him shelter. This was one moment of his life; when he was small, helpless, yet, as he believed, protected and safe; and when he was willing enough to say that 'the existence of God is absolutely and necessarily insusceptible of a scientific demonstration, and that Scripture has so represented it. For it commands us to believe in one God. *I am the Lord thy God: thou shalt have none other gods but me*.'[1] Still, there was another moment. And *then*, he was incapable, as Keats said, 'of remaining content with half-knowledge'; he could not live without 'irritable reaching after fact and reason'; *then* he must explain and understand. He may say, *now*, that he distrusts metaphysics, and in the interest of religious faith; but *now* dogma is not simple and single to him, and he cannot find its peace. But there is no way in which this humility of the heart and this pride of the mind may be reconciled; there can be no equilibrium here; each enfeebles the other. In the history of Europe, Romanesque gave way to Gothic. But Gothic always contained its dissolution within itself.[2] It was a compromise between the divine and the human which could not last; there is no coming to terms in this way. Therefore, in the English nineteenth century we see the order reversed. Coleridge's Gothic gives way to Newman's Romanesque.

[1] Notes on Baxter in *English Divines*, vol. ii, p. 52.
[2] That this is so, can, I think, be seen from study of the design and detail of Gothic building.

§ 13

I shall now return to Newman. In order to point out the vital contrast between him and Coleridge, I shall speak at some length of the two essays, *The Mission of St. Benedict* and *The Benedictine Schools*.[1] I have already drawn upon them in one connexion; they contain other considerations of great importance and interest for our present purpose.

Previously in this chapter I remarked that Newman praised the Benedictine Order for its disinclination to theological and philosophical speculation and its distrust of intellectual system. As he expounds the Benedictine life in these essays, this characteristic is symptomatic of a whole way of living and of a total sensibility. The core of this sensibility I have already tried to indicate; it is expressed in Newman's words, used in speaking of the Benedictine—'He does not analyze, he marvels; his intellect attempts no comprehension of this multiform world, but *on the contrary, it is hemmed in, and shut up within it*.'[2]

Now in the first of the two essays of which I am speaking, Newman draws a distinction, which he clearly regards as very important, between what he calls respectively the 'poetical' and the 'scientific'. These are Newman's words:

'Poetry, then, I conceive, whatever be its metaphysical essence, or however various may be its kinds, whether it more properly belongs to action or to suffering, nay, whether it is more at home with society or with nature, whether its spirit is seen to best advantage in Homer or in Virgil, at any rate, is always the antagonist to *science*. As science makes progress in any subject-matter, poetry recedes from it. The two cannot stand together; they belong respectively to two modes of viewing things, which are contradictory of each other. Reason investigates, analyzes, numbers, weighs, measures, ascertains, locates, the objects of its contemplation, and thus gains a scientific knowledge of them. Science results in system, which is complex unity; poetry delights in the indefinite and various as contrasted with unity, and in the simple as contrasted with system. The aim of science is to get a hold of things, to grasp them, to handle them, to comprehend them; that is (to use the familiar term), to *master* them, or to be superior to them. Its success lies in being able to draw a line round them, and to tell where each of them is to be found within that circumference, and how each lies relatively to all the rest. Its mission is to destroy ignorance, doubt, surmise, suspense, illusions, fears, deceits, according to the "Felix qui potuit rerum cognoscere causas" of the Poet, whose whole passage, by the way, may be taken as drawing out the contrast between the poetical and the scientific. But as to the poetical, very different is the frame of mind which is necessary for its perception. It demands,

[1] Both in vol. ii of *Historical Sketches*.

[2] *Historical Sketches*, vol. ii, p. 452; italics mine.

as its primary condition, that we should not put ourselves above the objects in which it resides, but at their feet; that we should feel them to be above and beyond us, that we should look up to them, and that, instead of fancying that we can comprehend them, we should take for granted that we are surrounded and comprehended by them ourselves. It implies that we understand them to be vast, immeasurable, impenetrable, inscrutable, mysterious; so that at best we are only forming conjectures about them, not conclusions, for the phenomena which they present admit of many explanations, and we cannot know the true one. Poetry does not address the reason, but the imagination and affections; it leads to admiration, enthusiasm, devotion, love. The vague, the uncertain, the irregular, the sudden, are among its attributes or sources. Hence it is that a child's mind is so full of poetry, because he knows so little; and an old man of the world so devoid of poetry, because his experience of facts is so wide. Hence it is that nature is commonly more poetical than art, in spite of Lord Byron, because it is less comprehensible and less patient of definitions; history more poetical than philosophy; the savage than the citizen; the knight-errant than the brigadier-general; the winding bridle-path than the straight railroad; the sailing vessel than the steamer; the ruin than the spruce suburban box; the Turkish robe or Spanish doublet than the French dress coat.' (pp. 386–8)

The relevance of this passage to an essay undertaking to speak of the nature of Romanticism will be clear to the reader. The aim of science is to comprehend and master; poetry is aware of objects as 'surrounding and comprehending' us. Poetry ends in the apprehension of the 'inscrutable and mysterious', indeed, it begins and ends in it; it is always looking up to and not, like science, looking down upon, its objects. And there follows the list of stock romantic objects, the savage, the knight-errant, the winding bridle-path, the ruin. We may indeed, legitimately enough, speak of Newman's 'Romanticism'. (We may observe also, in passing, that there emerges in this passage, what emerges in several other passages in these essays, Newman's disposition to see the child in the manner we are so familiar with in Wordsworth. Again, it is convenient to remark at this juncture how in these writings Newman glorifies the life of the country and expresses his abhorrence of the town. When he speaks of the life of the monk as 'Virgilian' he says, 'When Virgil chooses the country and rejects the town, he shows us that a certain aspect of the town is uncongenial with poetry, and that a certain aspect of the country is congenial. Repose, intellectual and moral, is that quality of country life which he selects for his praises; and effort and bustle, and excitement is that quality of a town life which he abhors. Herein then, according to Virgil, lies the poetry of St. Benedict, in the "secura quies et nescia fallere vita", in the absence of anxiety and fretfulness, of schemes and scheming, of hopes and fears, of doubts and disappointments.' (p. 409))

But we are less concerned here with these more familiar, obvious and, as we may say, hackneyed notes of Romanticism, than with those deeper notes which are the main theme of the passage from Newman which I have quoted. If Newman is near enough to Coleridge and Wordsworth when he speaks of children, savages, ruins, and the life of the country, he is equally near to them when he speaks of the 'poetical' apprehension of objects in contrast to the 'scientific'. Yet we must look further for differences. Newman is so far Romantic; but we quickly see that his romanticism is not identical with that of Coleridge. For if Coleridge is sharply removed from the ideal Newman has in mind by his impassioned researches in philosophy and science, Newman is sharply removed from Coleridge by the antipathy he felt for Gothic. Now as we may see, Newman's dislike of Gothic is deeply bound up with his disinclination for speculation and the life of reason. Consider, for example, the following passage in which again Newman is speaking of the Benedictine monk as he conceived him:

'He ploughed and sowed, he prayed and meditated, he studied, he wrote, he taught, and then he died and went to Heaven. He made his way into the labyrinthine forest, and he cleared just so much of space as his dwelling required, suffering the high solemn trees and the deep pathless thicket to close him in. And when he began to build, his architecture was suggested by the scene,—not the scientific and masterly conception of a great whole with many parts, as the Gothic style in a later age, but plain and inartificial, the adaptation of received fashions to his own purpose, and an addition of chapel to chapel and a wayward growth of cloister, according to the occasion, with half-concealed shrines and unexpected recesses, with paintings on the wall as by a second thought, with an absence of display and a wild, irregular beauty, like that of the woods by which he was at first surrounded.' (p. 427)

In the first place, we notice that Newman speaks of the forest trees and the deep thickets *enclosing* the monk. There is the *height* of the trees and the *depth* and *pathlessness* of the thickets. Under this height and within this depth, the monk is *closed* in. The elements of height and depth do not serve to create any impulse to mastery in the monk; in the face of them he is bowed down and humbled; he accepts them as that by which he is 'comprehended'.

Now Gothic, says Newman, when it came, was 'scientific and masterly'. If Coleridge is right (as we may well believe him to be) in saying that the Gothic cathedral owes its inspiration to the forest, it is an inspiration very different from that which the monk, in Newman's eyes, derived from it. Gothic is organized and planned as a whole in its very act of reaching up into the infinite; it is altogether deliberate in its act. But this was not the note of the Benedictine. Newman is careful to remark that Benedictine architecture is 'suggested by the scene', and is also an 'adaptation of received fashion'; it has 'waywardness', 'unexpectedness', 'second thoughts', 'irregularity', none of them the typical notes of Gothic. It retains so much of Roman architecture, conserving something of its quietness and power, yet also having little, in its total design, if the word 'design' is permissible at all, of self-containment and completeness. It has a certain childlikeness and innocence, compared with which Gothic is adult and masterful.

The monk's architecture was not in any sense *contrived*; he did not desire, says Newman, 'any new architecture of his own invention'. Moreover, we may believe that the monk of Newman's imagination found in Roman styles something congenial to his spirit. Between classical and Gothic styles Coleridge discerned an absolute difference. But the monk did not reject the classical, while changing it. If his architecture lost, as time went on, the completeness and symmetry of the classical, it yet retained the element of composure in the classical; if it did not gain the mounting power of Gothic, it had simplicity, resolution, and quietness. In the sensibility of these earlier Christian centuries something of the classical remained; and yet it was united with the recognition of the mysterious and unexpected.

This continuity with the classical is exhibited also, Newman is at pains to point out, in the scheme of Benedictine studies. The Benedictine did not seek novelty in study any more than in architecture; he studied the Scriptures and the Fathers and was expert in transcription, illumination, and binding, and we have spoken of his strong historical interests. In accordance with this spirit, he took up, says Newman, 'the Roman curriculum, professed the Seven Sciences, beginning with Grammar, that is, the Latin Classics, and, if he sometimes finished with them, it was because his boys left him ere he had time to teach them more. The subjects he chose were his fit recompense for choosing them. He adopted the Latin writers from his love of prescription, because he found them in possession. But there were in fact no writings, after Scripture, more congenial, from their fresh and natural beauty and their freedom from intellectualism, to the monastic temperament.' (p. 454) That Newman himself understood this attraction is obvious from the tenderness which always arises in his writings when he speaks of Virgil.

That the monks were not disposed to novelty in their architecture and in their studies and avoided its excitement, is the clue to the whole tenor of their life. They avoided *undertakings*; they were essentially not men of power. In the first instance they did not feel called upon even to be teachers; and when they were teachers they taught not in the atmosphere of the later universities, 'of disputes and emulations'. But ideally the monk is not even a teacher; and Newman quotes St. Jerome's remark that 'a monk's office is not a teacher's but a mourner's, who bewails either himself or the world'. The greatest 'poetry' is reached in those lives which, so far as possible, are unplanned, but which yet are composed, which do not order ahead, but which yet are quiet. 'They whose duty lies in what may be called *undertakings*, in science and system, in sustained efforts of the intellect or elaborate processes of action,—apologists, controversialists, disputants in the schools, professors in the chair, teachers in the pulpit, rulers in the church,—have a noble and meritorious mission, but not so poetical a one.' (p. 409) The 'poetical' life consists in 'living for the day without solicitude for the morrow, without plans or objects, even holy ones, here below; working, not (so to say) by the piece, but as hired by the hour; sowing the ground with the certainty, according to the promise, of reaping; reading or writing this present week without the consequent necessity of reading or writing during the next; dwelling among one's own people without distant ties; taking each new day as a whole in itself, an addition, not a complement, to the past; and doing works which cannot be cut short, for they are complete in every portion of them'. (p. 409)

The reader will now perceive that if Coleridge's romanticism was a reversion to Gothic, Newman's romanticism looked to a yet earlier phase of civilization. Coleridge's romanticism carried 'militant banners'; but he must also accept the perpetual paradox of Gothic in which bearing its 'banners militant', it yet 'struggles for no spoils'. He accepts the paradox, shown in him among other ways by his denial of any powers to the speculative reason and by his endless pursuit of metaphysics; and so does Wordsworth so far as the lines I have quoted express him. But 'hope that can never die, effort, and expectation, and desire' are not the words that describe Newman's monk. They suggest an ardour and a bustling excitement far removed from the early Benedictine, who was primarily a mourner, who waited and watched. Militancy was the last thing he desired; the world was dying around him, and he did not propose to try to save it, nor to create another and better. He did not wish to acquire and exert power, spiritual or worldly. Newman's 'romanticism', therefore, does not yield to Coleridge's in its sense of the supernatural which over-arches the human, in its perception of the unseen, in what must remain mysterious and undisclosed; but it differs profoundly from it in its lowliness, its quietness, its revulsion from power, its abandonment of claim.

§ 14

We end then, with the monk, in his mourning and watching, his quietness and solitude, his poetry and simplicity. I have remarked on Newman's attitude to childhood; and Newman sees Benedictine monachism as the childhood of Christianity or at least of Christian monachism. He is speaking in very broad terms; and he sees St. Benedict, St. Dominic, and St. Ignatius as standing in turn for three mighty phases in the history of Christianity: Poetry, Science, and Practical Sense.

The passages in which he expounds this scheme are of great interest to the student of Newman, for they show Newman's deep historical sense risking, to say the least, a clash with his beliefs, and threatening a significant disturbance within himself. He has spoken of the three orders in the growth of civilization; 'but after having so described them, it certainly did strike me that I had unintentionally been illustrating a somewhat popular notion of the day, the like of which is attributed to authors with whom I have as little sympathy as with any persons who can be named'.[1] According to these authors, 'the life, whether of a race or of an individual of the great human family, is divided into three stages'; and he goes on to enumerate the stages into which, according to these authors, any life, whether of race or individual, may be divided.

'The youth makes his start in life, with "hope at the prow, and fancy at the helm"; he has nothing else but these to impel or direct him; he has not lived long enough to exercise his reason, or to gather in a store of facts; and, because he cannot do otherwise, he dwells in a world which he has created. He begins with illusions. Next, when at length he looks about for some surer footing than imagination gives him, he may have recourse to reason, or he may have recourse to facts; now facts are external to him, but his reason is his own: of the two, then, it is easier for him to exercise his reason than to ascertain facts. Accordingly, his first mental revolution, when he discards the life of aspiration and affection which has disappointed him, and the dreams of which he has been the sport and victim, is to embrace a life of logic: this, then, is his second stage,—the metaphysical. He acts now on a plan, thinks by system, is cautious about his middle terms, and trusts nothing but what takes a scientific form. His third stage is when he has made full trial of life; when he has found his theories break down under the weight of facts, and experience falsify his most promising calculations. Then the old man recognizes at length, that what he can

[1] *Historical Sketches*, vol. ii, p. 367.

taste, touch and handle, is trustworthy, and nothing beyond it. Thus he runs through his three periods of Imagination, Reason, and Sense; and then he comes to an end, and is not;—a most impotent and melancholy conclusion.'

He at once insists that this is but a flight of fancy, and in any case a 'heathen view of life' with which no Catholic can sympathize. Yet its appeal to his sense of individuality, of growth, of development is obviously strong.

Besides, it accords so well with what he sees as the outstanding qualities of the three orders. He pays his respects to the Jesuitical order; but he can with difficulty hide something of the distaste he feels for it, its watchword Prudence, its lack of 'the poetry of life', its most prosaic architecture, the weight of fact, disillusionment, and experience which it carries. Its sense of fact and reality expels science; still more it expels poetry. The imagination is the servant of the useful. He speaks of it as 'a wonderful religion'; but he passes on, and will not write of it. He will write of the Dominicans, but does not fulfil his promise. It is of the Benedictines he writes. But can Christianity grow old? Not so. 'It is true that history as viewed in these three Saints is, somewhat after the manner of the theory I have mentioned, a progress from poetry through science to practical sense or prudence; but then this important proviso has to be borne in mind, that what the Catholic Church once has had, she never has lost. She has never wept over, or been angry with, time gone and over. Instead of passing from one stage of life to another, she has carried her youth and middle age along with her, on to her latest time'—he will not say, 'old age' (p. 368). So he writes; and so no doubt he believes. He may not 'weep over time gone'; but his heart nevertheless is in the childhood of Christianity, its simplicity and poetry.

Besides, if Newman longed for the life of the Benedictine monk, in full escape from the burden of civilization, and if in this he is longing for the 'primitive', this early monachism was a return to the 'primitive age of the world, of which poets have so often sung, the simple life of Arcadia or the reign of Saturn, when fraud and violence were unknown'. (p. 385) We may smile over the 'Arcadia' and the 'reign of Saturn'; and think also of the primitive spontaneity for which Rousseau and Blake longed. Here is the hunger for primitive glory imaged in the Benedictine monastery and the life of the monk: a curious amalgam to one who has read the literature of Romanticism. 'It was a bringing back of those real, not fabulous, scenes of innocence and miracle, when Adam delved, or Abel kept sheep, or Noe planted the vine, and Angels visited them.' Here, in this life of abjuration, denial, discipline, and penance, Newman saw the life of 'innocence'. It is far removed from the innocence Blake sought through the fire of Orc, from the 'natural piety' of Wordsworth's lyric, from the perfection of humanity when tyrant and priest have been removed from Shelley's world. Yet Newman is near enough to the Romantic movement and sufficiently a part of it to want to speak in this connexion of 'innocence'; and to see in the 'innocence' of the Benedictine monk something of the innocence of Adam.

§ 15

Now it may be that we have come a long way from the naturalism of the early phases of Romanticism. Yet in Newman's delight in the solitude and *summa quies* of monachism we have something not wholly new in the life of Romanticism. For when Newman says of the early monks, 'They had retired into deserts . . . They had gone where the face of man was not, except as seen in pale ascetic apparitions like themselves', our minds may naturally recall Endymion and Alastor, pale enough apparitions, going where the face of man was not, even if their spirits were too tumultuous and clamouring to satisfy Newman's liking. But it is of Wordsworth I wish especially to speak now. There are very great differences between Wordsworth and Newman; yet there are some striking similarities which it is worth while to consider.

Now as Newman portrays his ideal monk, we see his preeminent need for solitude and silence. St. Basil and St. Antony alike sought to be alone. Now every reader of *The Prelude* knows of Wordsworth's passion for solitude, his intense desire to be alone. Moreover, this was no idle sentimental or 'Romantic' desire, and had little in common with Rousseau's lounging in the bottom of his boat on the lake of Bienne indulging his reverie; it had a quality of bleakness, severity, and courage such as Rousseau never knew. St. Basil (as quoted by Newman in the essay on the Mission of St. Benedict), says that

'. . . each day as it comes, darkens the soul in its own way; and night after night takes up the day's anxieties, and cheats us with corresponding dreams. Now, the only way of escaping all this is separation from the whole world, so as to live without city, home, goods, society, possessions, means of life, business, engagements, secular learning, that the heart may be prepared as wax for the impress of divine teaching. Solitude is of the greatest use for this purpose, as it stills our passions, and enables reason to extirpate them. Let then a place be found such as mine, separate from intercourse with men, that the tenor of our exercises be not interrupted from without. . . . Quiet, then, as I have said, is the first step in our sanctification; the tongue purified from the gossip of the world, the eyes unexcited by fair colour or comely shape, the ear secured from the relaxation of voluptuous songs, and that especial mischief, light jesting. Thus, the mind, rescued from dissipation from without, and sensible allurements, falls back upon itself, and thence ascends to the contemplation of God.' (pp. 383–4)

So St. Basil. And here is Wordsworth.

When from our better selves we have too long
Been parted by the hurrying world, and droop,
Sick of its business, of its pleasures tired,
How gracious, how benign, is Solitude;
How potent a mere image of her sway;
Most potent when impressed upon the mind
With an appropriate human centre—hermit,
Deep in the bosom of the wilderness;
Votary (in vast cathedral, where no foot
Is treading, where no other face is seen)
Kneeling at prayers; or watchman on the top
Of lighthouse, beaten by Atlantic waves;
Or as the soul of that great Power is met
Sometimes embodied on a public road,
When, for the night deserted, it assumes
A character of quiet more profound
Than pathless wastes. (p. 663)

The first 'image of the sway of solitude' is of the hermit 'deep in the bosom of the wilderness'; the second of the votary alone in the 'vast cathedral'; the third the watchman set around by 'Atlantic waves'. To be surrounded by the vastness of wilderness, of cathedral, of ocean, and to be alone; and lest it still be thought that Wordsworth sought solitude for 'romantic reverie', we must take especial notice of the last lines:

Or as the soul of that great Power is met
Sometimes embodied on a public road,
When, for the night deserted, it assumes
A character of quiet more profound
Than pathless wastes.

Solitude is a Power; and Wordsworth sometimes saw it 'embodied on a public road', when solitude is also a profound quiet. Such an embodiment was the figure of the old soldier, described in lines I have already quoted, which cannot be too much studied.

There is another feature of Wordsworth's noble imagination which impresses the reader, and which is closely related to what we have said in the foregoing paragraph. I have briefly mentioned it at an earlier stage; its full significance will now be apparent. I mean, the great symbolic significance which roads held for

Wordsworth. The soldier embodied 'that great Power' on 'a public road'; and the sight of a 'public way',

> Familiar object as it is, hath wrought
> On my imagination since the morn
> Of childhood, when a disappearing line,
> One daily present to my eyes, that crossed
> The naked summit of a far-off hill
> Beyond the limits that my feet had trod,
> Was like an invitation into space
> Boundless, or guide into eternity. (p. 742)

We observe in these last lines that quality of Wordsworth's mind to which I have already called attention: 'beyond the limits that my feet had trod'. What we notice now is that the road as it crossed a 'naked summit' was to him a 'Power'. And he goes on (in book XIII):

> Yes, something of the grandeur which invests
> The mariner who sails the roaring sea
> Through storm and darkness, early in my mind
> Surrounded, too, the wanderers of the earth. (p. 742)

He is awed by the 'grandeur' and 'loveliness' of 'strolling Bedlamites'; and has fled in fear from 'uncouth vagrants'. These wanderers, pilgrims without home, who stand outside the civilized world, alone and poor, their abode the road, filled him with awe. In many lyrics he celebrates these figures, in their poverty, grief, desolation, simplicity, goodness, mildness. They are the pilgrims of the earth and have no abiding city.

Again, the monk as Newman describes him in the *Sketches*, is a worker with his hands. He is a countryman, repelled by the towns.

'They were not dreamy sentimentalists, to fall in love with melancholy winds and purling rills, and waterfalls and nodding groves; but their poetry was the poetry of hard work and hard fare, unselfish hearts and charitable hands. They could plough and reap, they could hedge and ditch, they could drain; they could lop, they could carpenter; they could thatch, they could make hurdles for their huts; they could make a road, they could divert or secure the streamlet's bed, they could bridge a torrent.' (p. 398)

They set no great store on learning, and what we like to call 'culture'. Now the grandeur which Wordsworth discerned in his Michael had at least a great deal in common with what Newman saw in his Benedictine monk—the countryman, unbothered by books,

> Intense, and frugal, apt for all affairs.

The poetry of Michael also was a 'poetry of hard work and hard fare, unselfish hearts and charitable hands'. Moreover, Wordsworth was not, any more than Michael, a 'dreamy sentimentalist' in love with 'melancholy winds and purling rills, and waterfalls and nodding groves'. Certainly Wordsworth never sought in nature any soft and sensuous beauty, and we know that Newman also turned away from it; Nature was to Wordsworth above all a 'discipline of fear', and as I have had occasion to say earlier, the great Wordsworth landscapes have the quality of high austerity and desolation.

> If from the public way you turn your steps
> Up the tumultuous brook of Green-head Ghyll,
> You will suppose that with an upright path
> Your feet must struggle; in such bold ascent
> The pastoral mountains front you, face to face.
> But, courage! for around that boisterous brook
> The mountains have all opened out themselves,
> And made a hidden valley of their own.
> No habitation can be seen: but they
> Who journey thither find themselves alone
> With a few sheep, with rocks and stones, and kites
> That overhead are sailing in the sky.
> It is in truth an utter solitude. . . . (p. 131)

That is the true Wordsworth landscape—'alone with a few sheep, with rocks and stones, and kites'. And when Wordsworth is in the great town, it is the hours of quiet 'when the great tide of human life stands still' which hold him; but (more especially for our present purpose) his faculties are possessed by the sight of dreary and deserted streets:

> . . . empty streets, and sounds
> Unfrequent as in deserts; at late hours
> Of winter evenings, when unwholesome rains
> Are falling hard, with people yet astir . . .

Here is the passage in which these lines occur:

> . . . scenes different there are,
> Full-formed, that take, with small internal help,
> Possession of the faculties,—the peace
> That comes with night; the deep solemnity
> Of nature's intermediate hours of rest,
> When the great tide of human life stands still;
> The business of the day to come, unborn,
> Of that gone by, locked up, as in the grave;
> The blended calmness of the heavens and earth,
> Moonlight and stars, and empty streets, and sounds
> Unfrequent as in deserts; at late hours

Of winter evenings, when unwholesome rains
Are falling hard, with people yet astir,
The feeble salutation from the voice
Of some unhappy woman, now and then
Heard as we pass, when no one looks about,
Nothing is listened to. (p. 697)

His imagination passes naturally from the peace of night and the calm of heaven and earth to deserted and rainy streets.

The 'poetical' character of the life of the monk, and of Wordsworth's shepherds, is then no easy and pleasant affair of delight in colour and form. From this they merely turned away, if indeed it occurred to them in a life of strenuous and unremitting toil. Both monk and shepherd are indeed countrymen, dwelling amidst the sublime forms of nature, far from the towns, 'knowing' as Newman says, 'the sweet soothing presence of earth, sky and sea'. The life of both was 'quiet'; and where, asks Newman, 'was quietness to be found, if not in reverting to the original condition of man, as far as the changed circumstances of our race admitted?' And here the story of the Romantic desire for the primitive comes to its conclusion, in no easy spontaneity and 'naturalness'; in living close to nature indeed, but in a life of frugality, labour, and loneliness.

§ 16

There is one further observation which I wish to make concerning Wordsworth. The reader will remember Hazlitt's well-known words with which his essay on Wordsworth begins: 'Mr. Wordsworth's genius is a pure emanation of the Spirit of the Age. Had he lived in any other period of the world, he would never have been heard of.' And he goes on to say at a later stage,

'. . . his poetry is founded on setting up an opposition (and pushing it to the utmost length) between the natural and the artificial, between the spirit of humanity and the spirit of fashion and of the world. It is one of the innovations of the time. It partakes of, and is carried along with, the revolutionary movement of our age: the political changes of the day were the model on which he formed and conducted his poetical experiments. His Muse (it cannot be denied, and without this we cannot explain its character at all) is a levelling one. It proceeds on a principle of equality, and strives to reduce all things to the same standard. . . .'

Now these words contain some truth; they also contain a great deal that is not true. It is true that Wordsworth opposes the natural, if by that we mean the life of the shepherd and the toiler in the country, to the artificial, if by that we mean the life of the town; the quiet of the one to the noise of the other; the silence of the one to, in the other, the gossip of the vulgar and the chatter of the educated; the forms and beauty of earth and sky to the judgements of 'manners studied and elaborate'. This is certainly true. And it is as true of Newman as it is of Wordsworth. It may very well also be true that Wordsworth would not have come to apprehend his values as he did, had he not lived at the close of the eighteenth century and during the first half of the nineteenth; it is true that he started from the revolutionary enthusiasm of his youth and might possibly never have come to what he was and saw in his maturity but for this. But to say this is not to say a great deal, unless we are mistaken enough to imagine that the greatest men do what they do in total independence of the age. Great men certainly and inevitably draw deeply upon their age; but their enduring greatness rests on their perception, under and through the influences which have played upon them, of what is permanent and universal in life, nature, and humanity. And this is the greatness of Wordsworth. To see in him one who 'would never have been heard of' in any other period of the world is a profound failure of perception; to say of him that he is a 'pure emanation of the Spirit of the Age' is to have missed what is essential and universal in his genius. It simply is not true that Wordsworth's art 'proceeds on a principle of equality'; that his mind moved within the circle of a hackneyed concept. It may be true, as we have suggested, that revolutionary idealism played its part in making the mature Wordsworth; but this is very different from saying that it was the essence of Wordsworth's genius. Wordsworth transcends his age, and does so absolutely, as all the greatest writers have done.

In what then does his transcendence of his age and his universality consist? This question I can best answer by calling attention to the eighth book of *The Prelude*. Briefly, the answer is that Wordsworth's imagination, like the imagination of all the greatest poets, beheld, above all,

> . . . images of danger and distress,
> Man suffering among awful Powers and Forms.

The eighth book of *The Prelude* is called 'Love of Nature leading to Love of Man'. 'Shepherds were the men that pleased me first', he says; and he goes on to explain what he does *not* mean by 'shepherds':

> Not such as Saturn ruled 'mid Latian wilds,
> With arts and laws so tempered, that their lives
> Left, even to us toiling in this late day,
> A bright tradition of the golden age;

Not such as, 'mid Arcadian fastnesses
Sequestered, handed down among themselves
Felicity . . . (p. 701)

The priest of the Roman Church, brooding over a world lapsed by an awful catastrophe from God, will pay, in the security of his freedom from foolish illusions, a kind of homage to a pretty romanticism by speaking of the monastic state as a return to 'that primitive age of the world, of which poets have so often sung, the simple life of Arcadia in the reign of Saturn, when fraud and violence were unknown'. But Wordsworth, the Romantic poet, will not sing of these things. His shepherd is no Saturnian or Arcadian figure. Newman can safely take the risk of speaking of his monk in this fanciful manner; Wordsworth will take no such risks with his shepherd. The priest may indulge fancy; the Romantic poet sticks to the facts.

Nor is it the village of the maypole dance and pretty customs which Wordsworth celebrates; instead, it is a life . . .

Intent on little but substantial needs,
Yet rich in beauty, beauty that was felt.
But images of danger and distress,
Man suffering among awful Powers and Forms;
Of this I heard, and saw enough to make
Imagination restless. . . . (p. 701)

Certainly, his imagination was not given ease by what he saw of the shepherd's life; 'restlessness' was what it knew. 'Fancy might run wild', peopling with handsome shepherds 'the banks of delicate Galesus' and 'Adria's myrtle shores'. But Wordsworth keeps his eyes on 'skies less generous, less serene'—

. . . hail to you
Moors, mountains, headlands, and ye hollow vales,
Ye long deep channels for the Atlantic's voice,
Powers of my native region! Ye that seize
The heart with firmer grasp! Your snows and streams
Ungovernable, and your terrifying winds,
That howl so dismally for him who treads
Companionless your awful solitudes! (p. 702)

This is what is *not* a pure emanation of the age. It is a vision of the spirit of man, companionless in awful solitudes, set around by ungovernable and terrifying powers, grasped by fear. The shepherd 'waits upon the storms'; and 'severest solitude'

Had more commanding looks when he was there.

Thus does Wordsworth glorify the shepherd in his life of danger and toil, a creature

. . . spiritual almost
As those of books, but more exalted far;
Far more of an imaginative form
Than the gay Corin of the groves . . .

and he was,

. . . for the purposes of kind, a man
With the most common; husband, father; learned,
Could teach, admonish; suffered with the rest
From vice and folly, wretchedness and fear. (p. 703)

He is an average man enough, and there is no false idealization. Yet, as he stepped . . .

Beyond the boundary line of some hill-shadow,
His form hath flashed upon me, glorified
By the deep radiance of the setting sun:
Or him have I descried in distant sky,
A solitary object and sublime,
Above all height! like an aerial cross
Stationed alone upon a spiry rock
Of the Chartreuse, for worship.

Thus we see that the shepherd, as Wordsworth sees him, is a symbol of man's life, without 'the trappings of a gaudy world', confronted in loneliness with a vast unknown, and uncontrollable powers. 'Terrifying winds howled dismally' for Lear also who trod 'awful solitudes' in his loneliness; and on seeing Edgar, he exclaimed, in the loneliness and illumination of his insanity, 'Ha? here's three on's are sophisticated; thou art the thing itself; unaccommodated man is no more but such a poor, bare, forked animal as thou art. Off, off, you lendings!' Lear was speaking of Edgar; but he was also speaking of himself whom he now saw for 'the thing itself'. The lendings of society are torn away by his imagination; he beholds himself, alone and helpless, 'before the extremity of the skies'. Shakespeare was no product of a revolutionary age which played with the opposition of natural and artificial; but he too looks from the 'sophisticated' to 'the thing itself'. So did Wordsworth, whose shepherds in their exposure and danger were men who, like Lear, 'suffered with the rest'

From vice and folly, wretchedness and fear.

Lear, I said, was speaking of Edgar; but we see, as Lear speaks, not Edgar and poor Tom but Lear himself. He has become 'the thing itself'; but although 'a poor, bare, forked animal', he is also sublime, a titanic thing, in its very smallness, which yet will not break in feebleness and self-pity. In Lear, as in Wordsworth's shepherd, the spirit of man is glorified, and glorified in its pitiableness and sorrow. Lear comes out of the storm into the redeeming love of Cordelia in her superhuman beauty; and when Wordsworth contemplates his shepherd in his loneliness and danger, he sees him glorified against the setting sun; and in doing so, the image of the Cross occurs in his mind, of a Cross

Stationed alone upon a spiry rock
Of the Chartreuse, for worship.

Now we read, at an earlier stage (in book VI) in *The Prelude*, of the Chartreuse Cross, and I shall conclude what I have to say of Wordsworth by referring to this earlier passage. Wordsworth is in France in the full tide of his revolutionary ardour. He reaches the Chartreuse some little time before 'riotous men' of the Revolution who will expel the monks. He and his friend

. . . ere twice the sun had set
Beheld the Convent of Chartreuse, and there
Rested within an awful *solitude*:
Yes; for even then no other than a place
Of soul-affecting *solitude*[1] appeared
That far-famed region . . . (p. 681)

They know that the Revolution will seek to overthrow

That frame of social being, which so long
Had bodied forth the ghostliness of things
In silence visible and perpetual calm.

The despoilers are drawing near. It was a striking moment in Wordsworth's life; and we may well be thankful that he recorded it in some detail. It shows the clash between the Wordsworth who was the 'emanation of the Spirit of the Age' and the Wordsworth who was not. He gives his salute to the Revolution:

Honour to the patriot's zeal!
Glory and hope to new-born Liberty!
Hail to the mighty projects of the time!
Discerning sword that Justice wields, do thou
Go forth and prosper.

This is the one Wordsworth. Here is the other:

But oh! if Past and Future be the wings
On whose support harmoniously conjoined
Moves the great spirit of human knowledge, spare
These courts of mystery, where a step advanced
Between the portals of the shadowy rocks
Leaves far behind life's treacherous vanities,
For penitential tears and trembling hopes
Exchanged—to equalise in God's pure sight

[1] The italics are Wordsworth's own.

> Monarch and peasant: be the house redeemed
> With its unworldly votaries, for the sake
> Of conquest over sense, hourly achieved
> Through faith and meditative reason, resting
> Upon the word of heaven-imparted truth,
> Calmly triumphant. . . .

Then, he asks that the monastery be redeemed by the

> . . . humbler claim
> Of that imaginative impulse sent
> From these majestic floods, yon shining cliffs, . . .
> These forests unapproachable by death,
> That shall endure as long as man endures,
> To think, to hope, to worship and to feel,
> To struggle, to be lost within himself
> In trepidation, from the blank abyss
> To look with bodily eyes, and be consoled. (pp. 681–2)

So we pass from the sanguine Revolution to the sense of man struggling and lost within himself in trepidation, looking from a blank abyss. That blank abyss is hidden from the eye of revolutionary humanitarianism; Wordsworth tried for a time to hide it from himself; but here, in his revolutionary time, it disclosed itself, the sense of it evoked by the eternal vocation of the monk. Then Wordsworth and his friend passed through 'Vallombre's groves'; and came out 'with uplifted eyes' to see

> The cross of Jesus stand erect, as if
> Hands of angelic powers had fixed it there,
> Memorial reverenced by a thousand storms. . . .

It is the image of this cross, symbolizing the life and worship of the monks of the Chartreuse, which occurs to Wordsworth when he contemplates his shepherd, standing in the setting sun. Thus is the shepherd of Wordsworth's imagination linked with one of the severest of the great monastic orders, which also cherished the tradition of the early Egyptian monks so dear to Newman's imagination. In December 1832, Dorothy Wordsworth wrote to Crabb Robinson, who had been abroad: 'My brother is very sorry that you should have missed the Chartreuse. I do not think that any one spot which he visited during his youthful travels made so great an impression on his mind: in my young days he used to talk so much of it to me.'

I said, earlier on, in speaking of Coleridge, that he has often been accounted a precursor of the Oxford Movement. When I think of Newman, and of the burden of so much of his writing, the greatness of the Benedictine Order and of the monks of the still earlier centuries, it seems natural to associate Wordsworth, more than Coleridge, with him. No doubt Coleridge did more than Wordsworth to renew Christianity in the nineteenth century; but if we think of Wordsworth in his strength, in his austere simplicity, in his independence of books, in his love of solitude and silence; and if we think of the great Wordsworth symbols, the wanderers and mourners in his poems who have no abiding city, we see, I think, that Wordsworth, more than Coleridge, leads on to Newman.

Therefore, had Hazlitt reflected a little more, he might have seen that what was most distinctive in the genius of Wordsworth was something Wordsworth shared with another North-countryman, who in the year 676 relinquished his rule over the monastery at Lindisfarne, took on the life of the recluse, and built for himself, on the Inner Farne, a cell from which he could see only the sky and hear only the sound of the waves breaking on the rocks.

EPILOGUE

§ I

IN looking back upon the Romantic movement as we have described it, we see it beginning in *Songs of Innocence* and then passing, with a quick and violent reaction, into antagonism to Christianity. But if it began in the naivety, joy, and simplicity of Blake's *Songs*, it ends in the brooding melancholy and wise sophistication of Newman.

What strikes the imagination is the quick, hurried, and agitated rhythm of the movement of Romanticism in England. It seems so short a time from the joy of Blake, and the revolutionary and sanguine ardour of Wordsworth and Coleridge, to the disillusion and wisdom of Wordsworth and Coleridge in their later years, and of Newman. And if we consider Keats, we almost regret, in so young a man, his maturity and freedom from illusion. In his early twenties, he speaks with the wisdom and balance of age; and he does so without a trace of priggishness. From the earliest days of his poetic life, he sought to face and understand human suffering; and he did not, for long, at any time, relax from these high labours. Also, if Shelley continued through his brief life to be the victim of excessive hopes, he passes from them suddenly and without warning to tragic despair.

Both Shelley and Keats died young. It is useless, but irresistible, to try to imagine what courses their imaginations would have taken had they lived. But when we consider Wordsworth and Coleridge, we can hardly fail to hear the growing elegiac note of their poetry as the years pass. Wordsworth finished *The Prelude* in 1805, when he was thirty-five; and in the twelfth book he had written:

> The days gone by
> Return upon me almost from the dawn
> Of life: the hiding-places of man's power
> Open; I would approach them, but they close.
> I see by glimpses now; when age comes on,
> May scarcely see at all. . . .

So, as early as 1802, Coleridge wrote:

> For not to think of what I needs must feel,
>   But to be still and patient, all I can;
> And haply by abstruse research to steal
>   From my own nature all the natural man—
>   This was my sole resource, my only plan:
> Till that which suits a part infects the whole,
> And now is almost grown the habit of my soul.

Certainly, Coleridge was to have more than 'abstruse research' for his comfort in later days; and we certainly have no right to complain of his work in the days after his poetry had ceased. But we cannot fail to be impressed by the similarity between these elegies of the two poets. And Newman was to say of himself that his soul resembled glass in transmitting the warmth of faith to others, itself remaining cold.[1] In the very wisdom and humility of these men there was also a certain awful wistfulness, a frost 'deep almost as life'. Wordsworth and Coleridge at least had their days of song. Newman, starting later, wrote verse over a long period of years; but his poetry, like that of Keble, who was greatly influenced by Wordsworth, was thin and cold.

It is little wonder if, after all, we look back and listen again to the voice of the indomitable titan in the Vale of Felpham, in all his errors, prejudice, and fury:

Rise up, O sun, most glorious minister and light of day.
Flow in, ye gentle airs, and bear the voice of my rejoicing.
Wave freshly, clear waters flowing around the tender grass;
And thou, sweet smelling ground, put forth thy life in fruits and flowers.
Follow me, O my flocks, and hear me sing my rapturous song.
I will cause my voice to be heard on the clouds that glitter in the sun.
I will call; and who shall answer me? I will sing; who shall reply?
For from my pleasant hills behold the living, living springs,
Running among my green pastures, delighting among my trees.
I am not here alone: my flocks, you are my brethren;
And you birds that sing and adorn the sky, you are my sisters.
I sing, and you reply to my song; I rejoice, and you are glad. (p. 441)

Or we may look back to Keats, in his confessed ignorance and doubt. In a movement which aged prematurely, we may fairly see him not only as the youngest but also as the wisest poet. Romanticism has its greatest value for us in its phases in which it expressed its sense of the unexplored sea around the island of life. After the limits the eighteenth century had imposed on the imagination, the Romantic poets felt themselves to be discoverers and adventurers bursting into strange and silent seas, alone. These seas Wordsworth faced, indeed, fairly robustly. Coleridge was terrified of them; and if he fled from them, he never forgot them. To Keats, quieter and more objective, they brought,

. . . in their priestlike task
Of pure ablution round earth's human shores,

in their very silence and inhumanity, a certain quietness and release.

[1] *Letters and Correspondence*, London, 1891, ed. Mozley, vol. i, p. 416.

§ 2

The story of Romanticism in England is, then, melancholy enough. It is a far step from the early confident days of the movement to Newman's longing, out of a world he saw moving quickly to catastrophe, for the shining days of a far-off monachism. But we must be careful also to keep a sense of proportion. For if the rhythm of the movement is, as I have suggested, agitated and hurried, we may perhaps be amused by the speed with which Romanticism came to rest itself, in its exhaustion and confusion, on the great Christian traditions. The quick return, in fright and dismay, from the banks of the Susquehanna to Geneva and Rome is not without its note of comedy. Shelley hurried back and fore between D'Holbach and St. Augustine; Coleridge pushes as far back as the Germany of the Reformation; and Newman sadly progresses through the Benedictine ages to the shores of the eastern Mediterranean in the early centuries. What is tragic and what is comic cannot indeed be separated out from each other.

§ 3

It is not our intention to speak more than a word of what came after the Romantic movement. I have had something to say of a book, *The Grammar of Assent*, which was published as late as 1870. But by that time Arnold had done most of his important work. Now of all the Victorians, it was Arnold who was most alive to the creative efforts of the Romantic writers. No doubt he was not in a position to see as much or as clearly as we in our time. Some of his criticism was just, some of it unjust and misplaced. But the importance of Arnold in the history of Romanticism is this. He was himself something of a Romantic, and he found himself writing lyrical and elegiac verse. He desired greatly (as Keats had desired, though Arnold did not know this) to pass beyond lyric to objective creation in narrative and drama. But he failed as Keats had failed, and turned to what he felt was then specially required, namely, a great critical endeavour. Now for a great deal of what he wished to do, and tried to do, Arnold was, as we know, ill-equipped. But there are in his critical effort three things of special interest for us when we see him in relation to the Romantic movement. The first is that he had an intense admiration for Newman and a great deal in common with him; but he rejected Newman's 'solution' (as he called it), and could not be in earnest with what may, with any respect to words, be called Christianity. Secondly, he exalted Goethe; and with that,

Spinoza reappears into view.[1] Thirdly, he also extolled the Greek mind and Greek models, and did so, to our mind, without realizing what a part Greek art had played in the making and in the failure of Romantic poetry. But in this last, there is another side to the picture. For Arnold liked also to speak of what he called the 'Celtic' element in poetry, and helped to give rise to the fatuities of the Celtic twilight.

Thus, if Arnold alone, in the nineteenth century, tried to grapple with critical issues raised by the Romantic movement, his writings are also the death-bed of Romanticism. He reacted from what was the consummation of the Romantic movement, namely, its rediscovery, in no mere spirit of archaeological zest, of Christian dogma. He also helped to bring it about that if Romanticism was to reappear, it would have all the qualities of an eccentric and self-conscious cult, which it certainly was not in those men of whom we have written.

It was, indeed, natural and inevitable that the Middle Ages, the great centuries of romance, should make their appeal to the Romantic writers—*Christabel* and *La Belle Dame* are enough to show this. But taking English Romanticism as a whole and as it is shown in its greatest representatives, it was no mere cult of the past; indeed, it began with a great deal of contempt for it and looked, all too cheerfully, to the future. In its later days, indeed, it came, in Wordsworth, Coleridge, and Newman, to an attitude of incomparably greater humility to what had gone before; and Newman had, what Coleridge, on account of his Protestantism, had less need of, a rich historical sense. But if in these writers Romanticism looked backward, it did so, not in any spirit of self-conscious cultivation, but on account of great spiritual need.

Again, having in mind English Romanticism as a whole, we cannot say of it that it cultivated the wonderful and marvellous. We may recall Keats's remark that wonders were no wonders to him. He preferred Chaucer to Ariosto, he said. Coleridge asked for his *Christabel* only the 'willing suspension of disbelief'; he did not try to bluff himself into believing in magic and witchcraft. The Romantic sense of the marvellous operated, in the writers of whom we have tried to speak, at too serious a level to allow feeble deception in these matters. 'Wonders' could not fail to interest them, but they knew what was only play, and what was not; and as time passed their sense of the mysterious and strange was increasingly satisfied in their contemplation of the mysteries of Christianity.

I have spoken of Arnold as rejecting Newman's 'solution'

[1] Cf. 'That much-decried idea of God as *the stream of tendency by which all things fulfil the law of their being*'.

But if Arnold helped to give rise to Yeats's Romanticism, he is also closely enough linked to another feature of life in our time. Mr. Eliot has somewhere shrewdly remarked on what he called Arnold's 'High Church atheism'—a glance at *St. Paul and Protestantism* is enough to show what Mr. Eliot had in mind; and along with Arnold's 'High Church atheism' went the crusade on behalf of 'culture'. In our own time, we have High Church theism with the same concern with 'culture'. But the considerable attachment to dogma which has become a feature of our time differs from that of the late Romantic writers in not having issued from a Romantic sensibility, and in having grown up along with a 'Classicist' way of feeling. Thus, if Arnold is in some degree responsible for Yeats's Romanticism, he may also be thought to be partly responsible for the Anglo-Catholic and Classicist orthodoxy of our time. Thus have Romanticism and Christianity taken their separate ways. They lived together in Wordsworth, Coleridge, and Newman; they continued to do so in Arnold, beneath the panoply of his classicism and unbelief. Then they parted, the one to find flamboyancy and colour, if not flesh and blood, in a Celtic twilight, the other to more sober and fastidious paths, in which it resists the vulgarities, attractions, and dangers of Romance.

INDEX

PRINTED BY WESTERN PRINTING SERVICES LTD. BRISTOL

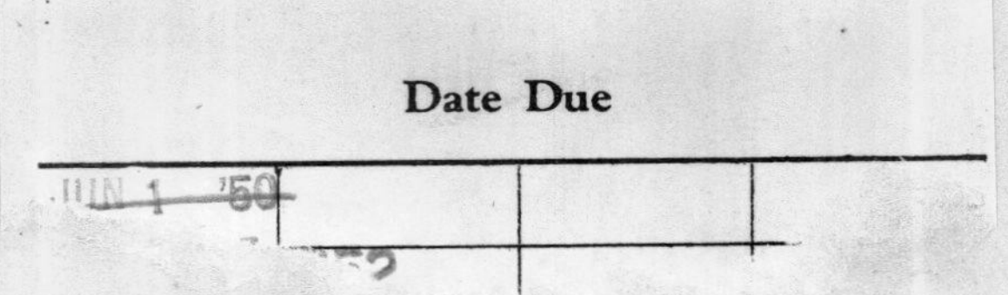